LABORED

WRITING PROGRAM ADMINISTRATION
Series Editors: Susan H. McLeod and Margot Soven

The Writing Program Administration series provides a venue for scholarly monographs and projects that are research- or theory-based and that provide insights into important issues in the field. We encourage submissions that examine the work of writing program administration, broadly defined (e.g., not just administration of first-year composition programs). Possible topics include but are not limited to 1) historical studies of writing program administration or administrators (archival work is particularly encouraged); 2) studies evaluating the relevance of theories developed in other fields (e.g., management, sustainability, organizational theory); 3) studies of particular personnel issues (e.g., unionization, use of adjunct faculty); 4) research on developing and articulating curricula; 5) studies of assessment and accountability issues for WPAs; and 6) examinations of the politics of writing program administration work at the community college.

BOOKS IN THE SERIES

The Framework for Success in Postsecondary Writing: Scholarship and Applications edited by Nicholas N. Behm, Sherry Rankins-Robertson, and Duane Roen (2017)

Labored: The State(ment) and Future of Work in Composition edited by Randall McClure, Dayna V. Goldstein, and Michael A. Pemberton (2017)

A Critical Look at Institutional Mission: A Guide for Writing Program Administrators edited by Joseph Janangelo (2017)

A Rhetoric for Writing Program Administrators edited by Rita Malenczyk, 2nd ed. (2016). First ed., 2013.

Ecologies of Writing Programs: Program Profiles in Context edited by Mary Jo Reiff, Anis Bawarshi, Michelle Ballif, & Christian Weisser (2015)

Writing Program Administration and the Community College by Heather Ostman (2013)

The WPA Outcomes Statement—A Decade Later, edited by Nicholas N. Behm, Gregory R. Glau, Deborah H. Holdstein, Duane Roen, & Edward M. White (2012). *Winner of the CWPA Best Book Award*

Writing Program Administration at Small Liberal Arts Colleges by Jill M. Gladstein and Dara Rossman Regaignon (2012)

GenAdmin: Theorizing WPA Identities in the 21st Century by Colin Charlton, Jonikka Charlton, Tarez Samra Graban, Kathleen J. Ryan, and Amy Ferdinandt Stolley (2012). *Winner of the CWPA Best Book Award*

LABORED

THE STATE(MENT) AND FUTURE OF
WORK IN COMPOSITION

Edited by Randall McClure, Dayna V. Goldstein,
and Michael A. Pemberton

Parlor Press
Anderson, South Carolina
www.parlorpress.com

Parlor Press LLC, Anderson, South Carolina, USA
© 2017 by Parlor Press
All rights reserved.
Printed in the United States of America on acid-free paper.

S A N: 2 5 4 - 8 8 7 9

Library of Congress Cataloging-in-Publication Data on File

1 2 3 4 5

1-60235-891-5 (paperback); 1-60235-892-3 (hardcover); 1-60235-893-1 (PDF); 1-60235-894-X (ePub); 1-60235-895-8 (iBook); 1-60235-896-6 (Kindle)

Writing Program Administration
Series Editors: Susan H. McLeod and Margot Soven

Cover image: by Todd Quackenbush © 2014. Used by permission from Unsplash.
Copyeditor: Jared Jameson.
Cover design: David Blakesley

Parlor Press, LLC is an independent publisher of scholarly and trade titles in print and multimedia formats. This book is available in paper, cloth and eBook formats from Parlor Press on the World Wide Web at http://www.parlorpress.com or through online and brick-and-mortar bookstores. For submission information or to find out about Parlor Press publications, write to Parlor Press, 3015 Brackenberry Drive, Anderson, South Carolina, 29621, or email editor@parlorpress.com.

Contents

Acknowledgments   *vii*

Introduction: Labor Practices, the *Statement*, and the Future of Work in Composition   *ix*
     Randall McClure, Dayna V. Goldstein, and Michael A. Pemberton

Section 1: The Statement in Context   1

1 Reflections of an Anonymous Graduate Student on the Wyoming Conference Resolution   *3*
     Susan Wyche

2 I Stand Here Ironing   *14*
     Chris M. Anson

3 My War on the *Statement*   *29*
     Valerie Balester

4 Elegy for a *Statement*   *52*
     Jeanne Gunner

Section 2: The Statement and Present-Day Labor Conditions   67

5 One of Many: The *Statement* in the Context of Other Position Statements on Academic Labor   *69*
     James C. McDonald

6 The jWPA: Caught Between the Promises of Portland and Laramie   *93*
     Timothy R. Dougherty

7 The Missing Piece: Where Is the Labor-Related Research at the Research Network Forum?   *115*
     Risa P. Gorelick

8 A State of Permanent Contingency: Writing Programs, Hiring Practices, and a Persistent Breach of Ethics   *126*
     Casie J. Fedukovich, Susan Miller-Cochran, Brent Simoneaux, and Robin Snead

9 Contingency, Access, and the Material Conditions of
Teaching and Learning in the *Statement*   147
    Holly Hassel and Joanne Baird Giordano

Section 3: Rescripting the Statement   167

10 Rethinking the "Legitimate" Reasons for Hiring Adjunct
Faculty: A Recension Statement of Its Own   *169*
    Evelyn Beck

11 Recognizing Realities   *187*
    Barry Maid and Barbara D'Angelo

12 A Focus on Reading as an Essential Component
of the Next *Statement*   *207*
    Alice S. Horning

13 Going Digital: Ideas for Updating CCCC's
Statement for a Digital World   *225*
    James P. Purdy

14 Out of Print: Revising the *Statement* for
More Inclusive Storytelling   *244*
    Joseph Janangelo

15 Strengthening the *Statement*: Data on Working
Conditions in College Composition   *268*
    Randall McClure, Dayna V. Goldstein,
    and Michael A. Pemberton

16 Afterword   *285*
    Joseph Harris

Appendix: Data Enhanced Version of the *Statement
of Principles and Standards for the Postsecondary
Teaching of Writing* (1989)   *289*

Contributors   *309*

About the Editors   *315*

Index   *317*

Acknowledgments

We are grateful to the contributors of this book for sharing their wisdom and for providing valuable insights aimed at improving the labor practices and working conditions for future generations of writing teachers. David Blakesley was kind enough to support this project, and we appreciate his belief in it and enthusiasm for it. We thank everyone at Parlor Press, especially Terra Bradley, for their stellar editorial assistance and proofreading, and we thank our students and colleagues, who continue to inspire our work and demonstrate what it means to be a writing studies professional.

Randall thanks his co-editors Dayna and Michael for their friendship and their patience; his family and friends for their unwavering support; his Lord for His mercy and blessing; and his wife, Christine, and his children—Connor, Aislinn, Rowen, and Flynn—for reminding him why he writes and why he lives.

Dayna thanks her collaborators for their ongoing fortitude and encouragement with this project; Valenia Boteva for her early work running DAS reports; the CCCC committee that funded the initial project; and the many adjuncts, part-timers, and contingent faculty whose humanity is the concern of this endeavor.

Michael thanks, first of all, Randall and Dayna for bringing him in to help with this project, which has been as exciting in its development as the topic has been timely and important; his colleagues and friends in the Department of Writing and Linguistics for their collegiality, good spirits, and support; and his family—J. Marie, Elizabeth, and Kara—for their enduring love, even as he gets older and greyer every year.

Introduction: Labor Practices, the *Statement*, and the Future of Work in Composition

Randall McClure, Dayna V. Goldstein, and Michael A. Pemberton

The *Statement of Principles and Standards for the Postsecondary Teaching of Writing* (hereafter the *Statement*), published in 1989 as a result of the Wyoming Conference, has long stood as the core document addressing staffing conditions in Rhetoric and Composition. The original *Statement* was an attempt by the field's foremost professional organization, the Conference on College Composition and Communication (CCCC), to argue for equitable treatment of composition professionals working in higher education. It has long been considered the "go to" document for Writing Program Administrators (WPAs), department chairs, other administrators, and faculty of all ranks as they attempt to create just employment conditions for an increasingly diverse labor pool in a rapidly changing workplace.

At the time the *Statement* was created, it reflected current working conditions for writing teachers in the academy and departments of English in particular. Ben W. McClelland noted in his 1981 *WPA: Writing Program Administration* article, "Part-Time Faculty in English Composition: A WPA Survey," that a high percentage of the composition workforce consisted of underpaid, non-benefited adjuncts, and the Introduction to the 1989 *Statement* identified this sad reality as one of its primary motivating causes:

> More than half the English faculty in two-year colleges, and nearly one-third of the English faculty at four-year colleges and universities, work on part-time and/or temporary appointments.

> Almost universally, they are teachers of writing, a fact which many consider the worst scandal in higher education today. These teachers work without job security, often without benefits, and for wages far below what their full-time colleagues are paid per course. Increasingly, many are forced to accept an itinerant existence, racing from class to car to drive to another institution to teach. (330)

By focusing on the working conditions necessary for quality writing instruction, the *Statement* challenged this oppressive model and worked to alleviate the inequities that full-time, part-time, temporary, and graduate student writing teachers had endured for many years. However, as most of us know all too well, the "contingent labor problem" is as pressing a concern today (in 2017) as it was in 1989. The biggest difference between then and now may be that the labor pool is even better qualified, skilled, and trained for the professional positions they occupy. While more than 40 percent of the schools surveyed by McClelland required that adjuncts only hold some type of undergraduate degree (13), most programs are now able to hire contingent faculty with masters and PhD credentials in the field. If anything, this makes the enduring inequities—in pay, in support, in office space, in development, in professional respect from colleagues—even more disturbing.

Of course, the environment for academic employment has also changed dramatically since the publication of McClelland's article and the adoption of the *Statement* in the 1980s. A nationwide recession in the 2000s empowered economically conservative state legislatures to slash support for higher education, and these Draconian measures in turn enabled—and in some cases required—institutions to cut expenses, reduce their number of full-time tenure-track positions, and increasingly rely on non-benefitted adjunct labor to meet instructional needs. Writing programs and writing instruction have been particularly vulnerable to these staffing shifts because WPAs and department chairs have often found it difficult to make persuasive cases that the resulting oppressive working conditions affect the quality of instruction and, ultimately, undermine the institution's educational mission (see, for example, Harris's "Afterword" in this volume). Professional manifestos alone are generally insufficient to support such arguments, and present-day administrators, prompted by internal and external fiscal pressures and strong calls for "evidence-based decision making," are likely to dismiss position statements from professional organizations if they lack concrete supporting data. Simply put, because data drives the decision-making culture common in colleges and universities today, the *Statement* may appear—to some—to be little more than a document "full of *sound and fury,* Signifying nothing."

The following email, posted by James Porter to the WPA-L listserv in 2010, illustrates the need for useful—and accessible—quantitative and qualitative research data about writing instruction:

> Does anyone know of any research—in the field of composition or in other fields—that addresses the relationship between quality of instruction and the appointment type of the instructor? In other words, is there any research on the question of whether using full-time faculty to teach composition (either tenure-line faculty or lecturers) correlates with a higher or lower quality of instruction than with part-time instructors (either adjuncts or graduate TAs)? And if not research per se, do folks have institutional data they'd be willing to share addressing this sort of question? How have you argued, in your own program, for the advantage of one type of appointment versus another in regards to teaching composition?
>
> "Quality of instruction," now there's a slippery variable. I've seen some research related to retention rates: e.g., as reported in a recent IHE article—> "Adjuncts and Retention Rates" (IHE, June 21, 2010), http://www.insidehighered.com/news/2010/06/21/adjuncts. There has also been some work on student perceptions of instruction. But what about research related to quality of outcomes—i.e., student writing performance—or to content knowledge?
>
> Also related to this: Has the WPA ever issued a policy statement regarding use of various types of instructors for first-year composition? Of course CCCC has a policy statement somewhat related to the nature of composition appointments—> Statement of Principles and Standards for the Postsecondary Teaching of Writing http://www.ncte.org/cccc/resources/positions/postsecondarywriting. This statement, however, does not refer to any research . . . and it really needs to be updated for current conditions (it's from 1989). I guess partly the question is, Are there any research studies, particularly recent studies and studies specific to writing

performance, that might support the CCCC policy regarding teaching appointments in composition?

We agree with Porter's implicit call to action. Not only it is time for a reinvigorated *Statement*, borne of the same passion for equity for all writing teachers as the original document but it is also time for a *Statement* that includes data and discussions responsive to the conditions of work in the early twenty-first century university. This volume is a first step toward that ultimate aim, a step that seems all the more necessary since a revised version of the *Statement*, authored by the Task Force to Revise the CCCC Principles and Standards for the Teaching of Writing, replaced the original in November 2013.

The new *Statement*, now titled *Principles for the Postsecondary Teaching of Writing*, is dramatically different from the 1989 version. Though it does not completely abandon the issue of labor practices and workplace inequities, the 2013 *Statement* is much more explicitly focused on research-based pedagogies and best practices in the writing classroom. It emphasizes the importance of rhetoric, audience, genre, response, technology, and the social nature of writing in its opening section on the "Principles of Sound Writing Instruction," while the bulk of the 1989 *Statement*'s focus on labor issues and workplace conditions necessary for quality writing instruction is relegated to a two-paragraph bullet point later in the document (as part of "The Enabling Conditions for Sound Writing Instruction").

The new *Statement* is a welcome testament to principles of writing instruction that we, as a field, have researched and embraced over the last twenty-five years. We (the editors) commend the committee for including numerous links and references to documents that support the pedagogical and other principles outlined in the *Statement*, though we are somewhat disheartened to see that the majority of outside sources cited are position statements drafted and adopted by other professional organizations (e.g., the Two-Year College English Assocation's *Statement on the Characteristics of a Highly Effective Two-Year College English Instructor*, the Modern Language Association's *Statement on Non-Tenure-Track Faculty Members*, and the *NCTE-WPA White Paper on Writing Assessment in Colleges and Universities*). As we indicated earlier, we are skeptical that position statements alone will be able to bring about real change, especially when they rely largely on other position statements for support.

We are further disappointed to see that labor issues have become a mere subsidiary point in the new *Statement*, erasing much of the original document's emphasis on the material conditions that directly impact teaching and the working lives of composition professionals. This could not come at a worse time, as labor conditions for the majority of professionals in our field have, arguably, not improved since 1989, and may, in fact, have gotten much worse (see Fedukovich et al. in this volume). In that respect, then, we feel that the perspectives of this book's contributing authors—and the research data they provide to support their claims—are as relevant and timely now as they were before the *Statement*'s latest revision.

This collection is divided into three sections, representing the past, the present, and the possible future of the *Statement* in our field. In the opening section, "The *Statement* in Context," we begin with two reflective pieces that recall the history and origins of the *Statement*. First, Susan Wyche, in "Reflections of an Anonymous Graduate Student on the Wyoming Conference Resolution," offers a retrospective account about attending the conference as an emerging professional, full of wonder and hope, and then becoming the "anonymous" focal point of a disciplinary movement. Next, in "I Stand Here Ironing," Chris Anson offers an imagined dialogue with the profession on the issues at the heart of the 1989 *Statement* as he reflects on the sometimes divisive debates and discussions that took place both as the document was being drafted and as members of the discipline responded to its subsequent adoption.

One facet of those debates is described in Valerie Balester's chapter, "My War on the CCCC *Statement*." Following up on her 1992 critique of the *Statement* in *College Composition and Communication* and using her own writing center as a primary exemplar, Balester reminds readers that the original *Statement* failed to recognize writing centers as important sites for writing instruction and, as a consequence, poorly served members of that professional community. Balester argues that a revised version of the *Statement* can and should reflect the scholarly tradition in writing center work and assert that such work is "a form of teaching and learning [and/or] scholarly service" that demands professional recognition. By doing so, "the *Statement* would provide a much-needed impetus for wider recognition in departments and colleges [e.g., English, Humanities, and Liberal Arts] that currently have a significant say over working conditions for writing center professionals."

In contrast to the hopeful note Balester strikes for a beneficial revision, Jeanne Gunner in "Elegy for a *Statement*" contends that from the very moment the *Statement* was composed, she and many other composition professionals felt that it "co-opted the spirit and intention of the *Wyoming Resolution* as well as our voices," and through its reification of power in an elite class of tenured and tenure-track composition professionals "look[ed] backward to a world order that had already become obsolete." The status of many composition professionals has certainly changed since 1989, but Gunner sees this change as an ideological liability, a means by which some privileged rhet/comp scholars have been absorbed into an oppressive status quo instead of being the agents of change they might once have envisioned. Rather than revise the *Statement*, she argues, it might be better "to eulogize it as a failed model" and recompose the document entirely, revisiting the initial tensions about credentialing and professional knowledge that were invoked in Wyoming.

The second section of this volume, "The *Statement* and Present-Day Labor Conditions," situates the *Statement* in discussion with other documents and data sets and provides commentary on how the *Statement* accounts, either successfully or unsuccessfully, for today's labor conditions. The section opens with a chapter by one of the *Statement*'s champions, James C. McDonald, who considers the value of professional statements as a genre in "One of Many: The CCCC *Statement* in the Context of Other Position Statements on Academic Labor." Putting the *Statement* into conversation with similar documents that confront disciplinary labor practices, McDonald identifies areas of consensus and dissensus and discusses how these documents might be used to inform and develop a new version of the *Statement*. While McDonald compares multiple statements in closely related (if not completely contiguous) fields, in "The jWPA: Caught Between the Promises of Portland and Laramie," Timothy R. Dougherty focuses on two highly recognized, discipline-driven documents in particular: the *Wyoming Resolution* and the *Portland Resolution*. Drawing on extended interviews with current high-profile, junior, untenured writing program administrators, Dougherty helps readers understand how the *Statement* could (and should) be amended to incorporate important parts of the *Portland Resolution* and further protect jWPAs in their already tenuous positions.

Moving from statements to locations, Risa P. Gorelick in "The Missing Piece: Where is the Labor-Related Research in the Research Network Forum?" takes readers on a journey into the history of one of today's most popular venues for new research in writing studies, the Research Network Forum (RNF) at the annual CCCC. Gorelick examines the trends in research from the vantage point of the RNF and identifies the degree to which research on labor issues and working conditions has been presented at the forum. From "examining RNF's archives of past work-in-progress presenters along with our list of well-published researchers who often serve multiple years as discussion leaders," Gorelick concludes that "one sees a 'Who's Who' list of distinguished members of the writing studies field. And while some discussion leaders have tackled the important work of exploring how the *Statement* has impacted labor practices and working conditions at different points in their careers, few have come to RNF to speak directly about their research." After considering why such research has not found its place in the field, Gorelick offers an avenue for bringing this research to RNF and, through RNF, to writing studies.

In a similar fashion, Casie J. Fedukovich, Susan Miller-Cochran, Brent Simoneaux, and Robin Snead remind readers that contingent appointments, one of the most tenuous of all academic positions, contradict the both the letter and the underlying spirit of the original *Statement*. In "A State of Persistent Contingency: Writing Programs, Hiring Practices, and a Permanent Breach of Ethics," Fedukovich and her co-authors examine four universities that make extensive use of contingent academic labor in their programs: a private and public university in the Southeast, a public university in the Southwest, and a private university in the West. Noting that two of these four universities have been named winners of the *CCCC Writing Program Certificate of Excellence*, even though they have seemingly ignored the *Statement*'s mandate to avoid normalizing full-time non-tenure-track positions, the authors argue that "the *Certificate* is implicated in accepting these unethical hiring practices while potentially masking new ways of seeing contingency." Through interviews and surveys of previous and current program directors and faculty members, Fedukovich and her co-authors consider the rationales used to justify such contingent faculty roles and propose modifications to the *Statement* that explicitly address them.

While Fedukovich and her co-authors take a firm stance against virtually any and all contingent labor, Holly Hassel and Joanne Baird Giordano take a more moderate stance. In "Contingency, Access, and the Material Conditions of Teaching and Learning in the *Statement*," they use findings from the scholarship of teaching and learning to argue that contingent faculty members can be trusted with the imperatives of the institution—they are not perpetual novices who require extensive supervision. The authors suggest that the *Statement* endorse the cultivation of a program mentality where all department members contribute to program development, regardless of employment status or type of institution. Echoing Anson's call in chapter two, Hassel and Giordano maintain that a revised *Statement*, rather than simply condemning the practice of hiring adjunct laborers, should make a point of encouraging professional development opportunities for all instructors.

Contributors to the final section, "Rescripting the *Statement*," see the *Statement* as a document that is clearly in need of review and revision to align it with current research and a twenty-first century context. They imagine how those revisions might occur and consider what advantages might be achieved by doing so. Evelyn Beck, in "Rethinking the 'Legitimate' Reasons for Hiring Adjunct Faculty: A Recension Statement of Its Own," begins this discussion by introducing us to a new class of contingent workers that did not exist—at least not in significant numbers—in 1989: the virtual, online writing teacher. While the original *Statement* characterizes adjunct, part-time teaching as a dead-end career path, an indefensible exploitation of struggling professionals who long for full-time positions, Beck asserts that the growth of online and distance offerings has actually created a new class of independent, freelance laborers. For this reason, she argues, the *Statement* needs to include another "legitimate" reason for hiring part-time faculty: faculty only interested in contingent employment, notably those teaching online at a distance. Beck identifies this "new breed" of contingent faculty as those "who are redefining what it means to be independent contractors in higher education."

Barry Maid and Barbara D'Angelo, in "Recognizing Realities," blend alternate constructions of contingent labor with the suggestion that renewed attention should be paid to making sure that all faculty members, both full-time and part-time, across the country have appropriate working conditions. Echoing Anson and Hassel and Giordano, they contend that these efforts would include but not be confined to an appropriate salary, benefits eligibility, access to professional development, and job security. Although Maid and D'Angelo recognize that local conditions control many of these issues, they offer a snapshot of what appropriate working conditions might look like and discuss alternative ways of delivering quality classroom instruction. Maid and D'Angelo assert that the *Statement* is really about recognizing reality: taking a pragmatic approach to the difficult labor conditions detailed in this section, and coming up with the best model to fit that reality.

Updating the *Statement* to reflect current working conditions and economic contexts is important, necessary work, but two contributors to this collection believe the *Statement* needs to do even more. In "A Focus on Reading as an Essential Component of the Next *Statement*," Alice S. Horning argues that the *Statement* should extend its focus beyond the teaching of writing to include reading instruction as well. Horning cites growing evidence that suggests most students' reading skills are weakening. According to Horning, every sort of data, from direct testing to careful diary-based data on students' reading activities, shows that many students have a "'don't, won't, can't' problem" with reading. They don't read very much, they won't read when it's required, and as a consequence, they can't read texts in the ways we expect of them. For these reasons, she argues, extensive professional discussion focused on reading should be an essential component of a revised *Statement*. In a similar vein, James P. Purdy considers ways the *Statement* could be revised to account for changes in writing instruction, practice, and particularly technologies in "Going Digital: Ideas for Updating the *Statement* for a Digital World." In addition to making the *Statement* a digitized document, Purdy argues that it needs to account for digital writing/scholarship, articulate the demands of digitally-delivered writing instruction, and identify and argue for the infrastructure necessary for producing and teaching digital writing.

Embracing the opportunity for ongoing revision that digital technologies make possible, Joseph Janangelo advocates a textual studies approach to revising the *Statement* in "Out of Print: Revising the *Statement* for More Inclusive Storytelling." This approach positions the text as less of a finished "go to" document for WPAs and more as "going forward" document for all writing teachers. Janangelo envisions the *Statement* as an in-process public document that perpetually accrues credibility and utility by deliberately anticipating and inviting further refinements, data, and rewrites by its users. He also suggests ways that the *Statement* could be rhetorically reimagined for online delivery and viral circulation.

As one step in the direction Janangelo suggests, Randall McClure, Dayna V. Goldstein, and Michael A. Pemberton discuss their data-supported version of the *Statement* (which appears at the end of this volume) in "Strengthening the *Statement*: Data on Working Conditions in College Composition" and identify areas for future research into the working conditions of postsecondary writing teachers. Through an examination of several national reports and studies that offer supporting data on tenure-track appointments, faculty workload, and class size, McClure, Goldstein, and Pemberton build the framework for a more robust, representative, persuasive, practical, and data-supported *Statement* that is open to further expansion as relevant research becomes available.

Following this chapter, and because we believe it important to emphasize data in understanding the conditions under which a revised *Statement* might be most effective, we conclude this volume by offering our version of what a data-enhanced *Statement* might look like. Working line by line through the original *Statement*, we include support from a range of national reports and studies on teaching conditions. We offer this enriched version of the *Statement* not as a finished product, but as a beginning, an opportunity, a means for jumpstarting the process.

In the book's "Afterword," Joseph Harris considers the many positions advocated by contributors and argues that the *Statement* is not persuasively affecting the landscape of labor conditions because one of its central premises—that fully-employed writing teachers create better writers—is as yet unsupported by clear, rigorous research data. Without such evidence, says Harris, the *Statement* falls flat as an argument for improved working conditions of temporary faculty and as a reassertion of the value of tenure-track faculty. We note that this afterword once again reinforces the need for practical, compelling research that not only attests to the value and effects of our work but also substantiates it in ways that are meaningful to outside audiences.

In sum, we believe that the discussions, debates, perspectives, and suggestions offered in this book make clear (with a few dissenting voices) that the *Statement* is widely recognized as a landmark document in the field, one that has helped to shape the teaching of college composition, particularly in regards to labor issues and workplace practices. Now more than twenty-five years after its genesis, the *Statement* is also recognized as a document in need of a makeover. The newly adopted 2013 *Statement* deemphasizes labor issues and focuses instead on pedagogical best practices; for this reason, it may be an opportune time to revisit the new version and, perhaps, resurrect the spirit of the 1989 *Statement* in a new twenty-first century form. This collected volume opens up this discussion, and we hope that doing so will lead to improved working conditions for all writing teachers.

Works Cited

CCCC Executive Committee. *Statement of Principles and Standards for the Postsecondary Teaching of Writing. College Composition and Communication*, vol. 40, no. 3, 1989, pp. 329–36.

McClelland, Ben W. "Part-Time Faculty in English Composition: A WPA Survey." *WPA: Writing Program Administration*, vol. 5, no. 1, 1981, pp. 13–20.

NCTE-WPA White Paper on Writing Assessment in Colleges and Universities. National Council of Teachers of English and Council of Writing Program Administrators, 2014, wpacouncil.org/whitepaper.

Porter, James. "Research on Teaching Appointment and Quality of Instruction." *WPA-L Archives*, 22 June 2010, lists.asu.edu/cgi-bin/wa?A2=WPA-L;68cdc550.1006.

Statement on Non-Tenure-Track Faculty Members. Modern Language Association, December 2003, www.mla.org/Resources/Research/Surveys-Reports-and-Other-Documents/Staffing-Salaries-and-Other-Professional-Issues/Statement-on-Non-Tenure-Track-Faculty-Members.

Task Force to Revise the CCCC Principles and Standards for the Teaching of Writing. *Principles for the Postsecondary Teaching of Writing*. National Council of Teachers of English, March 2015, www.ncte.org/cccc/resources/positions/postsecondarywriting.

Two-Year College English Assocation. *Statement on the Characteristics of a Highly Effective Two-Year College English Instructor.* National Council of Teahers of English, March 2012, www.ncte.org/library/NCTEFiles/Groups/TYCA/Characteristics_Statement.pdf.

SECTION 1: THE STATEMENT IN CONTEXT

1 Reflections of an Anonymous Graduate Student on the Wyoming Conference Resolution

Susan Wyche

Sitting in a college cafeteria on a Pacific tropical island, listening to two teachers discuss their classes, I feel as if I have just awakened from a twenty-five year nap.

I work as the Special Projects Coordinator for the Chancellor of University of Hawai'i Maui College. I like to say that I work on whatever the college intends to do next: I develop new ideas, propose new programs, and then write the grants or develop the partnerships that will fund them. It's an interesting job, but one that keeps me sequestered in administrative circles.

When I have time for lunch, I join a table of faculty members who eat every day in the cafeteria. Most are in their 50s or 60s and have been at this institution since its early days as a junior college. Occasionally we are joined by a lecturer or one of the newly-minted PhDs, those hired after the college added its four-year programs.

The group gossips about this or that, complains about or praises students, chats about personal stories—the usual stuff that teachers talk about at lunch. Though I'm not a teacher anymore, sitting with the group is one of my ways to connect with broader circles on the campus.

What's strange to me, though, is that the conversation is nearly identical to conversations I had at other cafeteria tables twenty-five years ago, albeit with a few changes: Now we have an African-American U.S. President, most of the teachers teach online as well as face-to-face, gay couples can marry (in some states), and I can get sushi five days a week in the cafeteria.

What hasn't changed is the sense of disenfranchisement. Most of the folks around the table teach a 6/6 load, unless they have administrative duties. One teacher who has been here for fourteen years is just now up for tenure, after many years spent as a lecturer before transitioning to the tenure track. Budgets are balanced on cutbacks in faculty salary, lecturers are crammed into offices—three or more to a desk—and the few tenured faculty shoulder heavy loads for curriculum development, assessment, program review, and advisement on top of their already heavy teaching loads. Support staff is equally overworked.

These conversations strike me afresh, because over ten years ago I hung up my academic robes, resigned my tenured position, and exited a West coast institution that I helped build from the ground up. I was disheartened at the time by internal politics, start-up exhaustion, and budget cutbacks, and longed for something different. I returned to school in landscape architecture and spent ten happy years designing gardens before the recession killed my profession. When I applied for a job at the local college, I wondered if I would be out of touch with the new issues, challenges, and technologies that had transformed academe in my absence. But I needn't have worried. Though technology has improved, and teachers are more open to it than they used to be, nothing much else has changed, especially the working conditions.

I am particularly sensitive to issues of working conditions because of my own, mostly unknown, role in the story of working condition activism in our profession. I was the anonymous graduate student who stood up at the Wyoming Conference twenty-five years ago and challenged an auditorium full of teachers and leaders in composition studies to address the inequities of our work lives. My tearful challenge was a catalyst that brought the members of that conference together to develop the *Wyoming Resolution*, which in turn rippled out to the professional associations of the Conference on College Composition and Communication (CCCC), the Council of Writing Program Administrators, and the Modern Language Assocation (MLA), albeit with checkered results. The story has been told in various publications, but I was not identified by name—an effort to protect me from my own institution until I was able to finish my doctorate. This is the first time that I've written about the events myself, events that could have occurred just as easily now as they did twenty-five years ago.

I was a graduate student in English at the University of Washington (UW) at Seattle. I'm pleased to make that identification now because the institution's identity was also protected to protect me. I was studying Composition and Rhetoric and had been teaching Basic Writing for two years. At that time, I worked with a classroom of diverse English language learners—African-American and Hawaiian football players whose game was better than their writing skills, the children of immigrant workers in Washington State's agricultural industry whose itinerant lifestyles impacted their education, and Vietnamese "boat people," the last gasp of refugees after the Vietnam War ended. Even to my then naïve self, I recognized the many ways in which both my specialization and the students I taught were ghettoized within the English department. One of the department's many literary theorists once remarked at the end of my seminar with him, "Susan, you have such promise. Why in the world would you waste your talents teaching writing?"

Of course most graduate students angled to get the few literature courses that were handed out, but the bulk of teaching assignments were comprised of Freshman Composition or Basic Writing. The teaching of writing at UW obviously played a significant role in the working conditions of tenure-track faculty and their ability to spend time researching and teaching graduate-level courses in their areas of interest. At the time, nearly three hundred graduate students started the program each year, over sixty with the coveted teaching assistantships. Each quarter, the survivors watched their ranks dwindle to the handful that would eventually complete their doctorates. The year before I graduated, the "Survey of Earned Doctorates" reported that the total time to degree from the baccalaureate to the doctorate had crossed over the ten-year mark. As long as the graduate students didn't offend and made some progress on their thesis or dissertation, they could languish in the system for years. There were few professors who cared, and those who did seemed to have a higher than normal incidence of failure to achieve tenure. The graduate students tried to organize several times, but most were too scared of losing their assistantships to participate openly.

In this atmosphere, my best friend and fellow teaching assistant, Connie Hale, was invited to meet with the Department Chair on the second week after classes began. She was told that a professor who had been given leave from teaching to be an editor for a professional journal had not been replaced in an upper-division writing course (the scheduling error was discovered only after the students finally decided to complain that no one had shown up to teach the course). The department needed someone to replace her immediately. Would my friend take it on?

Though graduate students were not supposed to teach upper-division courses, the Chair said that the administration would make an exception, given the circumstances. She was also told that the department had no funds to pay her for the additional course. With a full load as a graduate student, a full teaching load already assigned, and a job as a waitress on the side to make ends meet, she declined. But the Chair was insistent, adding that her assistance would be remembered when she came up for re-appointment next year. Of course, this suggested that her refusal would be remembered as well. Not wanting to endanger her next appointment, she reluctantly agreed.

Two weeks later, my friend became seriously ill. I drove her to the hospital, waited while she underwent emergency surgery, and then met with her class. Afterward, I informed the Chair that my friend would be out for several weeks recuperating. He listened quietly, and said that since I had already met with the class he would make me the same offer he'd made her: Teach the course without pay and my willingness to help the department would be remembered when I came up for re-appointment. The entire conversation took place in less than ten minutes, and like Connie, I felt I had no choice but to agree. I met with the class, Connie helped respond to the papers when she began feeling better, and we finished teaching the class together after she had recovered enough to return to campus.

Though Connie and I both recognized that the Chair's pressing us into unpaid service was unethical, we felt there was nothing we could do. Worse, this event seemed only another example of the department's general attitude towards its TAs; ours was not the only incident that year.

A few weeks later—around a campfire at the kick-off of the Wyoming Conference on English at the University of Wyoming—we told our story to a mix of English teachers from a variety of institutions, large and small. However, our storytelling did not elicit the commiseration we expected. Instead, one of the listeners, Sharon Crowley, dragged us over to tell our tale to a couple of the keynote speakers, Andrea Lunsford, at that time at the University of British Columbia, and Jim Raymond, then editor of *College English*. They listened seriously and advised that we had a legal case, should we choose to pursue it. This had not occurred to us—that we had rights, that perhaps there were some higher powers to which we could appeal, and that such treatment was not accepted as part of the usual abuse of graduate students.

For the next two days, our story and those of others at the conference—not just graduate students, but lecturers, untenured junior professors, and even tenured professors with national recognition—were shared in and around the official events of the conference. We even joked about the revolution brewing in the "ladies' room," because so many of us with tales to share were female. To a young graduate student, used to keeping quiet about the inequities of work, these conversations were empowering, if not intoxicating.

On the second evening of the conference, a joint session was held with several keynote speakers. This was a turning point in my life, and for professional standards in the world of composition.

I don't remember in what order the presenters spoke: James Sledd gave a tough talk about working conditions in the profession, and the emergence of "boss compositionists." Sledd believed that these directors of writing programs served the broader social institutions of power by controlling a curriculum designed to produce literate workers rather than citizens who engaged critically within the frameworks of a capitalist society. He spoke about working conditions for the graduate students and part-time teachers hired into this system, and how such a system disempowered both teachers and students.

Sledd's talk made me mildly uncomfortable with its Marxist rhetoric, yet he described with great accuracy the conditions of my own teaching. The audience clapped long and hard, and clearly his talk struck a chord among other participants.

Linda Flower then gave her talk about a research-based approach to the study of the writing process, a very apolitical talk that, under other circumstances, I would have enjoyed. The audience applauded politely, but without the gusto that had greeted Sledd's rousing talk.

The two presentations could not have been more different and, when Jim Reither, the moderator, opened the floor for questions, I waited to see what people would say.

To my surprise, no one responded to Sledd's presentation. Instead, the audience asked a series of questions regarding Flower's methodology and results. As I listened to these exchanges, my indignation grew. Why was the audience avoiding Sledd's strong presentation? Why was no one discussing now—in an official forum—what had been discussed nonstop between sessions since we arrived? When the moderator asked for one last question, my hand shot up, and he called on me.

As I stood to speak from the back of the auditorium, I realized that what I intended to say was somehow breaking a code of silence—something that one spoke of in the "ladies room," but not in mixed society. I realized that I was just a graduate student, and what I was going to say was publicly critical of my institution and my profession. I thought about my Chair hearing of this, and knew I might lose my assistantship. The enormity of what I was going to do hit me and I choked. People turned around in their seats to look at me, waiting. I either had to speak or sit down.

I took a deep, shaky breath, and forced the words out from the back of my throat, giving them an unintended weight and edge. I said I was a graduate student in composition, and oppressed, and that I taught basic writers, who were also oppressed. I turned to the audience and tearfully asked: "Why aren't you all talking about this?" Then I sat down.

For what seemed a long time, there was only silence. Then Reither said loudly, "This session is adjourned." Later, he told me that his one thought was that I needed to be able to leave the auditorium. As friends hustled me out the back door, other people turned and shouted at Jim, some cried, and most were stunned that a conference event had become so highly charged.

Perhaps the incident would have ended there, but that year the conference had integrated a classroom technique called "inkshedding" that Jim Reither had developed with colleagues at St. Thomas University. At the end of each day's sessions, people could write up their reflections and questions and those would be typed and circulated the next day (a pre-Twitter social media solution). The inksheddings provided a unique window into the minds of people at the conference—not just those who were brave enough to speak up in the Q & A sessions. That night, the room next to the auditorium filled up with people madly inkshedding, and many were angry that Jim had ended the earlier session so abruptly. More stories of situations at other own institutions were recorded— my desire for a public exchange about working conditions had struck a chord.

I have to rely on the accounts of others for how the chaos of that moment got transformed into a decision to act, to take the emotion that my question had released and turn it into the *Wyoming Resolution*. Jim Reither had been right: After I sat down, all I wanted to do was escape. Connie had taken me to our shared dorm room, and we were unaware of what was taking place among the other participants. Then, a couple of hours later, Sharon Crowley came by and said that they needed me to pull myself together and come to a bar downtown where people had gathered. In addition to Crowley, the group at the bar included Linda Robertson and several of the keynote speakers: Jim Slevin, the Chair of the English Department at Georgetown University, Jim Raymond, and later Tilly Warnock, the Conference Director.

Crowley and Robertson saw this as an opportunity to prepare a statement on professional working conditions, and Slevin, who was networked with the more powerful MLA and East coast circles of higher education, knew how such a statement could be routed through the various professional organizations to give the statement some clout. Together, they strategized that they could use the events of the conference to build momentum for a labor movement. Tilly Warnock agreed to make room in the schedule for participants to work collaboratively on a draft resolution. And the conversation continued into the wee hours of the morning.

For two days the resolution was drafted, debated, and revised in small groups and larger sessions. On Friday morning, the last day of the conference, the *Wyoming Conference Resolution*—the work of many people attending the conference that year—was formally presented. The plan was to send the *Resolution* forward from Wyoming to the next meeting of the CCCC. Jim Raymond agreed to publish the story of the *Resolution* in *College English*, so that others who were not there could understand its genesis.[1] One detail would be kept out, however, and that was the identity of the graduate student whose shaky challenge shook things up. Robertson and Slevin told me that I should remain anonymous.

Years later, I met a graduate student from Berkeley who gave a talk about the "anonymous graduate student" in the *College English* article, and others that followed. She argued that even as the profession addressed working condition issues for faculty and non-tenure-track instructors, the anonymous graduate student represented the desire to disappear graduate student issues. But that was not the case at all. Those authors (all who knew me personally) protected my identity because they were concerned for what might happen to Connie and me in the aftermath of the events at Wyoming.

As it turns out, those concerns were well founded. When we returned to UW a week later, we ran into the Chair almost immediately. He told

---

1. See Robertson, Linda R., et al. "The Wyoming Conference Resolution Opposing Unfair Salaries and Working Conditions for Post-Secondary Teachers of Writing." *College English*, vol. 49, no. 3, March 1987, pp. 274–80.

us that he had heard about what happened in Wyoming, that he had friends who had called him right away to let him know what his graduate students had said; then he walked away. Two weeks later, he told Connie that the Department had found some year-end funds, and that it was only right that she receive something for helping the department out. It was only $500 (full payment would have been a couple of thousand), but he hoped that it would help. When she asked about me, he suggested that she could pay me out of her funds (a secretary later called to say that the checks were ready, and that there would be one for me as well).

When Connie and I went to the Cashier's Office to pick up the checks, typed on the back was a statement that, in signing for the funds, we relinquished all rights to further grievance. We knew what that meant; the Chair had figured out that what he had done was a grievable action. Before we left the conference, Andrea Lunsford and Linda Robertson both warned us that we should not file a grievance if we wanted to finish our PhDs at UW. We were poor, we knew weren't likely to see any other settlements, and we couldn't talk anyway because of our vulnerable positions, so we signed.

For the next year, Connie and I worked with our fellow graduate students to address working conditions in our department. Slevin even came out at his own expense to offer a presentation on graduate student issues for our graduate student organization. Ironically, faculty asked to attend this meeting—the first time they had ever shown interest in graduate student forums. A few weeks later, my dissertation director, William Irmscher, advised me that it was easy for a student's scholarly work to be found wanting, and it was not always easy to tell who might take umbrage with political activities. He thought I should leave graduate school and finish my dissertation "out of sight," returning only to defend. I understood that he was not threatening but warning me, so I took his advice and found a job ABD at San Diego State University. I finished my dissertation a year later and returned to the UW campus only for the three short hours it took to hold my defense and file my papers.

After I had the PhD safely in hand, I was invited by Andrea Lunsford and Sharon Crowley to join the Committee on Professional Standards at CCCC, where the work on the resolution had migrated. By then the *Resolution* had become the in-process *Statement of Principles and Standards for the Postsecondary Teaching of Writing*, and it had run into resistance and division between those wishing to use tenure as an anchor for the *Statement* and those non-tenure-track teachers who felt their livelihoods threatened by that focus. I joined the Executive Committee in hopes of developing greater interest for the emerging *Statement*, but the committee was mired in other political issues of the day and the work on professional standards took a backseat. My colleague at San Diego State, Shirley Rose, suggested that we put together suggestions for ways in which people could implement the spirit of the *Wyoming Resolution* at their individual campuses, and that became the inspiration for our "One Hundred Ways to Make the Wyoming Resolution a Reality: A Guide to Personal and Political Action" article published in *College Composition and Communication* (*CCC*).[2]

After that, I became a "boss compositionist" in my own right at a far more humane department than my graduate school *alma mater*. Though I tried to improve working conditions for the graduate students and lecturers for whom I had responsibility, I found that I could not resolve the economic and political issues that arose from the way in which composition and rhetoric were structured within English departments and the institution more broadly.[3] In the fifteen years that I served as a director of writing at two institutions, I watched as conditions nationally not only failed to improve but also deteriorated significantly. Tenure-track positions were strategically replaced with non-tenure-track options, and institutions worked to become more flexible and less tied to their faculty base. Online teaching, with all of its amazing promise, attracted the interest of administrators as a tool for meeting growing demand and shrinking budgets, with the capability to further fragment faculty power.

Now, having a seat in the Chancellor's Office of a small college, I see daily the struggle that administrators have to support teaching and learning. It's a numbers game, and a loaded one at that. Like other colleges around the nation, our enrollments have grown dramatically due to

---

2. See Wyche-Smith, Susan, and Shirley K Rose. "One Hundred Ways to Make the Wyoming Resolution a Reality: A Guide to Personal and Political Action." *CCC*, vol. 41, no. 3, October 1990, pp. 318–24.

3. James Sledd, in his characteristically blunt way, lays the blame on the some of the same people who wrote the *Resolution* for later weakening it as it moved through the process that led to the *Statement*. Though I agree with Sledd's biting analysis of English departments, based on my experience at UW, I know that Slevin and others on the CCCC's committee did not intentionally "emasculate" the document—the issues were far more complex than they imagined when the *Resolution* was first drafted. See Sledd, James. "Why the Wyoming Resolution Had To Be Emasculated: A History and a Quixoticism," *Journal of Advanced Composition*, vol. 11, no. 2, 1991, pp. 269–81.

the last recession, but our budgets have not. We live in a rural area where the dollars per student are half that of urban campuses. We live on an island, where the labor pool is captive and there's no market competition. The liberal arts program, which enrolls the largest numbers of majors on the campus, is also the least visible when it comes to administrative interest—unless issues of retention bring it into focus. Though our employer partners tell us that communication and critical thinking are the two skills they value most, somehow the emphasis in funding flows to vocational and technical programs. Math, computer science, and other language-based programs have similar issues to those of composition. The most basic needs are also the least glamorous. Yet, the administrators I work with care about the lecturers, know them as neighbors (the other side of being in a small, rural community), and the institution's treatment of them is more enlightened than many institutions at large urban campuses—though that's not saying much.

Topics that seemed innovative in the 1980s—collaborative writing, writing groups, inkshedding—have now become mainstream or been replaced by innovations we couldn't imagine then. Peter Elbow once said that it takes approximately twenty-five years for what is "innovative" in the institution to become fully accepted (though he was talking about pedagogical concepts, not computer hardware). Perhaps he's right. I believe composition was the "canary in the coal mine" for higher education as a whole, and the working condition issues in composition twenty-five years ago—now spread to all other departments—must be re-engaged as a mainstream issue for all campuses, and all disciplines. The *Statement* is desperately in need of change.

I have glimmers of hope that maybe accreditation can still make a difference or technology will throw the whole thing over and some new shining way of learning will emerge from the ashes, providing economic recognition for the value that writing teachers bring to college education.[4] But those are hard visions to hold on to in the current academic climate, and as the political sphere in which higher education operates becomes more conservative and corporate-driven each year. The events

---

4. Obviously, neither accreditation nor technology—both tools that can be used for good and not-so-good purposes, educationally speaking—can deal with the broader social issues that shape institutions and internal hierarchies. See Leatherman, Courtney. "Do Accreditors Look the Other Way When Colleges Rely on Part-timers?" *The Chronicle of Higher Education*, 7 November 1997, p. A12.

leading up to the *Wyoming Resolution* addressed a time and a place from which all have moved on. Maybe it's time for the "anonymous" teachers of institutions today to speak out about the new realities of teaching and learning in postsecondary writing, in league with their fellow workers in other disciplines.[5] I'd like to think that the conversations we have can change and that our institutions can evolve as well.

---

5. One of the strongest voices on these issues today is that of Eileen Schell, author of two books, *Gypsy Academics and Mother-Teachers: Gender, Contingent Labor, and Writing Instruction* (Boynton/Cook-Heinemann, 1998) and *Moving a Mountain: Transforming the Role of Contingent Faculty in Composition Studies and Higher Education* (NCTE, 2001), and many conference presentations. Because our identities were kept quiet, many people do not know that the other graduate student, Connie Hale, was Eileen Schell's Freshman English teacher—and Connie's treatment as a non-tenure-track teacher by her institutional employers was part of Eileen's awakening to these issues.

2 I Stand Here Ironing

Chris M. Anson

> "... what you asked me moves tormented back and forth with the iron."
>
> —Tillie Olsen

I met my first adjunct in 1988. I was newly tenured at a major research university and had therefore earned the right (and the protection) to take my turn as the director of the composition program, which was staffed mainly by more than 90 graduate teaching assistants. That responsibility came with oversight of the only non-tenure-track faculty (NTTs) in the program, a dozen instructors assigned to sections of introductory composition or advanced courses in discipline-based writing taught through the extension division once a week in the evening.

Wait a minute. You met your "first adjunct." You talk about them as if they're hardly human.

Well, the writing program where I did my doctoral work didn't employ adjuncts. So my first close professional encounter with them really was several years into my position as a faculty member. In some ways, in that program they were already marginalized by default; it wasn't my intention to create a context where they weren't part of the mainstream.

Weren't you in control of their working conditions?

Partly. My wise colleagues who had founded the program and served as its directors before me insisted that the cohort of our NTTs be kept small, so for years their numbers held at twelve. That helped a little as I prepared for my first encounter with them on a weekday evening before the academic year started. The annual welcome-back meeting with the rest of the program had rattled me a little because of its sheer size—we held it in a lecture hall. This meeting with the adjuncts would be much more intimate. I ordered coffee and cookies from the university food service. Wearing the guise of new confidence in my appointment as director, I marched into the room. However, I wasn't quite ready for this group of instructors, all with some years on me and one old enough to be my father.

Oh, how exotic! Twelve rare others, so different from the TAs!

Sarcasm will become self-defeating, I think.

But non sequiturs won't? Again: Didn't you have control over their working conditions?

In many ways, these dozen adjuncts were a kind of shadow personnel and there was little any of us could do to change that. They had no office space—though eventually I managed to find them a common area where they could meet with students or prepare for class. They had to use a pay parking lot. And because most of them held full-time jobs elsewhere, they were unable to attend orientation meetings, faculty-development workshops, and other activities that we organized for the TAs during the day. They lived in a kind of parallel universe, cut off from the social and academic life the rest of us enjoyed. That wasn't our fault.

This is exactly what's wrong at so many places that employ both part-time and full-time NTTs. The field has fretted for decades over the poor pay, lousy working conditions, and exclusionary practices that NTTs suffer. (Look at Daniel Kovalik's expose in the Pittsburgh Post-Gazette *from a couple years ago about the 83-year-old adjunct instructor at Duquesne, who died of heart failure in abject poverty, unable to pay for the health care she needed as a cancer sufferer. She was making around $3,000 per course on a semester-to-semester contract, with no benefits.) Didn't you care?*

Of course. I did my best to find ways to involve our NTTs. They had ID cards that gave them various benefits and privileges, such as access to the library, which several of them appreciated.

Benefits? Like health insurance and retirement?

No, because they were hired on annual contracts to teach just one or two courses. But they could use the recreational facilities—you know, the pool, the gym—or eat at the faculty dining club. It's at least something. And in spite of the modest pay and the lack of other benefits, they really prized their teaching appointments.

But they were invisible.

That's true, sort of. The three or four meetings a year were usually the only times I saw them unless I happened to be around in the evening. Hardly a TA knew that they existed. This was a fact they just accepted. But look, the self-guilt is unproductive.

They didn't remain just an afterthought, though. Or did they?

Not for me. Our occasional meetings were friendly and helpful, and gave them a sense of purpose. I also communicated with them a lot in writing about their courses and spoke on the phone with some who wanted to chat now and then. I really liked them. In fact, they told me that things felt better once I took the reins, so I'm guessing they were happy. And they seemed to *want* these jobs. They panicked whenever a budget shortfall threatened to eliminate any of their appointments.

Sure. That could mean not being able to pay the rent.

Hold on a minute. One was a retired community college teacher in his early 70s—an affable, kind man dedicated to his students. He and his wife lived in a pleasant home in a quiet, attractive neighborhood—I once took him his students' papers when he was sick. And although they were living modestly as retirees, they weren't by any means poor. Two more were well-paid, tenured faculty members at different community colleges (one of them was even a division chair), and their sections just earned them a little extra discretionary money. Another was employed full-time at a local company and taught our course in business writing, mostly because he enjoyed it and had a lot of real-world expertise to share with our students. Another had taught at several colleges but decided to retire from full-time work and teach one course per quarter to keep busy and make use of her strong teaching skills. Her husband had a high-paying job in a local firm and the last thing she cared about was the money. Yet another was a tenured associate professor in the school of management who had opportunities to teach evening courses in his own department on overload—but he preferred our business writing course. See, they *wanted* to teach these courses, but most of them didn't *have to*. Only two of the adjuncts were barely piecing together a living wage by teaching five or six sections at various institutions on renewable-term contracts. And I really did worry about them. Their profiles were similar to the ones Frances Ruhlen McConnel described in her essay "Freeway Flyers: The Migrant Workers of the Academy."

So you're saying that they were OK with these sub-standard jobs. That's not a reason not to ask whether the jobs can be improved. That's like saying migrant farmworkers who toil in appalling conditions for nothing are "OK" with it because they do it.

Not quite. Most of those NTTs wouldn't have become homeless if they didn't pick up a section or two. Look, *I* taught extension courses at night. I did so at least once or twice a year, and banked the extra money for my kids' college education.

And you were "OK" with it, of course. Heck, you were a salaried tenured professor. And your extra sections provided "discretionary" money, not checks for groceries or the electric bill.

How is that so different from many of those adjuncts? I never complained about the modest per-section pay I got for the evening courses. It seemed reasonable. In that respect, I was just like the adjuncts who had full-time day jobs.

You could meet with students in your nice office. You had a phone and computer there. You could attend meetings of the faculty senate, participate in discussions, vote on major curricular or personnel changes. You had travel support to attend conferences. Access to the copy machine.

True, but I'm not sure those small deficits turned this group of adjuncts into a permanent underclass of exploited people. Some of those perks are pretty easily provided and many institutions provide them.

"Perks?" Not "essential tools for teaching?" Regardless, this specific and rather unusual case is not characteristic of what happens across this country. Many hundreds of NTTs are living close to the poverty line, and that's unconscionable when we think about the educational service they're providing. Have you calculated how much your institution pays you per course as a tenured professor? Just take your salary and divide it by your sections per year.

Not fair. Our NTTs had zero responsibilities beyond their one or two sections. They arrived in the early evening, met before class with students in the common space we procured, taught, and went home. I'm heavily burdened as a professor, and when I directed that program, it was like having three jobs. I worked seven days a week and often late into the night. Except for the ones who held faculty lines (and were accountable) elsewhere, none of our NTTs had to publish and didn't want to go to conventions, and I don't think any of them worried at all about not attending the faculty senate meetings or voting on personnel decisions in our department. Who cares when you're teaching once a week at night? Only one or two of them even showed up at our annual picnic—and that was on a Saturday.

Maybe they just didn't feel like part of the program. Can you blame them?

Not at all; they must have felt a little alienated. But we did try. Still, imagine deciding to teach at another, different college once a week at night for extra pay. How eager would you be to spend a lot of time there when you have other responsibilities on your home campus or at your main job?

But you're avoiding the larger systemic problem again. In addition to part-timers, there are thousands of full-time temporary faculty working at institutions across the country, and their only job is to teach many sections of composition at pay so low they could take home more money operating the fry machine at McDonald's. Where they teach is their institution. Shouldn't they be treated better? Shouldn't they have a voice?

Many full-time NTTs *do* have a voice and *are* treated at least respectably even if not identically to tenure-line faculty. But now you've revealed an important principle: We can't talk about NTT faculty as if all their situations are uniformly bad. Think of "material conditions" as a function of someone's life, not just the narrow activity of their teaching. Compare the part-time teacher who has a household income of $250,000 because of a partner or another job—who teaches for the satisfaction of it—with the so-called freeway flier who lives alone, on the poverty line. These are completely different circumstances.

It's utterly wrong to justify the terrible working conditions established by an institution on the basis of who can make ends meet under such conditions.

Understood. Again though, there's a danger in assuming that all teachers working in such jobs *feel the same way* about their employment. It's like when politicians talk about how "the American people" feel about an issue. It's insulting that they pretend to speak for everyone. They don't have a clue what individual people think. Nor should we assume to speak for every NTT about their work.

Which means that no one should have spoken out about the exploitations of child labor because some kids had more food on the table than others when they trudged home in the darkness after a 15-hour day of exhausting, mindless work?

Not a valid comparison. Besides, no one has proposed laws to "protect" NTTs from exploitation. They choose these positions. In fact, from a social Darwinist perspective, their availability and willingness to sign on only encourages institutions to hire them. Don't we all hunt around for the least expensive service people when we need them? And without caring about their conditions of employment?

Service people? Seriously?

I'm thinking institutionally. If a university advertises a job that doesn't pay all that well yet many credentialed people apply for it, then it's easy to see why that institution would be reluctant to dramatically increase the pay or reduce the section loads or provide elegant office space. You can call them evil or self-interested but not irrational. It's not exactly the institution's fault that there's a ready market of willing teachers.

It is. They overproduce the very people they then exploit. A Marxist materialist perspective would suggest…

But those people freely choose to be overproduced.

Unbelievable. Probably a good idea to take a tea break.

***

Where were we? Oh, right, not speaking *for* people but trying to understand how they think about their own conditions.

Someone has to speak for them.

Not always—unless you want to be patronizing and infantilizing. Take the CCCC Committee on Professional Standards for the Teaching of Writing, which was formed on the heels of the famous *Wyoming Resolution*. Its leaders and members, people like Sharon Crowley and Jim Slevin, worked tirelessly to understand the mass of interconnected issues surrounding the employment of NTT faculty in composition. The committee included members who represented various ranks—tenure-track assistant professors, full professors, part-time and full-time NTTs. That experience was transformative for most of the members because no one had to speak *for* anyone. They spoke for themselves, representing their own perspectives. And not even uniformly as groups: The NTTs didn't agree among themselves on some of the solutions.

But by that point, hadn't the Wyoming Resolution morphed into the Statement of Principles and Standards for the Postsecondary Teaching of Writing? *And that document, as Jeanne Gunner pointed out in "The Fate of the Wyoming Resolution: A History of Professional Seduction," seemed to alienate the very cohort of exploited instructors that the Resolution had tried to support. The Wyoming Resolution got defanged by the committee.*

But the sands were shifting. The field of composition studies had taken a turn, starting in the mid-1980s, toward issues of professionalization. All sorts of people had signed on to CCCC chair Maxine Hairston's call to "break our bonds" with the departments that controlled us. We were participating in the development of a field supported by research and theory and professional journals and burgeoning graduate programs. It was all very compelling. Then, once the conversation turned to the question of who was providing the lion's share of writing instruction in college—especially to first-year students—the NTT faculty issue came back in a different form.

What, no longer about working conditions? No longer about exploitation?

Those issues never disappeared. For example, the committee explored the possibility of censuring institutions that violated certain basic conditions of employment when hiring NTTs to teach composition. That was one of the original charges of the *Wyoming Resolution*—to establish a process for dealing with institutional "noncompliance." It got complicated fast. Legal consultants were brought in to help the committee understand the issues. The committee imagined blacklisting various institutions and publicizing the names. But on what basis? Through whose investigations, and with what permission to investigate? And with what effects on the already powerless instructors, who might have feared sharing anything about their conditions? Eventually, the idea was found to be far too expensive, complex, and legally risky for an organization like the CCCC to pursue. Meanwhile, the field was experiencing a kind of collective angst about the way we ourselves were tolerating—even *participating in*—the exploitation of contingent faculty. The labor issues were all bound up with other field-related grievances, such as the helplessness of writing professionals to *do* anything with so much external control, especially from literature-dominated English departments where composition was usually housed.

Boss compositionists by way of compliance.

Oh, don't quote that cranky James Sledd to me. Lord knows, there have always been outstanding composition directors who are determined to support their instructors—and not just NTTs. However, new worries entered the conversation as the field was maturing and developing disciplinary force, and the treatment of NTTs was a source of embarrassment.

Because NTTs didn't fit the mold of the fully-informed scholar, the kind of person who boasted a tenure-track position in composition studies, did research on writing and published books and articles about it, and held membership at the higher reaches of the academic hierarchy. Yes?

Partly. If we couldn't bring the labor conditions of NTTs closer to those of tenure-track faculty, then (so the argument went) we shouldn't have NTTs. Especially part-timers. Or we should dramatically reduce our reliance on them. Hence Sharon Crowley's and Robert J. Connors's introduction of an "abolitionist" movement, a highly-charged term for the highly-controversial idea of getting rid of the nearly universal American higher education requirement of a first-year writing course. Tossing the requirement virtually eliminates the NTT faculty problem at that level.

And throws hundreds of teachers out on their ears. Great. But why couldn't you reform their working conditions? It sounds like a grand acquiescence. Ironic, in the midst of all this concern about wielding power and control.

There was more to it. How could we—members of the profession—argue for our disciplinary status if we could hire non-scholars, people who were not steeped in the literature, not engaging in new inquiry, not following new advances in research, not privy to the conversations taking place at conferences and in the pages of journals, to teach composition? "Hey, we're very important scholars in a very important discipline! So important that anyone can do what we profess to do."

Many boss compositionists hardly taught.

OK, then: "So important that anyone can enact what we profess to know." Look, I was always sympathetic to the challenges that NTTs faced. But even I occasionally heard a small voice in my head that said, "You paid your dues. You *earned* the right to be a tenured faculty member. You specialized in what you teach. You killed yourself working long hours to produce and publish scholarship. You played by all the rules the system had established for advancement. You *sacrificed*. Why should someone come along and get 90% of what you have without your acquired credentials?"

Oh, boy, the grand narrative. "We suffered so much on the high seas before we took their lands."

Mockery won't help either. I said a *small* voice.

But so many did have credentials—PhDs that were also earned the hard way. They just couldn't find tenure-track positions.

PhDs in literature or other fields—not in composition studies. I wouldn't have expected to get a tenure-track position in medieval studies just because I had some language and linguistics background and had taken a course in Old English.

And what about those who did obtain degrees in composition studies and still resigned themselves to jobs as NTTs?

At some point we need to acknowledge differences in preparation and ability. Many with a law degree hanging on their wall don't get much beyond a meager income writing up wills in a ramshackle office. And then there are those who refuse, at any salary, to move away from the area where they earned their PhD. They settle for NTT status instead and hope, year after year, that something better opens up within a two-hour driving radius.

But preparation to teach writing isn't so binary, then. These are PhDs in composition studies, yet still they must accept depressing positions that lay waste to all their earlier ambitions. Hard to say that they didn't pay their dues, yet look at them.

Market forces. Often cruel, but we can't live in a fantasy world.

Further to the issue of credentials, many would argue that teaching writing effectively doesn't really require all that scholarly knowledge. Giants in the field of composition—Don Murray, for one—were excellent writers and craftspeople, and amazing teachers, without more than an MA. It's a practice, an art. Besides, doesn't it rely more on writing experience, on being a good writer and knowing about writing, than publishing or reading a bunch of essays drawing on arcane theory inaccessible to most teachers and of little relevance to good pedagogy?

Talk about binaries! Almost everything I study informs what I do as a teacher, enriches it, gives me new perspectives, makes me a "reflective practitioner," as Donald Schon would say.

So how, then, can there be so many uncredentialed—by your definition, anyway—NTTs teaching composition if they don't have the drive, training, or time to pursue all that "enriching" scholarship?

I'm not suggesting that it's impossible to teach writing effectively without access to cutting-edge research in the field. A lot of what's learned about pedagogy trickles down into textbooks, curricular materials, lore, and so on. Besides, many NTTs are teaching within a program whose goals and outcomes, course designs, textbook options, and even common pedagogical approaches are formulated and articulated by the experts who run them. But let's face it, the evidence is very strong that better teaching comes from access to a knowledge base and opportunities to focus intentionally and systematically on pedagogy.

But according to the Statement document, the underlying goal was to support the creation of tenure-track positions and gain disciplinary legitimacy. Keep the contingents at bay.

Well, yes. It recommended not relying on either part-time or full-time temporary faculty, phasing them out over time. This was the source of perhaps the most intense debate surrounding the document, the sense that an "elite" kind of professional within an intellectual hierarchy was favored against a lower-order "worker" whose lack of preparation, commitment to the field, certification, participation, and status would negatively affect students' learning. As Gunner put it in her "Elegy for a

Statement," the document was more about institutional power than disciplinary authority.

Compare the dull, uninspired teaching of a member of the "elite" with the brilliant, student-centered work of one of the proles struggling to make ends meet.

True, and easy enough to show, though not systematically. The debate between the "knowing that" of composition studies and the "knowing how" of strong teaching continues without resolution. The *Statement* raised—yes, problematically—the question of who should teach composition, and what credentials they should have, and how or whether that "credentialing" contributed to the development of students' writing abilities. And intellectually, that was one of the important contributions of the *Statement*.

Over time, then, the Statement failed to realize its rhetorical life force, to remove contingent faculty from the scenes of composition instruction in favor of building a respectable discipline populated by scores of writing scholars, bestowed with disciplinary legitimacy—and tenure—while making the case that those scholars were best equipped, and supported, to teach students effectively.

That's probably an accurate assessment. Fortunately, it also precipitated much experimentation: At least some programs have successfully converted NTT lines into permanent lines. At least some attention has been paid to creating a kind of de facto tenure for a class of teaching faculty who do more in the classroom but are not expected to engage in much original scholarship. At least some attention has been focused on improving the working conditions of NTTs, including higher pay, benefits, and longer-term contracts. At least some attention has been directed at avoiding hiring teachers by the section and the term. Further, some innovative programs have emerged, such as the one created by Joseph Harris at Duke, which hires and highly supports NTT post-doctoral fellows for five-year maximum terms while helping with their continued search for permanent, full-time positions. And don't forget about the effects of institutional consulting, especially through the Council of Writing Program Administrators' Consultant-Evaluator Service. For decades, its evaluators have advocated for improved NTT faculty working conditions on the campuses they visit.

But in the larger economic scheme of things, nothing has dramatically improved. So, what to do?

Let's think on it.

***

So, what now?

For one thing, the landscape of higher education has changed so much that the *Statement* seems almost impotent in the face of new pressures its authors could hardly have imagined. However, many things have come to pass: Writing studies is a discipline and growing internationally. Although unions are under attack from the right, many college and university NTTs continue to work under union contracts, which allow for arbitration to improve pay and benefits and other employment conditions. Dozens of programs have gained independence and departmental status, which means that their administrators no longer bow in submission to composition-disfavoring department chairs.

A dean is better?

Not always, but deans are also not always privy to the history of English or embroiled in the struggles to define "writing" within and beyond the traditions of literature and belles lettres. Additionally, tenure-track positions in composition have remained comparatively plentiful even though competition for them increases. And the perceived need for writing preparation continues unabated.

Under these circumstances, it's astonishing that the Statement's goals of improving working conditions fell flat. What's needed is a coherent plan of action, a set of guiding principles and practices—maybe even another document, but one that's taken forward much more publicly and lobbied for and worked toward, collectively.

How would that be an improvement?

The original Statement *implied a relationship between one's position and the ability to provide "quality" education—to serve the needs of undergraduate writers. "Higher education," it reads on page 329, "traditionally assures this quality by providing reasonable teaching loads, research support, and eventual tenure for those who meet rigorous professional standards." However anyone in the field of composition studies and many beyond it will see the false assumption here—that quality comes from institutional status.*

Well, tenure-line scholars aren't going away. So then what about programs that evaluate and reward faculty on different terms but at similar levels—a strong focus on teaching versus a partial focus on teaching and a partial focus on research? Quite attractive. Any solution, though, must be addressed beyond composition. Significant economic pressures, including widespread reductions in legislative appropriations to state universities, have forced administrations to look anywhere to cut costs, even as tuition skyrockets. As a result, we're experiencing the adjuncting of all of higher education. According to the American Association of University Professors, in 1975 NTT faculty—part-time and full-time—held 43% of all teaching positions in higher education. Today, NTT faculty have grown to 70%, and the numbers continue to rise as retiring tenured faculty are replaced by NTT appointees.

How interesting that now the current and future tenure-track faculty are the ones to feel nervous about being replaced.

No kidding. Though some lines of defense continue to protect the professoriate, such as accreditation, graduate programs, and high-level research.

Making them a smaller and even loftier elite, a new class of one-percenters eventually, while hordes of underemployed instructors with advanced degrees labor on their behalf, keeping their institutions afloat.

But back to the principles. If we can assume that teachers of writing do need access to the field, as complex and multifaceted as it's become, then perhaps "institutional status" could be replaced with "opportunities and support for engaging in faculty development." That should be a guaranteed condition of employment for all instructors, and an expectation. A recent study published in the *American Behavioral Scientist* found that part-time adjunct instructors save time by using teaching techniques that are less effective than the techniques used by their tenure-track (and full-time non-tenure-track) counterparts (Baldwin and Wawrzynski). The problem stems from what NTTs are asked (and paid) to do. Without support, we create a cycle of mediocrity and exclusion: Program directors can't move pedagogy forward based on new scholarship if they don't provide the time and incentive for teachers to learn and to talk about their work. This is especially true in the area of emerging technologies. We need to make this problem heard.

Yes, yes. More continuity. Longer-term renewable appointments that allow teachers to become dedicated to their institutions. Pay commensurate with effort. Time and space for more individualized work with students. Opportunities to be part of the professional conversation at conferences and elsewhere.

Exactly. And participation in the administration of the program.

And formative evaluation systems that encourage peer collaboration around teaching.

Not to mention the creation of a sympathetic and welcoming culture, where faculty of all ranks work and socialize together.

Yes, a sort of breakdown of the educational class divisions. As Harris has argued, "Improving working conditions needs to be posed not simply as a labor issue but also as a means of improving the quality of undergraduate education. We cannot just pay part-timers more and then hope that this added income will somehow improve their teaching. We need, rather, to be willing to make the training, supervision, and review of adjunct instructors part of our own regular work as faculty" (58 –59).

Precisely. He also makes a good case that tenure-line faculty should teach the first-year course alongside the TAs and NTTs, to break down the hierarchies implicit in *what's* taught as well.

And let's not forget about a voice in the broader campus discussions about personnel, work, and equity.

Exactly. But all of this may be moot. If we're to believe some of the predictions about the future of higher education, employment—across the board—will become more fragmented. A recent report from KnowledgeWorks, *Recombinant Education: Regenerating the Learning Ecosystem*, sees a trend toward "de-institutionalized production," in which "activity of all sorts will be increasingly independent of institutions as contributions become more ad hoc, dynamic, and networked." Essentially, that's a high-level and more highly-rewarded kind of freeway flying—much of it e-flying. For all of us. We're seeing it already as dozens of for-profit start-ups enter the educational marketplace, eroding the traditional model of the public university.

A bit too futuristic for the moment. Back to more immediate solutions.

More solutions? Well, clearly, above it all—a meta-principle—is that writing program administrators should be much more reflective about all these issues, and especially the kinds of NTT positions they oversee.

My God. More reflective? The history of writing program administration already reads like the chronicle of an unsettled species in an old Star Trek *episode.*

That's not futuristic? But go on . . . I don't see the relevance.

The story goes like this: Beleaguered by genetically related but hostile cousins on a neighboring planet, attacked regularly by unthinking, Borg-like galactic tyrants, writing program administrators are forced to roam nomadically in search of a place they can call home and live peacefully doing what they do best. The pages of the journals are filled with anecdotes of one bad deed or another wrought upon them, and the angst-ridden solutions to their plight betray every psychological coping mechanism from resignation and implosion ("abolitionism," "quitting," "stopping") to anger and resistance *("fighting back," "declaring independence")*. *And interwoven throughout is a near-constant thread of self-immersion, a relentless questioning of their identity, practices, and purpose in a confusing and unsympathetic universe, psychologically driven by their complicity in treating some of their own unfairly.*

Phew. Too true.

In other words, stop reflecting, back and forth with the iron, and do something!

Agreed. Let's stop.

Works Cited

"AAUP Policies & Reports." *American Association of University Professors*, www.aaup.org/reports-publications/aaup-policies-reports.

Baldwin, Roger G., and Matthew R. Wawrzynski. "Contingent Faculty as Teachers: What We Know; What We Need to Know." *American Behavioral Scientist*, vol. 55 no. 11, 2011, pp. 1485-1509.

CCCC Executive Committee. *Statement of Principles and Standards for the Postsecondary Teaching of Writing*. College Composition and Communication, vol. 40, no. 3, 1989, pp. 329–36.

Connors, Robert J. "The New Abolitionism: Toward a Historical Background." *Reconceiving Writing, Rethinking Writing Instruction*, edited by Joseph Petraglia, Lawrence Erlbaum, 1995, pp. 3–26.

Crowley, Sharon. *Composition in the University: Historical and Polemical Essays*. U of Pittsburgh P, 1998.

Gunner, Jeanne. "The Fate of the Wyoming Resolution: A History of Professional Seduction." *Writing Ourselves Into the Story: Unheard Voices from Composition Studies*, edited by Sheryl I. Fontaine and Susan Hunter, Southern Illinois UP, 1992, pp. 107–22.

Harris, Joseph. "Meet the New Boss, Same as the Old Boss: Class Consciousness in Composition." *College Composition and Communication*, vol. 52 no. 1, 2000, pp. 43–68.

KnowlegeWorks Forecast 3.0. "Recombinant Education: Regenerating the Learning Ecosystem." KnowledgeWorks and Saveri Consulting, 2012, knowledgeworks.org/sites/default/files/Forecast3_0_0.pdf.

Kovalik, Daniel. "Death of an Adjunct." *Pittsburgh Post-Gazette*, 18 Sept 2013, www.post-gazette.com/opinion/Op-Ed/2013/09/18/Death-of-an-adjunct/stories/201309180224.

McConnel, Frances Ruhlen. "Freeway Flyers: The Migrant Workers of the Academy." *Writing Ourselves Into the Story: Unheard Voices from Composition Studies*, edited by Sheryl I. Fontaine and Susan Hunter, Southern Illinois UP, 1992, pp. 40–58.

Schon, Donald. *The Reflective Practitioner: How Professionals Think in Action*. Temple Smith, 1983.

Sledd, James. "Why the Wyoming Resolution Had to Be Emasculated: A History and a Quixoticism." *Journal of Advanced Composition*, vol. 11, 1991, pp. 269–81.

"WPA Consultant-Evaluator Service for Writing Programs." Council of Writing Program Administrators, wpacouncil.org/consultant.

3 My War on the *Statement*

Valerie Balester

INTRODUCTION

The *Statement of Principles and Standards for the Postsecondary Teaching of Writing* (hereafter the *Statement*) was not universally welcomed by writing center professionals in 1992. Even so, the document proved to have a significant positive influence on how composition was structured within institutions and most certainly contributed to improved conditions for some writing centers. However, writing centers have continued to struggle for professionalization. In this chapter, I argue that a revised *Statement* can further assist in efforts to professionalize writing center work by aligning centers with writing programs rather than setting them apart as support services. I also argue that writing center professionals need to use the *Statement* more often and more effectively, especially in bids for tenure and promotion.

I was one of the naysayers when the original *Statement* appeared. In fact, it was said that I had declared war on the *Statement* (DeCiccio et al. 27). In my view, the *Statement* had positioned writing centers as supplemental to faculty and to English departments. For one thing, it mentioned writing centers only briefly, almost as an aside:

> The effectiveness of classroom writing instruction is significantly improved by the assistance students receive in writing centers. Centers provide students with individual attention to their writing and often provide faculty and graduate students with opportunities to learn more about effective writing instruction. Because these centers enhance the conditions of teaching and

learning, their development and support should be an important departmental and institutional priority.

The above quote, the *Statement*'s only explicit mention of writing centers, came in a section labeled "Teaching Conditions Necessary for Quality Education." Thus, nothing pointed toward the status or working conditions of writing center professionals. Another problem for me was that the *Statement* positioned writing centers as supplemental to classroom learning: Even though the language seemed a step forward for writing centers, they were being recognized as important to "assist[ing]" student learning (335). We would never describe a writing class as "assisting" learning, nor as a training ground for teachers (even though it often is). I declared that the *Statement* promoted "an image of writing centers as supplemental to the English department curriculum, useful for training graduate teaching assistants and lightening the burden on faculty for giving their students individual attention, in other words, for service" (Balester 167). This positioning of writing centers as service units left it unclear who staffed them and how their work counted within institutions of higher learning. At the time, I wanted more recognition for the complex teaching and learning occurring in writing centers, and more understanding that writing center professionals were suffering from low status, with attendant low wages, lack of job security, and low morale.

Any revision of the *Statement* represents an opportunity for the profession at large to recognize and celebrate writing centers as sites of teaching and learning and to explicitly include them as sites of professional activity staffed by writing professionals. Before doing so, it is important to realize how important both physical and online writing centers have become in the composition landscape. Preliminary results from a recent survey of 925 professionals representing 734 four-year colleges and universities (45% response rate) found that 99% of the schools had a writing center or learning center with writing tutors (Gladstein et al. 16 Jan 2014). Writing centers also exist at high schools and in two-year colleges, although it is more difficult to document their numbers. Writing centers have not only increased in number but also have extended beyond English departments and support for English classes to reach a wide array of students. A cross-institutional assessment of writing center exit surveys in three institutions (one a large, public institution; one a medium private institution; and one a small liberal arts college) found writing center patrons are "consistently across institutions, a diverse group of students" (Bromley et al. 21). In addition, "all three institutions see substantially more racial/ethnic minorities and multilingual writers than their institutional demographics would suggest" (22).

It is important that the revised *Statement* heed the advice of James C. McDonald in this volume to "no longer assume that it operates in English departments that consist only of composition and literature faculty but recognize that writing teachers work in departments of writing and rhetoric, language and literature, and humanities, and in departments of English that usually include a wider range of disciplines than it now assumes." In fact, the revised *Statement* should go even further to no longer assume that writing teachers work only within academic departments and that writing instruction takes place only within classrooms; writing professionals also work in writing and learning centers, and they function to *extend* rather than merely *support* classroom learning. In addition, I suggest that the revised *Statement* specifically clarify the position of writing center professionals as included in the term *writing program administrator* and writing centers as included in the term *writing program*.

Such revisions would extend gains made by writing centers in their status and working conditions over the last two decades and provide them a document they can use to live up to the promise afforded by their growth. The *Statement* should be a document writing centers can reference to argue for better working conditions, professionalization of staff, and funding of initiatives that promote literacy. In turn, writing center professionals should embrace the power afforded by the *Statement*'s bold claim that tenure and promotion can be assigned for the work they do as administrators and teachers (i.e., service) as much as for the work they do as scholars or researchers. As Michael Day and his colleagues have argued, scholarly activity, for which tenure is awarded, includes the administration of writing programs and centers (186). Because no "officially sanctioned document" currently exists that addresses the work of writing center directors (Day et al. 197), it is crucial that writing center professionals advance their professional standing by doing the empirical research advocated in this volume. By advocating as it does for changes in how we award recognition and tenure to faculty, the *Statement* holds great promise for writing center professionals.

Elevating the Status of Writing Center Professionals

Writing center professionals have almost obsessively debated their status and working conditions, no doubt because their status has been at issue (Healy; Lerner, "Time Warp"; Lunsford and Ede; Wallace and Wallace). In some places, they are still claiming status as faculty, an effort the *Statement* can support by including them under the umbrella of writing teachers. This inclusion has to be explicitly spelled out because so often writing center professionals are excluded from the concept *writing teacher*, with *tutor* being seen as something else, a support role, not a teaching role. Dave Healy has made the strongest case for the importance of writing tutors being seen as teachers and writing centers as sites of learning in their own right: "Being able to talk about and work on assignments with people who have no grade-giving power (or interest) is important in helping students develop intrinsic motivations for their studies" (23).

In fact, it is interesting that in the aforementioned cross-institutional assessment of writing center exit surveys students reported an array of reasons for visiting the writing center:

> [W]hile over 40% of the students from each institution did report that they came to the writing center, in part, because they thought it might help them get better grades, less than 4% of the students selected this as the only reason for their visit. Instead, several factors motivate students [. . .]: an instructor recommended that they do so [. . .]; they see the writing center as a place where they can improve their writing in general [. . .]; they want to make sure they are on the right track with their assignment [. . .]; and they see their visit as a regular part of their writing routine." (Bromley et al. 26)

These reasons suggest that at least some students regard the writing center as a site of learning in its own right. This is further suggested by the finding that almost all students surveyed planned to visit the center more than once and would recommend it to a friend (27), and almost all felt writing center sessions were productive and addressed their concerns (30). The breadth of work writing centers perform further argues for them as sites of learning in their own right and highlights the array of professional skills their directors must possess. A recently-completed census of writing program and writing center directors revealed some preliminary data from 493 writing center directors showing the following services offered, among others: face-to-face consultations (99%); online synchronous tutoring (29%); online asynchronous tutoring (37%); assistance with oral presentations (49%); assistance with presentation software (46%); assistance with new media (25%); assistance with leading class discussions (10%); assistance with preparing poster presentations (21%) (Gladstein et al. 22 Sep 2013). It is imperative that writing centers are mentioned in the *Statement* under the heading "Teaching Conditions Necessary for Quality Education," and it is equally important that the *Statement* revise the wording so that writing centers do not seem supplemental. So instead of declaring "Because these centers enhance the conditions of teaching and learning [. . .]," (336), the *Statement* should read "Because these centers are sites of teaching and learning [. . .]."

Just as the *Statement* needs to be explicit about writing centers as sites of teaching and learning, it needs to be explicit about the term *writing programs* to include writing centers. The Council of Writing Program Administrators (CWPA) now includes writing center directors among their ranks. For example, the membership statement on its website reads:

> The Council of Writing Program Administrators offers a national network of scholarship and support for leaders of college and university writing programs. Members include directors of freshman composition or undergraduate writing, WAC coordinators, *writing center directors*, department chairs, and so on. [Italics mine]

However, it was not always so, nor has this acceptance always been recognized by the profession at large, mainly due to how the position of writing center director has been perceived historically and how writing centers have been funded and staffed.

In "Time Warp: Historical Representations of Writing Center Directors," Neal Lerner traces historical representations of writing center directors, defining the director as the person responsible in an institution for offering one-to-one writing instruction, including the "laboratory approach" prominent in the 1920s and early 1930s and various forms of writing clinics and centers that have existed before and since. Lerner observes that the expense and difficulty of individualized instruction, coupled with a high demand for it, often resulted in less-than-optimal solutions such as hiring untrained, unqualified staffs and directors. By the 1950s, more tenured or tenure-line faculty were serving as directors, but even into this decade and beyond, writing centers would compete with first-year and other writing programs for resources such as space, budget, and staff, complicated by the tendency to staff any composition work with less-than-secure academic workers:

> [T]he phenomenon of the writing laboratory continued to exist largely because of its relatively low cost and flexibility in staffing. [. . .] it was quite easy for a department head or dean to divert one of those staff [i.e., part-time instructors, adjunct faculty, or graduate students] to the writing laboratory. This staffing pattern was coupled with a thinly veiled hostility toward students most likely to need the services of a writing laboratory. [. . .] This attitude [. . .] is likely to be familiar to the contemporary writing center director. (8–9)

While Lerner goes on to point out far happier conditions at some institutions, he also acknowledges conditions at many writing centers still mirrored marginal status at the time he wrote the article (2006). Fortunately, however, he noted that since the 1970s there had been a slow but steady increase of acknowledgement that writing center directors need to possess highly specialized knowledge and be current in the scholarship of literacy, rhetoric, and composition.

As a case in point, in 1985, Jeanne H. Simpson, working with the National Writing Centers Association (now the International Writing Centers Association [IWCA]), published a statement on professional concerns that clarified the highly specialized nature of the writing center director's work. The brief mention of writing centers in the 1989 *Statement* suggests that, at that time, Simpson's statement had not been widely read outside writing center circles. The *Statement*, unfortunately, reflected what writing center professionals often perceived as their status within English departments. Relegated, for the most part, to servicing faculty and classes, often staffed by non-tenure-track faculty or graduate students, with minimum budgets, stuffed into basements or old classrooms, writing centers seemed to be an afterthought, of little consequence to the intellectual work of departments (Healy; Lerner, "Time Warp"; North; Harris, "Centering"; Wallace and Wallace; Waldo).

Writing center literature reflects the fact that the definition of writing center directors as writing program administrators (WPAs) remains in flux. In 2000, Michael A. Pemberton, Doug Hesse, and Kathleen Blake Yancey worked on an initiative to add two representatives from the

IWCA to the Consultant Evaluator team of the CWPA, an addition approved by the organization's governing board. According to Pemberton, they were attempting to address a tendency to exclude writing center directors from writing program administrator status (personal note). This notion of *exclusion*, a phenomenon in which writing center directors, often in staff positions, are not perceived as writing program administrators by colleagues in their departments and professional organizations, including the CWPA, was noted around the same time by Carol Peterson Haviland and Denise Stephenson (378). As an example of exclusion, theirs is the only article devoted to writing centers in *The Writing Program Administrator's Resource*, a volume of 538 pages.

Still, there were some signs that perceptions were beginning to change and that writing center directors were increasingly being accepted by WPAs as colleagues. Muriel Harris, an iconic writing center director, claimed title to being a writing program administrator in "Diverse Research Methodologies at Work for Diverse Audiences," more than once using the phrase "writing center directors, like other writing program administrators" (1, 2). Linda Myers-Breslin's introduction to *Administrative Problem Solving for Writing Programs and Writing Centers: Scenarios in Effective Program Management* recognizes writing center directors as part of a "third generation" of WPAs (ix), increasingly working beyond the boundaries of English (x). To make a related point, writing center work is represented throughout the volume; for example, the first chapter investigates teaching assistant training, while the second investigates writing center training.

Around the same time that Pemberton, Hesse, and Yancey were making their case to the CWPA, James C. McDonald and I, having both worked as writing program administrators and in writing centers, were curious about whether writing center directors were seen as colleagues or as subordinates within programs or institutions where separate director positions existed. We surveyed writing center directors and writing program directors (defined as directors of writing programs such as composition, writing across the curriculum [WAC], and writing in the disciplines [WID]) to get a view of their status and relationships. We wanted to know if writing center directors were getting the support they needed to achieve tenure and fulfill their missions, especially support from other writing program administrators, and if they were perceived as subordinate to those other administrators. Our survey, published in 2001, suggested mixed results: "[I]nstitutions tend to grant writing program directors more status than writing center directors, often significantly more," yet "writing program directors regard writing center directors more as partners and less as helpmates" (76). While the *Statement* reflects this view that writing center professionals were not really faculty (much less real teachers), the results we saw in the late 1990s when we began the survey work suggested that writing *program* directors had received tenure or were in tenure-track positions more often than writing *center* directors.

Seeking Institutional Status

While the Conference on College Composition and Communication (CCCC) and the *Statement* were largely silent on professional status issues for writing center professionals, the writing center community was pondering them and sometimes coming up with solutions of their own. Back in 1992, Byron Stay, noting that the *Statement* provides only a "bland, three-sentence reference" to writing centers (2–3), was suggesting action. In a *Writing Lab Newsletter* article, he proposed that writing centers realign themselves with institutional, not departmental, goals. English departments generally focused on fulfilling institutional "service obligations" by getting students through writing programs efficiently. Scarce resources were allocated to their own majors and research. Stay declared that institutional realignments would better match writing centers' missions of service to students in the form of improving writing instruction. He suggested thaht writing centers move outside English into departments of rhetoric and writing or up the chain at an institutional level outside academic departments and within academic affairs (3).

In the 1990s, some writing centers were just beginning to explore independence from English departments, often stimulated by institutional missions to create WAC programs. In 1993, Mark Waldo declared that a freestanding writing center with a well-trained staff and a tenured director was the "last best place" for a WAC program. Although he acknowledged that some writing centers still mirrored the "ghetto" image I invoked in my 1992 response to the *Statement*, Waldo saw a "new breed" of center arising (16).[1] At a panel at the 1993 CCCC, Steve Braye asked Jeanne Simpson if nonhierarchical, liberatory writing center goals conflicted with institutional goals. They took their discussion to email,

---

1."Rather than describing our place in the profession as a 'niche,'" I lectured, "we might describe it as a 'ghetto'" (Balester 166).

where Simpson declared: "Given the institutional posture of many Eng. Depts. via-a-vis writing, the more natural thing to do is to get away from an English dept. as fast as possible and get a larger, institutional profile" (Simpson et al. 157). Simpson also stated that writing centers provided a unique learning experience for students (156).

Throughout the 1990s, writing centers were enacting Stay's, Simpson's, and Waldo's advice to forge alliances outside English. For example, Molly Wingate of Colorado College was figuring out how to make institutional alliances to benefit her writing center. Learning to collaborate within her college, unmediated by a department head, gained her access to opportunities that resulted in an online writing center, more computers for her center, and the opportunity to argue for better salaries and staff with specialties such as English as a Second Language. Susan McLeod counseled that WAC programs "should be housed appropriately—in a writing center, in the office of the chief academic officer, in a campus writing program office," and not in an English department (110). Howard Tinberg described a two-year college writing center as the appropriate place for institution-wide assessment (69). Joan Mullin described the creation of a WAC program/writing center at the University of Toledo situated within the College of Arts and Sciences. Sara E. Kimball described how, in 1999, the writing center at the University of Texas at Austin had moved out of English and reported to the new Department of Rhetoric and Writing as a key player in a cross-disciplinary writing program. At the University of North Carolina at Chapel Hill, Kimberly Town Abels ran a writing center that was moved from an English department to an academic services unit within a college; she built a competent staff, developed online writing lab software, made connections across campus, and kept records of the work done—creating over time a center that is still going strong (399–400). At my institution, Texas A&M University, the question of where to house a cross-disciplinary campus writing program was being asked by our faculty senate in 1998. The writing center was selected as the site of the program, outside the English Department and within Academic Affairs, under the auspices of the Associate Provost for Undergraduate Studies.

However, moving out of a traditional English department was not always seen as the optimal solution by writing center directors, often because they identified strongly with their English department roots. In 1994, Stephen North's "Revisiting 'The Idea of a Writing Center'" provided a dose of cynicism[2] to quell the optimistic view of writing centers others were promoting. He claimed that his earlier vision of writing centers was wrong, and found it "laughable" that he had envisioned them as "centers of consciousness about writing on campus" (14). This sort of writing center could only work, if at all, on smaller campuses because the tutor-to-student ratio needs to be small. Rather than being a center of consciousness about writing, such a site would be one of conscience: "the place whose existence serves simultaneously to locate a wrongness [. . .] in a set of persons [. . .] to absolve the institution from further consideration of such persons" (15). My own declaration of war was repudiated by some writing center colleagues, who called my idealism a "wonderful vision," but warned against my approach, which they saw as divisive. They felt that I risked "alienating colleagues in the English department" by implying "that we can teach them how to teach writing" (DeCiccio et al. 27). My colleagues also worried that if writing centers repudiated a service role, students sent to them for servicing by classroom teachers would be confused. If writing centers were not meant as a supplement to writing classrooms and helpmates to writing instructors, as they were implicitly cast in the *Statement*, these colleagues asked, what else could they be?

Haviland and her colleagues pointed out that while freestanding writing centers "have the greatest autonomy and access to resources if they are viewed favorably and have short reporting lines," they may also experience another, somewhat unique problem: isolation from colleagues or the academic mission (88). In fact, this fear was sometimes realized. Mullin and her colleagues described the isolation Mullin experienced as a result of being hired as an administrator rather than as faculty, and she speculated that the writing center at Toledo would have been better protected as a university-level rather than a college-level unit (232–33). More dire was the prediction of Terrance Riley in 1994: By professionalizing, writing centers would compromise their values, "recreating most of the debilitating hierarchies that we wished to escape." In converting to "just another academic unit" (150), he speculated, writing centers really lose independence. Better, he thought, to stay marginalized within English than to leave the safety of an academic department. Peter Carino sounded another caution: Non-English faculty perceptions of the writing center as an editing service may be at least as damaging as those

---

2. See Haynes-Burton, Cynthia. "Letter to the Editor." *The Writing Center Journal*, vol. 15, no. 2, 1995, pp. 181–83.

from English, and the resources for expanding the mission to the whole university may not be provided (8–9). If English does not value work of writing center professionals, why should the university? Indeed, such cautions are worth attending to, and represent yet another good reason that any revised *Statement* needs to make the case for writing centers as independent sites of learning and teaching and that writing center professionals need to use it to argue for tenure and promotion.

In spite of these cautions, by 2000, writing centers were changing location and in turn political affiliations. Optimism was re-emerging in the writing center literature. Joyce Kinkead and Jeanette Harris predicted a rosier outcome than North had foreseen:

> Writing centers will [. . .] be viewed as the "guardians" of writing—places where writing and talk about writing are central. In fact, we believe that writing centers will no longer be viewed only as support programs but will assume on many campuses a major role in the teaching of writing. [. . .] The struggle to cast off our remedial image and marginal status may finally end as writing centers become central to the teaching of writing. (23)

That, I believe, was an accurate prediction. By mid-decade (2006), Mullin and others recognized multiple writing center locations—within an English department, half in/half out, and freestanding (227).

Over the last decade, many writing centers have developed strong programs and have become central to rhetoric and literacy instruction on campuses of all sizes; many, serving as the locus for WID programs, not only teach colleagues in English about how to teach writing but also teach colleagues from across the disciplines. Much of this progress has been the result of writing centers pulling away from perceptions that they are handmaidens to English departments and aligning themselves with institutional goals to improve retention, graduation rates, or communications skills at their institutions. For example, we know that student success and persistence is linked to a balance between challenging students academically and providing adequate support to help them meet this challenge (Laird et al. 96). Online writing centers, because they provide students with easy access to writing and speaking assistance, undoubtedly play a role in retention and persistence, a fact recognized in the CCCC position statement on online writing instruction. Although, true to the CCCC, this statement tends to stress the *support* role of online writing centers, it does recognize them as central to writing instruction: "Tailored, personalized feedback from peer or professional tutors can afford invaluable learning opportunities for student writers" (CCCC Committee for Best Practices in Online Writing Instruction). Other research confirms that tutoring positively correlates with retention, persistence, and higher academic performance, especially for at-risk students (Rheinheimer et al.), and with retention for undeclared students (Rheinheimer and McKenzie).

As writing centers have moved into more independent positions and aligned themselves with institutional missions outside English, their directors have situated themselves to highlight their status as writing professionals worthy of the protections the *Statement* champions. The independent writing center is not an anomaly but representative of widely-occurring changes in the academy and in the teaching and learning of writing. As Mauriello and his colleagues put it in the introduction to *Before and After the Tutorial: Writing Centers and Institutional Relationships*, the sixteen chapters in their book are "united in their efforts to expand writing centers beyond their long-recognized borders. More plainly put, they seek to build and sustain local relationships, reaching into every corner of the university and even into the local community in order to find them" (3). As writing centers forge new alliances, then, they take the teaching of rhetoric and writing well beyond the boundaries of English departments, and even sometimes beyond the boundaries of institutions of higher education. Further, writing centers can be sites of research with a mission to enhance and promote literacy education, and the *Statement* should explicitly call for writing center professionals to be included with the writing program administrators and writing faculty it seeks to support in such missions.

Using the Statement to Gain Tenure and Promotion

The reality is that independence does not fully protect writing center professionals in the way that tenure and promotion do. While they have worked hard to rectify an image of writing centers as mere service units, writing center professionals have also aspired to achieve tenure and promotion through their scholarship and research activities. In 2002, Barry M. Maid noted that WPAs, including writing center directors, would be best protected with tenure, and thus some institutional power, and he advised they acquire primary access to control over "faculty, curriculum, and budget" (38). Unfortunately, tenure has been elusive for writing center directors and most likely will remain so unless we redefine how we award it; in 2001, only about 17% of the writing center director positions in one survey were tenure-track (Balester and McDonald 67). In a more recent survey of 278 writing center directors, only 31% were classified as tenured or tenure-track, while others were classified as full-time non-tenure-track faculty (23%); part-time non-tenure-track faculty (2%); full-time faculty/staff (12%); part-time faculty/staff (2%); full-time staff (28%); and part-time staff (2%) (Gladstein et al. 12 Sep 2013).

The *Statement* as it stands can be used to support arguments writing center professionals need to make to gain tenure and promotion: (1) it calls for recognition and rewarding of the research of scholarship and teaching (Boyer)[3] and (2) it calls for writing professionals to be given access to or claim resources (time and status) in a manner that allows them to conduct scholarship and research. However, again, it should be noted that writing centers may or may not be assumed to be part of the composition programs or composition specialists mentioned in the *Statement*: "Whenever possible, faculty professionally committed to rhetoric and composition should coordinate and supervise composition programs. Evidence of this commitment can be found in research and publication, participation in professional conferences, and active involvement in curriculum development and design" (331). The *Statement* goes on to say that research should include activities such as publishing composition textbooks, collaborating on interdisciplinary publications, conducting workshops or seminars for faculty, and performing "the particularly demanding administrative service that is often a regular part of a composition specialist's responsibilities" (331). I would add assessing writing programs to this list, an activity that not only takes much time for writing center directors but also leads to insights that improve their ability to teach writing in the writing center context.

In general, the writing center literature shows agreement that producing publishable research is a desirable goal for writing center professionals, but one that is difficult to attain. *The Writing Program Administrator as Researcher* presents Harris's claim that the writing center is a productive site for research, that center directors should do such research, and,

---

3. See the argument made by Jackson and colleagues (134) that suggests that writing center research has to validate its differences from other research in composition (i.e., more collaborative, more practical), as well as Singh-Corcoran's observation that "institutionally specific work has its own value and is as significant as work that deepens the field" (35).

in turn, that institutions should reward it (3–4), an argument that runs through the volume. Elsewhere, Nancy Grimm argues that when a writing center is perceived as providing a service to faculty, such efforts at research are hindered ("Service"); thus, the center needs a research mission. Her call for the writing center as a site for research was taken up again by Stephen Ferruci and Susan DeRosa, who reimagine writing center spaces as divorced from service, "where research, sometimes done collaboratively with the students and tutors who use the center [. . .] informs our work" (31). Margaret J. Marshall argues that writing centers should not only do research but also sell it by packaging it for their colleagues who might not understand it because it tends to be "invisible" service work (75).

The writing center community has successfully increased the research profile of many writing center professionals. Writing center literature has grown a great deal, with books such as *Good Intentions: Writing Center Work for Postmodern Times* (Grimm), *The Center Will Hold: Critical Perspectives on Writing Center Scholarship* (Pemberton and Kinkead, eds.), *Noise from the Writing Center* (Boquet), *The Everyday Writing Center: A Community of Practice* (Geller et al.), *Facing the Center: Toward an Identity Politics of One-to-One Mentoring* (Denney), and *The Online Writing Conference: A Guide for Teachers and Tutor* (Hewett) moving us forward in theoretical approaches. Rebecca Day Babcock and colleagues have mapped the qualitative studies done on writing centers from 1983–2006, while Babcock and Terese Thonus advocate evidence-based practice for writing centers in a 2012 book. Recent edited collections, all affording publishing opportunities, include *Writing Centers and the New Racism: A Call for Sustainable Dialogue and Change* (Rowan and Greenfield), *The Successful High School Writing Center: Building the Best Program with Your Students* (Fells and Wells), and *Before and After the Tutorial: Writing Centers and Institutional Relationships* (Mauriello, Macauley, and Koch).

Much of this burgeoning research activity comes from a deliberate nurturing of new generations of scholars. The IWCA and various regional affiliates have taken on responsibility for mentoring new scholars by offering scholarships to their conferences, hosting the annual summer institute, and providing advice on publishing in the *Writing Lab Newsletter* and *The Writing Center Journal*. A 2010 call for proposals from the *Journal* invited peer tutors to contribute, and the National Conference on Peer Tutoring in Writing provides opportunities for young scholars to try their hands at research before graduate school. Natalie Singh Corcoran noted in 2008 that a growing number of students attracted to rhetoric and composition have worked in, and want to continue working in, writing centers, even in spite of the efforts of some English faculty to discourage them (35). In 2003, Rebecca Jackson and her colleagues documented the development of twelve graduate courses that included or focused on writing centers, such as the one that I taught at Texas A&M. Three graduates of that course, including Jackson, went on to write dissertations on writing centers and to work in rhetoric and composition.[4]

Pemberton conducted a follow-up study in 2011, as he traced his interest in training writing center and writing program directors to his own experiences as a harried assistant professor, trying to balance his administrative duties with his obligation to publish scholarship (256). At that time, in 1991, his investigations revealed a problem:

> [I]n spite of the "unstated truth" that rhetoric/composition scholars would almost certainly be expected to perform some WPA work in their new faculty positions, there were no courses in any of the writing programs [. . .] researched [. . .] that trained graduate students in how to fulfill those duties. (257)

His results paid particular attention to whether writing center administration was specifically addressed. He found sixteen courses of this type, including my course at Texas A&M (which, incidentally, has not been taught for years and is unlikely to be taught again), prompting him to observe "a certain degree of ambivalence about their perceived importance to graduate study in rhetoric and composition" (263). The lesson from Pemberton is that the effort to professionalize administrative work is an uphill battle, one that can be helped by the *Statement*'s acknowledgment of the importance of the scholarship of teaching and the need for research time.

There remain many writing center directors who, given their institutional realties, do not have tenure or the possibility of tenure as long as it is defined as mostly research with a smattering of teaching or service. Greater recognition of service or teaching in granting promotion and tenure should be an option, and here I do not simply mean the scholarship of teaching as defined by Ernest L. Boyer, but actual teaching. The *Statement* needs to reaffirm its original stance on how tenure and

---

4. Besides Jackson, now at Texas State University, Susan Wolf Murphy and Diana Cardenas, both now at Texas A&M University Corpus Christi, took that course with me.

status are conferred and reassert its claim that "postsecondary institutions should develop flexible standards governing tenure, standards that accurately reflect the mission of the institution" (332). Even more crucial and to date not often called for within the writing center community is the *Statement*'s stance on alternative routes to tenure and promotion: "At the vast majority of colleges and universities, and even at research institutions, *distinguished teaching and service should warrant serious consideration for tenure and promotion*" (332; my emphasis). How has the writing center community missed this important fact? While we have been consumed by our attempts at visibility and identity, obsessed by producing research equivalent to teacher/scholars, I believe that we have missed the opportunity to advocate for tenure and promotion based on what we do daily: distinguished service or, if you prefer, administration and distinguished teaching.

Researching Our Way Up

Despite the impressive proliferation of writing center scholarship and research, knowledge about writing centers as sites of teaching and learning has not yet advanced in a way that is going to significantly improve the status of writing center professionals. Randall McClure, Dayna V. Goldstein, and Michael A. Pemberton (this volume) call writing centers to action by reminding us that we are operating in a highly competitive environment that demands evidence for our claims of efficacy. It is up to writing center professionals to gather the evidence these authors call for. As they explain, "Accumulated, rigorous scholarship on the valuation of quality teaching and its relationship to student learning could provide much of the support needed on labor conditions in composition that decision makers find compelling."

Elizabeth Boquet and Neil Lerner examined writing center research and scholarship between 1998 and 2008 and conclude that little had been accomplished in the way of theory and less in the way of research that could inform composition studies or gain writing centers recognition and status. Writing center literature seems stuck in the reactionary pose, unwilling to "go beyond mere assertions of identity" (185). They add, "We must seek this information not only because our annual reports, accrediting agencies, or funding agencies expect it—but because it is our scholarly work and the sites where it happens are the intellectual breeding grounds for our research" (186). Assertions of identity persist because writing centers, in spite of gains, continue to struggle for status. Yet this is not a productive stance. McClure and his co-authors would say that when it comes to improving their status, writing center professionals are stuck in dissensus, "a perpetual emphasis on the local and idiosyncratic."

Boquet's and Lerner's findings were further validated by Dana Lynn Driscoll and Sherry Wynn Perdue, who studied articles from *The Writing Center Journal* (1980–2009) for evidence of well-designed empirical studies (defined as replicable, aggregable, and data supported). Although they found a steady increase over time in empirical research, they found only fifteen out of a total of 270 articles could be coded as replicable, aggregable, and data supported. While much empirical research of this type is occurring, it is not being published in the field's premier journal and is not always being done by writing center professionals or focused specifically on writing centers. They advocate "serious shifts in how writing center scholars conceptualize, conduct, compose, and support research" (29). As they state, "the field must embrace such change to validate our practices, to secure external credibility and funding, and to develop evidence-based practices" (29).

So what do we need to know? We have a start in some exemplary research that explores what really happens in tutoring sessions, how particular tutors and students interact in specific settings, how one-to-one learning happens, what motivates students to use a writing center, and what tutors and students gain from their experiences (Bromley et al.; Thompson; Thonus; Williams and Takaku). Further, many other worthy studies can be found in the estimated 33 dissertations on writing centers completed in the 1990s and 75 from 2000–2008 (Lerner, "Introduction" 6). Finally, Shannon Carter has outlined a productive stance for writing center research that we have yet to explore: "[I]nvestigating the power nexus involved in acquiring new literacies" (136), in essence using the position of being between the student and the many literacies the institution promulgates. In the daily administration of a writing center, there are ample opportunities to document and to investigate practices. If we take the *Statement*'s stand on tenure as a guide, we might also argue for strategic plans, annual reports, and the reports of assessment undertaken to improve our practice being valued as research or as evidence of exceptional service.

Terms of a Truce

Writing centers have moved beyond an identity that positions them as merely "enhanc[ing] the conditions of teaching and learning" (*Statement* 336). They are, instead, sites for teaching and learning in their own right that champion literacy and cultivate a climate that advocates for literacy education throughout the curriculum. Writing centers engage in individualized teaching, attend to students whose classroom teachers may not be equipped or have time to help them, and provide help to colleagues from across the disciplines in writing pedagogy. Writing center directors, in turn, handle complex organizations with staffs that need significant professional development and with budgets that require creativity. They are thrust into partnerships across campus, and they meet demands for evidence-based assessment. By recognizing this work as a form of teaching and learning or as scholarly service and by openly acknowledging that writing center directors are included in the term *writing program administrator*, the *Statement* would provide a much-needed impetus for wider recognition in departments and colleges that currently have a significant say over working conditions for writing center professionals.

It's time, too, for writing center directors to meet the challenge to demonstrate effectiveness. One way to approach this is to respond to the visions, goals, and needs of the institution in which they are situated. A goal that exists at any institution is the need for literacy instruction (including instruction in the rhetorical arts of writing, oral communication, or multimedia communication). Other common goals include boosting retention and increasing student engagement through strong campus support services and high-impact practices (like interaction with faculty, writing-intensive courses, and collaborative learning). Writing centers will succeed if they demonstrate they can help institutions meet these goals and if, as Carter has argued, we can help faculty members from across the disciplines understand that all students, even graduate students, need feedback and individualized instruction as they negotiate the complex demands of various literacies.

Works Cited

Abels, Kimberly Town. "The Writing Center at the University of North Carolina at Chapel Hill: A Site and a Story under Construction." *The Writing Center Director's Resource Book*, edited by Christina Murphy and Byron L. Stay, Lawrence Erlbaum, 2006, pp. 393–402.

Babcock, Rebecca Day, et al. *A Synthesis of Qualitative Studies of Writing Center Tutoring 1983–2006*. Peter Lang, 2012.

Babcock, Rebecca Day, and Terese Thonus. *Researching the Writing Center: Towards an Evidence-Based Practice*. Peter Lang, 2012.

Balester, Valerie. "Symposium on the 1991 Progress Report from the CCCC Committee on Professional Standards: Revising the 'Statement': On the Work of Writing Centers." *College Composition and Communication*, vol. 43, no. 2, 1992, pp. 167–71.

Balester, Valerie, and James C. McDonald. "A View of Status and Working Conditions: Relations between Writing Program and Writing Center Directors." *WPA: Writing Program Administration*, vol. 24, no. 3, 2001, pp. 59–82.

Boquet, Elizabeth. *Noise from the Writing Center*. Utah State UP, 2002.

Boquet, Elizabeth, and Neal Lerner. "After 'The Idea of a Writing Center.'" *College English*, vol. 71, no. 2, 2008, pp. 170–89.

Boyer, Ernest L. *Scholarship Reconsidered: Priorities of the Professoriate*. Carnegie Foundation for the Advancement of Teaching, 1990.

Bromley, Pam, et al. "How Important Is the Local, Really? A Cross-Institutional Qualitative Assessment of Frequently Asked Questions in Writing Center Exit Surveys." *The Writing Center Journal*, vol. 33, no. 2, 2013, pp. 13–37.

Carino, Peter. "Beyond Supplementation: Leaving Composition Programs." *The Politics of Writing Centers*, edited by Jane Nelson and Kathy Evertz, Boynton/Cook-Heinemann, 2001, pp. 5–14.

Carter, Shannon. "The Writing Center Paradox: Talk about Legitimacy and the Problem of Institutional Change." *College Composition and Communication*, vol. 61, no. 1, 2009, pp. 133–52.

CCCC Executive Committee. *Statement of Principles and Standards for the Postsecondary Teaching of Writing*. College Composition and Communication, vol. 40, no. 3, 1989, pp. 329–36.

Conference on College Composition and Communication Committee for Best Practices in Online Writing Instruction. *A Position Statement of Principles and Example Effective Practices for Online Writing Instruction (OWI)*. National Council of Teachers of English, March 2013, www.ncte.org/cccc/resources/positions/owiprinciples.

Day, Michael, et al. "What We Really Value: Redefining Scholarly Engagement in Tenure and Promotion Protocols." *College Composition and Communication*, vol. 65, no. 1, 2013, pp. 185–208.

Denney, Harry. *Facing the Center: Toward an Identity Politics of One-to-One Mentoring*. Utah State UP, 2010.

DeCiccio, Albert C., et al. "Walking the Tightrope: Negotiating between the Ideal and the Practical in the Writing Center." *Writing Center Perspectives*, edited by Byron L. Stay et al., NWCA, 1995, pp. 26–37.

Driscoll, Dana Lynn, and Sherry Wynn Perdue. "Theory, Lore, and More: An Analysis of RAD Research in The Writing Center Journal, 1980–2009." *The Writing Center Journal*, vol. 32, no. 2, 2012, pp. 11–39.

Fells, Dawn and Jennifer Wells, editors. *The Successful High School Writing Center: Building the Best Program with Your Students*. Teachers College Press, 2011.

Ferruci, Stephen, and Susan DeRosa. "Writing a Sustainable History: Mapping Writing Center Ethos." *The Writing Center Director's Resource Book*, edited by Christina Murphy and Byron L. Stay, Lawrence Erlbaum, 2006, pp. 21–32.

Gladstein, Jill, et al. "Re: Preliminary data for WCDs from the WPA Census (subtitle: please take the census!)-Deadline extended to 9/30." WCENTER listserv, 12 September 2013.

—. "What services do writing centers offer?" WCENTER listserv, 22 September 2013.

—. "WPA Census including a little data." WCENTER listserv, 6 January 2014.

Geller, Anne Ellen, et al. *The Everyday Writing Center: A Community of Practice*. Utah State UP, 2006.

Grimm, Nancy. "In the Spirit of Service: Making Writing Center Research a 'Featured Character.'" *The Center Will Hold: Critical Perspectives on Writing Center Scholarship*, edited by Michael A. Pemberton and Joyce Kinkead, Utah State UP, 2003, pp. 41–57.

—. *Good Intentions: Writing Center Work for Postmodern Times*. Boynton/Cook, 1999.

Harris, Muriel. "Centering In on Professional Choices. *College Composition and Communication*, vol. 52, no. 3, 2001, pp. 429–40.

—. "Diverse Research Methodologies at Work for Diverse Audiences: Shaping the Writing Center to the Institution." *The Writing Program Administrator as Researcher: Inquiry in Action and Reflection*, edited by Shirley K. Rose and Irwin Weiser, Boynton/Cook, 1999, pp. 1–17.

Haviland, Carol Peterson, et al. "Politics of Administrative and Physical Location." *The Politics of Writing Centers*, edited by Jane Nelson and Kathy Evertz, Boynton/Cook-Heinemann, 2001, pp. 85–98.

Haviland, Carol Peterson, and Denise Stephenson. "Writing Centers, Writing Programs, and WPAs: Roles by Any Other Names?" *The Writing Program Administrator's Resource: A Guide to Institutional Practice*, edited by Stuart C. Brown and Theresa Enos, Lawrence Erlbaum, 2002, pp. 377–92.

Healy, Dave. "A Defense of Dualism: The Writing Center and the Classroom." *The Writing Center Journal*, vol. 14, no. 1, 1993, pp. 16–29.

Hewett, Beth L. *The Online Writing Conference: A Guide for Teachers and Tutor*. Boynton/Cook, 2010.

Jackson, Rebecca, et al. "(RE)shaping the Profession: Graduate Courses in Writing Center Theory, Practice, and Administration." *The Center Will*

Hold: Critical Perspectives on Writing Center Scholarship, edited by Michael A. Pemberton and Joyce Kinkead, Utah State UP, 2003, pp. 130–50.

Kimball, Sara E. "Computers in the Writing Center." *Administrative Problem-Solving for Writing Programs and Writing Centers: Scenarios in Effective Program Management*, edited by Linda Myers-Breslin, National Council of Teachers of English, 1999, pp. 133–45.

Kinkead, Joyce, and Jeanette Harris. "What's Next for Writing Centers?" *The Writing Center Journal*, vol. 20, no. 2, 2000, pp. 23–24.

Laird, Thomas F. Nelson, et al. "Classroom Practices at Institutions With Higher-Than-Expected Persistence Rates: What Student Engagement Data Tell Us." *New Directions for Teaching & Learning*, vol. 2008, no. 115, 2008, pp. 85–99.

Lerner, Neal. "Time Warp: Historical Representations of Writing Center Directors." *The Writing Center Director's Resources Book*, edited by Christina Murphy and Byron Stay, Lawrence Erlbaum, 2006, pp. 3–11.

—. "Introduction to a List of Dissertations and Theses on Writing Centers 1924–2008." *The Writing Lab Newsletter*, vol. 33, no. 7, 2009, pp. 6–9.

Lunsford, Andrea, and Lisa Ede. "Reflections on Contemporary Currents in Writing Center Work." *The Writing Center Journal*, vol. 31, no. 1, 2011, pp. 11–24.

Maid, Barry M. "Working Outside of English." *The Allyn and Bacon Sourcebook for Writing Program Administrators*, edited by Irene Ward and William J. Carpenter, Longman, 2002, pp. 38–46.

Mauriello, Nicholas, et al., editors. *Before and After the Tutorial: Writing Centers and Institutional Relationships*. Hampton Press, 2011.

Marshall, Margaret J. "Sites for (Invisible) Intellectual Work." *The Politics of Writing Centers*, edited by Jane V. Nelson and Kathy Evertz, Boynton/Cook-Heinemann, 2001, pp. 74–84.

McClure, Randall, et al. "Strengthening the *Statement*: Data on Working Conditions in College Composition." *Labored: The State(ment) and Future of Work in Composition*, Parlor Press, 2017, pp. 268–284.

McLeod, Susan. "The Foreigner: WAC Directors as Agents of Change." *Resituating Writing: Constructing and Administering Writing Programs*, edited by Joseph Janangelo and Kristine Hansen, Boynton/Cook, 1995, pp. 108–16.

Mullin, Joan. "Writing Across the Curriculum." *Administrative Problem-Solving for Writing Programs and Writing Centers: Scenarios in Effective Program Management*, edited by Linda Myers-Breslin, National Council of Teachers of English, 1999, pp. 97–111.

Mullin, Joan, et al. "Administrative (Chaos) Theory: The Politics and Practices of Writing Center Location." *The Writing Center Director's Resource Book*, edited by Christina Murphy and Byron L. Stay, Lawrence Erlbaum, 2006, pp. 225–36.

Myers-Breslin, Linda. *Administrative Problem-Solving for Writing Programs and Writing Centers: Scenarios in Effective Program Management.* National Council of Teachers of English, 1999.

North, Stephen. "The Idea of a Writing Center." *College English*, vol. 46, no. 5, 1984, pp. 433–46.

—. "Revisiting 'The Idea of a Writing Center.'" *The Writing Center Journal*, vol. 15, no. 1, 1994, pp. 7–19.

Pemberton, Michael A. Personal note to author, 24 July 2013.

—. "Revisiting 'Tales Too Terrible to Tell': A Survey of Graduate Coursework in Writing Program and Writing Center Administration." *Before and After the Tutorial: Writing Centers and Institutional Relationships*, edited by Nicholas Mauriello et al., Hampton Press, 2011, pp. 255–74.

Pemberton, Michael, and Joyce Kinkead, editors. *The Center Will Hold: Critical Perspectives on Writing Center Scholarship.* Utah State UP, 2003.

Rheinheimer, David C., et al. "Tutoring: A Support Strategy for At-risk Students." *The Learning Assistance Review*, vol. 15, no. 1, 2010, pp. 23–33.

Rheinheimer, David, and Kelly McKenzie. "The Impact of Tutoring on the Academic Success of Undeclared Students." *Journal of College Reading and Learning*, vol. 41, no. 2, 2011, pp. 22–36.

Riley, Terrance. "The Unpromising Future of Writing Centers." *The Writing Center Journal*, vol 15, no. 1, 1994, pp. 20–34. Reprinted in *The Allyn and Bacon Guide to Writing Center Theory and Practice*, edited by Robert W. Barnett and Jacob S. Blummer, Allyn and Bacon, 2001, pp. 139–52.

Rowan, Karen, and Laura Greenfield, editors. *Writing Centers and the New Racism: A Call for Sustainable Dialogue and Change.* Utah State UP, 2011.

Simpson, Jeanne H. "What Lies Ahead for Writing Centers: Position Statement on Professional Concerns." *The Writing Center Journal*, vol. 5, no. 2, Spring/Summer 1985, pp. 35–39.

Simpson, Jeanne et al. "War, Peace, and Writing Center Administration." *Composition Studies/Freshman English News*, vol. 22, no. 1, 1994, pp. 65–95. Reprinted in *Landmark Essays on Writing Centers*, edited by Christina Murphy and Joe Law, Hermagoras, 1995, pp. 151–78.

Singh-Corcoran, Natalie. "You're Either a Scholar or an Administrator." *E(M)erging Identities: Graduate Students in the Writing Center*, edited by Melissa Nicolas, Fountainhead Press, 2008, pp. 27–35.

Stay, Byron L. "Writing Centers on the Margins: Conversing from the Edge." *The Writing Lab Newsletter*, vol. 17, no. 1, 1992, pp. 1–4.

Thompson, Isabelle. "Scaffolding in the Writing Center: A Microanalysis of an Experienced Tutor's Verbal and Non-Verbal Strategies. *Written Communication*, vol. 26, no. 4, 2009, pp. 417–53.

Thonus, Terese. "Triangulation in the Writing Center: Tutor, Tutee, and Instructor Perceptions of the Tutor's Role." *The Writing Center Journal*, vol. 22, no. 1, 2001, p. 59.

Tinberg, Howard. "Examining Our Assumptions as Gatekeepers: A Two-Year College Perspective." *Administrative Problem-Solving for Writing Programs and Writing Centers: Scenarios in Effective Program Management*, edited by Linda Myers-Breslin, National Council of Teachers of English, 1999, pp. 62–70.

Wallace, Ray, and Susan Lewis Wallace. "Growing Our Own: Writing Centers as Historically Fertile Fields for Professional Development." *The Writing Center Director's Resource Book*, edited by Christina Murphy and Byron L. Stay, Lawrence Erlbaum, 2006, pp. 45–51.

Waldo, Mark. "The Last Best Place for Writing across the Curriculum: The Writing Center." *WPA: Writing Program Administration*, vol. 16, no. 3, 1993, pp. 15–26.

Williams, James D., and Seiji Takaku. "Help-seeking, Self-efficacy, and Writing Performance among College Students." *Journal of Writing Research*, vol. 3, no. 1, 2011, pp. 1–18.

Wingate, Molly. "Their Institutions." *Resituating Writing: Constructing and Administering Writing Programs*, edited by Joseph Janangelo and Kristine Hansen, Boynton/Cook, 1995, pp. 100–07.

4 Elegy for a *Statement*

Jeanne Gunner

INTRODUCTION

During its process of development and through its ultimate publication so many years ago, the *Statement of Principles and Standards for the Postsecondary Teaching of Writing* (hereafter the *Statement*) evoked deep and often divided feelings. In the late 1980s, I was part of the hopeful non-tenure-track faculty who believed the *Wyoming Resolution* would lead the Conference on College Composition and Communication (CCCC) to endorse an inclusive statement on professional standards and working conditions. Although even today reading the document that emerged from such hopes is an upsetting experience for me, others who also expected a touchstone document reflecting our professional identity and ethics might find themselves needing the Kübler-Ross scale to parse out their feelings of anger and depression over its ineffectiveness. Serious consideration of updating the principles in it can only lead us through the remaining stages of denial, bargaining, and acceptance.

Many factors militate against the original *Statement*'s resurrection, perhaps most obviously the sea-change of the digital age, for the *Statement*'s assumptions about literacy and teaching are simply outmoded, as James P. Purdy and others in this volume address. Equally apparent is the transformation of the nature and function of faculty in higher education, the result of economic and cultural shifts over the last several decades. The professional conversations about working conditions since the *Statement* appeared have by now helped demonstrate how completely the *Statement* failed to anticipate—or how it ignored—the massive economic restructuring already well underway in 1989. We can see this economic paradigm shift in a wide variety of metrics, including statistics (see chapters by McClure et al. along with others in this volume) on tenure-track/non-tenure-track positions and percent of college courses taught by adjunct faculty; the rise of for-profits[1] and the new economic model they represent, routinely structured outside of the traditional system and adjunct-dependent;[2] and the shifting economic model for public higher education, with institutions moving from state-supported, to state-assisted, to self-sustaining over this time period.[3]

In this chapter, then, I present an argument against recension, first by reviewing the ways in which the *Statement* began its life cycle as *already* a revision of the *Wyoming Resolution*, subverting the *Resolution*'s original goals and voices in order to serve the interests of the then more culturally-powerful tenure-line professional. Pursuing the path of further revision(ism), I argue, would leave unresolved the original professional ills that prompted the *Statement*. It would also leave unchanged the *Statement*'s need to smooth over conflicts within the profession, an inevitable outcome of professional organization sponsorship. I suggest that we instead revisit the original *Statement* to see where and how it suppresses serious questions of disciplinary identity, membership, and managerial responsibility, and then consider the viability and worth of revision in the context posed by continual, disruptive changes in the contemporary system of higher education overall.

THE ORIGINAL REVISION

Those who resisted the *Statement* (and I belonged to this camp) and who saw it as a professional betrayal[4] might find in an attempt at revision a kind of professional repetition compulsion: Why consider reviving a statement that in its original incarnation spoke for so few of us?

---

1. According to *The Economics of Higher Education*, "Approximately 9 percent [of college students] attend a private for-profit (i.e., "proprietary") institution. Enrollment growth is fastest at for-profit schools, which have increased in size from 200,000 students in the late 1980s to nearly 2 million students today."

2. See Suevon Lee's "For-Profit Higher Education: The Industry, By the Numbers" for statistics on for-profit figures for recruitment, executive compensation, and academic progress.

3. See Howard Fine's "UC President OKs UCLA Anderson Self-Sufficiency Plan" and description of Responsibility Center Management models, used at Ohio State, Kent State, and other universities, in "Learning about RCM."

4. For a discussion of such objections to the *Statement*, see Jeanne Gunner's "The Fate of the Wyoming Resolution: A History of Professional Seduction."

Perhaps like the Freudian melancholic, we're drawn to identify with it, even as originally and much more so over time its image of the composition professional badly misrepresents actual writing instructors. In "The Spirit and Influence of the Wyoming Resolution: Looking Back to Look Forward," James C. McDonald and Eileen E. Schell document the hostility and divisions that the *Statement* excited as it transmogrified from the *Wyoming Resolution*. The *Wyoming Resolution* was itself the product of deep frustration and resentment (see John Trimbur and Barbara Cambridge, who, writing at the time, noted that "the resolution was drafted [. . .] following a remarkable release of the anger and bitterness so deeply felt in the rank and file of writing teachers—anger about the poor conditions that make it difficult to teach properly and bitterness about the insecurity and powerlessness of so many who teach writing" [13]). Because the anger it evoked then may now seem mystifying, with the marginalization of writing instructors today being so well and publically known, rereading it along with the *Statement* might help provide a clarifying context.

Recall that the *Wyoming Resolution* charged the CCCC Executive Committee with three steps[5] intended to help ameliorate the unfair working conditions of marginalized writing instructors. Believing the CCCC intention was to advance the *Wyoming Resolution* agenda, many whose voices the *Resolution* represented found the resulting *Statement* a revisionist document—already, in fact, a recension—that served the professional self-interest of the academically privileged. Few of those in later rhetoric/composition generations have witnessed organization-wide scenes of equivalent deep emotion as those described in McDonald and Schell. Those of us who opposed the *Statement* in 1989 were angry because it co-opted the spirit and intention of the *Wyoming Resolution* as well as our voices. These feelings—the sense of hope followed by what seemed a direct rebuke of it, and this from our own professional organization—came at a time and point of critical field formation, where the stakes, or so we believed, were real, with potential material effect. The camaraderie that characterized the *Wyoming Resolution*—both at the

---

5. "To formulate, after appropriate consultations with post-secondary teachers of writing, professional standards and expectations for salary levels and working conditions of post-secondary teachers of writing [and] establish a procedure for hearing grievances brought by post-secondary teachers of writing [. . . and] establish a procedure for acting upon a finding of noncompliance"; see appendix in Trimbur and Cambridge (18).

conference at which it was formulated and in the reception it received when it was published—was shredded by the unexpected professional class system the *Statement* proposed.

In sum, the *Wyoming Resolution* and the *Statement* embody radically differing models of how contingent workers should inhabit the profession, and the anger resulted from the completely unexpected privileging of a hierarchical system. The *Statement* smacked of professional parvenuism on the part of tenure-line rhetoric/composition colleagues, an aspiration to equality with the then-prevailing literary scholarly elite, where adjunct ranks retained the whiff of old-school spousal hires, unlike the "marginalized faculty" of the composition world, who, in their shameless numbers, "damag[ed] the quality of education" (330). It seemed to suggest that ragtag composition itinerants were to step aside and allow the field to claim a disciplinarily gentrified status, with scholar-kings in top-tier institutions as the formulator-guardians of what professional-strength rhetoric/composition is and the institutional forms it should take. What galled so in the *Statement* was this overt insistence on a connection between rank and excellence, an academic institutional Social Darwinism complete with implied threats of mongrelization ("Quality in education is intimately linked to the quality of teachers" (329); "the commitment to quality education requires that the number of part-time writing teachers [. . .] be kept to a minimum" (333).

In its effort to consolidate professional status and economic security, the primary authors sought to preserve the interests of the literature departments in which most composition programs were then housed, and which depended on the full-time equivalencies and graduate teaching assistants of the writing program for their literature graduate students. In what was an era of bitter relations between literature and composition professionals, the *Statement* closed ranks with the literary-landed gentry rather than with the marginalized instructors the *Wyoming Resolution* represented:

> The teaching of writing courses need not be limited [. . .] to those faculty members whose primary area of scholarship is rhetoric and composition. *Because of the significant intellectual and practical connections between writing and reading, composition and literature, it is desirable that faculty from both areas of specialization teach in the composition program.* (331, my emphasis)

By attempting to assuage any territorial fears in and about the dominant English department economy, the *Statement* had to soft-pedal its claim for a field with a distinct literature of its own: The consumption/appreciation model of student reading and writing common to literature pedagogy would be considered apt professional preparation for the teaching of writing. This concession came, minus consensus, despite the serious philosophical and practice-based conflicts that then-common approaches to writing instruction presented to then-current efforts to theorize rhetoric/composition as a discipline. One such example is Richard Fulkerson's first overview of theoretical approaches, "Composition in the Eighties: Axiological Consensus and Paradigmatic Diversity," published in 1990, in which he notes the decline of expressivism, formalism, and mimeticism, with the rhetorical instead displacing these approaches (411–14).

A concession of this professional magnitude fatally undercut the *Wyoming Resolution*. More important for critical weighing of a revival effort today, the *Statement*'s subversion of the *Wyoming Resolution* also illustrates how an organizationally-sponsored statement of any kind is vulnerable to political conservatism for reasons that much less directly affect non-affiliated entities (like, one might note, a gathering on the order of the Wyoming Conference on English, which was not connected to CCCC).

The Shelf Life of Timeless Values

In its call for exclusive control of the terms of work, the *Statement* projected what today we might call a nation-state conception of the field, a sovereign, united entity necessary for its efficient organization and security. From the opening line, the *Statement* posits that the goal of writing instruction is to enable the presumably natural end of democracy to flow from students' critical reading and writing ability: "A democracy demands citizens who can read critically and write clearly and cogently" (329), and the "loyalty" of a marginalized faculty to this cultural truth would inevitably be compromised, a scenario in which "[a]ll lose: teachers, students, schools, and ultimately a democratic society that cannot be without citizens whose education empowers them to read and write with critical sophistication" (330). Interfering with the "tradition[al]" (329) teaching environment—which the *Statement* assumes to be the working conditions supplied by tenure-track positions—would, the *Statement* implies, disrupt the inherent order of a democratic system. Only where "those freedoms established as the right of full-time tenurable and tenured faculty" (330) apply can students be "empowered," the *Statement* goes on to argue, and only students empowered by tenure-line faculty can embody a democratic society. The logic of the Enlightenment and of the founders themselves provides the philosophical and historical proof of the design. These truths are to appear as self-evident, and the increasing divergence from them, in the form of non-tenure-track faculty, would thus self-evidently produce a "crisis [that] dramatically affects the public interest" (330). The *Statement* depicts a world out of balance, an affront to the natural order.

In making this teleological move, the *Statement* relies on institutional power rather than disciplinary authority. It looks backward to a world order that had already become obsolete, as forces of globalization were reordering institutions and social power through economic revaluation of traditional institutions. Print literacy was becoming just one of many literacy forms, and increasing access to technology was fuelling democratic growth and economic empowerment beyond the dreams of any first-year course, led by a tenured professor or not. The *Statement* thus debuted as an exercise in professional nation-building in what was even then an ever more transnational world. Especially considering the *Statement*'s poststructural era, this kind of always already outmoded argument is an appeal to conservatism. In its call to sustain the principles and standards of an earlier age, the *Statement* follows the conservative strategy that Jeff Rice outlines in "Conservative WPAs": an attempt to maintain the status quo, the familiar, and to suppress the new, the diverse, and all of that which dissents, in a discourse that "settles in general on already established, uniform practices and beliefs even as it *often argues otherwise*" (4).

Claiming to represent the democratic and professional interests of marginalized writing instructors, the *Statement* actually works to preserve the status and working conditions of tenure-track faculty, as James Sledd famously argued in "Why the Wyoming Resolution Had to Be Emasculated." He coined the term "boss compositionists" to name this phenomenon. In language far harsher than is the polite norm of today, Sledd criticized the "newly risen compositionists, who are full of praise for themselves and their freshly bedoctored students but contemptuous of mere 'practitioners,' the teachers who do the work that the compositionists theorize about" (274–75): "[T]he most irritating characteristic of the boss compositionists is their contempt for the real teachers of composition" (275). Sledd saw and attacked the caste system that is implicit in the *Statement* and derided the notion that there was any revolutionary content to it: "I clearly see that a new group of academic entrepreneurs has achieved some degree of comfort and status. I clearly see that the old exploitation of temporaries and teaching assistants continues" (276).

How could such a status quo statement be materially effective in an environment already embracing the heteroglossic, the hypertextual, the open-ended, the destabilized, multiplicity, hybridity, the nonlinear, indeterminacy, anti-foundationalism, the socially constructed, the decentered, the postmodern, the asymmetrical, the intertextual, the queer? In every line, the *Statement* deconstructs itself. In theories of composing and pedagogy, from social constructionism to post-process; in emerging fields, from new media to World Englishes and cultural perspectives, from postcolonialism to rhetorics of color; in the calving of new disciplines—technical and professional writing, new media studies, English as a second language, writing program administration; in the theorizing of alternative, digital, and visual discourses in new methodologies, from ethnography to narrative inquiry: Those in the field continued to contribute to its proliferating practices and identities, confuting the teleological claims of the *Statement*. It was not even a document of its time, and the idea of reviving it, of reimagining it in now-relevant form, seems at best a quest for the quixotic.

COMMUNITY, INC.

Further, a revised *Statement* is a quest that, unsurprisingly, is already a deliverable, as they say, issued by the professional organizations. The *Statement on the Status of Working Conditions of Contingent Faculty*, CCCC-approved in 2010, reiterates much of the last two pages of the *Statement*—and notes the failure of its call for tenure-line appointments. Likewise, on its website, the American Assocation of University Professors (AAUP) offers an "issues" statement on contingent faculty ("Background Facts on Contingent Faculty") that substantially reflects the CCCC statements: the exploitative nature of the positions; the presumed excellence of contingent faculty but assertion of the inevitable damage to students; the need to set limits on the positions and increase the proportion of tenure-line appointments.

This is what professional organizations do: They issue statements that produce more statements, and any preceding rhetorical failures do not interrupt the flow. That is because the material effects of such statements have little to do with their topics and infinitely more to do with organizational credibility and survival, for organizations demonstrate their viability in the issuing, not the results. They operate necessarily on a corporate model—they are corporations, after all—with an economic imperative as the central mission.

The professional organization is subject to the same market forces that are altering the forms and values of our professional labor. Professional higher education organizations must accommodate their primary constituency, which now for the CCCC consists or soon will consist of an overwhelmingly contingent faculty, content deliverers, and online facilitators, increasingly outside of rhetoric/composition leadership. The changing membership profile is becoming evident even for the Modern Language Assocation (MLA), whose 2012–2013 President, Michael Bérubé, in a *Chronicle of Higher Education* interview noted the need for the MLA to "reach out to the growing number of scholars who are working in 'alt-ac,' academic jobs that are off the tenure track. [. . .] How can [I] encourage more non-tenure-track faculty members to join the MLA?" (Patton). Professor Bérubé based his appeal to potential members on professional ethos: "[T]he association must retool itself and assume more of an advocacy role."

With a membership that is increasingly contingent, the organization is not going to be an agent of change against the very conditions that sustain its membership base. This is not a charge of organizational corruption, but merely an economic reality. The CCCC has been particularly sensitive to its dues table, for instance, and the MLA's dues rate is tied to income level, but these policies result from a market concern, not altruism, and they reflect the common business practice of planned flexibility designed to maintain and, ideally, increase membership. As the available membership changes, the organization does so as well in order to remain a solvent concern. With such careful management, the professional organization will thrive despite the end of tenure and the privatization of research. Thus, long after state forms of higher education are stripped down, vocationalized, virtualized, and branded in contradistinction to elite private institutions, the corporate ethos of organizations such as the AAUP, CCCC, and MLA will remain, as each necessarily adapts to the free-market-induced new labor conditions by aiming their advocacy efforts at insuring the numbers needed for solvency. To look to another statement to alter professional conditions is, once again, to badly misread the corporate context from which such statements emerge.

In what ways have we as a discipline, especially those of us who have been involved in its managerial functions, accommodated the processes that bring us to the current statistics on contingent faculty and the associated commodification of the writing process that enables the reformulation of teaching into facilitation and delivery? Examining the facts of success and failure, we see that scholarly work and academic administration have prospered and the teaching of writing has become more marginalized. This new reality marginalizes the faculty function in higher education: "If the U.S. is to reclaim its position as the most-educated nation in the world, federal policy needs to shift from paying for and valuing time to paying for and valuing learning" (Laitinen). The willingness of adjuncts and non-tenure-track faculty to teach despite the now-systemic conditions likely reflects an economic imperative and a professional desire, and in any case the arrangement is, by this point, systemic. As the tenure system and full-time faculty proportion decline, and as working conditions remain unstable at best and exploitative as routine, the question of the relationship between composition instructors and rhetoric/composition scholar-researchers becomes ever more tenuous.

What Is to Be Done?

Frequently, and more intensely of late, I have felt pressure to be "less hopeless" and adopt a more positive register and a fix-it mode. Yet, daily reports and articles, in professional and public sites, in print and online, document the fundamental, global changes in the structures and values of higher education, driven by the usual economic goals of reduced costs, greater efficiency, increased effectiveness; by profit-seeking, political agendas—"creative disruption" and innovation being an unquestionable good; by retiring tenured professors replaced by contract (or casual) faculty; by the outsourcing of programs and the corporate agenda of MOOCs and virtual classrooms—a litany of faculty marginalization and curricular standardization accompanied by and enabling management growth and ever-increasing, breathtaking gaps in compensation.[6]

---

6. A situation neatly summarized by Steven Ward in "A Machiavellian Guide to Destroying Public Universities in 12 Easy Steps."

Neurotically, I often revisit the StraighterLine website to read its description of its English composition "course":

> The online English composition course examines five fundamental types of writing: compare and contrast, argumentative, persuasive, narrative, and descriptive. Lessons in this online English course also highlight the importance of proper grammar, punctuation, and spelling, and explain effective research techniques, editing, and revision.

For an additional fee, one can have e-mail contact with a "professor"; for English Composition, this is an individual who "received a Bachelor of Science in Human Services and Management and a Master of Arts in Education/Adult Education and Training/E-Learning from University of Phoenix." Models of this sort do not make me feel creatively disrupted, but they do dampen my hopes about the efficacy of further revision to any statement on working conditions.

I don't know that the situation is fixable, and it may be that the later twenty-first century model of higher education will better fit the social and economic structures of a flattening earth. I do think the income gap and redistribution of wealth[7] will be reflected in that model, and we will have greater equity at last by virtue of a more equally shared disenfranchisement of faculty. Perhaps, then, it is time not to recompose the *Statement* but to eulogize it as a failed model, a testament to prior values and efforts, and instead to reckon with a new reality.

We could, of course, accept the status quo, since our field is less affected by these shifts than most. Even if 100,000 PhDs are produced and only 16,000 tenure-track jobs are available,[8] a large number of those jobs are in rhetoric/composition, and so we should be optimistic for our

---

7. "Household income, adjusted for inflation, has grown 12X more for the top 1% than for the middle 20% [. . .] and 24X more than the bottom 20%" (Thompson); "As of 2010, the top 1% of households (the upper class) owned 35.4% of all privately held wealth, and the next 19% (the managerial, professional, and small business stratum) had 53.5%, which means that just 20% of the people owned a remarkable 89%, leaving only 11% of the wealth for the bottom 80% (wage and salary workers)" (Domhoff).

8. "[Hacker and Dreifus] report that America produced more than 100,000 doctoral degrees between 2005 and 2009. In the same period there were just 16,000 new professorships" ("Disposable Academic").

graduate students. Personally, I cannot feel the joy here. We exist in a social context, as our usual rhetorical refrain has it, and changes to the higher education edifice may produce a delayed effect on us—but they will affect us.

We could adapt to the increasing dominance of the non-tenure-track model, providing data on how poor working conditions affect not academic quality but institutional mandates in the form of "access, completion, and success" and detailing ways to enhance contingent faculty conditions and inclusiveness, as noted educational researcher Adrianna Kezar does in "Spanning the Great Divide between Tenure-Track and Non-Tenure-Track Faculty." She has to sidestep some crucial issues, however: "I am not arguing that it is desirable to staff colleges and universities with [non-tenure-track faculty]—only that their increasing numbers on college campuses is the reality that we must deal with." The authors of the *Statement* were adaptable in the same way, making free with intellectual and professional concessions in order to produce a management-friendly document that had no real impact on established practice.

We could jettison the teaching of writing as part of the field of rhetoric and composition, focusing instead on research and theory. This would lessen pressure on writing instructors who, for example, out of economic necessity or enthusiasm for innovation, find it hard to avoid or to distinguish between advancing new technologies/pedagogies and fostering change that undermines disciplinary and faculty authority. It would also let us follow Kezar in solving a problem by omitting its fundamental complication or the *Statement* by occupying both sides of the divide: "[Research in rhetoric and composition] is fundamentally necessary to the quality of education at all levels" (332), but don't forget that "[w]hile insisting on the importance of research in rhetoric and composition, we join with those professional associations who have affirmed that postsecondary institutions should develop flexible standards governing tenure [and agree that] distinguished teaching and service should warrant serious consideration for tenure and promotion" (332).

Dealing with hybridity, we must admit, is not our strong suit, even as the connection between teaching and research has been and remains a contentious professional borderlands. Thus, one could claim that the more ethical or strategic path is to reconceptualize the teaching and administering of writing as an academic area different from rhetoric and composition. In *Postcomposition*, Sid Dobrin argues against the "ethically abhorrent" implications of seeking to "improve" student writers while being oblivious to the role of colonizer that such a mission entails (13) and for a "writing-without-students position" (15). He urges a move to "the intellectual work of writing studies, specifically the work of writing theory, an endeavor likely best removed from the academic work of pedagogy and administration" (24). By the second path in a process I have elsewhere discussed as a "purification of/purification to" approach to disciplinary content ("Disciplinary Purification"), Dobrin's powerful argument has the value of, if not resolving the paradox, at least theoretically justifying the Kezar approach of removing the conflicting element, and it does not flinch, as the *Statement* does, from backing a single position.

Or we could revise the *Statement* but this time at least name the difficult issues that mobilized the reaction against the 1989 version of it. A revision effort that does not take these issues into account threatens to continue to bequeath to later rhetoric/composition generations the fatal foundational ill of suppressing professional matters not only of material working conditions but also of professional knowledge and identity that the original *Statement* left unresolved. If a revised statement assumes a largely traditional institutional and organization-based structure and does not renounce the impossible dream of articulating stable principles and standards, it, too, will be an already outmoded one. A revised statement, then, would need at a minimum to account for:

- The existence of a large, mainstream faculty not tied to the literature and practices of the rhetoric/composition field as characterized by CCCC intellectual sponsorship, with many of these largely contingent faculty working out of different theoretical/methodological frames, a lore-based agglomerative approach, or a corporation-authored curriculum.

- The challenge of inclusive faculty governance as the path to improved professional equity, reducing or ending the historical privilege of tenure-line faculty in governance matters, including in hiring and curriculum the changes in the nature and form of professional credentials.

- The changes in the nature and form of professional credentials and so of the vocational values that shape the writing curriculum inside and outside the conventional institutional model.

- The restrictions on curricular authority that assessment driven by accreditation organizations further produces.

- The growing redefinitions of academic credit away from seat-time in conventional classrooms in the form of such practices as competency-based credit, creating a faculty-free learning zone.

Such an undertaking asks a great deal of ourselves. Are we willing to acknowledge alternative sources for professional knowledge, validating routes that do not involve attending our graduate rhetoric/composition programs, such as those listed for the StraighterLine instructor? How willing are we—and how much agency is involved, in any case—to take into account today the heterogeneous nature of writing instructors and their workplaces, instructional formats, and pedagogical practices—and so many of these corporate, not academic? As Sledd so vehemently noted, Maxine Hairston identified issues of this order, and she, vehement in her own way, gave blunt statement to them. As her argument makes clear, the relationship of tenure-line to contingent faculty includes issues of professional knowledge, an issue that the *Statement* attempts to deny, dismiss, and defer. Sledd quotes these lines from Hairston:

The overwhelming majority of college writing teachers in the United States [. . .] are not

> professional writing teachers. They do not do research or publish on rhetoric or composition, and they do not know the scholarship in the field; they do not read the professional journals and they do not attend professional meetings such as the annual Conference on College Composition and Communication; they do not participate in faculty development workshops for writing teachers. (78–79)

Hairston is in the unusual position of having become correct over time, and it may be that we have to recognize that the profession of rhetoric/composition as the *Statement* represents is a very marginal one, and acknowledge other representations, including those more posthuman in nature and delivered in remote relation to what we do as scholars of rhetoric/composition. Trimbur and Cambridge argued in 1988 that

> the Wyoming Resolution raises a series of issues which cannot be resolved and makes a series of demands which cannot be met under current conditions. [. . .] To implement the Wyoming Conference Resolution would change what it means to study and teach reading and writing, literature and composition. It

would require a reallotment of resources and personnel and a revision of the current hierarchy. (16–17)

More recently, Donna Strickland argued that "rather than represent composition studies as connected to material, hierarchical workplaces, most histories of composition studies have instead offered histories of ideas [. . .] that more or less presume an audience of professionally secure teachers" (5). Any new statement cannot afford to situate itself in this idea camp; however, thus far, we have not shown a willingness to acknowledge that the assumptions in the *Statement* form an idea of faculty and their work that is outside of history.

At this stage in the disruption of higher education, dissensus on the principles and standards of the profession has more to offer us than consensus does. Thus this is an elegy without the generic final reconciliation, for the *Statement* is not worth grief, nor should it inspire hope, and emotion management is not progress.

Works Cited

"Background Facts on Contingent Faculty." American Association of University Professors (AAUP), www.aaup.org/issues/contingency/background-facts.

CCCC Executive Committee. *Statement of Principles and Standards for the Postsecondary Teaching of Writing. College Composition and Communication*, vol. 40, no. 3, 1989, pp. 329–36.

"The Disposable Academic." *The Economist*, 6 December 2010, www.economist.com/node/17723223.

Dobrin, Sid. *Postcomposition*. Southern Illinois UP, 2011.

Domhoff, G. William. "Wealth, Income, and Power." *Who Rules America?* February 2013, www2.ucsc.edu/whorulesamerica/power/wealth.html.

The Economics of Higher Education. Department of the Treasury with the Department of Education, December 2012, www.treasury.gov/connect/blog/Documents/20121212_Economics%20of%20Higher%20Ed_vFINAL.pdf.

Fine, Howard. "UC President OKs UCLA Anderson Self-Sufficiency Plan." *Los Angeles Business Journal*, 28 June 2013, labusinessjournal.com/news/2013/jun/27/ucla-anderson-gets-ok-mb-self-sufficiency-plan/.

Fulkerson, Richard. "Composition in the Eighties: Axiological Consensus and Paradigmatic Diversity." *College Composition and Communication*, vol. 41, no. 4, December 1990, pp. 409–29.

Gunner, Jeanne. "Disciplinary Purification: The Writing Program as Institutional Brand." *JAC*, vol. 32, no. 3–4, Spring 2012, pp. 615–43.

—. "The Fate of the Wyoming Resolution: A History of Professional Seduction." *Writing Ourselves into the Story: Unheard Voices from Composition Studies*, edited by Sheryl Fontaine and Susan Hunter, Southern llinois UP, 1992, pp. 107–22.

Hairston, Maxine. "The Winds of Change." *College Composition and Communication*, vol. 33, 1982, pp. 76–88.

"Learning about RCM." Kent State University, 2015, www.kent.edu/budget/learning-about-rcm.

Lee, Suevon. "For-Profit Higher Education: the Industry, By the Numbers." *Huffington Post*, 9 August 2012, www.huffingtonpost.com/2012/08/09/for-profit-higher-educati_n_1761369.html.

Kezar, Adrianna. "Spanning the Great Divide Between Tenure-Track and Non-tenure=Track Faculty." *Change: The Magazine of Higher Learning*, November–December 2012, www.changemag.org/Archives/Back%20Issues/2012/November-December%202012/spanning-great-divide-full.html.

Laitinen, Amy. "Cracking the Credit Hour." New America Foundation and Education Sector, September 2012, www.cbenetwork.org/sites/457/uploaded/files/Cracking_the_Credit_Hour_Sept5_0.pdf.

McDonald, James C., and Eileen E. Schell. "The Spirit and Influence of the Wyoming Resolution: Looking Back to Look Forward." *College English*, vol. 73, 2011, pp. 360–78.

Patton, Stacey. "New MLA President Pledges to Improve Conditions on the Nontenure Track." *The Chronicle of Higher Education*, 26 January 2012, chronicle.com/article/New-MLA-President-Pledges-to/130471/.

Rice, Jeff. "Conservative WPAs." *The Writing Program Interrupted*, edited by Donna Strickland and Jeanne Gunner, Heinemann Boynton/Cook, 2009, pp. 1–13.

Sledd, James. "Why the Wyoming Resolution had to Be Emasculated." *Journal of Advanced* Composition, vol. 11, no. 2, 1991, pp. 269–81.

Strickland, Donna. *The Managerial Unconscious in the History of Composition Studies*. Southern Illinois UP, 2011.

Thompson, Derek. "A Giant Statistical Round-Up of the Income Inequality Crisis in 16 Charts." *The Atlantic*, 12 December 2002, www.theatlantic.com/business/archive/2012/12/a-giant-statistical-round-up-of-the-income-inequality-crisis-in-16-charts/266074/

Trimbur, John, and Barbara Cambridge. "The Wyoming Conference Resolution: A Beginning." *WPA: Writing Program Administration*, vol. 12, no. 1–2, 1988, pp. 13–18.

Ward, Steven. "A Machiavellian Guide to Destroying Public Universities in 12 Easy Steps." *The Chronicle of Higher Education*, 2 October 2013, chronicle.com/blogs/conversation/2013/10/02/a-machiavellian-guide-to-destroying-public-universities-in-12-easy-steps/.

SECTION 2: THE STATEMENT AND PRESENT-DAY LABOR CONDITIONS

5 One of Many: The *Statement* in the Context of Other Position Statements on Academic Labor

James C. McDonald

INTRODUCTION

The Conference on College Composition and Communication's (CCCC) *Statement of Principles and Standards for the Postsecondary Teaching of Writing* (hereafter the *Statement*) aimed to change dramatically the employment practices of English departments and writing programs, to establish professional standards for an emerging but often unrespected discipline, and to reverse the trend of hiring composition teachers as contingent faculty with poor salaries and benefits, difficult working conditions, and little job security. In 1989, when it was drafted and approved, it was rare for a professional academic association to set standards for faculty working conditions within a discipline. Disciplinary associations normally left it to organizations like the American Association of University Professors (AAUP) to develop standards for faculty working conditions.

However, even as the *Wyoming Resolution* provided a popular mandate for CCCC to set standards not only for composition scholars but also for all writing teachers, professional associations were already beginning to take responsibility for addressing the widespread problems in writing teachers' working conditions. In 1987, for example, CCCC came out with a statement of criteria for evaluating faculty scholarship in the new field of composition studies, and in 1986 the National Writing Centers Association published a statement establishing acceptable working conditions and professional expectations for writing center directors (Simpson). Inspired most by the *Wyoming Resolution*, which explicitly linked teachers' working conditions to the quality of instruction that their students receive, the drafting and publication of the *Statement* created a rhetorical occasion for a national discussion of higher education's exploitation of contingent faculty and helped to launch a labor reform movement within academia.

Publications of a draft and a final version of the *Statement* in *College Composition and Communication* (*CCC*) in 1989 propelled many faculty to participate in hotly debated sessions about the *Statement* at several CCCC meetings, and *CCC* devoted parts of two issues, October 1991 and May 1992, to arguments about the *Statement*, which also was the subject of articles in other publications. In addition, CCCC distributed copies of the *Statement* to several thousand department heads around the country (Committee on Professional Standards 61) and encouraged members to organize public discussions about it on campuses and at conferences and to use it in generating arguments about working conditions with campus administrations and accrediting associations. At the same time, CCCC initiated discussions with AAUP, the Modern Language Association (MLA), the Association of Departments of English (ADE), and several accrediting associations to increase support for the standards articulated in the *Statement* in an attempt to persuade colleges and universities to implement them.[1]

Today, the *Statement* functions more quietly as one of many position statements by professional associations that set standards for working conditions—faculty salaries, benefits, teaching loads, merit raises, class sizes, tenure and promotion criteria—and addresses both the value of tenure-line faculty and the continuing exploitation of contingent faculty. The labor standards of professional associations became more important in the late 1990s with the formation of the Coalition on the Academic

---

1. See James C. McDonald and Eileen E. Schell for a history of the *Wyoming Resolution*, the drafting of the *Statement*, and the early arguments about the *Statement*. In its February 1989 "CCCC Initiatives on the Wyoming Conference Resolution: A Draft Report," the CCCC Committee on Professional Standards for Quality Education described their work with representatives of the AAUP, the Council on Postsecondary Accreditation, and the American Federation of Teachers, as well as their communications with the six associations who made up the English Coalition, including MLA and ADE, and the Directors of the Regional Institutional Accrediting Bodies (66–68). ADE endorsed the *Wyoming Resolution* in 1987 (Slevin 50).

Workforce (CAW), an alliance of the AAUP and the major disciplinary associations, including CCCC and MLA. At this time, the CAW collected and disseminated data on faculty working conditions in each discipline, urged associations to create their own standards for faculty working conditions, and coordinated a campaign to educate the public about the exploitation of contingent faculty. The CAW February 2010 issue brief, *One Faculty Serving All Students*, lists four "principles" to guide faculty, administrators, and others working to improve academic labor conditions, especially for contingent faculty:

- All faculty members need to receive compensation and institutional support and recognition commensurate with their status as professionals.
- *All faculty members should be aware of the recommended standards and guidelines for the academic workforce issued by their professional associations and faculty organizations.*
- All faculty members should have access to key information on academic staffing in their departments and institutions and use this information—along with recommended targets for staffing, contracts, compensation, and working conditions—to advocate for change.
- All long-term faculty members need to be fully enfranchised to participate in the work and life of the department and institution. (2, my emphasis)

In urging faculty to learn about their disciplinary associations' labor standards, the CAW realized that professional associations' coordinated involvement in the academic labor movement would increase the number of faculty participating in the movement, join faculty commitment to their discipline to the academic labor movement, strengthen the authority behind the arguments for labor reform, and urge associations to educate their members about labor standards and problems. Just as CCCC recognized the need to address the specific labor issues and situations of writing teachers, the CAW and its associations understood that they must set standards that recognize the particular nature and circumstances of each discipline's scholarship, teaching, and service.

In publishing standards for faculty working conditions in their disciplines, professional associations also recognize the need to stand together to improve working conditions for all faculty and oppose the exploitation of contingent faculty. Many organizations argue for standards that address what is unique about their members' work, even as their statements echo each other in their reiterations of the importance of research and teaching in all fields and in their calls for equitable treatment of all faculty. As a group, these texts demand respect for the diversity of faculty work and scholarship and for a sense of shared purpose in urging institutions to provide fair and equitable working conditions for all faculty.

This chapter provides an overview of the documents of professional associations in disciplines that are often represented in English departments, comparing them to the *Statement* and discussing the need for awareness of all these statements, even when we rely on the *Statement* in arguing for better faculty working conditions. I comment throughout and I close with recommendations for revising the *Statement*, given what arguments and evidence exist in other professional standards documents.

SITUATING THE *STATEMENT*

In first situating the *Statement*, it should be noted that the text considers only writing programs located within English departments and tends to assume that English departments include only two fields of study and two programs:

> Because of the significant intellectual and practical connections between writing and reading, composition and literature, it is desirable that faculty from both areas of specialization teach in the composition program. Ideally, faculty from each area should have the training and experience necessary to teach in both the literature and composition programs. (331)

However, on every campus, the *Statement* operates alongside other disciplinary documents that try to influence how faculty are evaluated and treated, depending on whether writing programs are located in departments of writing, English, English and modern languages, communication, or humanities and in consideration of what disciplines are contained within the unit. Because English departments may include faculty and programs in linguistics, creative writing, English as a second language (ESL), and folklore, faculty and administrators who set policies governing academic working conditions, therefore, need to be aware not only of labor standards authored by AAUP, CAW, CCCC, the National Council of Teachers of English (NCTE), MLA, and ADE, but possibly also those by the Association of Writers and Writing Programs

(AWP) for creative writing, the Linguistic Society of America (LSA), the American Folklore Society (AFS), and Teachers of English to Speakers of Other Languages (TESOL), Inc., as well as the Council of Writing Program Adminstrator's (CWPA) *"The Portland Resolution": Guidelines for Writing Program Administrator Positions* (Hult et al.) and the writing center position statement adopted by the International Writing Centers Association (IWCA) (Simpson). In fact, more than two dozen position statements on faculty working conditions have been published by these twelve associations.[2]

When read in the context of an English department, these statements as a group paint a picture of large, complex, and fragmented English departments in which colleagues may have little knowledge or respect for each other's fields. The statements resist the assumption that English studies is a hierarchy of disciplines with literary studies establishing the paradigm for "normal" scholarship, teaching, and faculty work, a paradigm that often has faculty in other fields struggling for visibility, respect, and the job security, salaries, merit raises, tenure, promotions, research support, and even office space that comes with this recognition. Documents setting standards for the working conditions of writing faculty and writing program administrators (WPAs), linguists, creative writers, linguists, folklorists, TESOL specialists, and contingent faculty emerged out of a history of discrimination against scholars outside of literary studies, administrators below the level of department chair, and contingent faculty, as well as a sense of alarm about decreasing numbers of tenure-track faculty and increasing reliance on poorly paid and supported contingent faculty.

Most labor position statements contain the following: criteria for evaluating faculty and their work, standards on the hiring and treatment of contingent faculty, and comprehensive standards. Most of these documents try to educate an audience of both faculty and graduate students within the discipline and other faculty and administrators with power in determining hiring practices, working conditions, and evaluation practices, although a few texts narrow their target audience to readers such as department chairs or job seekers. Two statements important to composi-

---

2. For this article, I am limiting my study to professional statements by associations that may represent specific faculty within an English department. Thus, I am not considering statements of AAUP and CAW or of some faculty who may be employed in a humanities, communications, or languages department or in a unit beyond the department level.

tion specialists, however, fall outside these categories: the *MLA Recommendation on a Minimum Wage for Full-Time Entry-Level Faculty* and the *ADE Guidelines for Class Size and Workload for College and University Teachers of English: A Statement of Policy*. Each addresses a single issue, and each illustrates interesting problems and choices that associations face in defining labor standards.

The MLA minimum wage recommendation stands out among other standards on salaries and benefits in its specificity and its concern with academic rank. First published in 2002 and updated every year since, it recommends minimum salaries for entry-level instructors ($58,000 in the April 2016 version) and entry-level assistant professors ($72,000 in April 2016), and suggests that higher education institutions provide health insurance with employer contributions along with "a portable retirement plan." Most other documents that discuss salaries, including the *Statement* and other MLA policy documents, avoid numbers in defining fair professional salary and benefits, instead arguing that salaries and benefits for one category of faculty, such as ESL specialists or contingent faculty, should be the same as what other faculty with comparable duties, experience, and credentials receive.

Although the principle of comparability takes local situations into account in a way that the MLA minimum wage recommendation does not, it is a difficult principle to define, and none of the texts in this study attempt to define comparability or to argue how comparable salaries should be determined when there are differences in rank, responsibilities, and credentials. In many institutions where the rank of instructor is non-tenure-track (NTT) by definition,[3] some labor documents provide no option but to take entry-level assistant professor salaries as the standard for determining salaries of non-tenure-track instructors. The documents also often justify lower salaries for NTT faculty based on differences in credentials and responsibilities outside the classroom, as the *Statement* does in stating that part-time faculty "should receive a salary that accurately reflects their teaching duties and any duties outside the classroom they are asked to assume. Compensation, per course, for part-time faculty should never be lower than the per-course compensation for full-time faculty with comparable experience, duties, and credentials" (334). In trying to account for different responsibilities among the tenure-track and non-tenure-track, the *Statement* makes the questionable

---

3. The Board of Regents in my state of Louisiana, for example, made the rank of instructor untenurable in all state colleges and universities in the 1970s.

assumption that faculty and administrators can calculate how much of full-time tenure-track faculty salary is compensation for teaching—per course—and how much is for research and service.

The MLA minimum wage recommendation does not distinguish between tenure-track and non-tenure-track positions and so applies to visiting assistant professors as well as full-time non-tenure-track instructors. It thus supports implicitly the practice of many institutions that use rank to justify salary differences between tenure-track and non-tenure-track faculty while at the same time calling for significantly higher salaries than many entry-level and non-tenure-track faculty now earn. The MLA minimum wage statement also implicitly opposes the common practice, in arguments about faculty salaries on campuses, in statehouses, and in the media, of setting salary standards by determining the average salaries of faculty for each rank in similar institutions in a region, such as Southern community colleges or Midwestern comprehensive research universities. Although this common practice is sensitive to regional differences in the cost of living, it often justifies large disparities among salaries of tenure-track and non-tenure-track faculty with similar credentials and responsibilities in neighboring institutions. The MLA document may be an implicit argument against this practice, but implicit arguments usually do little to persuade those who determine faculty salaries.

The ADE class size and workload statement, published in 1992, interestingly, uses other associations' standards to enhance its authority and provides a variable definition of ADE's standards. As the *ADE Guidelines* explain, professional associations have been setting standards for class size and teaching load since at least 1966—and the ADE statement explicitly reaffirms the principles and standards set by NCTE, AAUP, and the National Junior College Committee as well as silently reaffirms the *Statement*. ADE, like CCCC, holds that no college teacher should teach more than three sections of writing classes and no more than sixty students or forty-five developmental writing students altogether in a single term and recommends that writing class sizes be limited to "fifteen or fewer, with no more than twenty students in any case." ADE appears to make no distinction between composition and creative writing courses, which would make its recommended class sizes for creative writing workshops higher than the standards set in the *AWP Guidelines for Creative Writing Programs & Teachers of Creative Writing*, which recommends a limit of 15 students in workshops and states "that 12 be viewed as desirable and most effective." ADE also recommends class sizes no larger than 35 for literature courses, 25 if a literature course is "writing intensive," and 15 for honors classes and "seminars that require students to conduct research and to produce sustained critical essays [. . .] because close individual guidance is essential." ADE further recommends that in a literature course, "[f]or each additional thirty-five students, a teacher should have a qualified assistant to help with the evaluations of written assignments."

The ADE and CCCC strategy of setting one optimum standard for class sizes alongside a second higher but acceptable standard and ADE's call for the hiring of graders when literature class sizes far exceed its standards recognize that many programs may find the optimum standard unrealistic. By offering two sets of standards, the statements try to resolve the tension between providing politically/economically achievable goals and setting high standards that a majority of institutions would find costly and impractical.

While the *Statement* and the *ADE Guidelines* recommend the same standards for composition class sizes and teaching loads and while both statements should be used in constructing arguments on working conditions, the more comprehensive ADE standards make its document more useful here. ADE covers class sizes not only for writing courses but also for other courses that a faculty member might teach as well, and it addresses the entirety of his or her teaching load in recommending no more than twelve hours in the classroom per week for those teaching undergraduates exclusively and no more than nine hours for those also teaching graduate students. ADE also calls for lower teaching loads for faculty with publishing expectations, especially junior faculty seeking tenure. Even the *ADE Guidelines* could be more useful, however, if it set standards for other English courses, especially in grammar and linguistics.

Statements Defining Standards for Evaluating Faculty

Guidelines on faculty evaluation fall into two categories: statements setting tenure and promotion criteria for faculty in a particular discipline (CCCC's *Scholarship in Composition: Guidelines for Faculty, Deans, and Department Chairs* and the *AFS Position Statement on Promotion and Tenure Standards and Review*) and statements that consider one issue impacting faculty evaluation, such as work with technology (the *CCCC Promotion and Tenure Guidelines for Work with Technology*), service

(MLA's *Making Faculty Work Visible: Reinterpreting Professional Service, Teaching, and Research in the Fields of Language and Literature*), and institutional assessment (the *ADE Statement of Good Practice: Teaching, Evaluation, and Scholarship*). Statements in the first category assume that one group of faculty—writing teachers or folklorists—are part of a unit dominated by faculty who may have little knowledge or appreciation of their colleagues' research or the genres in which they write. *Scholarship in Composition*, in fact, is explicitly addressed to "faculty, deans, and department chairs" outside composition studies. Moreover, it continues to be published on the CCCC website, despite that the *Statement* expresses the same principles for evaluating composition scholars, perhaps because, with its narrower focus, it may be offered to these readers when evaluations take place.

Both the CCCC and AFS statements on evaluating scholarship call for those who evaluate faculty for tenure, promotion, and merit raises to recognize genres and forums for publishing and disseminating research beyond the academic book and article, to include "innovative textbooks, computer software and programs, and curricular development" and "conducting workshops" (*Scholarship in Composition*), or "[t]he production of exhibitions, festivals, archives, audio recordings, videotapes/films, and digital media works" (*AFS*). In addition, *Scholarship in Composition* calls for faculty evaluations to respect that composition scholars often publish "in academic journals cutting across traditional academic boundaries." Similarly, the AFS statement argues that the nature of folklore research often leads folklorists to disseminate their research in forums that challenge the academy's distinction of scholarship from service—an argument that compositionists and the *Statement* could use when arguing for pedagogical and assessment workshops and curriculum development to be evaluated as scholarship.

Both statements also argue that faculty evaluations must respect the kinds of research that compositionists and folklorists conduct, emphasizing differences from literary research and criticism. Therefore, both the CCCC and AFS statements argue in support of collaborative research and empirical or field research, and *Scholarship in Composition* makes arguments for evaluations to respect the interdisciplinary nature of much composition research and its practical and pedagogical purposes. Further, both the CCCC and AFS statements recommend that evaluations take into account that scholars in these fields may appear to be less productive than their colleagues. *Scholarship in Composition* recommends that those evaluating the scholarship of WPAs realize that the time required of administrative work "may result in lower scholarly productivity than in beginning faculty members without comparable administrative responsibilities"—therefore recommending that "administrative contributions should be given significant weight during tenure and salary reviews" and that outside evaluations of administrative service be included along with reviews of faculty's research and teaching records. Likewise, the AFS statement argues that the nature of folklore research—that "many folklorists expend great effort to gather their own primary information through direct, extended contact with individuals and communities outside academe"—affects "the speed with which folklore scholarship may come to fruition."

A second category of statements on faculty evaluation includes those that focus on a single problematic aspect of faculty work, and the publication of such a statement usually reflects a change in working conditions or evaluation procedures. The 1998 *CCCC Promotion and Tenure Guidelines for Work with Technology* supplements the *Statement* and *Scholarship in Composition*, both published in the late 1980s before computers became a central part of composition teaching, research, administration, and service. The *Statement* lists four "kinds of professional activity" for scholars in rhetoric and composition that are "sometimes undervalued" by English departments: textbook publication, "collaborative research," "professional activities such as workshops and seminars for faculty at all levels," and administrative work (331). Although the *Statement* does not represent this list as comprehensive, the list offers little support to faculty trying to make a case that tenure and promotion committees should regard electronic publications and the creation of instructional software or design of an online course as important scholarship. The 1998 statement on work with technology somewhat fills this gap.

Similarly, the *ADE Statement of Good Practice*, published in 1993, was crafted in response to increasing calls for formal assessments of faculty work and programs, often with arguments that universities should reduce their research mission in order to give more attention to teaching. Stating that "hasty adoption of reductive assessment measures is more likely to impair than to improve teaching," that "[g]ood evaluation requires sensitivity, judgment, and significant time and effort," and that standards of evaluation must reflect the individual nature of each institution ("What is appropriate in a research university may be limiting and even destructive in other settings"), the ADE statement argues for regular "qualitative, multiple measures" such as teaching portfolios, classroom observations, and evaluation forms that "emphasize qualitative measures and discursive formats" for evaluating both individual faculty and programs, instead of reliance on one-shot quantitative measures such as student evaluation surveys.

Opposing the popular view that teaching and research are separate and disconnected activities, the ADE statement argues that "[s]cholarship—the effort to advance knowledge—is a distinguishing feature of higher education" and that "teaching and scholarly activity are mutually reinforcing." These principles led ADE to adopt a broad definition of scholarship in which research and teaching are closely connected. With this definition, the ADE statement recommends that faculty scholarship should be evaluated not just by an examination of academic books and articles but also of scholarly work such as presentations, "instructional materials," and reviews of works by other faculty—and that "[s]cholarship on teaching—its methods, assessment procedures, and ways to improve it—should be valued on a par with traditional forms of scholarship." As a result, the ADE statement goes beyond recommendations of criteria for conducting program assessment and faculty evaluations to urge English departments to encourage diverse kinds of research and career paths besides that of researchers who publish frequently.

Making Faculty Work Visible, by the MLA Commission on Professional Service is not actually a position statement, but a 54-page report and argument calling for a better way of describing, evaluating, and rewarding service. It, however, functions like a position statement by providing arguments that enable faculty to persuade department chairs and tenure and promotion committees to recognize and reward parts of faculty work that are usually "invisible or undervalued" and, like the AFS statement, calling for those who evaluate faculty work to rethink the triad of scholarship, teaching, and service. The MLA Commission on Professional Service argues for replacing the triad with a "new model" that defines "*intellectual work* and *academic and professional citizenship* as the primary components of faculty work" (2), although the Commission also suggests how its principles can be incorporated into evaluations governed by the scholarship, teaching, and service model. *Making Faculty Work Visible* supplements other position statements on evaluating faculty, which generally have little specific to say about service. Even when a position statement declares that service is an important part of faculty work, the document often fails to discuss service as an area where faculty work is undervalued in ways that often lead to exploitation.

As a group, statements of standards for faculty evaluation suggest several subjects for revision in the *Statement*. A revised *Statement* obviously should incorporate and perhaps update the standards in the *CCCC Promotion and Tenure Guidelines for Work with Technology* (for discussion on possible and specific revisions to the *Statement* related to digital technologies, see James P. Purdy's chapter in this collection). A revision might include an argument, such as the one in the AFS statement, that criteria for evaluating research productivity should recognize that some research, such as ethnological and longitudinal studies, may require more time to produce publishable results than other research in English. Also, considering the amount of committee work, assessment, and other faculty service that go into writing programs, the *Statement*, like MLA's *Making Faculty Work Visible*, should also include a stronger position on the scholarship involved in much of the service in writing programs in arguing for fair evaluation of service and in incorporating NCTE's call, in its *Position Statement on the Status and Working Conditions of Contingent Faculty*, to compensate part-time faculty for committee work and other service.

The ubiquity of institutional assessment in higher education also makes it important for a revision of the *Statement* to provide guidelines of good and bad practices in the use of institutional assessment in faculty evaluations, as ADE has done. The *Statement* presents arguments for rewarding collaboratively-written works, scholarship on pedagogy, online publications and software, textbooks, workshops, and other forms and genres that composition scholars employ so that faculty evaluations take the special circumstances of composition scholarship into account. However, the *Statement* could also show how its guidelines are consistent with popular arguments that scholarship and publication be defined in broad and diverse terms, that higher education encourage scholarship on teaching, and that research, teaching, and service are too intertwined in many faculty's work to evaluate them fairly. Institutions assume that these three kinds of work can be separated neatly and easily—and they often can't be.

STATEMENTS ON THE HIRING AND TREATMENT OF CONTINGENT FACULTY

A large number of labor statements set standards on the hiring and treatment of contingent or non-tenure-track faculty. A total of nine statements by disciplinary associations connected to English studies address contingent faculty exclusively: four by MLA, two by ADE, one by NCTE, one by AWP, and one by LSA. These statements testify to the recognition by many of the associations connected to English studies of the growing overreliance on and exploitation of contingent faculty as a critical problem that requires the involvement of faculty of all disciplines to solve (for more discussion on the state of "permanent contingency," see the chapter by Casie J. Fedukovich and colleagues in this collection). Since the CCCC's comprehensive *Statement* was drafted in 1989, the percentage of contingent faculty has grown substantially throughout higher education, particularly in English departments and writing programs, despite the fact that the number of tenure-track composition positions has increased. English departments' practices in hiring, tenuring, and promoting WPAs and composition specialists appear to show an acceptance of the scholarship in composition studies, and some would contend that departments have improved how teaching assistants are prepared to teach writing as advocated in the *Statement* (see Risa P. Gorelick's chapter in this collection). The intractability of contingent faculty problems, however, has caused many associations to address these problems in separate statements.

The 1994 *MLA Statement on the Use of Part-Time and Full-Time Adjunct Faculty* states the basic principle behind these statements succinctly: "All adjunct faculty members should be treated as professionals." To this end, the nine statements mentioned in the previous paragraph agree on most aspects of the working conditions for contingent faculty: salaries and benefits comparable to that of their tenure-track colleagues and a work environment that incorporates non-tenure-track faculty "into the life of the department to the fullest extent possible," as MLA words this second principle in its 2003 *Statement on Non-Tenure-Track Faculty Members* and its 2011 *Professional Employment Practices for Non-Tenure-Track Faculty Members: Recommendations and Evaluative Questions*. The most typical of the nine statements is probably LSA's *The Employment of Part-Time and Temporary Teaching Staff*. Like other signatory associations in the CAW in 1999 and 2000, LSA explicitly adopted the

Standards for Employment of Part-Time Faculty drafted by the American Historical Association. The LSA statement's requirements for contingent faculty include "equitable salaries," "access to basic benefits" (retirement, sick leave, health and life insurance), travel funds to conferences and workshops, "seniority for hiring and pay raises after the probationary period," and access to computers, phone, office space, supplies, and other support.

The September 2010 NCTE *Position Statement on the Status and Working Conditions of Contingent Faculty*, however, provides the most detailed standards of any statement. It calls for

- Appointment letters that "clearly describe the position and identify workload distributions"—a requirement also addressed by the principle in the 2003 MLA *Statement on Non-Tenure-Track Faculty Members* that "NTT faculty members should be fully informed of their terms of employment and fully aware of the possibilities and consequences of departmental review."
- "[T]imely" (rather than last-minute) appointments.
- Yearly evaluations.
- Per-course salaries equivalent to that of tenure-track faculty with "comparable experience, duties, and credentials."
- Benefits and raises comparable to those offered to tenure-track faculty.
- Material support such as offices, telephone and computer access, copying, and secretarial help.
- Invitations to serve on "relevant" committees.
- Compensation for committee work and other service.
- Access to other support provided to tenure-track faculty such as travel funds, grants, sabbaticals, mentoring, and faculty development.

The *MLA Recommendation on Minimum Per-Course Compensation for Part-Time Faculty Members*, which is updated annually, goes beyond the salary standards of the other contingent faculty statements. For 2016–2017, it recommended, based on "a review of best practices in various institutions," a minimum pay of "$9,670 for a standard 3-credit-hour semester course or $6,440 for a standard 3-credit-hour quarter or trimester course." Its recommendation for a minimum full-time salary of three courses a semester (six per year) or three courses per quarter (nine per year) was $42,540–$42,570, based on the recommendation for entry-level instructor salaries in the *MLA Recommendation on a Minimum Wage for Full-Time Entry-Level Faculty Members.*

The problem of defining fair and achievable per-class salary standards is illustrated by Evelyn Beck's essay in this collection discussing contingent faculty working exclusively online. Beck writes that many online adjuncts earn less than $2,500 per class (181), an amount significantly below the MLA recommendation. It is true that faculty can teach online for colleges and universities throughout the country and accept or decline any adjunct position offered. Yet at $2,500 per class, an instructor would need to teach ten classes a year to exceed the U.S. Census Bureau's 2015 estimated weighted poverty threshold for a family of four that includes two children under eighteen ($24,036). At the same time, the standard that contingent faculty be paid a per-course salary at least equivalent to that of an entry-level full-time faculty member—a standard that appears in the *Statement* and most other statements addressing contingent faculty working conditions—may be meaningless at an institution like Jones International University, where adjunct faculty, according to Beck in this volume, outnumber full-time faculty 125 to 6 (175).

The problem of pay standards is also intertwined with the issue of job security. As Larry D. Singleton writes in his study of contingent composition faculty working conditions in the University of Louisiana system, salaries, on average, are highest for full-time tenure-track faculty and lowest for faculty hired by the semester and by the class. Permanent full-time non-tenure-track faculty generally make less money than tenure-track faculty but more than full-time faculty with multi-year contracts, who average higher salaries than full-time faculty with one-year contracts (46–49). Although the *Statement* should set a standard for per-course salaries, a revision should be guided by the knowledge that exploitation of contingent faculty is greatest when they are hired by the course.

MLA's definition of a full-time teaching load (three classes per term) is lower than the four- or five-class per semester load of many full-time instructors, a fact that MLA acknowledges in recommending higher salaries for full-time non-tenure-track faculty with larger teaching loads. The MLA salary recommendation for part-time faculty also lays out other conditions under which part-time faculty should be paid higher than its recommended minimum:

- based on "ancillary duties, including but not limited to: recruitment; supervisory role and responsibilities; research, publication, other forms of professional development, and curriculum development"—a stance that goes somewhat beyond other associations' calls for paying contingent faculty for committee work and service;

- based on "years of experience and professional degrees or other qualifications"—a standard in agreement with other statements;
- when institutions do not provide health insurance or a retirement plan for part-time faculty, calling for an "equivalent add-on premium or stipend" so that these faculty can pay for health insurance and pay into an independent retirement fund;
- for less-secure appointments "where contracts or appointments are for one year or less and not renewable, have no provision for a career path consisting of a sequence of appointments leading to longer-term contracts, or (after a reasonable probationary period) provide no rights to due process procedures after termination";
- based on "Instructional workloads: number of contact hours, class size, advising and method for evaluating student work and assigning grades (e.g., labor-intensive reading and commenting on student papers)."

The standards proposed by all the associations are consistent in these regards as they adhere to the principle that contingent faculty should be compensated and treated as professionals and should work under the same conditions and with comparable pay and benefits as tenure-track faculty. The extent of the disciplines' agreement in these standards could be read (in fact, should be read) as a kind of "industry standard" for English departments that a revised *Statement* should now reflect.

There is less agreement about how contingent faculty should be hired, however, and association standards have been evolving since 1989. The *Statement*, in fact, takes a hard line: that no more than 10% of a department's classes should be taught by part-time faculty and that it is "exploitative" to employ full-time non-tenure-track faculty "to provide instruction that is a regular part of the institution's curriculum" (335). The *Statement* emphasizes the latter position by italicizing a quotation from AAUP policies: "*The permanent use of temporary faculty is a contradiction in terms*" (334). This position drew protests in the 1990s from contingent faculty negotiating for greater job security without tenure lines (McDonald and Schell 371–72), and it does not recognize the practice of hiring permanent faculty outside the tenure system—although many contingent faculty have fought hard for the security of such positions.

This said, labor statements have evolved over the last quarter century to recognize other categories of contingent faculty based on existing hiring practices, and they have tried in their own ways to realistically account for the existence of full-time contingent faculty as a "fact on the ground," as the 2003 MLA *Statement on Non-Tenure-Track Faculty Members* puts it. In contrast to the *Statement*, MLA explicitly states that a standard that calls for virtually all faculty positions to be tenure-track generally does little to guide institutions in their hiring of contingent faculty, as some hiring practices are much more exploitive than others. Recent statements now call for departments to give "equal consideration" if not preference to their contingent faculty when they conduct searches for tenure-track positions.[4] The *Statement*'s position that contingent faculty should teach no more than 10% of a program's classes is softened in other statements. The 2002 policy statement *Ensuring the Quality of Undergraduate Programs in English and Foreign Languages: MLA Recommendations on Staffing* suggests "that institutions show their commitment to quality in undergraduate education when the percentage of undergraduate course sections taught by full-time faculty is above average for a given type of department." The average percentage in 1999 for PhD-granting departments, according to this statement, was 46%, 62% for MA-granting departments, 72% for BA-granting departments, and 53% for AA-granting departments. MLA's *Statement on Non-Tenure-Track Faculty Members* does not provide percentages but instead recommends that contingent faculty be "hired by means of long-term planning whenever possible, to provide for extended terms of appointment consistent with institutional needs, thereby also providing sufficient job security to encourage and support continuing involvement with students and colleagues." This standard would "ideally" mean three-year renewable contracts for contingent faculty and eligibility for "long-term review" after six years followed by "longer (five- or six-year) contracts" and participation "in departmental governance regarding NTT lines"—and any revision to the *Statement* should consider such.

A revised *Statement* must do a better job of contending with present realities in setting standards on tenure and job security for writing teachers. The MLA standards are far from ideal, but MLA's statements appear

---

4. MLA's *Statement on Non-Tenure-Track Faculty Members* adds the qualifier "presuming that their home institution is not their PhD-granting institution."

to be written with a realization that professional standards must evolve as working conditions and economic situations change in higher education. While tenure lines for all faculty should remain a long-term goal, the *Statement* must not defend tenure at the expense of helping contingent faculty win longer and stronger guarantees of employment outside the tenure track along with the improvements in salaries and benefits that come with these guarantees.

STATEMENTS OF COMPREHENSIVE STANDARDS FOR FACULTY WORKING CONDITIONS

Faculty who teach writing and direct writing programs have access to several comprehensive statements on labor practices and working conditions, including the *Statement*, CWPA's *Portland Resolution* (Hult et al.), IWCA's *What Lies Ahead for Writing Centers: Position Statement on Professional Concerns* (Simpson), the *AWP Guidelines for Creative Writing Programs & Teachers of Creative Writing*, and TESOL, Inc.'s *Position Statement on Professional Equity for the Field of Teaching English to Speakers of Other Languages*. These statements attempt to cover almost everything that impacts the working conditions of faculty in the discipline, including salaries and benefits, job security, hiring criteria, tenure and promotion criteria and respect for the field's scholarship, support of faculty scholarship (travel funds), faculty development opportunities, teaching conditions (class sizes and teaching load), and material support (office space, computer, telephone, and supplies). The scope of these statements varies widely, however. The *Portland Resolution* and the IWCA statement have the narrowest scopes, setting standards for administrators that often apply to only one member of a department. The TESOL, Inc. and AWP standards are restricted to faculty in their disciplines—TESOL specialists and creative writers, respectively. The *Statement*, however, is much broader, covering scholars of rhetoric and composition, graduate students, and all faculty—tenure-track and non-tenure-track—who teach writing classes regardless of their primary discipline. The fact alone that WPAs and writing center directors have their own statements reveals how difficult it is for the *Statement* to adequately cover such a diverse faculty.

The simplest of the comprehensive statements is the TESOL, Inc. position statement, a 143-word document that states opposition "to policies that treat ESL/EFL instructors and faculty differently from their counterparts with specialized credentials in other disciplines" and calls for "commensurate salaries, benefits, working conditions, and workloads across disciplines in order to foster academic and intellectual equity and integrity in academic institutions and in society at large." Other comprehensive statements are much more detailed. The *Statement*, *AWP Guidelines*, *Portland Resolution*, and IWCA documents all, in some way, deal with faculty credentials and the hiring process. AWP, for example, offers a vehement argument suggesting that departments treat the MFA degree as equivalent to the PhD in filling creative writing positions and that creative writers with a substantial record of publishing are qualified for creative writing positions without a graduate degree.

The composition statements, on the other hand, reflect a history of English departments appointing literature specialists to direct writing programs, staffing composition classes with graduate students and literature specialists, and graduating far more literature PhDs than PhDs in composition studies. For this reason, the *Statement* includes standards regarding English graduate students, who should teach composition "as an essential part of their training for future professional responsibilities" (332) and an argument that "it is desirable" for literature faculty to teach composition courses (331). It also establishes, however, important territory for composition studies within English, defending rhetoric and composition as a "legitimate field of scholarship with standards comparable to other academic fields," calling for "training and experience" of English faculty in both composition and literature, and arguing that WPAs should be "faculty professionally committed to rhetoric and composition" (331). The *Statement*'s wording recognized that, because rhetoric graduate programs were a new phenomenon in 1989, many veteran composition scholars and WPAs had literature PhDs and there were not enough composition specialists to staff every WPA position.

Although the *Statement* includes "the particularly demanding administrative service that is often a regular part of a composition specialist's responsibilities" as one of four kinds of "undervalued" professional activity that English departments "should count seriously" (331), it does not otherwise provide standards for WPA or writing center director positions. While the *Statement* states that, in some institutions, composition faculty members "are given administrative duties without the authority needed to discharge them; at others, they are asked to meet publication standards without support for the kind of research that their discipline requires" (329), the *Statement* does not provide standards for supporting the administrative work and research of WPAs and writing center directors or for defining reasonable administrative responsibilities. The *Portland Resolution* and the IWCA statement help to fill this gap. The two statements are similar, often using the same wording. Both call for institutions to provide a written description of the position before hiring or appointing faculty to the position, and much of the text in both statements provides guidelines for defining the responsibilities of the position as well as informing an institution's faculty and administrators in detail of the workload of these positions. Both statements argue that the position "should carry sufficient stability and continuity" for sound planning and development of the program or center. Both recommend tenure-track lines for faculty in these positions with well-defined evaluation criteria and procedures that consider their work as scholars, administrators, and teachers realistically and fairly. Both call for a sufficient budget and resources for the program or center, such as release time, clerical support, travel funds, supplies, computers, and office space, and both recommend similar preparation for these positions, especially knowledge of and/or experience in "teaching composition and rhetoric," "theories of writing and learning," "research methods," and "evaluation methods."

One feature that distinguishes CWPA's and IWCA's statements from the others is a detailed concern with the preparation of WPAs and writing center directors. Both statements list what the *Portland Resolution* calls "desirable supplemental preparation" (Hult et al.) and IWCA includes experience with business matters such as "accounting," "business administration," "grant writing," "information systems," "personnel management," and "records management" along with education areas such as "curriculum design," ESL, and educational psychology among its "appropriate" preparation list (Simpson). The *Portland Resolution* expands on the writing center statement to include not only "language and literacy development," "local and national developments in writing instruction," "various MLA, NCTE, and CCCC guidelines and position statements," and "writing, publishing, and presenting at conferences" as part of the expected preparation of WPAs but also "public relations," basic writing, and "testing and evaluation" as areas of recommended supplemental preparation (Hult et al.). Neither statement makes clear to what extent graduate programs should take responsibility for providing this preparation for WPAs and writing center directors, to what extent institutions should provide this preparation for their administrators, or to what extent this preparation is an individual responsibility. My sense of the genre of position statements on faculty labor conditions, which are primarily concerned with institutional responsibilities to faculty, suggests that the statements expect institutions to take some of the responsibility for preparing faculty for these administrative positions, but the detail and range of knowledge and experience required or recommended in the two statements strongly implies that graduate programs need to provide much of this preparation.

CONCLUSION AND RECOMMENDATIONS

The *Statement* operates in a context of many disciplinary position statements on faculty working conditions. These statements exist not to reinforce existing institutional standards, but to persuade faculty and administrators to change widespread practices that exploit faculty and encourage unjustified preferential treatment of some faculty over others. Based on my analysis of the *Statement* in the context of other statements of labor standards in English studies, I have a few recommendations. The *Statement*, I believe, would be more persuasive if it drew on and enhanced the collective authority of disciplines in English and the academy. The *Statement* should no longer assume that it operates in English departments that consist only of composition and literature faculty but recognize that writing teachers work in departments of writing and rhetoric, language and literature, and humanities, and in departments of English that usually include a wider range of disciplines than it now assumes. The *Statement* should take advantage of the fact that many of its standards are in agreement with other associations' standards by informing its readers about standards that have wide support. CCCC should use other professional statements to supplement the *Statement*, offering more detailed guidelines for supporting and evaluating faculty in administrative positions, evaluating faculty service and work with technology, compensating contingent faculty for additional responsibilities, and providing fair alternative standards for hiring full-time contingent faculty when establishing more tenure-track lines is not possible. If the *Statement* cannot fully address the labor issues of WPAs and writing center directors, then it should clearly endorse the *Portland Resolution* (Hult et al.) and the IWCA *Position Statement on Professional Concerns* (Simpson), although these two documents also need to be updated. At the same time, CCCC should take advantage of the central importance of writing instructors in higher education and CCCC's well-known commitment to ending the exploitation of contingent faculty to improve on existing standards and so influence the positions of other associations.

Composition faculty need to be aware of the position statements of their colleagues and learn how to use them in conjunction with the *Statement* to strengthen institutional commitment to the principles embodied in most of these statements: equitable treatment of faculty of all disciplines, tenure-track and non-tenure-track; a broad definition of scholarship that values teaching, encourages research that contributes to the teaching mission of higher education, and treats much service and administrative work as important intellectual activity; respect for diverse kinds of scholarship in faculty evaluations; the importance of recognizing and fairly compensating all the work that faculty do; and the need for job security and, whenever possible, tenure protections for faculty to instruct their students and contribute to their institutions effectively.

Works Cited

ADE Guidelines for Class Size and Workload for College and University Teachers of English: A Statement of Policy. Association of Departments of English, March 1992, ade.mla.org/Resources/Policy-Statements/ADE-Guidelines-for-Class-Size-and-Workload-for-College-and-University-Teachers-of-English-A-Statement-of-Policy.

ADE Statement of Good Practice: Teaching, Evaluation, and Scholarship. Association of Departments of English, March 1993, ade.mla.org/Resources/Policy-Statements/ADE-Statement-of-Good-Practice-Teaching-Evaluation-and-Scholarship.

ADE Statement on the Use of Part-Time and Full-Time Adjunct Faculty Members. ADE Bulletin, vol. 132, Fall 2002, pp. 76–77.

AFS Position Statement on Promotion and Tenure Standards and Review. American Folklore Society, www.afsnet.org/?page=PromotionTenure.

AWP Guidelines for Creative Writing Programs & Teachers of Creative Writing. Program Director's Handbook. Association of Writers & Writing Programs, www.awpwriter.org/guide/directors_handbook_guidelines_for_creative_writing_programs_and_teachers_of_creative_writing.

AWP Recommendations Regarding Non-Tenure-Track Faculty. Program Director's Handbook. Association of Writers & Writing Programs, www.awpwriter.org/guide/directors_handbook_recommendations_regarding_non_tenure_track_faculty.

Beck, Evelyn. "Rethinking the 'Legitimate' Reasons for Hiring Adjunct Faculty: A Recension Statement of Its Own." *Labored: The State(ment) and Future of Work in Composition,* edited by Randall McClure et al., Parlor Press, 2017, pp. 169–186.

CCCC Executive Committee. *Scholarship in Composition: Guidelines for Faculty, Deans, and Department Chairs.* National Council of Teachers of English, 1987, www.ncte.org/cccc/resources/positions/scholarshipincomp.

—. CCCC Executive Committee. *Statement of Principles and Standards for the Postsecondary Teaching of Writing. College Composition and Communication,* vol. 40, no. 3, 1989, pp. 329–36.

Conference on College Composition and Communication Committee on Computers and Composition. *CCCC Promotion and Tenure Guidelines for Work with Technology.* Conference on College Composition and Communication, National Council of Teachers of English, November 1998, www.ncte.org/cccc/resources/positions/promotionandtenure.

Conference on College Composition and Communication Committee on Professional Standards for Quality Education. "CCCC Initiatives on the Wyoming Conference Resolution: A Draft Report." *College Composition and Communication,* vol. 40, no. 1, February 1989, pp. 61–72.

The Employment of Part-Time and Temporary Teaching Staff. Linguistic Society of America, February 2000, www.linguisticsociety.org/sites/default/files/lsa-stmt-parttime-teaching-staff.pdf.

Ensuring the Quality of Undergraduate Programs in English and Foreign Languages: MLA Recommendations on Staffing. Modern Language Association, 2002, www.mla.org/Resources/Research/Surveys-Reports-and-Other-Documents/Staffing-Salaries-and-Other-Professional-Issues/Ensuring-the-Quality-of-Undergraduate-Programs-in-English-and-Foreign-Languages-MLA-Recommendations-on-Staffing

Hult, Christine, et al. *"The Portland Resolution": Guidelines for Writing Program Administrator Positions. WPA: Writing Program Administration,* vol. 16, no. 1/2, Fall/Winter 1992, pp. 88–94.

McDonald, James C., and Eileen E. Schell. "The Spirit and Influence of the Wyoming Resolution: Looking Back to Look Forward." *College English,* vol. 73, no. 4, 2011, pp. 360–78.

MLA Recommendation on Minimum Per-Course Compensation for Part-Time Faculty Members. Modern Language Association, March 2012, www.mla.org/Resources/Research/Surveys-Reports-and-Other-Documents/Staffing-Salaries-and-Other-Professional-Issues/MLA-Recommendation-on-Minimum-Per-Course-Compensation-for-Part-Time-Faculty-Members.

MLA Recommendation on a Minimum Wage for Full-Time Entry-Level Faculty Members. Modern Language Association, April 2016, www.mla.org/Resources/Research/Surveys-Reports-and-Other-Documents/Staffing-Salaries-and-Other-Professional-Issues/MLA-Recommendation-on-a-Minimum-Wage-for-Full-Time-Entry-Level-Faculty-Members.

MLA Statement on the Use of Part-Time and Full-Time Adjunct Faculty Members. Modern Language Association, February 1994, www.mla.org/Resources/Research/Surveys-Reports-and-Other-Documents/Staffing-Salaries-and-

Other-Professional-Issues/MLA-Statement-on-the-Use-of-Part-Time-and-Full-Time-Adjunct-Faculty-Members.

Modern Language Association Commission on Professional Service. *Making Faculty Work Visible: Reinterpreting Professional Service, Teaching, and Research in the Fields of Language and Literature.* Modern Language Association, December 1996, www.mla.org/content/download/3227/81262/profserv96.pdf

Modern Language Association Committee on Contingent Labor in the Profession. *Professional Employment Practices for Non-Tenure-Track Faculty Members: Recommendations and Evaluative Questions.* Modern Language Association, June 2011, apps.mla.org/pdf/clip_stmt_final_may11.pdf.

One Faculty Serving All Students: An Issue Brief by the Coalition on the Academic Workforce. Coalition on the Academic Workforce, February 2010, www.academicworkforce.org/CAW_Issue_Brief_Feb_2010.pdf.

Position Statement on Professional Equity for the Field of Teaching English to Speakers of Other Languages. Teachers of English to Speakers of Other Languages, Inc., Octobert 2003, www.tesol.org/docs/pdf/11222.pdf?sfvrsn=2.

Position Statement on the Status and Working Conditions of Contingent Faculty. National Council of Teachers of English, September 2010, www.ncte.org/positions/statements/contingent_faculty/. Also printed in *College English*, vol. 73, no. 4, March 2011, p. 356–59.

Simpson, Jeanne H. "What Lies Ahead for Writing Centers: Position Statement on Professional Concerns." *Writing Center Journal*, vol. 5.2/6.1, 1985, pp. 35–39.

Singleton, Larry D. "University of Louisiana System Freshman Composition Faculty: Instructor Working Conditions and Student Learning Conditions." Dissertation, University of Louisiana at Lafayette, 2004.

Slevin, James F. "A Note on the Wyoming Resolution and ADE." *ADE Bulletin*, vol. 87, 1987, 50.

Standards for Employment of Part-Time Faculty. American Historical Association, 2003, www.historians.org/jobs-and-professional-development/statements-and-standards-of-the-profession/standards-for-employment-of-part-time-faculty.

Statement on Non-Tenure-Track Faculty Members. Modern Language Association, December 2003, www.mla.org/Resources/Research/Surveys-Reports-and-Other-Documents/Staffing-Salaries-and-Other-Professional-Issues/Statement-on-Non-Tenure-Track-Faculty-Members.

United States Census Bureau. "Poverty Thresholds." U.S. Department of Commerce, 3 February 2016, www.census.gov/hhes/www/poverty/data/threshld/.

6 The jWPA: Caught Between the Promises of Portland and Laramie

Timothy R. Dougherty

> *The WPA is, on most campuses, the logical person to champion the kinds of changes envisioned by the CCCC's "Statement." Unfortunately, the WPA is just as likely to be a 97-pound weakling, ill-equipped to kick sand in anyone's face.*
>
> —Duncan Carter and Ben McClelland

INTRODUCTION

Published in 1992 alongside the official unveiling of the Council of Writing Program Administrators' (CWPA) *"The Portland Resolution": Guidelines for Writing Program Administrators* (Hult et al.; hereafter the *Portland Resolution*), Carter and McClelland's words above continue to carry a haunting resonance amidst the current state of labor affairs in postsecondary writing programs. Just as the field as a whole continues to struggle to live up to the standards set forth in the Conference on College Composition and Communication's (CCCC) *Statement of Principles and Standards for the Postsecondary Teaching of Writing* (hereafter the *Statement*), recent WPA scholarship suggests that it also continues to struggle to help WPAs gain the job security and institutional clout needed to advocate for better working conditions and programmatic quality.

More than twenty years ago, this reality led CWPA to draft the *Portland Resolution* as a document that would function as a sort of *Statement* for WPAs (Carter and McClelland 81).[1] Yet today, untenured faculty members are still tapped for administrative roles so often that Alice Horning, in the introduction to her and Debra Frank Dew's edited collection entitled *Untenured Faculty as Writing Program Administrators*, coined a term for this unique institutional location: the junior WPA (jWPA) (4). Further, as the jWPA narratives in both Dew and Horning's collection and Theresa Enos and Shane Borrowman's edited volume *The Promise and Perils of Writing Program Administration* indicate, the perils that the *Portland Resolution* sought to mitigate for untenured WPAs seem to be continuing apace.

Despite the hopeful interventions of the *Portland Resolution* two decades ago, the WPA too often remains Duncan and McClellan's "97-pound weakling" in today's university. While the *Statement* and the *Portland Resolution* may have helped to secure more tenure-track WPA positions,[2] the increasingly popular jWPA position reveals that many WPAs are still often untenured, and potentially laboring without clear and fair evaluation procedures that adequately account for their hefty administrative loads. Though their institutional location at the helm of writing programs would still seem to make them "the logical person" to give teeth to the *Statement* on an individual campus, a jWPA's own murky tenure picture and unprotected status can create a particularly unsafe atmosphere for attempting to kick the shifting sands of today's university on behalf of the working conditions in their programs.

Wedged between the responsibility to lead advocacy for labor justice as outlined in the *Statement* and their own precarious and disempowering job security situation that originally gave rise to the *Portland Resolution*, how do jWPAs understand, negotiate, and work through this predicament? Are they aware of these professional statements and the responsibilities and protections encoded in them? How do they see their institutions living up to the calls that have issued forth from these framing documents? How do they simultaneously seek to work toward better labor conditions in their programs and better chances at tenure in their own professional lives? Finally, what do their experiences suggest about how to

---

1. For a thorough discussion of the related yet separate ground covered by the *Portland Resolution* and the *Statement*, see James C. McDonald's chapter in this volume.

2. As Dew and Horning's collection attests, even this is not guaranteed. Following Martha D. Patton and Jo Ann Vogt, Dew writes, "Nontenure-track faculty WPA appointments remain as prevalent as jWPA lines, and they are arguably more problematic" (288).

revise or strengthen the *Statement* and the *Portland Resolution* in order to achieve better working conditions for writing teachers and program administrators alike?

To begin answering these questions, this chapter reports findings from a series of interviews with ten jWPAs. While these jWPAs' experiences cannot be generalized to all locations, I offer their responses here as a way to understand the challenges and opportunities for ethical action currently being navigated by jWPAs in their particular institutional contexts. These interviewees' responses offer the field a deeper look into jWPAs' lived realities at the crux of composition labor's rock and hard place, and suggest a strong correlation between a jWPA's familiarity with these disciplinary statements and their institution's current performance at aligning with the principles codified in each statement. Further, despite large differences in institutional context, there are important shared themes running through the narratives of the jWPAs whose institutions are gaining traction on the labor promises laid out in both the *Statement* and the *Portland Resolution*, insights which beg for revisions to the statements themselves.

In what follows, I first provide more background about the emerging jWPA professional location as it intersects with the history, purposes, and language of both the *Statement* and the *Portland Resolution*, followed by some contextual information about the study's design and a description of the study's participants. Building from participants' responses, I then report on these jWPAs' familiarity with the *Statement* and the *Portland Resolution* as well as their assessment of their institution's current performance according to the standards outlined in both documents. I close this section with an exploration of the two most important shared characteristics of the high-performing programs described by interviewees: long-term planning and collective effort for labor reform.

I conclude the chapter with some concrete recommendations for the revision of the *Statement* based on these jWPAs' experiences. Namely, the *Statement*'s section on "tenure-line faculty" must be revised to account for the unique circumstances facing jWPAs and, following the *Portland Resolution*, must actively discourage institutions from hiring untenured faculty to run their writing programs. However, since the jWPA is likely a permanent professional category in our field—as Dew says, "the train is out of the station" (279)—both the *Statement* and the *Portland Resolution* must also emphasize a hiring institution's material responsibility to provide extra professional development support for a jWPA hire.

Background

The *Portland Resolution* was a primary outcome of the 1991 CWPA conference that sought to assess the challenges presented by *The Wyoming Conference Resolution Opposing Unfair Salaries and Working Conditions for Post-Secondary Teachers of Writing*, better known as the *Wyoming Resolution*, and the *Statement* that followed it. As James C. McDonald notes in this volume, members of CWPA recognized that more specific protections needed to be drafted to account for the unique circumstances facing untenured faculty working as WPAs. The *Portland Resolution* filled that gap, and was designed to work in lockstep with the *Statement*. Yet, as stated in the chapter's opening, the practice of hiring untenured faculty as WPAs continues at such a pace that we now have a term for the unique location: jWPA. Part of the fault for the growth of this professional category might even be pinned on the language of the *Statement* and the *Portland Resolution* themselves.

On the one hand, the *Statement*'s most overt nod to the importance of writing program administration comes in the section on "tenure-line faculty." This section begins by stating, "departments offering composition and writing courses should rely on *full-time tenured or tenure-track faculty members* who are both prepared for and committed to the teaching of writing" (331). While a failure to distinguish between the circumstances facing tenured and tenure-track faculty may have negligible consequences for the teachers of writing in programs, many scholars have argued that those consequences can become quite serious when it comes to writing program administration. Rather than qualifying this distinction in its brief discussion of administration in the very next point, though, the *Statement* actually removes all markers of tenure altogether. It states only that "Whenever possible, faculty professionally committed to rhetoric and composition should coordinate and supervise composition programs" (331). Of course, all sorts of folks can call themselves "professionally committed to rhetoric and composition." Indeed, the varied contributors to Dew and Horning's collection show that jWPAs can be graduate students, tenure-track faculty, non-tenure-track (NTT) faculty, and even nonacademic administrative staff. Horning notes in the collection's introduction that she and Dew had originally meant the term jWPA to solely refer to tenure-track faculty, but their experience of soliciting pieces for the collection led them to define the term much more broadly, as "everyone else who serves as a WPA *outside* of a regular, full-time, tenured WPA faculty appointment" (4). Since there can be serious labor inequities between tenured, tenure-track, or non-tenure track writing program administration appointments, the *Statement* should be much more explicit here about the preferred institutional location for its envisioned administrator who's "professionally committed to rhetoric and composition."

On the other hand, the *Portland Resolution*'s pragmatic codification of best practices for hiring, tenuring, and promoting WPAs itself potentially invites growth in the number of jWPAs. Even though the document overtly states, "The WPA should be a regular, full-time, tenured faculty member" in section I.3, other sections of the document state that there should be clear evaluation criteria "in decisions involving salary increases, retention, promotion, and tenure" (I.2). If tenure is something for which a WPA might be evaluated, that invites the interpretation that tenure-track, untenured WPAs are an acceptable professional category. If we are serious about eliminating the use of jWPAs on ethical grounds, then the *Portland Resolution* should take a harder line and cut mentions of tenure evaluations altogether.

Of course, the jWPA position currently exists, and such mentions in the the *Portland Resolution* do provide professional protection to those negotiating their tenure cases at this very moment. What's more, not all scholars are convinced that the jWPA position is a bad thing. For instance, Richard C. Gebhardt argues in Dew and Horning's collection that a well-supported jWPA with terrific preparation from their graduate studies could be a revitalizing influence on an institution while simultaneously providing a compelling argument for composition's greater disciplinary prestige when, and if, they do win tenure (18). While many—if not most—folks will agree with Horning's counterstatement in the same volume that the jWPA professional location is ethically unacceptable (40), Suellyn Duffey reminds us in the very next chapter that institutional contexts as well as individual preparation and personality vary so widely that we should take great care before making such sweeping pronouncements official doctrine in documents like the *Statement* and the *Portland Resolution* (59).

Regardless, this robust conversation serves as a telling reminder that the conundrums the *Statement* and the *Portland Resolution* sought to remedy are still very much with us today. Frankly, both WPAs *and* postsecondary teachers of writing often continue to find themselves in tenuous labor situations. While WPA labor dynamics in recent years have caused scholars to increase their attention to the unique plight facing untenured WPAs, they have had less to say about how this increasing reliance on jWPAs is affecting the labor conditions for the teachers in these writing programs.³ How are jWPAs negotiating both of these aims, especially when these aims for personal job security and collective labor equity might be pulling them in different directions?

Context and Data Collection

To begin answering this question, I put out a call for participants in an interview study to jWPAs on the WPA listserv (WPA-L). All interviewees voluntarily responded to my call through the listserv. Each consented to the IRB-approved interview on a condition of anonymity, and all ten of the jWPAs interviewed direct first-year writing programs despite coming from a variety of institutional and geographical locations. Four hail from institutions in the South, all of which are described by the Carnegie Foundation as M4 (medium 4-year institutions). Three of those are public institutions, and one is private. One of those public institutions is a Historically Black University (HBCU). One respondent comes from a public M4 institution in the West. Two respondents come from the Midwest, one from a public S4 (small 4-year institution) and one from a private M4. Three respondents work in public institutions in the Northeast, two of which are M4 and one of which is an L4 (large 4-year institution).

Adding to this range of institutional and geographical diversity, the respondents are also at different stages of their career. Two have just completed their first year on the job, two their second, and two their third. One has just completed a fourth year, two have just completed their fifth, and one has begun a sixth year as WPA. These final three are up for major reviews this fall (2016): two for tenure, and one for permanent lecturer. These final three also happen to be the only respondents who have prior history with their institutions before starting their cur-

---

3. In addition to Dew and Horning's *Untenured Faculty as Writing Program Administrators*, Enos and Borrowman's *The Promise and Perils of Writing Program Administration* devotes two sections to the narratives of untenured WPAs, one to those on the tenure track and another to those on the non-tenure track. While both are essential reading and provide lots to ponder about the ethics of hiring jWPAs and the difficulty facing them in their own tenure cases, the texts have little specifically to say about the difficulty facing these jWPAs in working toward labor justice for the teachers working in their own programs.

rent roles, two as teachers in the program before becoming WPAs, and one as both teacher and WPA before earning a PhD and becoming a tenure-track faculty member. Consonant with the evidence of a steady and increasing national commitment to hiring "professionals committed to rhetoric and composition" to staff writing programs (McClure et al.; this volume), all ten interviewees cited rhetoric and composition as one of their primary areas of expertise. Eight of the ten possessed a PhD in rhetoric and composition. One interviewee had a literature PhD but cited a strong secondary interest and training in rhetoric and composition. The final interviewee possessed a rhetoric and composition MA, with no intention of pursuing a doctorate. Finally, all interviewees were white females.[4]

Though I followed the basic interview script in each session (see appendix), each respondent's answers prompted me to follow-up questions in order to clarify a point or push a particularly interesting idea further.

---

4. While I did receive two responses to my call from males, one was already tenured and replied to my call in order to offer suggestions and encouragement. The other was untenured, but currently holding a position as a writing center director. Though the final pool of interviewees was unplanned, it is also unsurprising, as Jillian Skeffington and colleagues' survey of WPAs reminds us that women continue to occupy the most tenuous positions in our discipline, still earning lower salaries than their male counterparts (18). Further, as Collin Lamont Craig and Staci Maree Perryman-Clark remind us in their essay "Troubling the Boundaries: (De)Constructing WPA Identities at the Intersections of Race and Gender," both the perceived membership of CWPA and the field's communicated professional ethos remains white-centric in the US. They call all of us in the discipline to think harder about, and to more publically assert, the ways that racial and gendered identity politics play a central role in how any of us navigate institutional and disciplinary structures (53–54). Indeed, while some interviewees mentioned "race" and "diversity" overtly or in passing about their student populations, the only interviewee to make her own whiteness central to the work she does also happened to be the only interviewee working at an HBCU. This seems to make Craig and Perryman-Clark's point more salient: Those marked racially as "other" in their institutional contexts are more likely to notice the ways in which race is potentially operating in each moment. While these aren't the only matrices of difference intersecting as WPAs go about their work in the academy, I do agree with Craig and Perryman-Clark's reminder that racial and gendered identity politics remain central to anyone's work of ethically negotiating institutional and disciplinary politics. In light of this understanding, the gender and racial homogeneity here is certainly a limitation of this study.

As such, my own interests and synergy with each interviewee produced particular results in particular moments based on our shared work in a particular medium (whether by phone or in person). Nevertheless, each interviewee answered the basic questions listed in the appendix.

Following Anselm Strauss and Juliet Corbin's grounded theory approach, I wrote memos after each interview to capture my initial impressions of the conversation, and to begin tracing out themes that were emerging in the conversations (198). This initial stage of memos led me to an additional focus for the study, as I noticed in an early conversation that even a jWPA who had a glowing report of her institution's performance in light of both the *Statement* and the *Portland Resolution*—and felt assured of her own tenure case—still told me she would not recommend the job to another untenured faculty person. This curious and foreboding admonition—in response to a throwaway question before we said goodbye—prompted me to add the inquiry as an official question to the other interviewees.

Program Performance and jWPAs' Working Knowledge of Professional Statements

In the tables that follow, I compare the interviewees' awareness of the disciplinary statements on labor best practices with their self-disclosed assessments of their institutions' performance along the principles outlined in each document. I begin with the *Portland Resolution* and then move on to the *Statement*. Though the correlation is not 100% across both documents, the shaded grey areas in each table show that the same interviewees who professed less awareness of the statement in question tended to also be the interviewees who held a negative assessment of their institution's performance according to the best practices outlined in the same document.

In Table 1, those interviewees I've categorized as "very familiar" with the *Portland Resolution* both used that term themselves. The respondent I've categorized as "familiar" gave an affirmative response of knowing about it. Of those I categorized as "slightly familiar," two said they were "a little bit" familiar with the document. The other interviewee I've categorized as "slightly familiar" professed that she was pretty sure she knew it, but needed to read it again and wished she'd done more homework on it before taking her job. Those I've coded as "familiar with EIW" spoke of intimate knowledge of the CWPA's sister document, *Evaluating the*

Intellectual Work of WPAs (*EIW*). Those who I've categorized as "not familiar" indicated no familiarity with either document.

Table 1. *The Portland Resolution*

The Portland Resolution					
Component	Coding Scheme				
Familiarity w/ statement	Very Familiar	Familiar	Slightly Familiar	Familiar w/ *EIW*	Not Familiar
	2	1	3	2	2
Job description	Had one	Officially Made one	Don't have one		
	2	2	6		
Clear evaluation	Clear	Clear but worried	Unclear		
	1	2	7		
Access to resources	Great	Good	Mixed	Bad	No Answer
	3	3	2	0	2
Access to stakeholders	Great	Good	Okay	Bad	
	3	4	3	0	

In asking jWPAs to speak toward their institution's performance on the *Portland Resolution*, I looked for mentions of four of the five crucial pieces of the *Portland Resolution*: a clear job description, a clear and fair evaluation process, access to resources for the program, and access to institutional stakeholders (Hult et al. 89–90). I left out the fifth criteria, defined by Hult and colleagues as "job security," because it is calling for long-term, professional stability in the role. Since each of my interviewees is on the track to a permanent appointment, this condition was already satisfied. Even for those interviewees who indicated they were quite familiar with this document, I repeated these four institutional conditions to aid them in their memory and in preparing their answers.

Only two of the interviewees came into the job with a job description. Two have officially made their own since taking the position, and the other six still do not have an official job description. Of those who were "very familiar," one of those entered the job with a clear job description and the other has officially now made one. The other WPA who had a job description was also the only other WPA who was immediately familiar with the *Portland Resolution*. The final WPA who's made an official job description knew the *EIW* well and used it to advocate for her job description, but was unfamiliar with the *Portland Resolution*. Those who professed slight familiarity or no familiarity with the *Portland Resolution* were also the group who had no job description and professed to have the fuzziest evaluation criteria. While familiarity with the *Portland Resolution* on the part of the WPA may not be sufficient to guarantee better working conditions, it does seem for this group of respondents to be a necessary prerequisite for a highly-functioning jWPA labor situation.

Table 2. *The Statement*

Statement of Principles and Standards for the Postsecondary Teaching of Writing					
Component	Coding Scheme				
Familiarity w/ Statement	Very Familiar 2	Familiar 3	Slightly Familiar 1	Not Familiar 3	Not Sure 1
Institution's Performance	Well 3	Improving 1	Mixed 1	Bad 5	

Table 2 shows the results of the interviewee's familiarity with the *Statement* as well as their self-disclosed assessment of their institution's performance. Just like the *Portland Resolution* question, I made sure to reiterate the basic tenets of the *Statement*, even to those who professed to be quite familiar with the document. For the sake of simplicity in the interview format, I emphasized the *Statement*'s call for no more than 10% of writing classes staffed by temporary labor, for benefits and secure contracts (if not tenure-track positions) for writing teachers, for equal access to material teaching resources for NTT faculty, for NTT faculty's ability to participate in the intellectual life of the department, and for course size caps at 15–20 per class and no more than sixty students per semester. Based on these aspects of the document, each respondent began with a qualitative judgment and continued to explain their position by describing facets of their program as they lined up with the *Statement*. Due to time constraints and the particular institutional challenges each interviewee faced, some chose to focus more or less on each of these facets. Some interviewees didn't mention certain aspects of the *Statement* at all, while others meticulously followed through on each category. Thus, unlike the *Portland Resolution* in Table 1, the institutional performance category is condensed into one measurement based on the interviewee's initial categorization and the examples they offered to illustrate this performance.

Both interviewees who professed to be "very familiar" with the *Statement* also categorized their departments as doing well in living up to the *Statement*'s expectations. The other interviewee who categorized her institution as performing well also professed to be "familiar" with *Statement*. Though each had a different configuration for meeting the *Statement*'s standards, these three programs were the only three of those I interviewed who were below the 10% part-time faculty marker that the *Statement* sets as its maximum acceptable level for part-time faculty (333). It should be mentioned, though, that while these are the only places that provided secure, full-time, benefitted contracts to nearly every one of their faculty members, none of them are living up to the *Statement*'s call for use of all tenure-track faculty. Still, these jWPAs described a high level of permanent job security and benefits for their teachers, strong access to the material and intellectual resources of the department, and class sizes/course loads in line with those outlined in the *Statement*. This finding suggests a possible revision for the *Statement* should expand the parameters for labor equity and high-performance beyond tenure lines alone. I return more fully to this idea in the conclusion.

The other two interviewees who professed familiarity with the *Statement* had mixed reviews of their department's performance. One of them declared her department as exactly mixed, saying that the social and intellectual aspects of the department are working quite well. In the financial and benefits for teachers portion of the *Statement*, however, her department—which relies on roughly 75% NTT, part-time labor—is doing "piss poor." The other jWPA who professed familiarity with the *Statement* saw a bit more progress in the material life of the department: Just over half of the department's adjuncts, who teach the lion's share of the courses, have access to benefits. However, the physical and social conditions for the adjuncts in the life of the department were described as "heartbreaking." On the whole, this jWPA's description placed her department in the "bad" performance category.

The jWPA who was "slightly familiar" with the *Statement* also said that her department is improving on its vision each year.

Across the board, those who were unfamiliar or unsure about their familiarity with the *Statement* also described their programs as having the lowest performance of those jWPAs I interviewed. Their responses ranged from an understated "Not good" to an exclaimed "Not working!" to even more damning indictments. One of these jWPAs, referring to her school's professed commitments to social justice, states, "We preach social justice, but don't practice it for our adjuncts." Another, in describing her institution's performance on the *Statement* resorted to expletives: "It f***ing sucks!"

For both the *Portland Resolution* and the *Statement*, then, there is a clear correlation between the jWPA's familiarity with these documents and their institution's performance. Part of this may be due to each jWPA's scholarly focus, and part of it seems aligned with the institutional cultures they've inherited. This said, it seems clear that a familiarity with the tenets of these disciplinary best-practice statements is a prerequisite for better programmatic labor conditions. Of course, I am neither implying that working familiarity with these disciplinary documents will magically improve jWPAs' labor situations in their programs, nor am I saying that such familiarity is itself a sufficient condition for high programmatic performance. This small sampling of jWPAs does suggest, though, that working familiarity with the contents of these documents may be a necessary condition for a program's alignment with the standards set in the *Statement* and the *Portland Resolution*. Just as Edward White has famously implored WPAs to use their power or lose it in an article aptly entitled "Use It or Lose It: Power and the WPA" (3), jWPAs must be aware of the disciplinary clout encoded in these documents in order to use them as part of a well-rounded arsenal of rhetorical strategies for bringing their institutions to heel. In other words, use them to your advantage, or lose a keen opportunity provided by these important inartistic proofs. While this finding does not directly bear on a revision of the *Statement* or the *Portland Resolution*, it does imply that the field must find better ways to help jWPAs become aware of the labor tools they have at their disposal.[5] In what follows, I'll tease out some of the shared qualities exhibited by the three programs performing well under both statements.

Profiling Shared Qualities in Successful Programs

Only three of the ten jWPAs represented their programs as performing at a high level under the conditions outlined in both statements, and these programs vary greatly in size, geography, organizational maturity,

---

5. For a similar recommendation, see McDonald's chapter in this volume.

and job structures. The first program, which I'll hereafter refer to as "Small Program," is located in an institution categorized by the Carnegie Foundation as an S4 public institution in the Midwest. "Small Program" jWPA has a long institutional history as a NTT teacher, writing center director, and WPA before being hired as a tenure-track faculty member and resuming her post as the WPA after completing her PhD in rhetoric and composition. The second program, hereafter referred to as "Medium Program," is located at an institution categorized as an M4 private college in the Southeast. "Medium Program" is the only jWPA I interviewed who is on the promotion track for a permanent lecturer position, and she taught at her institution for four years before earning the promotion to WPA. She holds an MA, which is considered the teaching degree at her institution, and is not planning to pursue a doctorate. Upon successful review this fall, she will be promoted to the lecturer equivalent of tenure. The third program, which I'll hereafter refer to as "Large Program," is located in an institution categorized as an L4 public institution in the Northeast. "Large Program" jWPA also has a rhetoric and composition PhD and, while having administrative experience elsewhere on the non-tenure-track, was hired here as a WPA on the tenure-track. Shortly after she arrived, her institution asked her to lead the transition of the writing program out of the English department and into a stand-alone, independent program in the university. While this has allowed her a great deal of access to stakeholders and resources for the program, her tenure case is still in the hands of the English department. Though she has a clear job description that she officially drafted herself, as well as clear and fair evaluation criteria, the political reality of this recent move does give her pause as she contemplates tenure.

While these programs have many differences, they do share two qualities that indicate clear benchmarks for success: collective effort toward institutional change and long-term planning for achieving the labor visions outlined in the *Statement* and the *Portland Resolution*. As for collective effort, this nod to the work of others isn't merely window dressing for the programs that are seeing success. Rather, it seems to be a fundamental prerequisite that bending a program's practices toward the standards outlined in the *Statement* and the *Portland Resolution* is a collective, multi-generational, and multi-leveled endeavor. Even the most charismatic and creative WPAs rely on help from their friends. In other words, based on these jWPAs' experiences, we can shelve any notions of a hero narrative. Institutional progress in the area of labor practices and working conditions appears to be a collective effort. In this way, these jWPAs ratify Bruce Horner's insights on labor in composition and writing program administration. In a critique of the way WPAs argue for their intellectual worth, Horner claims that the market-driven rhetorics of "utility" and the professionalism rhetorics of WPA "intellectual work" that WPAs often use to justify their programs and their labor tend to work against the collective reality of the work of composition and writing program administration. Rather than being commodifiable products of individual achievement, Horner argues, both composition and WPA work are inherently networked, collective endeavors (179–80). These jWPAs' stories confirm this insight, prompting the possibility that CWPA might fruitfully consider a revision to *Evaluating the Intellectual Work of Writing Administration*.

The other theme that emerged among the three programs deemed high performing in terms of the two statements—as well as in discussions with another jWPA who's begun building a more robust intellectual climate in her program—is the importance of planning for the long term. For the jWPAs whose institutions are already performing admirably under both statements, they have either inherited or built a program-wide long-term plan to achieve equitable labor conditions. For instance, "Small Program" is led by a jWPA who had the institutional and experiential benefit of serving as her department's jWPA before going back to school for her doctoral work. As such, she has twenty years of experience at this institution, first as NTT faculty NTT, then as NTT director of the writing center, and then as NTT WPA. Even before she became tenure-track faculty, then, she provided the stability needed to sustain her vision of full-time lectureships and renewable contracts for all NTT faculty in the program. She began with successful advocacy for updated computer technology in writing classrooms. Then, over a period of six years, she slowly hired permanent, full-time, and fully-benefitted professional writing teachers to staff her program's writing courses.

This long-term vision is mirrored in both "Medium Program" and "Large Program." "Medium Program," for instance, had two strong WPA leaders before its current jWPA, and the previous leaders laid a strong groundwork for the current jWPA. "Large Program" underwent a dramatic paradigm shift, yet the jWPA has instituted a long-term vision with plans to slowly convert their stable, renewable visiting assistant professor positions (with great salaries and benefits) to tenure-track positions. This planning insight demands a more robust nod to the scaffolding of labor reform in writing programs than the *Statement* currently provides, a notion I flesh out in the conclusion.

This penchant for planning extends past the established and successful programs to the ones who are slowly beginning to see some progress along the parameters of the *Statement* and the *Portland Resolution*. One jWPA, in her third year at a public M4 institution in the South, inherited a program staffed by roughly 70% of temporary instructors without benefits. In her three years—during a statewide economic downturn, no less—she's been able to successfully create five full-time, renewable instructorships with full benefits and competitive salaries. This results in a reduction of flexible labor from 70% to 50–57%, depending on yearly enrollment. She has ambitious, concrete plans in place to reduce this percentage to 20% over the next two years, and 10% in three years.

Still another jWPA, one just finishing her first year in the job at an M4 institution in the Northeast, knows her program has a long way to go. As previously stated, she describes the material conditions of office space, institutional visibility, and teaching support for adjuncts as "heartbreaking." In her planning, she has made it her first priority to seek to build a cohesive spirit of intellectual camaraderie and exchange for the teachers in the writing program. But she knows that more material markers of progress will require a longer haul: "I don't think we're going to get there anytime soon. But I'll keep my fingers crossed for the long term." Referring to other WPAs' stories about how long it took them to secure full-time lectureships for all their adjuncts, for instance, or to build an autonomous writing program, she states:

> I'm thinking ten years will probably be our long-term timeline. That means I'm post-tenure. That means we're starting to have conversations about these changes. In three years, very cautiously. Then, more explicitly after tenure, and with more force and momentum, hopefully, after six or seven years.

Recommendations for Revising the *Statement*

These jWPAs' experiences suggest the need for revision to the *Statement* along two lines: one for the working conditions of writing teachers in departments, and the other for the working conditions of jWPAs. I'll address the former first, and close with some recommendations for further protecting jWPAs. While it would be difficult to build specific guidelines into the *Statement* in order to reflect the need for long-term labor planning and a collective effort from numerous stakeholders in an institution, these themes do suggest that the *Statement* should prescribe some intermediate steps between the stated ideal of programs staffed entirely by tenure-track faculty and the stark reality of academic appointments for most jWPAs, these participants included. The *Statement* should scaffold its ideal vision by providing some long-range benchmarks for programs to plan for in the real continuum between absolute part-time labor exploitation and total tenure-line paradise.

Of the three high-performing programs, I found only one ("Large Program") was even able to envision—let alone implement—a viable possible future where it might convert its full-time, renewable visiting assistant professorships into permanent tenure lines. And this program is only able to do so because it relies on a large number of graduate student teaching assistants (TAs)—albeit TAs who are well supported and union organized. The other two jWPAs I interviewed whose programs were close to living up to the calls in the *Statement* and the *Portland Resolution* ("Small Prorgram" and "Medium Program") must currently content themselves with having built programs where their NTT faculty are at least accorded job security, full-time renewable contracts, and health benefits. The seven programs that lagged behind these high-performing programs are sometimes still dealing with labor situations where upwards of 70% or more of their classes are staffed by flexible adjunct labor. The *Statement*'s admonition, quoting the American Association of University Professors, that "The permanent use of temporary faculty is a contradiction in terms" (334) rings particularly hollow for the jWPAs I've interviewed, many of whom find themselves without their own clear job description while being handed programs that have grown quite financially dependent on staffing the majority of classes with flexible part-time labor. Although the *Statement* does allow that the "transformation to full-time tenure-track lines may have to proceed in stages" (335), it must do more to state reasonable, realistic means of achieving those stages.

To rectify this, the *Statement* should delineate some appropriate stages for an institution in transition from flexible labor to tenure-track security. It might declare that one possible first step to better working conditions, as I found in my interviews, is the full participation of all part-time faculty in the intellectual life, material support (in terms of office space and copying privileges, for instance), and long-term governance of the department. Once this is reasonably achieved, the second recommended step could be to begin a conversion process of part-time lines to full-time NTT lines equipped with full benefits and renewable contracts, similar to the "humane lectureship" location analyzed and critiqued by authors in composition (Brumberger) and technical and professional communication (Melancon and England). Barring a sea change in an institution like the one experienced by "Large Program" jWPA, the *Statement* could reiterate that this second step will have to be incrementally implemented over time, as budgets allow, until a department reaches the *Statement*'s benchmark of less than 10% of classes staffed by part-time labor. Once this is attained, step three could recommend that the department must then find a way to get this figure closer to 0%. At this point, the *Statement* could finally suggest that step four would have departments document a feasible strategy to converting these full-time, renewable lines into tenure-track appointments or their reasonable equivalent.[6] If a specific scaffolding step-by-step process like this proves too unwieldy a revision for the *Statement*, more global changes may be required to the document that do away with the separate sections on tenure-line and full-time temporary faculty, integrating them more gracefully to reflect this need for scaffolding and the reality that many programs are achieving solid forms of labor equity in their contexts without matching the *Statement*'s call for tenure lines or bust.

One of the most interesting moments of my interview process came when I asked if these jWPAs would recommend taking a jWPA job to others. Though each stated they felt reasonably assured that they would achieve tenure themselves, only one of the ten respondents offered an unqualified yes to that question. This resoundingly negative response seems curious given that each of the participants seemed confident in their own tenure case. Each participant expected to run the gauntlet of pre-tenure administration successfully, yet nine of ten wouldn't wish the experience on another colleague in the field. More research is needed on

---

6. By this, I follow "Medium Program" jWPA's experience: She herself is appointed on a lecturer track that awards the equivalent of tenure with a clear evaluation scheme weighted more for teaching than research. This option might be further trumpeted somehow in the *Statement* and the *Portland Resolution*, as it confers job security for those who are excellent teachers but otherwise uninterested in pursuing the PhD or a research tenure-track position. It also answers earlier critiques of the bias toward PhD professionalization encoded in the *Statement*'s all-or-nothing tenure plan (see also Hansen; McDonald, this volume; McDonald and Schell).

this point—both quantitative data on the percentage of jWPAs who are being denied tenure and qualitative data to better understand why so many seemingly successful jWPAs wouldn't recommend the experience to someone else. While that research is beyond the scope of this chapter, it does seem clear that the participants I interviewed almost unanimously believe that it's better to wait until tenure to take on an administrative role. As such, I suggest that the *Statement* must revamp its recommendations to the use of "faculty professionally committed to rhetoric and composition" (331) for administration in three ways:

- Add the word "tenured" to the phrase above in point 2 of the tenure-line faculty section, and refer directly to the *Portland Resolution*'s discouragement of the use of jWPAs here.
- Build another point immediately following that notes the institutional barriers at many schools to hiring a tenured faculty writing program administrator. Then, lay out clear parameters for the ethical hiring of jWPAs. This point would necessarily include the demand for clear job descriptions and fair evaluation structures that publically protect jWPAs for their additional service load as they work toward tenure. Finally, refer again to the *Portland Resolution* for further enhancement of disciplinary authority here.
- Declare that an institution has an ethical responsibility to provide the material resources for additional administrative training required for jWPAs to be successful. One way to say this is "We recommend that any institution who actively seeks to hire a junior faculty member to run its writing program must also provide adequate additional professional development funding to support this faculty member's success before they take over administrative duties. One possible development opportunity, but by all means not the only one, is CWPA's annual workshop for WPAs prior to the WPA Conference. The hiring institution must also provide a yearly monetary stipend for additional administrative professional de-

velopment in order to ensure the success of their junior hire in the demands of their role."[7]

The last point equally applies to the *Portland Resolution*, which should also encode more specific material responsibilities for institutions willing to hire jWPAs. While I agree with those who contend that graduate programs must also reform their professional training in order to prepare graduates for the likely eventuality that they'll have to accept a jWPA position,[8] I contend that our discipline must concomitantly and vociferously demand that any institution seeking to save money by hiring a jWPA must also pay the higher price of providing training funds to ensure a jWPA's success.

In the end, the current situation for these ten jWPAs is not all bad. Despite most of them not knowing the professional standards as outlined in the *Portland Resolution*, the majority of jWPAs I interviewed felt that they had good access to resources and higher-level administrators for the benefit of decision-making in their departments. This signals a positive change that, as McClure, Goldstein, and Pemberton state at the outset of this volume, can be bolstered by more hard data on writing program working conditions across the board. While this interview study provides only a small gesture in that direction, I hope to have demonstrated the correlation between administrator and institutional awareness of these disciplinary labor guidelines and better working conditions within programs. By adding more teeth and specificity to the *Statement* and the *Portland Resolution*—and coupling such revision with a more thorough effort to educate future jWPAs about these resources—we can continue to help jWPAs gain the necessary footing to collectively build better labor conditions in more writing programs. Indeed, data-based

---

7. Though there may be a danger of seeming self-serving by mentioning this CWPA professional service, this recommendation comes directly from one of the jWPAs I interviewed. While she offered a "qualified no" when I asked her if she'd recommend the jWPA job to someone else, she thought that one of the qualifications that would make a jWPA job more humane would be if the institution provided the funding to go to this "WPA bootcamp" before starting the job. This additional institutional support for administrative training was a desire echoed by a few other jWPAs I interviewed.

8. See Dew's terrific conclusion to the Horning and Dew collection, which provides a thorough overview of the current debate about how much graduate programs need to take responsibility for the administrative preparation of their students.

revisions like the ones outlined in this book could mean the crucial difference between weaklings kicking sand and empowered programs collectively building on stone.

Works Cited

Brumberger, Eva. "The Best of Time, the Worst of Times: One Version of the 'Humane' Lectureship." *Moving a Mountain: Transforming the Role of Contingent Faculty in Composition and Higher Education*, edited by Eileen Schell and Patricia Lambert Stock, National Counctil of Teachers of English, 2001, pp. 91–106.

Carter, Duncan, and Ben McClelland. "WPAs Assess the CCCC's 'Statement of Principles and Standards." *WPA: Writing Program Administration*, vol. 16, no. 1–2, 1992, pp. 71–87.

CCCC Executive Committee. *Statement of Principles and Standards for the Postsecondary Teaching of Writing. College Composition and Communication*, vol. 40, no. 3, 1989, pp. 329–36.

Craig, Collin Lamont, and Staci Maree Perryman-Clark. "Troubling the Boundaries: (De)Constructing WPA Identities at the Intersections of Race and Gender." *WPA: Writing Program Administration*, vol. 34, no. 2, 2011, pp. 37–58.

Dew, Debra Frank. "Conclusion: Ethical Options for Disciplinary Progress on the Issue of jWPA Appointments." *Untenured Faculty as Writing Program Administrators*, edited by Debra Frank Dew and Alice Horning, Parlor Press, 2007, pp. 279–91.

Dew, Debra Frank, and Alice Horning. *Untenured Faculty as Writing Program Administrators*. Parlor Press, 2007.

Duffey, Suellynn. "Defining Junior." *Untenured Faculty as Writing Program Administrators*, edited by Debra Frank Dew and Alice Horning, Parlor Press, 2007, pp. 58–71.

Enos, Theresa, and Shane Borrowman. *The Promise and Perils of Writing Program Administration*. Parlor Press, 2008.

Evaluating the Intellectual Work of Writing Program Administrators. Council of Writing Program Administrators, wpacouncil.org/positions/intellectual-work.html.

Gebhardt, Richard C. "The Importance of Untenured Writing Administrators to Composition and to English Studies." *Untenured Faculty as Writing Program Administrators*, edited by Debra Frank Dew and Alice Horning, Parlor Press, 2007, pp. 15–39.

Hansen, Kristine. "Face to Face with Part-Timers: Ethics and the Professionalization of Writing Faculties." *Resituating Writing: Constructing and Administering Writing Programs*, edited by Joseph Janangelo and Kristine Hansen, Boynton/Cook, 1995, pp. 23–45.

Horner, Bruce. "Redefining Work and Value for Writing Program Administration." *JAC*, vol. 27, no. 1–2, 2007, pp. 163–84.
Horning, Alice. "Ethics and the jWPA." *Untenured Faculty as Writing Program Administrators*, edited by Debra Frank Dew and Alice Horning, Parlor Press, 2007, pp. 40–57.
—. "Introduction: What is Wrong with THIS Picture?" *Untenured Faculty as Writing Program Administrators*, edited by Debra Frank Dew and Alice Horning, Parlor Press, 2007, pp. 3–14.
Hult, Christine, et al. *"The Portland Resolution": Guidelines for Writing Program Administrator Positions*. *WPA: Writing Program Administration*, vol. 16, no. 1/2, Fall/Winter 1992, pp. 88–94.
McClure, Randall, et al. "Strengthening the *Statement*: Data on Working Conditions in College Composition." *Labored: The State(ment) and Future of Work in Composition*, Parlor Press, 2017, pp. 268-284.
McDonald, James C. "One of Many: The *Statement* in the Context of Other Position Statements on Academic Labor." *Labored: The State(ment) and Future of Work in Composition*, edited by Randall McClure et al., Parlor Press, 2017.
McDonald, James C., and Eileen E. Schell. "The Spirit and Influence of the Wyoming Resolution: Looking Back to Look Forward." *College English*, vol. 73, no. 4, 2011, pp. 360–78.
Meloncon, Lisa, and Peter England. "The Current Status of Contingent Faculty in Technical and Professional Communication." *College English*, vol. 73, no. 4, 2011, pp. 396–411.
Patton, Martha D. and Jo Ann Vogt. *"The Center Will Not Hold: Redefining Professionalism in the Academy." Untenured Faculty as Writing Program Administrators*, edited by Debra Frank Dew and Alice Horning, Parlor Press, 2007, pp. 40–57.
Skeffington, Jillian, et al. "Living in the Spaces Between: Profiling the Writing Program Administrator." *The Promise and Perils of Writing Program Administration*, edited by Theresa Enos and Shane Borrowman, Parlor Press, 2008, pp. 5–20.
Strauss, Anselm, and Juliet Corbin. *Basics of Qualitative Research: Grounded Theory Procedures and Techniques*. Sage Publications, 1990.
White, Edward. "Use It or Lose It: Power and the WPA." *WPA: Writing Program Administration*, vol. 15, no. 1–2, 1991, pp. 3–12.

Appendix: Interview Script

1. As a plate spinner at this point in your career, when someone inside and outside of the academy asks what you do, what do you say? How do you describe it?

2. How familiar are you with the CWPA *Portland Resolution*? How does this match your experience at your institution?

3. How familiar are you with the CCCCs *Wyoming Resolution* and *Statement of Principles and Standards for the Teaching of Postsecondary Writing*? How does this match your experience at your institution?

4. How have you seen your department balancing these ideals?

5. How have you sought to balance these ideals of Portland and Wyoming, given your institutional location?

6. What role do you play in the staffing decisions for the writing program in your department?

7. What lessons have you learned from being in this role?

8. Given your location and experience, would you recommend junior faculty jump into WPA work?

9. What conditions would need to prevail for the jWPA position to be an acceptable, or desirable, or equitable position?

10. What advice do you have for jWPAs already negotiating this role, who find themselves in the tricky position of needing to advocate for labor reforms for their staff while continuing to work for their own job security?

7 The Missing Piece: Where Is the Labor-Related Research at the Research Network Forum?

Risa P. Gorelick[1]

Introduction

The Research Network Forum (RNF) at the Conference on College Composition and Communication (CCCC) is a community of inquiry originally conceived in 1986 by Charles Bazerman, Cheryl Geisler, and Susan Jarratt, among others. Its original intent was to bring current research to the forefront of CCCC, and RNF met for the first time in 1987. Over time, RNF's mission has shifted in that it provides mentoring on research in writing studies more broadly conceived, bringing together graduate students, full-time and part-time faculty, and nationally-acclaimed writing scholars. RNF participants are often in the midst of grappling with the character of research and with what it means to identify oneself as a *researcher*, or one's work as *research*.

Since its beginnings in 1987, the year following the 1986 Wyoming Conference on English that was the impetus of the 1989 *Statement on Principles and Standards for the Postsecondary Teaching of Writing* (hereafter the *Statement*), participants in RNF at CCCC have examined not only the theoretical and technical aspects of our work in writing studies but also its wider social and cultural implications. Indeed, RNF was founded so that a wide range of participants might benefit from

---

1. The author wishes to acknowledge the helpful feedback from Research Network Forum Co-Chair Gina M. Merys and the research analysis of past RNF programs provided by Mark Sutton.

the fruits of current, ongoing research from all areas of the discipline, making theory, research, and practice integrated through one event. Participants come from all sectors of the profession: graduate students beginning their first tentative ventures into research; experienced classroom teachers who wish to begin using their cumulative experience and current sites as foundations for teacher-research projects; scholars at the beginning, middle, and later stages in their careers conducting both traditional and experimental research; nationally-acclaimed researchers who wish to share their current interests while providing guidance to new researchers. All come together to discuss how we might better study and understand the nature of discourse and how we might use that understanding in our research, teaching, and service.

The forum begins each year with a set of talks from plenary speakers who discuss their specific research area in light of the conference theme. The plenary addresses are followed by a morning and an afternoon session of work-in-progress presenters who share their research in thematic roundtables of four to six researchers and one to three discussion leaders. For the most part, discussion leaders have terminal degrees and are established in the field as researchers; many discussion leaders have also served as writing program, writing center, and writing across the curriculum administrators. Some discussion leaders have also held other administrative posts, including department chair, dean, and provost. From its organization alone, the gathering of such a group of people to discuss current research topics in writing studies would appear to be an ideal place to address issues of labor practices for postsecondary teachers of writing.

The combination of insightful plenary talks and small-group working sessions creates an energetic dialogue among this wide range of scholars, professors, and students. Each working group discusses how the questions offered in each year's CCCC's call for proposals can be explored in the context of specific research areas. The result is an ongoing process of experimentation and application, intent on enriching all who participate. The design of RNF encourages participants to leave with new ideas and understanding that can materially benefit the many stakeholders at their institutions and beyond through completed theses, dissertations, and other publications. Viewed this way, RNF could serve as the ideal site to discuss research on labor practices and working conditions in postsecondary writing. This chapter examines the trends in research from the vantage point of RNF, identifies the degree to which research on labor issues and working conditions has been presented at the forum, considers why such research has not found its place in the field, and offers an avenue for bringing this research to RNF and, through RNF, to writing studies.

Research Trends and the RNF

Since 1995, I have served as chair/co-chair of the Research Network Forum. Looking through past RNF programs over the last nineteen years offers an interesting lens into the postsecondary teaching of writing. Some research trends include digital technologies (cyberspace, moos, hypertext, OWLs, wikis, blogs, social media, MOOCs), first print then electronic portfolios, service-learning, ESL, Literacy Studies, Disability Studies, Women's and Gender Studies, and a host of takes on theory, many of which started as dissertation projects and matured through RNF work-in-progress sessions into publication in a range of academic venues.

RNF Executive Committee Member Mark Sutton has started to examine works-in-progress that appeared on RNF's program over specific years and tracing their post-RNF life. To date, Sutton has studied RNF programs and work-in-progress presenters' proposals/abstracts from the following years: 1998–1999, 2001–2005, and 2008–2010. The RNF Executive Committee is trying to determine if there are accurate attendance records, as not everyone who appears on the program actually shows up and presents on their work-in-progress (though most do). Additionally, while the proposal/e-proposal form asked work-in-progress proposers to submit a title and research abstract to better place presenters at thematic tables, not all proposers submit abstracts. Therefore, there are often more people on the program presenting work-in-progress than the number of abstracts. Despite these potential drawbacks, Table 1 summarizes Sutton's findings on the presence of labor practices and working conditions in the research presentations offered at RNF.

Table 1. Proposed RNF work-in-progress (WIP) presentations dealing with labor issues.

Year	Total RNF WIP Abstracts	Number of RNF WIP Abstracts that Deal with Labor Issues	% of RNF WIP Abstracts that Deal with Labor Issues
1998	55	1	1.82
1999	21	0	0
2001	74	0	0
2002	46	1	2.17
2003	42	1	2.38
2004	57	2	3.50
2005	107	3	2.80
2008	42	2	4.76
2009	113	5	4.42
2010	120	5	4.17
TOTALS	**677**	**20**	**2.95**

(Sutton, Unpublished RNF Research)

Of the 677 total RNF abstracts Sutton has reviewed, he has found only twenty that possibly dealt with labor issues, accounting for just 2.95% of the research presented at RNF. Sutton has also attempted to determine what happened to the work-in-progress post-RNF. At this point, Sutton has only been able to confirm a handful of publications—defined as full-fledged conference presentations, completed dissertations, published journal articles, book chapters, and books—on the issue of labor resulting from work presented at RNF. One of the pieces was Sutton's own research project on "Training Programs for Part-Time Composition Faculty: An Exploratory Study," which was presented at CCCC. Another published research project was Toby Coley's "Religious Restraint in Graduate Student Professionalization," which was published in a 2010 issue of *Rhetoric Review*. Rochelle Rodrigo's and Chris Vassett's RNF work-in-progress presentations, according to Sutton, which possibly dealt with labor-related topics, were completed as dissertations, and Gloria McMillian brought her "National Adjunct Writing Faculty Survey (2003–2008)" to RNF over a period of years and presented on her findings at a number of conferences post-RNF.

Despite a few attempts to discuss labor practices and working conditions, investigations that align (or fail to align) with topics in the *State-*

ment have been largely absent at RNF. After examining RNF's archives of past work-in-progress presenters along with our list of well-published researchers who often serve multiple years as discussion leaders, one sees a "Who's Who" list of distinguished members of the writing studies field. And while some discussion leaders have tackled the important work of exploring how the *Statement* has impacted labor practices and working conditions at different points in their careers, few have come to RNF to speak directly about their research. Despite offering hundreds of research projects over the last twenty-seven years, Sutton's initial findings appear to confirm that RNF work-in-progress presenters and discussion leaders have stayed away from any research on labor practices and working conditions, particularly data-driven research and analysis on the principles and standards outlined in the *Statement*.

While the majority of participants over the last several years have been graduate students, RNF still has a fair amount of participation from full-time faculty as well, yet even they have not been addressing labor practices at RNF (though they may be presenting on this topic at other venues). This finding suggests that, despite the attention the topic is given on listservs and in committees, research on labor issues and working conditions continues to be a topic that is largely overlooked by scholars in writing studies.

Piecing Together the Missing

Perhaps the research question we have been afraid to ask over the past three decades is whether our national organizations (CCCC, the National Council of Teachers of English [NCTE], the Modern Language Association [MLA], the American Assocation of University Professors) have the authority to really improve our situation, particularly as national media stories, academic new sources (e.g., *The Chronicle of Higher Education* and *Inside Higher Ed*), and comments on social media outlets continue to signify that labor conditions in many academic institutions have deteriorated significantly. In 2011, the MLA Committee on Contingent Labor in the Profession published a booklet entitled *Professional Employment Practices for Non-Tenure-Track Faulty Members: Recommendations and Evaluative Questions*. In it, the committee states the obvious: "non-tenure-track faculty members now constitute a majority of the faculty in higher education in the United States and Canada" (1). The document "endorses and extends" MLA's 2003 *Statement on Non-*

Tenure-Track Faculty Members and 2008 *Education in the Balance: A Report on the Academic Workforce in English* and "offers recommendations in five general areas for improving the professional standing of faculty members who hold non-tenure-track appointments": hiring and assessment, compensation and professional advancement, professional rights and responsibilities, professional development and recognition, and integration into the life of the department and institution (3). Similar to the *Statement* and other professional recommendations from groups in years prior to these latest employment guidelines, however, organizations like MLA appear to lack the power and/or motivation to enforce compliance. Moreover, not one of the organizations listed above has attempted to censure colleges and universities whose labor practices violate any of their suggested practices.

During the Fall 2013 semester, for example, social media turned the tragic death of Margaret Mary Vijkto, an MLA member and adjunct professor of French for twenty-five years who died of a heart attack while undergoing cancer treatment, into a viral story of the plight of all adjuncts and unfair labor practices. Since Vijkto did not have health benefits as an adjunct, when she became ill, she lost her teaching contract and she was on the verge of homelessness (Kovalik). Stories emerged later suggesting that Vajtko's former employer, Duquesne University, did reach out and offer her housing and health care assistance, but whether or not that is true, this story provided more national discussion on many adjuncts' fates than most other research on the topic had done in years. From the amount of attention this story received, there is hope that scholarship on working conditions will be more fruitfully engaged. But should it take this kind of tragic event to spur more scholarship about labor practices? And, more importantly, will such research really seep into the administrative forces of the Ivory Tower to make an impact on the working conditions in English, writing, and other departments that rely more and more heavily on contingent faculty?

It was on a similar note that the 15th Annual Wyoming Conference, where the *Statement* was first drafted, began. As James C. McDonald and Eileen E. Schell chronicle, "Several noted scholars in composition had been denied tenure. Despite a robust job market for new PhDs in rhetoric, many feared that their research and work as WPAs would not be recognized when they came up for tenure" (362). Further, James Slevin reported in his keynote that "sixty percent of new PhDs in English could not find tenure-track jobs" (McDonald and Schell 362–363).

McDonald and Schell point out that "addressing labor issues was not part of the agenda for the 1986 Wyoming Conference, but labor exploitation became an important topic" (363).

James Sledd, presenting in a general session at the event, stated, "Teachers alone can never change the system of corporate control which pays them rather badly in the expectation that they will preserve, protect, and defend it" (qtd. in McDonald and Schell 364). He suggested a "social revolution" and a "departmental revolution to break the departmental dominance of the literati" (qtd. in McDonald and Schell 365). The result of Sledd's remarks and the question/answer session that followed created the impetus for drafting the *Statement*.

A few years later, Sledd continued to examine labor practices in the field with his article, "Why the Wyoming Resolution Had to Be Emasculated: A History and a Quixotism." In it, he suggests that labor issues go back to the 1930s "composition bums" who were "perpetual instructors" who labored beside teaching assistants (269–70). As graduate programs grew and more people entered college post-WWII, the labor divide between the tenured and non-tenured increased. Sledd cites Ray Kytle from the 1970s who noted that "composition was taught almost exclusively by 'slaves,' that is, by graduate students [. . . and] composition is taught primarily by 'serfs'—untenured and, by present criteria, untenurable instructors" (qtd. in Sledd 273). Sledd suggests that English departments created "boss compositions" who were "admitted to the worshipful company of privileged researchers"—the literature professors—but the price they paid was to administer "the teaching of writing to the contingent workers and teaching assistants" (275). Sledd believes that "boss compositionists" had "contempt for the real teachers of composition" (275). Whether or not "boss compositionists" had contempt for those who taught composition, most had little power to change the employment landscape on their campuses or operationalize much less enforce the tenets of the *Statement*.

Sledd's narrative reveals that he attempted to "encourage a little democracy" by petitioning MLA with a request that the organization "give some practical effect to its expressed concern for literacy by prompt, strong action against the continuing exploitation of graduate students and part-timers as teachers of composition, the principal workers for literacy in higher education of the United States" (277). However, he claims MLA "officers had not known what to do with the petition," and while "hundreds" signed the petition, nothing came of it (277). What

Sledd especially liked about the *Wyoming Resolution* that came later was the third part of the document, which requested "'a procedure for acting upon a finding of noncompliance': institutions running a slave trade were to be publically exposed and rebuked" (277). CCCC took the *Statement* to a committee, chaired by Slevin, who decided "the CCCC could not at this time become involved in the censure of institutions" (CCCC Committee qtd. in Sledd 278). Without the power to censure institutions for their labor practices, Sledd and others believe the *Statement* did not have the backbone to make substantial changes in hiring practices.

RNF Executive Committee, Discussion Leaders, and Plenary Speakers

It takes more than backbone to make substantial changes in the labor practices in the postsecondary teaching of writing. RNF has been fortunate to have a number of high-profile scholars and researchers who have published on labor issues in the field and served as discussion leaders and plenary speakers over the years. Stuart C. Brown and Theresa Enos's edited collection, *The Writing Program Administrators Resource: A Guide to Reflective Institutional Practice,* addresses many labor-related issues, and many of the collection's contributors, including Louise Wetherbee Phelps, Gail Stylgall, Ed White, Susan McLeod, Duane Roen, Chris Anson, Greg Glau, Shirley Rose, and Irwin Weiser have served as RNF discussion leaders and/or plenary speakers. However, RNF archives do not show that any of the scholars who spoke as plenary speakers addressed the RNF group on issues of labor or writing program administration.

Plenary speakers are invited annually to RNF by the Executive Committee, comprised of the chair/co-chairs, the table coordinators, work-in-progress coordinators, discussion leader coordinators, journal editor coordinators, plenary coordinators, publicity coordinators, assessment coordinators, Graduate Research Network liaison, and past chairs. There is also an open call at RNF for anyone interested in helping to plan the following year's meeting, including the selection of plenaries. This group reviews feedback from RNF participants on each year's plenary speakers and determines who would best fit the following year's call. For a group of its size, it is shocking given the realities of labor practices and working conditions in the field that there has not been a single suggestion over the past nineteen years to invite anyone to specifically address labor issues. Now that this missing piece has been identified, it is my hope that we will someday soon hear a plenary address on labor issues in composition.

As John Trimbur, who regularly served as an RNF discussion leader, and Barbara Cambridge point out in "The Wyoming Conference Resolution: A Beginning," politics always come into play in higher education, and, as we have seen in writing programs for decades, the working conditions in our field, even post-*Statement*, have not improved much in the past twenty-five years (15). Despite the fact that when it first appeared in 1989 the *Statement* made bold moves to professionalize teaching college-level writing, it seems all the more prudent now to research and subsequently address in another revision of the *Statement* the working conditions of postsecondary teachers of writing, as work in the academy has likely changed dramatically since the late 1980s. Without it, many teachers, especially graduate students and other contingent faculty, may lack the mechanisms of support requisite for success. Particularly given their presence at the event, RNF could become *the* venue to explore this type of research on the conditions articulated in the *Statement*.

SUGGESTIONS TO BRING LABOR ISSUE RESEARCH TO RNF

If RNF is the research arm of the field and labor issue research is not being brought to RNF, is there perhaps a more suitable venue for such research, or is this research just not being pursued? It is clear that the study of labor issues has been missing from the Research Network Forum at CCCC for far too long. While RNF does not have the power to dictate research, it would welcome the opportunity to have those who are interested in labor issues bring their work-in-progress to present at RNF. In addition to the discussion that RNF can generate, scholars can focus on data-driven research, which tend to have a more positive impact on hiring/labor decisions beyond the department level. If researchers start examining labor conditions quantitatively, perhaps the working conditions for all postsecondary teachers of writing will improve.

Graduate students, however, should be cautioned about the politics of researching labor issues in their dissertations and theses and then turning these projects into job talks or other publications without having the quantitative data to support their claims. It would simply not be politically savvy to focus on poor labor practices and create a job talk on them. In addition to working closely with their advisors to consider the politics of their research topics, graduate students should present the implications of their research questions and findings at RNF thematic roundtables with experienced discussion leaders. Still, it is true that research in and around graduate student training and administrative work has increased at RNF, particularly when looking back through presentations over the past nineteen years. This research trend around graduate student labor could act as a seed for research on other labor issues down the road. I am hopeful that this line of inquiry will prove beneficial to the field and to the working conditions of those employed by postsecondary writing programs. With steady growth in participation over the past twenty-five years,[2] RNF has become *the* introduction to the professional side of the field, particularly for the graduate student demographic. It has turned into the unofficial mentoring arm of CCCC, and it could serve as a venue to support research into working conditions, particularly those of graduate teaching assistants.

As seen in the list of contributors to this collection, labor issues are important to a wide variety of scholars in writing studies, and bringing this research to RNF will allow more people to enter the conversation and attempt to tackle some of the labor issues that impact so many teachers and students across the country. Such a discussion would be fruitful to many and, by working together with the network established by the Research Network Forum, we may be able to gain some political power to actually make a stronger impact in labor practices for graduate students and contingent workers. Until then, there will continue to be a missing piece, and the goals of the *Statement* will continue to remain largely unmet.

Works Cited

Brown, Stuart C., and Theresa Enos. *The Writing Program Administrator's Resource: A Guide to Reflective Institutional Practice*. Lawrence Erlbaum Associates, 2002.

CCCC Executive Committee. *Statement of Principles and Standards for the Postsecondary Teaching of Writing. College Composition and Communication*, vol. 40, no. 3, 1989, pp. 329–36.

Conference on College Composition and Communication Committee on Professional Standards. "A Progress Report from the CCCC Committee on

---

2. In 1994, there were approximately 30–40 total participants (work-in-progress presenters and discussion leaders). In 2013, RNF welcomed 305 participants from 157 universities, nine colleges, and five community colleges, which included 250 work-in-progress presenters and ninety-one discussion leaders.

Professional Standards." *College Composition and Communication*, vol. 42, no. 3, 1991, pp. 330–44.

Kovalik, Daniel. "Death of an Adjunct." *Pittsburgh Post-Gazette*, 18 September 2013, www.post-gazette.com/Op-Ed/2013/09/18/Death-of-an-adjunct/stories/201309180224.

McDonald, James C., and Eileen E. Schell. "The Spirit and Influence on the Wyoming Resolution: Looking Back to Look Forward." *College English*, vol. 73, no. 4, March 2011, pp. 360–78.

Modern Language Association Committee on Contingent Labor in the Profession. *Professional Employment Practices for Non-Tenure-Track Faculty Members: Recommendations and Evaluative Questions*. Modern Language Association, June 2011, apps.mla.org/pdf/clip_stmt_final_may11.pdf.

Sledd, James. "Why the Wyoming Resolution Had to Be Emasculated: A History and a Quixotism." *Journal of Advanced Composition*, vol. 11, 1991, pp. 269–81.

Sutton, Mark. "The Influence of the Research Network Forum on Composition/Rhetoric Scholarship." Sixty-Third Annual Conference on College Composition and Communication, St. Louis, March 24, 2012.

Trimbur, John, and Barbara Cambridge. "The Wyoming Conference Resolution: A Beginning" *WPA: Writing Program Administration*, vol. 12, no. 1–2, Fall/Winter, 1988, pp. 13–18.

8 A State of Permanent Contingency: Writing Programs, Hiring Practices, and a Persistent Breach of Ethics

Casie J. Fedukovich, Susan Miller-Cochran, Brent Simoneaux, and Robin Snead

INTRODUCTION

For decades, scholars in rhetoric and composition have discussed, debated, and agonized over the role(s) of contingent faculty in writing programs. These discussions often include justifiable hand-wringing over how the structure of writing programs and the first-year writing requirement permit (and even sanction) unethical employment practices. More often than not, however, such discussions do not include practical, realistic solutions to the dilemma. Several scholars have thoughtfully discussed the ethical considerations of the problematic hiring practices of first-year writing programs (Bousquet et al.; Crowley; Schell), yet the complex notion of contingency continues to grow increasingly complicated.

Several institutions of higher education have begun to reimagine the role of contingent writing faculty by creating renewable, full-time positions. At these institutions, such positions often follow a non-tenurable teaching track that seeks to be parallel to, in some cases, the traditional, research-based tenure track. These positions, some contend, are ones in which contingent faculty are better supported as members of the scholarly community through engagement in professional development and the scholarship of teaching and learning. We argue, however, that even the most equitable of these full-time teaching-track positions seem to contradict the standards set forth in the Conference on College Composition and Communication's (CCCC) *Statement of Principles and Standards for the Postsecondary Teaching of Writing* (hereafter the *Statement*) as well as its very premise: to address the fact that "More than half the English faculty in two-year colleges, and nearly one-third of the English faculty at four-year colleges and universities, work on part-time and/or temporary appointments," creating what the *Statement* calls "an enormous academic underclass" (330). Although strides have been made to improve conditions for non-tenure-track faculty, these faculty are still typically employed on renewable contracts and do not benefit from the same job security and protection of academic freedom provided by tenure.

Contract positions—permanently contingent positions, in a sense—have become ever more prevalent in writing programs around the country, and they point to competing values and logics about academic labor within our field. In this chapter, we use the term "contract faculty" and "contingent faculty" interchangeably. We have made this choice consciously, emphasizing the potentially temporary (and therefore contingent) nature of any contract appointment that is made at the will of an institution, in contrast to the security of employment and permanence offered by a tenure-track position. Certainly there is a vast difference between full-time, renewable, benefits-bearing, contract positions and part-time, semester-by-semester, contract positions. Such full-time positions are still potentially temporary, however, so our goal in this chapter is to explore whether they satisfy the intentions of the *Wyoming Resolution*, which is linked inextricably to the *Statement*. As part of this exploration, we examine the brief history of the *CCCC Writing Program Certificate of Excellence*, which should arguably exemplify the standards of the professional organization.

We start with the *Wyoming Resolution* as a moment when the competing values and logics of academic labor came to the fore: values about the professionalization of the discipline (What does it mean to be a professional in the field of academic writing?) and values about how/when voices become audible through policies, procedures, and systems (Who is heard in the current system?). Our history since that moment sheds light on an internal disciplinary paradox: the field's persistent striving for ethical—equal?—working conditions for the contract faculty who teach in writing programs and its recognition of the reality of the institutional contexts in which these faculty teach. This chapter draws upon the development of the *Statement*, the historical and political context leading up to its development, and the actions that CCCC has taken since its adoption to address questions of contingent employment that continue to challenge the field. We ask: Is it possible to create full-time positions, still governed by renewable contracts, that do not violate the standards set forth in the *Statement*? If so, is the *Statement*, and the historical context from which it arose, still relevant to hiring practices in contemporary writing programs?

The activist spirit that led to the drafting of the *Wyoming Resolution* gradually eroded as its tenants were adapted into the *Statement*. The complex adaptation from resolution to institutional position statement meant that the very real costs—financial as well as logistical—of censure must be accounted for; the *Statement* can support ethical practices but it cannot, as an institutional position statement, require them. Further, to require institutions to provide full support to contract faculty may have overburdened programs and resulted in unforeseen negative consequences, including the dissolution of entire programs (Anson and Gaard). The result, then, is a *Statement* that appears toothless, "emasculated" (Sledd), and ineffective in stemming the tide of contingency. Initiatives like the *Writing Program Certificate of Excellence*, however, work to address these gaps by rewarding exemplary programs instead of censuring offending ones. However, the *Certificate* cannot escape the context set by our current labor crisis, so even programs recognized as "excellent" may rely heavily on contract labor. By tracing the *Statement*, from its emotional origin in Laramie through its influence on the *Certificate*, we offer suggestions for programmatic changes that may recapture some of the spirit of Wyoming and fill the ethical gaps left by the *Statement*.

Acknowledging a Grassroots Exigence: The *Wyoming Resolution*

While the history of the *Wyoming Resolution* has been well rehearsed (e.g., McDonald and Schell; Robertson et al.; Wyche), it is worth briefly revisiting this moment—a moment in which competing values and logics of academic labor come to the fore. The *Wyoming Resolution* begins by making explicit the unfair working conditions endemic to the teaching of writing: excessive teaching loads, unreasonable class sizes, inadequate salaries, lack of benefits and professional status, and barriers to professional development. Labor conditions were a concern for many writing teachers in the years leading up to the Wyoming Conference, and they have remained unresolved. The Wyoming Conference called individuals into collective action and provided a sense of urgency, as attendees shared experiences across programs and institutions. The Wyoming Conference allowed the systemic inequities of non-tenure-track labor to emerge in narrative, and the call for solutions became insistent. As James C. McDonald and Eileen E. Schell note, the *Wyoming Resolution* "has served as a symbolic and material location from which to argue for improved working conditions for contingent faculty, WPAs, and others in the profession" (373). Experiences and working conditions that were once seemingly personal and invisible were now shared and public.

The *Wyoming Resolution* intended to make visible the systemic inequities of composition teachers and suggest new systems and procedures to directly address these inequities. In short, the *Wyoming Resolution* proposed systems and procedures to support contingent faculty who, while teaching the majority of the courses in first-year writing, receive the least institutional support. Three primary provisions make up the *Wyoming Resolution*:

1. To formulate, after appropriate consultations with postsecondary teachers of writing, professional standards and expectations for salary levels and working conditions of postsecondary teachers of writing.

2. To establish a procedure for hearing grievances brought by postsecondary teachers of writing—either singly or collectively—against apparent institutional non-compliance with these standards and expectations.

3. To establish a procedure for acting upon a finding of non-compliance; specifically, to issue a letter of censure to an individual institution's administration, Board of Regents or Trustees, State legislators (where pertinent), and to publicize the findings to the public at large, the educational community in general, and to our membership.

CCCC adopted the *Wyoming Resolution* in 1987, and the CCCC Committee on Professional Standards[1] was then charged with address-

---

1. Committee membership initially included James Slevin (Chair), Vivian Davis, Ben McClelland, James Raymond, Linda Robinson, Audrey Roth, and James Vincent.

ing its three tenets. Despite the fact that the *Wyoming Resolution* passed "without dissent" ("CCCC Initatives"), there were unofficial "conflicting opinions" that faced the committee (McDonald and Schell 368). These conflicts centered on two issues: 1) disagreement over a "two-tiered" faculty system—one tier for tenured and tenure-track "research" faculty, and another for non-tenure-track "teaching" faculty, and 2) dissention over the continued employment of part-time faculty. While some committee members believed that academic freedom hinged on all faculty lines being tenure-eligible, others argued for faculty who were excellent teachers but were not interested in the research and service requirements of tenure lines, including those not interested in full-time work.

Additional tensions surrounded the censure provision of the *Wyoming Resolution*. Despite the vehement advocacy of Sharon Crowley and Vivian Davis for censure procedures, American Association of University Professors lawyers in consultation with the committee pointed to problems with enforcement and a lack of real consequences for censured institutions, and the CCCC Executive Committee ultimately opposed censure (McDonald and Schell 369–70). As the committee reported in February 1989, it was decided that "the CCCC could not at [that] time become involved in the censure of institutions" (65). Although James Sledd writes that the decision to eliminate censure, among other changes, "emasculated" the *Wyoming Resolution*, Chris M. Anson and Greta Gaard point out that this decision may have saved writing programs at some universities, noting, "while some schools may be embarrassed or threatened into compliance, it may be simpler for a financially strapped college to do away with freshman composition entirely—as it may do away with its athletic programs—in order to quell a national offensive against its practices" (172).

The question of censure drew forth the complexity in making the tenets of the *Wyoming Resolution*, as crafted from their emotionally-charged genesis, into policy. While committee members and other vested parties all vied for the same purpose—to better serve contract writing instructors—the context produced logistical and ideological roadblocks along with potential pitfalls. Therefore, the controversy surrounding competing values and logics of academic labor continued.

Developing Policy: Moving the Personal into the Political through the *Statement*

Out of these discussions about the *Wyoming Resolution*, the CCCC Committee on Professional Standards drafted the *Statement* in order to offer those who wished to argue for improved conditions in their own departments an authoritative policy statement on which to base their arguments. Its development and adoption has been well-documented (see, for example, McDonald and Schell), and, like the *Wyoming Resolution*, the *Statement* was not received without controversy. The 1991 "Progress Report from the CCCC Committee on Professional Standards" acknowledges that the *Statement* "met with disinterested, puzzled, or angry reactions" from college administrators as well as "resistance from the very people whose working conditions it was intended to improve" (332).

In discussing these reactions, the committee, chaired by Crowley, suggested that adoption of the provisions of the *Statement* be based on *choice* and noted "not all institutions will find all the provisions of the *Statement* to be applicable to their local situations" (CCCC Committee on Professional Standards 332). This commentary significantly weakened the initial *Statement*, however, by asserting that those departments "satisfied with their professional *status quo*" (332) could simply disregard the standards it outlines. Although the report "caution[s] that institutions should not accept the judgment of the tenured and tenurable in such matters" (332), the fact is that tenured and tenurable faculty, along with administrators, were those with voice and decision-making power. Those with the least power to argue for change, who might previously have been supported in their fight by the *Statement*, could now be met with the counterarguments of others who were "satisfied" and saw no need to change.

Two specific criticisms of the *Statement* are addressed in the 1991 "Progress Report," the first involving the stance on part-time positions (a concern that carried over from the *Wyoming Resolution*). Although the report reaffirms the need to increase tenure lines for writing instruction, citing issues of academic freedom not afforded to those with tenuous employment situations, it simultaneously advocates for the possibility of long-term, non-tenure-track positions. The report states, specifically, "while the language of the document emphasizes tenure, we *strongly support*, as moves toward equality, alternative models of employment and faculty governance that, in different ways, serve the same ends—that grant writing teachers the rights, privileges, and protections traditionally enjoyed by tenure-line faculty" (335, emphasis added).

This possibility was taken up in more detail in the National Council of Teachers of Education's (NCTE) 2010 *Position Statement on the Status and Working Conditions of Contingent Faculty*, a statement that acknowledges the widespread prevalence of such positions and therefore sets out to determine "fair" working conditions. The final tenet of the *Position Statement* addresses the unlikelihood that permanent positions could be mandated in writing programs, stating, "[i]nstructors should be afforded the opportunity to earn tenure, or, in the alternative, 'long-term security of employment' as teaching specialists." Problematically, the 2010 NCTE document fails to set forth a workable definition for "long-term security of employment." This absence produces gaps through which unethical hiring practices can, and do, slip.

The second criticism of the 1989 *Statement* addressed in the 1991 "Progress Report" concerns the "mandate for professionalizing the field of Rhetoric and Composition" (337). The *Statement* affirms that "part-time teachers of writing should [. . .] demonstrate professional involvement with composition theory and pedagogy" (333) and "should have access to research support and travel funds to attend professional conferences" (334). While the committee cites issues of territoriality within departments as the locus of the objections to professionalization, William S. Robinson claims that the language of the *Statement* itself contributes to arguments against the professionalization of the field. Robinson calls attention to the following clause in the *Statement* regarding marginalized faculty: "Even when, as it [sic] often the case, these faculty bring to their academic appointments the appropriate credentials, their low salaries, poor working conditions, and uncertain futures mar their effectiveness" (330). He questions the negatively framed spirit of the clause, writing, "*[E]ven when* they have the appropriate credentials? Aren't we concerned that, like teachers in every other field, they *always* have the appropriate credentials?" (347). Such language, Robinson explains, emphasizes the fact that many without appropriate credentials teach writing courses, which works against any sense of professionalization, as does the assertion that "whenever possible, faculty professionally committed to rhetoric and composition should coordinate and supervise composition programs," a statement that he argues is analogous to saying "Whenever possible, trained chemists should supervise chemistry labs" (347).

In a nod to the second and third provisions of the *Wyoming Resolution*, the committee concludes its 1991 "Progress Report" with three "Recommendations to the Membership" addressing grievance and censure. In the second of these recommendations, the committee defines programmatic "compliance" with the *Statement* "as any genuine effort by an institution to improve the status and situation of writing teachers and writing programs" and argues that noncompliance is "resistance" to such "efforts of reform" (342). The criteria for "genuine" effort are not specifically outlined and, without a means of censuring an institution for noncompliance, such expectations carry little weight. The committee continued to work on the notion of censure at least through 1993, when then co-chairs Chris M. Anson and M. Elizabeth (Betsy) Sargeant suggested working with accrediting agencies and engaging in advocacy in Washington, DC, but that plan was rejected by the Executive Committee, perhaps because it required significant funding to carry out (Anson).

In the years since the publication of the *Statement*, little has changed in the staffing of writing courses. If anything, the percentage of contingent faculty teaching writing has increased. According to the 2008 report of the 2007 Association of Departments of English's (ADE) Ad Hoc Committee on Staffing, between 1993 and 2003, there was a 10.7% decrease in tenure-line faculty in English, while non-tenure-line faculty increased by an almost equal 10.5% (5). The ADE committee, chaired by David Bartholomae, found that "most tenured and tenure-track faculty members' efforts are concentrated in teaching the upper-division undergraduate and graduate curricula," while "most non-tenure-track faculty members are concentrated in the lower division" (7), particularly in first-year writing. Of the first-year writing courses offered in public colleges and universities, 61.3% were taught by part-time or full-time non-tenure-track faculty (44). In institutions where first-year writing is a part of the English department, tenured or tenure-track faculty are reported to teach only 32.7% of the course sections, whereas in institutions where first-year writing is separated from English, the percentage rises to 56% (8). More recently, the Modern Language Association reported that in 2010, 60–80% of courses in English were taught by contingent faculty (Feal 5).

As colleges and universities have hired more and more faculty in non-tenurable lines, many departments have been divided into tenure-track research faculty and non-tenure-track teaching faculty. Some scholars believe that this division is not entirely negative. Michael Murphy, who advocates for a formalized, full-time teaching-intensive track for first-year writing, argues "the 'teaching substructure' existing now in composition and rhetoric has already begun to contribute substantially to the intellectual vitality and institutional standing of the discipline" ("New" 14). However, there are those who believe that there are more destructive motivations influencing the division of teaching and research faculty. In "Meet the New Boss, Same as the Old Boss: Class Consciousness in Composition," Joseph Harris points out the "routine contempt that English still holds for intellectual work in composition" and the "willingness of the English professoriate to participate in the ongoing exploitation of composition teachers" (44) because it serves their own interests. That interest, he suggests, is the interest of never having to teach first-year writing, a sentiment expressed nine years earlier by Sledd. Harris notes that English departments want the best of both worlds. They want credit for teaching composition, and they want the full-time equivalency it brings for budget and hiring, but the tenure-track and tenured faculty don't want to teach the courses (60).

Some scholars (Boe; Doe et al.; Nardo) argue that the division between faculty tiers is present through only two measures: who is rewarded with reduced teaching loads and who has financial support to complete their research. In spirit, the two-tiered system may release non-tenured faculty from the expectation of publication and other types of professional engagement, engagement supported by this reduction in teaching and research funding. However, Doe and colleagues argue that many non-tenure-track faculty engage in "research, artistry, and other forms of scholarly work" for which they "receiv[e] little or no recognition" and are "afforded virtually no time to carry out" (438). That is, these contract faculty are conducting the same kinds of professional activity as their tenured colleagues, but without departmental support or recognition and, in many cases, with a dramatically increased teaching load.

Like the staffing of writing courses, little has changed in the material conditions of many contingent faculty. The following *Statement* excerpt is, unfortunately, still descriptive of the day-to-day lives of many contingent faculty: "These teachers work without job security, often without benefits, and for wages far below what their full-time colleagues are paid per course. Increasingly, many are forced to accept an itinerant existence, racing from class to car to drive to another institution to teach" (330). The Great Recession of 2008 only exacerbated these practices, as at-will and just-in-time hiring was utilized in the face of massive institutional budget cuts. Kelly Ritter writes, "[T]he labor that has been required to keep the first-year course afloat has often been devised at the expense of best practices, a cost-saving response to socioeconomic conditions that have created an eager but often unsupported workforce that cannot do the work well under the social and material conditions provided by institutions" (388).

A 2012 study sponsored by the Center for the Future of Higher Education and the New Faculty Majority, titled "Who is Professor 'Staff,' and How Can This Person Teach So Many Classes," surveyed 500 contingent faculty across disciplines (Street et al.). The researchers noted that the humanities and arts proportionally rely on larger pools of contingent faculty, accounting for more than twice as many respondents as any other discipline (21). The report connects growing overreliance on contract labor with outcomes-driven public focus, arguing that lack of basic necessities for teaching—space, technology, even required textbooks—impact students' educational experiences. More importantly for the purposes of this chapter, the survey "[made] manifest the symbolic anonymity of the generic Professor 'Staff' designation, [and] reveal[ed] consistent patterns in the objective working conditions and subjective experiences of contingent faculty" (7). Participants described familiar scenes of insecure labor, unsupported teaching, aloof or hostile administrators, and cultural isolation.

Ann M. Penrose's 2012 study with untenurable faculty in a first-year writing program particularizes these experiences. Her research suggests that contract faculty acutely feel distinctions between tiers, particularly in the areas of community, expertise, and autonomy—the very aspects that define what it means to be a professional. "The material conditions of NTT teaching," Penrose writes, "clearly create the impression that NTT faculty are not members of the professional communities in which they work" (109).

Several authors, including Boe and Murphy, highlight the lack of a voice given to non-tenure-track faculty in departmental matters, including the lack of voting privileges (Boe, 35; Murphy, "Making" 59). Similarly, Bartholomae observes that contingent faculty not only lack a voice but also are often ignored. He states that although contingent faculty "are a primary point of contact in lower division courses [. . .] they remain largely invisible to all others in the department except the chair, the director of composition, and the director of undergraduate studies" (18). In many programs, the work of non-tenured faculty members becomes visible only in terms of review and evaluation, and then often when programs or individuals address unmet expectations.

Precisely how these conditions affect pedagogical practice remains unclear, however, and calls for research into the causal links between labor practices and pedagogy have grown more emphatic. Writing in *Forum*, Brad Hammer notes, "The economic contexts for causation are clear. What is less transparent is what can be/is being done" (A2) about the social and material conditions facing non-tenure-track faculty. He thus calls for a "strong push toward research (by those contingent faculty most disenfranchised with the academy)" (A3). Without such research, writes Hammer, "the causal links between labor practices and pedagogy will be ongoingly voiced by the needs and values of those steeped in administration and 'service' and outside the core values of compositionist literature" (A3).

Research such as Street and his colleagues' and Penrose's, as well as collections such as this one seek to place contract labor in historical, social, economic, ideological, and pedagogical context. Establishment of networks like the New Faculty Majority, which seeks to "educate the public about the impact of the contingent faculty crisis on educational quality and the public good, and to mobilize a broad coalition of constituencies to support ethical reform" provide organizational foundation for direct action and research. Feeling otherwise disenfranchised in their departments, contract faculty have begun connecting through these digital networks to share experiences and collect data.

Since its publication, the *Statement* has received continued attention in the literature and is evoked often in arguments focused on non-tenure-track faculty, but, as Sledd notes in his 1991 critique of the response to the *Wyoming Resolution*, we are left to question why "so much talk" has in some ways "produced so little action" (260). The *Statement* has been joined by the NCTE's 2010 *Position Statement on the Status and Working Conditions of Contingent Faculty*, which focuses specifically on the concerns of contingent faculty. The 2010 document reiterates many of the arguments of the original *Statement*; however, it does not strongly affirm the need to maintain traditional tenure lines for writing instructors. Instead, in many ways, it implicitly supports the establishment of untenurable teaching-track lines within composition programs by offering guidelines for how those lines should be defined.

Rewarding, not Censuring: The *CCCC Writing Program Certificate of Excellence*

CCCC has moved from talk to action through initiatives such as the *Writing Program Certificate of Excellence*. There is little, if any, discussion in the public literature about the rationale for initiating the *Certificate*, but it is clear that the *Certificate* holds origin in good faith. Kathleen Blake Yancey, Chair of CCCC when the *Certificate* was initiated, recalls that the exigence for the *Certificate* came from two perceptions: "(1) we don't honor our own work as much as we should; and (2) to date, all our awards were for individuals, but programs can achieve excellence as well, and given that [Rhetoric and Composition] is uniquely programmatic, we ought to have an awards program that would acknowledge and recognize excellence in that arena." The *Certificate* presented an opportunity for CCCC to reward programs that exemplified best practices in the administration, teaching, and assessment of writing. Plus, as the field continues to struggle against national anti-intellectual discourse and shrinking budgets, this move to make visible the work of writing programs may help build a future case for improved conditions for contingent faculty. As long as the intellectual labor of our programs remains mysterious, it remains all too easy to devalue. In this way, the *Certificate* holds much promise for renovating the status of all teachers of writing and especially for those unprotected by tenure or its equivalent.

While the *Certificate* was not designed to address the *Statement* directly, we see implicit connections among the *Certificate*, the *Wyoming Resolution*, and the *Statement*. In other words, if the organization could not engage either politically or fiscally with institutional censure, positive reinforcement offers a reasonable accommodation to promote the dictates of both the *Wyoming Resolution* and the *Statement*. The *Certificate* thus allowed CCCC to take on more prominence as a standards-bearing organization, and the national recognition granted to institutions by the award could elevate programs to support enrollment, status, and bargaining power.

According to the guidelines, *Certificate*-eligible programs "must be able to demonstrate" nine attributes of their programs, from the generative ("program imaginatively addresses the needs and opportunities of its students, instructors, institutions, and locale") to the logistical ("class size is appropriate"). Each point is framed in the positive—a list of *Dos*, instead of a list of *Thou Shall Nots*—yet each of the nine points in some way recalls the two-tiered employment system endemic to the teaching of first-year writing. For example, point three, "The program treats contingent faculty respectfully, humanely, and professionally," clearly outlines expectations for programmatic regard of non-tenure-track faculty.

This point takes contingency as a given, as an expected course of action in composition programs and a realistic assessment of current conditions. Considering the problematic internal paradoxes that we have described within the organization's own statements, however, it stands to question: Which practices are *best* practices? If the *Certificate* is intended to be a change agent that rewards practices to which other programs might aspire, should the criteria be written to be realistically achievable and/or aspirationally desirable? A *Certificate* with criteria no program could achieve might be irrelevant to the field, yet a *Certificate* with criteria that reflect compromises in ethical employment standards reifies existing problematic practices.

Couched in the language of protection, the requirement to "treat contingent faculty respectfully, humanely, and professionally" summarizes—and at the same time potentially reduces—many WPAs' long-fought battles with institutional politics and the national discourse on the role of higher education. In the move from the grassroots passion of the *Wyoming Resolution* through the *Statement* to the *Certificate*, the fundamental spirit of activism has faded. In its place, encoded in the guidelines for the *Certificate*, is the recognition of the problematic hiring practices common to many programs and, by proxy, an implied acceptance of these standards.

From Embodied Action to Policy to Reward: Building Unity, Masking Difference

Because the *Certificate* rewards "exemplary" work by writing programs, its guidelines offer insight into the values and logics held as best practices by CCCC. While the implication of the *Certificate* is positive—rewarding programs, making labor visible, reinforcing community—its language provides a troublesome set of metrics. Tracing the evolution of the *Certificate*, as detailed in previous sections, finds that the material concerns of the *Wyoming Resolution* became codified, and thus deemphasized, in a number of ways. Following S.I. Hayakawa's Ladder of Abstraction, the stories shared in Wyoming moved upward to abstraction from their material origins, through the *Statement* to their distillation in the guidelines for the *Certificate*. Programs are judged against the

Certificate's nine points of measure, and winners are assumed to have at least met—if not exceeded—these criteria. A judgment is the final say, a "conclusion" based on collections of data and vested in the sound ruling of a court of qualified persons. Judgments—as compared to reports and inferences—"stop thought" with the "temporary blindness they induce" (Hayakawa 27). A judgment constructs, revises, and reinforces a chosen reality while masking possible other realities. Although programs are expected to address each of the nine criteria in their application for the award, they are not necessarily required to demonstrate "excellence" in all areas. Therefore, less-than-excellent hiring practices may not disqualify an institution from being awarded if it excels in other ways the review committee deems meritorious.

The *Certificate* guidelines thus presume unequal treatment as ordinary and do not explicitly offer a measure for rewarding programs that actively work to *reduce* contingency, only those that seem to best *manage* contingency. To reward programs that "treat contingent faculty respectfully, humanely, and professionally," the *Certificate* is implicated in accepting these unethical hiring practices while potentially masking new ways of seeing contingency. Additionally, while some past *Certificate of Excellence* winners have earned the award because of their attention to ending unethical hiring practices in their programs, these decisions to do so are not detailed in the *Certificate*'s points of measure or in any accessible archive of the award committee's decision-making process. Further, because programs do not receive feedback on how they "measure up" to the points of measure, receipt of the award may imply that all of their practices are acceptable.

The performance of the *CCCC Writing Program Certificate of Excellence*—as it is written, assessed, and awarded—is thus potentially damaging in two ways: first, its baseline requirements implicitly support unethical hiring practices. Second, awarding the status of "Program of Excellence" to schools that still rely overwhelmingly on underpaid, time-poor contingent labor both normalizes and promotes practices against which many in the discipline are stringently fighting. For example, one of the recent *Certificate* winners, University of South Florida, is reported via The Adjunct Project to pay contingent faculty $2,200–2,800 per class with semester contracts. St. Louis Community College was also recognized in 2011–2012 for its ESL Program, even as its adjunct salary is reported at $2,094 per class. If the winners of the *Certificate* must demonstrate the nine points of measure, including "respectful, humane, and professional treatment" of contingent faculty, then compartmentalizing to such a degree carries potential ramifications. A revision of the *Certificate*'s rubric, and perhaps a consideration of transparency, could move this recognition closer to disciplinary values of fairness and equality of labor.

Explicit, public, detailed discussions of salaries and working conditions remain too risky for many contingent faculty. These absences speak to the veiled nature of contingency: Before crowdsourced documents like The Adjunct Project, New Faculty Majority, and large-scale research projects such as the Coalition on the Academic Workforce's (CAW) *A Portrait of Part-Time Faculty Members*, the material concerns of contract faculty members were relegated to the local and anecdotal. For example, the CAW study gathered responses from more than 10,000 adjunct faculty members, and it bears noting that when broken down by discipline, English language and literature gathered almost three times as many responses as the next largest discipline, Modern languages and literatures other than English. Anonymity is crucial in situations where employment can be terminated at-will.

As with the move from the impassioned experiences at the Wyoming Conference to the drafting of the *Wyoming Resolution* and the *Statement*, the *Certificate* seeks to unite a community under common values. The urgency of the *Wyoming Resolution* dimmed as it was written into the *Statement*. The *Statement*'s vigorous attention to the "enormous academic underclass" as "the worst scandal in higher education today" (330) is likewise defused by the *Certificate*'s passive acceptance of contingency. We argue that a revision to the nine measures for the *Certificate*, and perhaps a revision of the language in the *Statement* addressing and defining contingency, is essential for the discipline to move forward.

Ed Nagelhout and Julie Staggers argue in their opening statement in "Forum on the Profession" that policy and position statements from organizations such as CCCC and the Two-Year College English Association often lead to "miscast ideals of indoctrination and surveillance" and these

> documents, although well intentioned and not without merit, generally define good teaching in terms of doing 'more' without considering the reality of teaching as a contingent faculty member. They fail to consider lack of security; they fail to consider a standard workload; and, more important, they describe expectations in terms of 'characteristics' without considering the kinds

of support necessary to develop skills for good teaching over time. (Arnold et al. 414)

We consider the *Certificate* as participating in the same kinds of elision. CCCC's intention, to be sure, is not to support abuse. However, by rewarding programs that still utilize a majority of contingent faculty without notably working toward equivalence is to protect the system and induce "temporary blindness" through judgment (Hayakawa 27). CCCC can adjust this perception of disembodiment and bureaucratic distance by revising its existing *Writing Program Certificate of Excellence* award process to more actively address contingency in detail. If our goal is to make contract positions more equitable, then the *Certificate* and the *Statement* must be clearer about their standards.

The *Certificate* should be thus considered an aspirational document. Notably absent from its nine points of measure is acknowledgement that contingent faculty are anything more than a managed resource (see Bosquet; Bosquet et al.; Dobrin; Strickland). Is contingency a continuum of action and experience? Is contingency measured only materially? Or as Lisa Arnold argues in her opening statement in "Forum on the Profession," should we revise our documents to shift focus to better consider the "intellectual aspects of the work of the profession" (Arnold et al. 411)? A revision of the *Certificate*'s nine metrics that includes explicit attention to reducing contingency may provide programmatic support for institutions struggling with budgets and hiring decisions. As these programs approach administrators with arguments for better working conditions, they can then cite disciplinary expectations and a move to gain positive publicity for the institution. Part of this revision should include attention to whether adherence to ethical employment practices in a program (which we define in more detail below) should be a requirement for consideration for the award. In other words, is a program eligible for the *Certificate* if they meet some criteria and not others, or are some criteria—such as ethical employment practices—strict requirements for consideration?

The recent trend toward full-time, renewable contract positions in writing programs needs to be addressed in a revision to the *Statement* as well, to both indicate that there is a difference between full-time, renewable positions and part-time positions with no benefits, and also to clarify what guidelines for such positions CCCC condones. If CCCC intends to advocate for full-time, renewable contract positions that are parallel to traditional tenure-track positions as a viable option for writing programs, the *Statement* must be revised accordingly to clarify its standards for hiring practices. We recommend consideration of the following criteria, at a minimum:

- Full voting privileges on curricular and policy issues related to classes the faculty members teach;
- Salary equivalent to tenure-track faculty with the same credentials and graduate training;
- Support for scholarly activity and participation in professional organizations in the form of travel funding, sabbaticals, and other support available to tenure-track faculty;
- Possibility of promotion and merit raises, parallel to tenure-track counterparts;
- Elimination of language pertaining to the number of times a contract can be renewed.

Ideally such a revision would be preceded by in-depth study of programs that have used such contracts to see how faculty—both tenure-track and non-tenure-track—perceive their success in addressing the long-standing ethical problems of contingency.

Conclusion

The economic, discursive, and ideological riptide, as Lester Faigley notes, continues to carry programs away from the security of shared values: fair working conditions, programmatic freedom, and disciplinary support. Faigley asks, "What do you do when the tide seems to be running against you?" (41). His recommendations presage much of composition's current conversations: "You have to look outward [. . .] You have to look for opportunities to inform people about what you do. You have to practice what you preach and engage in public discourse. You have to form alliances [. . .] You have to organize" (41). We're beginning to see hints of these practices in composition, from the *CCCC Certificate* to The Adjunct Project to recent scholarship on activism and public rhetorics (Adler-Kassner; Rose and Weiser).

Writing program administrators and faculty alike struggle daily with the systemic inequalities handed down to programs by budgets and institutional bureaucracy. In the absence of large-scale changes, programs can still fight for these quickly eroding values, even as they encourage disciplinary organizations like CCCC to revisit their policies and public records to reflect a move toward better conditions.

One example of individual programmatic change involves borrowing from existing tenure processes. At many institutions, tenure-track faculty members already define on an individual basis the percentage of their effort in different areas. At North Carolina State University, for example, each faculty member negotiates a Statement of Mutual Expectations (SME) signed by both the faculty member and department head that outlines how much of that faculty member's effort is devoted to teaching, research, service, and administration. The faculty member can initiate a revision to an existing SME at any time, but the expectation still remains that, regardless of the percentage of effort defined in the SME, the faculty member must reach a specific qualitative and quantitative measure of publication to earn tenure. What would happen if a faculty member could negotiate an SME that had the power of defining that faculty member's requirements for tenure, instead of each faculty member having to write an SME that will guarantee that they meet an already prescribed publication quota? Could it then be possible for a faculty member to be primarily devoted to excellent teaching and still earn tenure?

A solution to this dilemma might be the development of a parallel teaching track that provides a path to tenure for faculty with a focus on teaching, even within a research university, and, ultimately, a revision to the *Statement* that provides for and describes this possibility. Definitions of what it means to be a scholarly teacher and to engage in the scholarship of teaching and learning (Boyer; Shulman) provide a roadmap for how we could define the parameters of such positions. We don't have to reject the importance of scholarship, discovery, and peer review in the academy to redefine what it might mean for a faculty member to have more of an emphasis on teaching than research—research and teaching, of course, are not mutually exclusive. The fact that we have not heard arguments for, or seen prominent examples of, permanent teaching-focused positions that also include tenure at research universities speaks to how we still find ourselves stuck in the nineteenth century model of the German research university, and how English departments—and writing programs in particular—still struggle to justify themselves as participating in an established discipline.

We believe that it is time for our discipline to take a public position, and offer a viable solution to the unethical hiring practices still prevalent in our field. Our field hasn't adequately addressed the problematic conditions that sparked the *Wyoming Resolution*, and in many ways, our responses to the *Statement* and our framing of the *CCCC Writing Program Certificate of Excellence* have reified some of the problematic practices that we sought to change. However, by working backward to recapture some of the spirit of the Wyoming Conference—through revisions to the *Statement* and *Certificate* criteria that can support grassroots programmatic attention, which trickles upward to inform disciplinary bureaucratic structures—we can begin to revise, slowly, our shared actions to better reflect our shared values and move away from a state of permanent contingency.

WORKS CITED

2007 Association of Departments of English (ADE) Ad Hoc Committee on Staffing. *Education in the Balance: A Report on the Academic Workforce in English*. Modern Language Association and Association of Departments of English, 2008, www.mla.org/Resources/Research/Surveys-Reports-and-Other-Documents/Staffing-Salaries-and-Other-Professional-Issues/Education-in-the-Balance-A-Report-on-the-Academic-Workforce-in-English.

Adler-Kassner, Linda. *The Activist WPA: Changing Stories about Writing and Writers*. Utah State UP, 2008.

Anson, Chris M. "Re: Question about the CCCC Committee on Professional Standards." E-mail to Robin Snead, 14 October 2012.

Anson, Chris M., and Greta Gaard. "Acting on the 'Statement': The All-Campus Model of Reform." *College Composition and Communication*, vol. 43, May 1992, pp. 171–75.

Arnold, Lisa, et al. "Forum on the Profession." *College English*, vol. 73, no. 4, March 2011, pp. 409–27.

Bartholomae, David. "Teaching on and off the Tenure Track: Highlights from the ADE Survey of Staffing Patterns in English." *Pedagogy: Critical Approaches to Teaching Literature, Language, Composition, and Culture*, vol. 11, no. 1, 2010, pp. 7–32.

Boe, John. "Don't Call Me Professor!" *Pedagogy: Critical Approaches to Teaching Literature, Language, Composition, and Culture*, vol. 11, no. 1, 2010, pp. 33–42.

Bosquet, Marc. "Composition as Management Science: Toward a University Without a WPA." *JAC*, vol. 22, no. 3, 2002, pp. 493–526.

Bosquet, Marc, et al., editors. *Tenured Bosses and Disposable Teachers: Writing Instruction at the Managed University*. Southern Illinois UP, 2004.

Boyer, Ernest. *Scholarship Reconsidered: Priorities of the Professoriate*. Carnegie Foundation for the Advancement of Teaching, 1990.

CCCC Executive Committee. *Statement of Principles and Standards for the Postsecondary Teaching of Writing. College Composition and Communication*, vol. 40, no. 3, 1989, pp. 329–36.

CCCC *Writing Program Certificate of Excellence*. National Council of Teachers of English, 2004, www.ncte.org/cccc/awards/writingprogramcert.

Conference on College Composition and Communication Committee on Professional Standards. "A Progress Report from the CCCC Committee on Professional Standards." *College Composition and Comminication*, vol. 42, no. 3, October 1991, pp. 330–44.

Conference on College Composition and Communication Committee on Professional Standards for Quality Education. "CCCC Initiatives on the Wyoming Conference Resolution: A Draft Report." *College Composition and Communication*, vol. 40, no. 1, February 1989, pp. 61–72.

Crowley, Sharon. *Composition in the University: Historical and Polemical Essays*. University of Pittsburgh P, 1998.

Dobrin, Sidney. *Postcomposition*. Southern Illinois UP, 2011.

Doe, Sue, et al. "Discourse of the Firetenders: Considering Contingent Faculty Through the Lens of Activity Theory." *College English*, vol. 73, no. 4, March 2011, pp. 428–49.

Faigley, Lester. "Literacy after the Revolution." *College Composition and Comminication*, vol. 48, no. 1, 1997, pp. 30–43.

Feal, Rosemary. "Contingent Faculty Members: More Alike than Different? *MLA Newsletter*, vol. 42, no. 2, 2010, pp. 5–6.

Hammer, Brad. "From the Editor: The Need for Research in 'Contingency Studies.'" *Forum: Newsletter for Issues about Part-Time and Contingent Faculty*, vol. 14, no. 1, 2010, pp. A1–A3.

Harris, Joseph. "Meet the New Boss, Same as the Old Boss: Class Consciousness in Composition." *College Composition and Comminication*, vol. 52, no. 1, 2000, pp. 43–68.

Hayakawa, S. I. *Language in Thought and Action*. 5th ed., Houghton Mifflin/Mariner Books, 1991.

McDonald, James C., and Eileen E. Schell. "The Spirit and Influence of the Wyoming Resolution: Looking Back to Look Forward." *College English*, vol. 73, no. 4, March 2011, pp. 360–78.

Murphy, Michael. "Making a Place for Teaching Faculty: Some Thoughts on David Bartholomae's 'Teaching on and Off the Tenure Track.'" *Pedagogy: Critical Approaches to Teaching Literature, Language, Composition, and Culture*, vol. 11, no. 1, 2010, pp. 57–62.

—. "New Faculty for a New University: Toward a Full-Time Teaching-Intensive Faculty Track in Composition." *College Composition and Comminication*, vol. 52, no. 1, 2000, pp. 14–42.

Nardo, Anna K. "Our Tangled Web: Research Mandates and Staffing Practices." *Pedagogy: Critical Approaches to Teaching Literature, Language, Composition, and Culture*, vol. 11, no. 1, 2010, pp. 43–50.

"New Faculty Majority Foundation." New Faculty Majority, 2012, www.newfacultymajority.info/equity/nfm-foundation.

Penrose, Ann M. "Professional Identity in a Contingent-Labor Profession: Expertise, Autonomy, Community in Composition Teaching." *WPA: Writing Program Administration*, vol. 35, no. 2, 2012, pp. 108–26.

A Portrait of Part-Time Faculty Members. Coalition on the Academic Workforce, June 2012, www.academicworkforce.org/CAW_portrait_2012.pdf.

Position Statement on the Status and Working Conditions of Contingent Faculty. National Council of Teachers of English, September 2010, www.ncte.org/positions/statements/contingent_faculty/. Also printed in *College English*, vol. 73, no. 4, March 2011, p. 356–59.

Ritter, Kelly. "'Ladies Who Don't Know Us Correct Our Papers': Postwar Lay Reader Programs and Twenty-First Century Contingent Labor in First-Year Writing." *College Composition and Comminication*, vol. 63, no. 3, 2012, pp. 387–419.

Robertson, Linda R., et al. "The Wyoming Conference Resolution Opposing Unfair Salaries and Working Conditions for Post-Secondary Teachers of Writing." *College English*, vol. 49, no. 3, 1987, pp. 274–80.

Robinson, William S. "The CCCC Statement of Principles and Standards: A (Partly) Dissenting View." *College Composition and Comminication*, vol. 42, no. 3, October 1991, pp. 345–49.

Rose, Shirley, and Irwin Weiser. *Going Public: The WPA as Advocate for Engagement*. Utah State UP, 2010.

Schell, Eileen. *Gypsy Academics and Mother-Teachers: Gender, Contingent Labor, and Writing Instruction*. Boynton/Cook, 1997.

Shulman, Lee. "From Minsk to Pinsk: Why a Scholarship of Teaching and Learning." *The Journal of Scholarship of Teaching and Learning*, vol. 1, no. 1, 2000, pp. 48–53.

Sledd, James. "Why the Wyoming Resolution Had to be Emasculated: A History and a Quixotism." *Journal of Advanced Composition*, vol. 11, Fall 1991, pp. 269–81.

Street, Steve, et al. "Who is Professor 'Staff' and How can this Person Teach So Many Classes?" *Center for the Future of Higher Education Policy Report #2*, August 2012, Center for the Future of Higher Education, www.insidehighered.com/sites/default/server_files/files/profstaff%282%29.pdf.

Strickland, Donna. *The Managerial Unconscious*. Southern Illinois UP, 2011.

Wyche, Susan. "Reflections of an Anonymous Graduate Student on the Wyoming Conference Resolution." *Labored: The State(ment) and Future of Work in Composition*, edited by Randall McClure et al., Parlor Press, 2017, pp. 3-13.

Yancey, Kathleen Blake. "Re: Question about the CCCC Writing Program Certificate of Excellence." E-mail to Susan Miller-Cochran, 2 November 2012.

9 Contingency, Access, and the Material Conditions of Teaching and Learning in the *Statement*

Holly Hassel and Joanne Baird Giordano

> *Quality in education is linked to the quality of teachers. Higher education traditionally assures this quality by providing reasonable teaching loads, research support, and eventual tenure for those who meet rigorous professional standards.*
>
> —Statement of Principles and Standards for the Postsecondary Teaching of Writing

Introduction

More than two decades ago, the *Statement of Principles and Standards for the Postsecondary Teaching of Writing* (hereafter the *Statement*) provided a framework for an ideal university writing program, one staffed with well-compensated, tenure-stream faculty trained in composition and rhetoric and provided with ample access to professional resources and autonomy in designing curricula. Arguing that "the responsibility for the academy's most serious mission, helping students to develop their critical powers as readers and writers, should be vested in tenure-line faculty," the *Statement* attempted to serve as a bulwark against the encroachment of an increasingly stratified labor force in composition, one with multiple tiers of employees who experienced varying degrees of status, benefits, and resources. Today, the *Statement* is out of line with the practical realities of modern American writing instruction, just as its "ideal" vision did not reflect working conditions for composition instructors in 1989.

In order to reflect the changing landscape of teaching writing at the college level in the twenty-first century, the next version of the *Statement* will need to account for the changing nature of the academic labor market, for new (or previously unacknowledged) student populations with varying levels of preparation and paths through first-year writing courses, and for growth in higher education at the two-year, open-access campus. To be successful at both reflecting and shaping the profession of teaching postsecondary writing, any revision of the *Statement* must extend its reach to account for the following:

1. The varying kinds of institutions at which most PhDs and MAs in English will be employed and where a revised *Statement* can influence the working conditions of writing teachers.

2. The ways we as a discipline and our institutions can reshape contingent labor status to enhance the overall quality of professional experience for all writing instructors (and to benefit our students).

3. The emphasis on student learning that should drive these two paradigm shifts.

An updated *Statement* will necessarily be something different from the original; however, it can still retain its initial purpose—to set standards and make recommendations about the material conditions under which writing instructors work—while simultaneously recognizing greater diversity within those conditions.

In this chapter, we provide an overview of changes in the employment status of postsecondary English faculty and the kinds of institutions in which they work, and we make recommendations for additions and revisions to the *Statement*. Those recommendations focus on adjusting the *Statement* to reflect growth in the number of instructors who teach in two-year colleges and who work off the tenure track. We make two other recommendations that emerge from the previous two changes, namely, the need for the *Statement*'s values and principles to emerge from a focus on student needs and student learning and the need for all graduate programs in English to prepare instructors with training in writing pedagogy; both recommendations will ultimately result in better teaching and learning conditions for instructors and students.

We further examine the professional resources available for instructors working in open-admission and two-year colleges, where the majority of first-year writing instruction takes place. We call into question the *Statement*'s assumption that contingency itself is problematic and instead argue for revisions to the *Statement* that acknowledge the relationship between material working conditions for instructors off the tenure track at open-enrollment campuses. We advocate for a *Statement* that makes recommendations for graduate training that prepares postsecondary educators in English for working conditions that involve teaching (likely off the tenure track) a broad range of students at nonselective institutions. Contending that working conditions for instructors are inextricably linked with student learning outcomes, we argue for specific revisions to the *Statement* that

- Have the power to inform material conditions for instructors;
- Support more robust training and professional development for all instructors;
- Establish the relationship between teaching conditions and student learning outcomes;
- Make a strong statement about graduate training that emphasizes composition pedagogy for all students in English graduate programs.

Such a statement will be of greater service to a wider range of instructors who teach in our postsecondary writing classrooms.

THE CHANGING LANDSCAPE OF TEACHING COLLEGE WRITING

The original version of the *Statement* argues for a workplace reality that reflects only a minority of instructors who teach first-year writing. Moreover, two shifts in employment status and institutional type make some of the original *Statement*'s recommendations obsolete. The existing *Statement* argues that "commitment to quality education requires that the number of part-time writing teachers [. . .] be kept to a minimum" and advocates for departments where no greater than 10% of sections are taught by contingent instructors (333). This position forecloses upon a professional conversation that accounts for the workplace reality in which about half of all teachers of writing in the United States work in a two-year institution where contingent status is the norm. Further, the current *Statement* makes no mention of the great number of varying institutional types and what those differences mean for the professional realities of the people who teach there. In its current incarnation, the *Statement* prescribes a kind of employment status that is increasingly unavailable to many writing faculty; therefore, portions of it are irrelevant to a majority of college writing instructors in making policy recommendations that would substantially change the conditions under which they teach.

Consequently, it's essential that a revision to the *Statement* fully accounts for the experiences of the vast number of tenure-line and contingent faculty who teach at open-access and/or two-year institutions. In 2008, the Modern Lanaguge Assocation (MLA) and the Assocation of Departments of English (ADE) documented, in detail, the employment status of instructors in English. David Laurence outlines in the MLA/ADE report, *Demography of the Faculty: A Statistical Portrait of English and Foreign Languages*, that of 82,400 respondents to the most recent National Study of Postsecondary Faculty, only 20.3% of the faculty members in English teach at Carnegie Doctoral/Research institutions; by contrast, "[a]lmost half of all faculty members in English (47.9%) teach in Carnegie Associate's institutions" (2). In other words, half of the English instructors in the US who teach at the postsecondary level are working at two-year colleges. This report acknowledges that "[d]espite the extraordinarily high percentage of faculty members teaching off the tenure track in two-year colleges, the 8,704 English faculty members holding tenured and tenure-track positions in two-year colleges outnumber the tenured and tenure-track English faculty in every other sector" (Laurence 2). In fact, the total number of instructors at two-year institutions (39,460) is nearly equal to the *combined total* of instructors at all other types (approximately 7,500 at baccalaureate; 16,750 at master's; and 16,740 at doctoral/research institutions). American college students are overwhelmingly taught by instructors—many tenure-track, many part-time, most contingent—in a two-year college setting.

A twenty-first century *Statement* on standards for teaching postsecondary writing must fully address the professional needs of writing instructors who work at two-year campuses, especially in providing for research-based pedagogical approaches and resources for teaching at institutions of access. Failing to acknowledge the centrality of teaching and learning first-year writing in two-year institutions means that we as a profession have an inaccurate understanding of what postsecondary writing teachers face in their classrooms and workplaces.

Addressing this misunderstanding is important for several reasons, one of which is that research in the field of writing studies often informs national policy and the position statements of our professional organizations. For the most part, current scholarship on teaching college writing does not adequately reflect the reality that half of the members of our profession teach in a two-year setting, and our discipline's publications frequently do not provide instructors at those institutions with scholarly texts that are relevant to their work. As a policy document, one of the *Statement*'s most important functions is to make visible the values and priorities of the field while at the same time working within the realities of a variety of institutional conditions (see Hassel and Giordano for further discussion of this topic).

A revised *Statement* could partially correct this lack of disciplinary attention to the needs of two-year college instructors by making those needs explicit. We see a critical need for language that makes visible two-year college teaching and learning and acknowledges that open-access colleges and selective colleges have important similarities in the learning outcomes students need to achieve in first-year writing but that non-selective institutions differ from selective programs in some important ways. These include the broader range of curricula (typically at least one and sometimes multiple non-degree credit writing courses intended to prepare students for a core, transfer-level course), the diversity of students who are more likely to attend two-year campuses (including US-educated multilingual students, returning adult students, and first-generation and low-income students), and those students' range of learning needs, as well as a mission focused on teaching in the lower division.

Off the Tenure Track

As economic shifts in the last two decades have constrained funding for public universities, many institutions have increasingly embraced corporate/business models for managing the work of the university, a change that has exacerbated the "problem" of contingent labor and the decline of tenure-line faculty positions in higher education.[1] As MLA/ADE's 2008 *Education in the Balance: A Report on the Academic Workforce in English* demonstrates, "only 32% of faculty members in English, across all institutions, hold tenured or tenure-track positions" (2007 ADE 4). Similarly, the MLA/ADE report *Demography of the Faculty* concludes that 60% of instructors at four-year institutions work off the tenure track, while the percentage of contingent faculty at two-year campuses is closer to 80% (Laurence 2). These findings stand in stark contrast with the 1989 numbers cited in the *Statement*: "More than half the English faculty in two-year colleges, and nearly one-third of the English faculty at four-year colleges and universities, work on part-time and/or temporary appointments" (330). In other words, and to be blunt, we work at institutions that are too deeply entrenched in the economic and political realities of staffing writing courses with contingent labor to think realistically that tenure-track faculty jobs in composition will be the prevailing position type at any kind of institution.

A revised *Statement* that is applicable to two-year institutions must recognize the dominance of contingent faculty who work in these settings. The *Statement* must make realistic recommendations within the context of institutional restrictions in the current economic climate—recommendations that will be taken seriously by policymakers and administrators who have the most direct influence on working conditions. Though pressing for more stable labor conditions for contingent faculty may come at the risk of weakening the push for more tenure-line faculty, the state of working conditions for those working off the tenure line requires that we move in this direction instead of continuing to hold out for the off-chance that our profession will create a workplace reality where the majority of instructors are tenure-line. The working conditions of our profession—employment instability for most instructors—affect our profession in profound ways that demand urgent redress.

The revision should fruitfully acknowledge and help shape the working conditions of instructors working off the tenure track, recognizing that almost no institution—particularly a two-year or proprietary institution—is going to adhere to the current *Statement*'s recommendation

---

1. Composition/rhetoric and English scholars more generally have been tackling the issue of part-time and contingent labor for quite some time. See Marc Bosquet, Bosquet et al., Eileen Schell, and Schell and Patricia Stock for arguments about the impact and roles of contingent labor in the university and in writing studies in particular.

that no more than 10% of course sections be taught by part-time faculty. Nor is this later recommendation likely to gain much traction with institutional leaders who make decisions about budgets and curricula: "Compensation, per course, for part-time faculty should never be lower than the per-course compensation for full-time faculty with comparable experience, duties, and credentials" (334), reaffirmed in the *Position Statement on the Status and Working Conditions of Contingent Faculty* in the March 2011 *College English*. While ideal, this position is out of touch with the realities of institutional budgets. What a revised *Statement* can effectively argue for is a living wage with benefits for contingent and part-time faculty, one that adequately compensates non-tenure-stream writing instructors for their work. Similarly, CCCC can make a strong statement against institutional policies or practices that prevent contingent faculty from having full-time employment with benefits.[2]

The *Statement* must advance a value system and take a position that argues for quality working conditions for all instructors, regardless of their employment status. The current version does not effectively do this. For example, the *Statement* endorses full-time tenure-track positions in composition courses, arguing that "To provide the highest quality of instruction, departments offering composition and writing courses should rely on full-time tenured or tenure-track faculty members who are both prepared for and committed to the teaching of writing" (331), a problematic recommendation that requires revision. Further, this language obscures the necessity of cultivating professionalism (including both the responsibilities and rewards) for all instructors of writing, regardless of their employment status. Whereas the current *Statement* asserts that "the excessive reliance on marginalized faculty damages the quality of education" (330) the next incarnation of the *Statement* must shift its focus to best practices for hiring, training, evaluating, compensating, and coordinating across position types because our profession will never again return to a situation in which the majority of writing courses are taught

---

2. For example, see a November 2012 story in *Inside Higher Ed* about Community College of Allegheny County's decision to "cut course loads and hours for some 200 adjunct faculty members and 200 additional employees to avoid paying $6 million in Affordable Care Act-related fees in January 2014" (Flaherty).

by tenure-line faculty.[3] Ultimately, we argue that CCCC and the framers of its policy statements must manage a paradigm shift—one in which the solution to the problem of "marginalized faculty" is not framed in terms of conversion to a bygone model but rather articulates methods for improving the professional status and working conditions of contingent faculty so that they are no longer marginalized.

Since the majority of first-year writing instructors do (and will) work off the tenure track, the revised *Statement* should endorse the cultivation of a program mentality where all department members contribute to the program's development regardless of employment status or type of institution. In this way, the revised *Statement* should reinforce the 1989 claim that contingent faculty "should be given a voice in the formulation of department policy regarding courses and programs in which they teach (for example, by voting at department meetings and by serving on curriculum and hiring committees)" and that "they should have the same right as full-time faculty to participate in the design of evaluation procedures" (334). We argue that the lack of tenure status is not what marginalizes instructors in contingent positions; what marginalizes those instructors is (1) exclusion from decision-making processes, (2) departmental and disciplinary attitudes toward contingent faculty that devalue their expertise and treat them as perpetual novices who can't make meaningful contributions to curriculum and program development, and (3) lack of access to professional (and sometimes basic) resources. These three factors prevent non-tenure-track faculty from participating in program development and department matters in the way that the current version of the *Statement* describes.

The *Statement* should include clear and direct language that addresses the first two issues, that of contingent faculty being excluded from institutional life and the disciplinary undervaluing of contingent faculty.

---

3. Though we do not have space to address the issue here, we have argued elsewhere (see Lisa Arnold et al.) that contingent faculty status is not in and of itself a problem. For example, as Laurence's report shows, of 37,500 instructors with part-time and non-tenure-track work, as many prefer part-time as full-time—49.9% versus 50.1% (3). Many instructors want the flexibility of a part-time instructional position, and contingency does not in and of itself marginalize instructors from a larger department or campus unit. Our current argument does not prima facie accept contingent faculty status as either inevitable or without problems; however, we argue that academic English and writing programs must adapt their culture to accommodate the majority of the labor force teaching first-year writing who work off the tenure track.

Specifically, the criteria that departments should prioritize when working on program development are evidence of instructors' reflective practice, professional activity, and institutional citizenship, not their employment status. Instructors working both on and off the tenure track should be represented on committees that contribute to textbook selection and develop supporting materials in first-year writing and should have access to professional development opportunities such as training, workshops, and seminars (see Arnold et al. for our discussion of the moral imperative to invite non-tenure-track faculty to participate in the governance life of English departments). Working conditions that promote and develop quality instruction should be equally available to non-tenure-track faculty as to tenure-line faculty; these include clear and transparent evaluation criteria, regular opportunities for feedback from colleagues on their work in the classroom, support and mentoring from colleagues, a voice in department governance, and material resources such as office space and technology.

The third issue, access to professional resources, can be addressed in several ways. When institutional infrastructure makes it nearly impossible to radically reshape the budgets and structures that have vested English departments heavily in relying on contingent labor to provide writing instruction, the success of the next version of the *Statement* depends on its effectiveness as a tool for creating inclusive, cohesive working environments that give professional dignity to both tenure-line and contingent instructors. This would, for example, involve providing professional development resources that are critical for the ongoing intellectual engagement of all writing instructors. A 2010 report endorsed by the Two-Year College English Association, *Research and Scholarship in the Two-Year College*, emphasizes that "at two-year colleges, good teaching matters most," yet affirms that scholarship is "a prerequisite and corequisite for good teaching—because teachers' scholarship legitimizes their expertise, informs their classroom practice, and provides their students with models for intellectual inquiry" (3–4). To neglect financial and institutional support for the majority of instructors who teach writing at most campuses in the country is to neglect the quality of our teaching and of student learning in the college writing classroom. The current *Statement* asserts: "As colleges have the right to expect of writing specialists the highest level of performance, so they have the obligation to extend the greatest possible support. To do less is to compromise writing instruction for future generations of American students" (330–31). A revised version must emphasize this commitment to professional support for non-tenure-track instructors much more emphatically, while avoiding the implied value system of the current *Statement*, which positions contingent faculty as less effective than tenure-line faculty.

Therefore, our next recommendation is to urge CCCC to make a strong and specific statement supporting institutionally-funded training on pedagogical, technological, and professional issues for all faculty, including part-time instructors. For example, a survey of 12,612 contingent faculty conducted by the Coalition on the Academic Workforce showed that just 8.7% of part-time contingent faculty have private office space while 59% have shared office space (*Portrait*). Further, just 11.8% of part-time contingent faculty had a private computer while slightly over half, 51.5%, had access to a shared computer, and nearly a third of part-time contingent faculty did not have library privileges at their teaching institution. If we are committed as a professional organization and as a discipline to supporting excellent teaching in the writing classroom, then resources must be available to all instructors who teach writing. These include small-scale opportunities (like grants to fund reading circles or workshops on relevant issues) and larger-scale research funding that supports instructors who want to pursue intellectual inquiry into teaching and learning in our field. This means that a revised *Statement* needs to eliminate language that suggests that instructors who work off the tenure track are inferior to those who work on it, such as that noted above. Finally, language asserting that all institutions should provide contingent faculty equal access to funding for ongoing professional development—for example, memberships in professional organizations, conference attendance, and access to disciplinary journals should be included in a revised *Statement*.

STUDENT LEARNING AND THE USES OF THE STATEMENT

Little space in the 1989 *Statement* discusses student learning, though certainly many other CCCC position statements address issues of outcomes or assessment. The omission of a thorough discussion of student learning would make it difficult for members of our profession to use a new *Statement* to show their institutions how instructors' working conditions decrease the quality of their institutions by affecting student learning outcomes. Consequently, any revision of the *Statement* is an opportune time for CCCC to develop a policy stance that accurately reflects the changing face of the profession and highlights the inextricable connections between teaching conditions and learning conditions. Other position documents by our professional organizations—notably the *WPA Outcomes Statement for First-Year Composition* first adopted in 2000 and revised in 2008 and again in 2014—have made student learning goals central to their work. Even more recently, the Council of Writing Program Administrators (CWPA), in collaboration with the National Council of Teachers of English and the National Writing Project, released the *Framework for Success in Postsecondary Writing*, which moved beyond academic outcomes to define the habits of mind that students need to be successful in college-level writing (4). These position statements, though useful on their own merits, are missing a key opportunity to make recommendations that recognize the intersections between the learning outcomes we hope students will achieve, instructors' working conditions, and the diverse institutions where both students and instructors do their work.

A revised *Statement* should be considered successful if it can be used to support quality working conditions for instructors which, in turn, create effective learning conditions for students. This means highlighting the relationship between the needs of the students at particular institutions and simultaneously creating quality working conditions. When instructors lack resources to meet student learning needs, working conditions deteriorate because those instructors or programs do not have the tools they need to satisfactorily perform their jobs.

What the revised *Statement* can fruitfully address are the intersections between the learning outcomes or habits of mind we hope students develop and the institutional material conditions that influence how successfully students achieve them. For example, some instructors teach a course load of five or more composition classes (particularly contingent faculty who are piecing together full-time work and a livable wage through employment at multiple institutions). Improved conditions for those contingent faculty seeking full-time employment options would make it more likely that they might become part of both the departmental culture and the profession. With divided employment obligations, those instructors may have less time to use a process pedagogy that involves feedback on multiple drafts of an essay, a key element in helping students achieve the outcome "that it usually takes multiple drafts to create and complete a successful text" that the CWPA recommends. As a further example, if an institution is impoverished in its resources and/or serves primarily low-income students, the students are less likely to have access to technology that allows them to achieve the CWPA outcomes associated with "composing in electronic environments"—whether that's due to the institution's or the students' lack of resources.

A revised *Statement* must be applicable across institution types and faculty ranks, supporting policies at institutions where diversity in student academic preparation is a central part of instructors' working conditions. Teaching writing at an open-access institution (which includes most two-year colleges and some four-year colleges) is a fundamentally different experience than teaching in a university with selective or even moderately competitive admission standards. Selective-admission baccalaureate or doctoral-granting institutions serve students who come to college with academic preparation that often includes a writing-intensive academic curriculum. At a bare minimum, students at these institutions provide evidence in their admissions applications to document basic competency in academic literacy. Like selective universities, two-year campuses enroll academically high-achieving students, but they more often serve a much broader range of college writers and often enroll significant numbers of learners who would not be admitted to other institutions due to their deficiencies in writing, often among other academic deficiencies. Therefore, policies supported by research and presented in a revised *Statement* may be of particular importance for instructors in these institutions.

In particular, the *Statement* needs to address the fact that working conditions at open-access institutions involve working with a wide range of students with serious academic and nonacademic needs. For example, writing instructors on our two-year campuses at the University of Wisconsin Colleges typically teach a core, transferable research course in a classroom of students with diverse educational backgrounds, ranging from high achievers (such as high school valedictorians) who would be admitted to any public institution in our state to marginally-prepared college writers who previously completed an introductory degree-credit composition course to students who took multiple intensive skills and remedial support courses in a lengthy process toward achieving the learning outcomes for our writing program. For this last group of students, *first-year* writing is a misnomer because the pathway toward completing our institution's core writing requirement lasts two or sometimes three years. Beyond their academic diversity, most open-admission campuses have students with a wide range of special needs: a large proportion of nontraditional students, multilingual students, and students with challenging personal (often socioeconomic) challenges that create barriers to college completion. For example, in a research study we conducted tracing students' transition from developmental writing to completion of the core writing requirement, just 42% of 93 students who began in basic writing ultimately completed second-semester composition, with an average time to completion of 3.3 semesters—notably, this is higher than our institutional completion rate of 31%. Further, all of the students who successfully completed the writing program sequence were still taking "first-year" writing in their second college year.

Therefore, sections of the *Statement* that are especially relevant here and that should be expanded in order to account for the different kind of work that instructors at open-admissions institutions encounter include the final section on "Teaching Conditions Necessary for Quality Education" and an additional section that lays out the minimum qualifications for teaching developmental/non-degree credit courses. For instructors in these institutions, it's critical that strong language be included that not only asserts "Remedial or developmental sections should be limited to a maximum of 15 students" (335), but also explains in detailed language that small class sizes for remedial courses are critical because of the significant academic needs these students have and points to research in the field on the relationship between class size, student retention, and student learning to support the recommendation. The same recommendation for a revised *Statement* that makes a strong, data-supported explanation for the importance of holding writing class sizes to 20 students also holds true for degree-credit writing courses. Our campus, like most two-year institutions, enrolls students who haven't taken any academic English courses or writing-intensive classes during their senior high school year; most of these writers encounter a substantial gap between their most recent educational experiences and the demands of even basic college-level reading and writing.

The current economic climate, the expanded expectation for more students across populations to attend college, and the presidential emphasis on "college for everyone"[4] all contribute to an educational landscape in which we can expect more students like ours to attempt higher

---

4. One of the stated goals of the Obama administration has been to support the efforts of community colleges and increase the number of students earning associate's degrees—or as *CHE* reports, "five million more Americans earning college degrees and certificates over the next decade" (Parry and Fischer).

education than ever before, particularly learners from first-generation and low-income backgrounds who are developing the cultural capital and academic literacy skills necessary to earn a college degree. Two-year, open-admission campuses are the most likely access point for nontraditional/place-bound students, students of color, multilingual students, and first-generation and working-class college students. For example, "Who Are the Undergraduates," a *Chronicle of Higher Education* (*CHE*) report profiling undergraduate demographics, shows that 12.07% of all undergraduates identify as coming from families making less than $20,000 per year, and of that group, 48% attend a two-year public college. Another 11.58% identify as coming from families that make between $20,000 and $40,000, and 52% of that group attend public, two-year campuses. We must recognize as a discipline that the institutions with the students requiring the greatest resources—in support centers, in qualified and skilled instructors, in economic terms—may right now have the fewest. Though we acknowledge that low-income students attend all kinds of institutions, *CHE* notes, "Just under 15 percent of the undergraduates at the country's 50 wealthiest colleges received Pell Grants in 2008–9, the most recent year for which national data are available." As Pell Grants are usually a barometer for the percentage of students from low-income families at a particular institution, this statistic should not surprise anyone.

We know that poor and minority students are disproportionately clustered in two-year and open-admission institutions; a more recent column in *CHE* illustrates the serious impact being a first-generation student has on the persistence and retention: "More than a quarter of [first-generation college students] don't make it past the first year, and almost 90 percent don't graduate within six years" (Greenwald). Students facing these sorts of challenges require a great deal of learning support, for example small class sizes near the optimal range; learning support courses that introduce students to academic literacy skills that help them be successful; composition tutorial or studio courses that can provide intensive, one-on-one instruction; and other, time-intensive practices that promote student success.

We suggest that the *Statement* incorporate language that accounts for this sort of work by providing not only recommendations but also a set of well-organized and robust resources that can assist instructors in communicating program needs (and the rationale for those needs) to their institutional leaders. The *Statement* should be accompanied by an easily-accessible, user-friendly database that writing program administrators and other writing studies professionals can use to provide institutional administrators with empirical evidence to support policy decisions that improve the professional lives of postsecondary writing instructors. For example, CWPA has developed a "Bibliography of Sample Research" and "Postsecondary Framework Representative Curricular Resources" to accompany the *Framework for Success in Postsecondary Writing*; a similar model might be used to help support the work of instructors at open-access institutions and contingent faculty. Further, supporting research in two-year colleges and open-admissions institutions that can document, using a systematic research design, the learning needs of students across the range of academic preparation and ability is critical for providing an evidence-based set of recommendations that will likely be more persuasive to policymakers and administrators. This would assist programs that are facing challenges like increased course maxima, elimination of contact hours in writing courses, or changes to placement or assessment methods that may hinder student learning. Rather than having to scramble to marshal resources to illustrate disciplinary best practice and research findings about the impact of policy decisions on students (which is the most persuasive focus when trying to influence policy), individual instructors and program leaders would have ready access to the information needed to make a case.

The *Statement* makes policy recommendations and, therefore, should be relatively brief. However, an appendix or easily accessible online documentation system about existing research in our field would provide writing studies professionals with substantial evidence that they can use to advocate for institutional practices and public policies that promote excellence in teaching postsecondary writing. For example, a web resource might offer supporting evidence about the relationship between class size and student learning or provide a compilation of research that illustrates how learning outcomes are affected by material conditions for contingent faculty that do not support their integration into the fabric of a program, department, or campus. Please see the chapters by McClure and colleagues, Maid and D'Angelo, and Janangelo for similar recommendations.

Graduate Training and Requirements for Teaching

Finally, CCCC must emphasize the importance of graduate training in English that includes coursework in composition pedagogy, teaching experience, and mentoring for all students who plan to have an academic career in English. This means that, even at the Master of Arts level, it is critical for programs to offer an increased emphasis on student learning and research-based best practices in teaching postsecondary writing. As *Education in the Balance* concluded, contrary to the working group's initial assumption that most contingent faculty hold a doctorate, the data collection showed that "master's degree seems to be the qualifying degree for teaching off the tenure track (and teaching in the lower division). [. . .] In general, it appears that an MA or an MFA is accepted across all institutional sectors, four-year as well as two-year, as an appropriate degree qualification for teaching the lower division" (2007 ADE 5). This finding may be unsurprising to those of us working at two-year and baccalaureate-granting institutions, but it "caught the committee by surprise" (5). This report highlights the importance of increased graduate training and experience in teaching writing for MA programs because those students do and will continue to make up a substantial portion of the contingent faculty at open-access institutions. Further, as discussed earlier, even tenure-stream faculty in English at two-year campuses and many four-year institutions can expect to spend a significant portion of their professional lives teaching first-year writing, regardless of their areas of graduate emphasis.

In order to account for this wide spectrum of students who now attend college, therefore, the *Statement* must not only address working and teaching conditions but also (1) the preparation and training that graduate programs should offer in order to effectively prepare instructors to thrive in such environments and (2) the minimum credentials instructors should possess in order to teach in both the non-degree and degree-credit curriculum. In order to be successful as a resource for writing instructors, department chairs, and administrators, the revised *Statement* must acknowledge that the conditions in which writing teachers teach at two-year campuses and other open-admission colleges are very different from those at selective institutions and that instructors with a strong background in pedagogy coursework, learning theory, and working with underprepared students are more likely to both be successful in and enjoy their work at institutions of access. For many instructors, teaching college composition most frequently means adapting to the learning needs of writers whose high school curricula and prior learning experiences are not a good match for what they will be asked to do in a college-level writing course. This reality does not alter the learning outcomes that most two-year programs expect students to achieve in first-year writing, but it does change the pace of instruction, the multiplicity of approaches required for meeting students' academic needs, and the time it takes for individual students to become proficient college readers and writers. Specific language might read, "All graduate programs offering the Master of Arts in English degree should require at least two graduate seminars on composition pedagogy, in addition to an elective course focused on a subspecialty within composition and rhetoric, such as rhetorical theory, writing center studies, reading pedagogy, developmental writing, or teaching English to speakers of other languages."

In this way, graduate students who find themselves, as most will, teaching off the tenure track and primarily in the first-year writing or developmental core sequence will have at least a foundational knowledge and understanding of the needs of students developing competency in college writing, a foundation they can build on with ongoing experience, training, and professional development specific to their needs and the needs of the institution at which they work. Realistically, graduates of MA and PhD programs will increasingly encounter the broad range of students who attend a two-year, open-admission campus and, as a result, will need to develop an agile pedagogical sensibility that they can adapt to teach students with varying needs in every classroom. This reality in higher education gives particular exigency and a new inflection to the 1989 *Statement*'s endorsement that "Each institution should provide adequate training and supervision of graduate writing instructors, and this training should be conducted by someone with appropriate preparation or experience in rhetoric and composition" (332).

Beyond training, mentoring, and supervision by faculty with backgrounds in writing studies, graduate programs in rhetoric and composition—indeed, in English more broadly—need to adapt to meet the changing demands of postsecondary teaching. A very small minority of graduate students can expect to move into positions like those held by their advisors, where they will teach only in their area of expertise, frequently in literature, and primarily to English majors or graduate students. Therefore, the revised *Statement* should endorse a systematic, national self-assessment on the part of graduate programs that rigorously evaluates the preparation given to graduate students in English, the vast majority of whom will find first-year writing is their primary teaching responsibility, frequently teaching to a diverse range of students. Such a *Statement* could then be used as a resource by campus change agents who hope to prepare their graduate students for a professional life beyond graduate school—and who aim to engage in an honest self-assessment of their programs' abilities to prepare students for the professional lives that they are most likely to experience. We suggest language such as

> Effectively assessing students' writing, placing them in appropriate courses, and providing them with instruction that addresses their individual needs as college readers and writers requires a program built on writing instructors who have expertise and graduate training in assessment and pedagogy and who can adapt their teaching to a wide range of learners. In order to provide graduates of both MA and PhD programs with the best preparation for the kinds of work they are likely to encounter, graduate programs must carefully assess placement rates and types for graduates of their programs and match departmental curriculum and degree requirements to the needs of these job opportunities.

In doing this kind of self-examination, English departments can produce graduates who are well-prepared to not only contribute but also succeed and thrive at institutions with open admission or nonselective admission policies.

Compared with previous position documents with similar goals, an updated *Statement of Principles and Standards for the Postsecondary Teaching of Writing* must address a more complex set of professional realities for college instructors. A revised list of standards must define what it means to be a postsecondary writing teacher in ways that depart from the traditional assumption that upper-division, tenure-stream work in a professor's graduate research specialty is the preferred and dominant college teaching position. It is essential that a revised, twenty-first century *Statement* reflect the diverse working conditions of all members of our profession, which includes a varied range of student populations, courses, employment statuses, types of institutions, and kinds of writing programs. A revision has the potential to influence departmental, institutional, statewide, and even national public policies and, thus, become a catalyst for change that will more effectively address the learning needs of college writers and graduate students in English. A *Statement* that fails to do this will be ineffective and irrelevant in supporting the majority of professionals who teach postsecondary writing.

Works Cited

2007 Association of Departments of English (ADE) Ad Hoc Committee on Staffing. *Education in the Balance: A Report on the Academic Workforce in English*. Modern Language Association and Association of Departments of English, 2008, www.mla.org/Resources/Research/Surveys-Reports-and-Other-Documents/Staffing-Salaries-and-Other-Professional-Issues/Education-in-the-Balance-A-Report-on-the-Academic-Workforce-in-English.

Arnold, Lisa, et al. "Forum on the Profession." *College English*, vol. 72, no. 4, March 2011, pp. 409–27.

Bousquet, Marc. *How the University Works: Higher Education and the Low-Wage Nation*. New York UP, 2008.

Bousquet, Marc, et al. *Tenured Bosses and Disposable Teachers: Writing Instruction in the Managed University*. Southern Illinois UP, 2004.

CCCC Executive Committee. *Statement of Principles and Standards for the Postsecondary Teaching of Writing*. *College Composition and Communication*, vol. 40, no. 3, 1989, pp. 329–36.

Committee on Research and Scholarship in the Two-Year College. *Research and Scholarship in the Two-Year College*. Two-Year College English Association, National Council of Teachers of English, 2010, www.ncte.org/library/NCTEFiles/Groups/TYCA/ResearchScholarship.pdf.

Flaherty, Colleen. "So Close Yet So Far." *Inside Higher Ed*, 20 November 2012, www.insidehighered.com/news/2012/11/20/college-cuts-adjuncts-hours-avoid-affordable-care-act-costs.

Framework for Success in Postsecondary Writing. Council of Writing Program Administrators, National Council of Teachers of English, and National Writing Project, 2011, wpacouncil.org/files/framework-for-success-postsecondary-writing.pdf.

Greenwald, Richard. "Think of First-Generation Students as Pioneers, Not Problems." *The Chronicle of Higher Education*, 11 November 2012, chronicle.com/article/Think-of-First-Generation/135710/.

Hassel, Holly, and Joanne Baird Giordano. "Occupy Writing Studies: Rethinking College Composition for the Needs of the Teaching Majority." *College Composition and Communication*, vol. 65, no. 1, September 2013, pp. 117–39.

Laurence, David. *Demography of the Faculty: A Statistical Portrait of English and Foreign Languages*. Modern Language Association and the Association of Departments of English, 10 December 2008, www.mla.org/content/download/25391/1163986/demography_fac2.pdf.

Parry, Marc, and Karin Fischer. "Obama's Ambitious Plan for Community Colleges Raises Hopes and Questions." *The Chronicle of Higher Education*, 15 July 2009, chronicle.com/article/Obamas-Plan-for-Community/47379.

A Portrait of Part-Time Faculty Members. Coalition on the Academic Workforce, June 2012, www.academicworkforce.org/CAW_portrait_2012.pdf.

Position Statement on the Status and Working Conditions of Contingent Faculty. National Council of Teachers of English, September 2010, www.ncte.org/positions/statements/contingent_faculty/. Also printed in *College English*, vol. 73, no. 4, March 2011, p. 356–59.

Schell, Eileen. *Gypsy Academics and Mother-Teachers: Gender, Contingent Labor, and Writing Instruction*. Boynton/Cook, 1998.

Schell, Eileen, and Patricia Stock. *Moving a Mountain: Transforming the Role of Contingent Faculty in Composition Studies and Higher Education*. National Council of Teachers of English, 2001.

"Who Are the Undergraduates?" *The Chronicle of Higher Education*, 12 December 2010, chronicle.com/article/Who-Are-the-Undergraduates-/123916/.

WPA Outcomes Statement for First-Year Composition. Council of Writing Program Administrators, July 2014, wpacouncil.org/positions/outcomes.html.

SECTION 3: RESCRIPTING THE STATEMENT

10 Rethinking the "Legitimate" Reasons for Hiring Adjunct Faculty: A Recension Statement of Its Own

Evelyn Beck

INTRODUCTION

Since the *Statement of Principles and Standards for the Postsecondary Teaching of Writing* (hereafter the *Statement*) was published in 1989, technology has had a tremendous impact on the teaching profession, including the teaching of writing—and especially in the opportunities created for adjunct faculty. Of course, they are far from the only ones affected. Technology has spurred what could become a seismic shift in employment. According to the U.S. Bureau of Labor Statistics, contingent workers make up 29% of the US workforce, and that ratio is expected to grow to 50% by 2020 (Vollmer 16). To cut costs, companies are increasingly relying on a freelance workforce because technology has made it possible to do so.

That this change has become a part of American culture is evident by the popularization of a new vocabulary for so-called "part-time" workers. Economists and other observers of how the job market is evolving regularly refer to independent contractors, perma-temps, and other members of the "1099 economy" or more frequently, "the Uber economy," the latter term spawned by the success of companies like Uber, which relies on ordinary people to serve as taxi drivers according to their own schedules. Granted, these terms are often used disparagingly as part of a grave concern for the loss of full-time jobs with benefits. Yet many younger workers don't want to trade the freedom of working at their convenience for the security of a steady paycheck and health insurance, and they have embraced the changes, part of a landscape in which the concept of "a job" has metamorphosized. This ongoing debate was discussed in an article about Uber in *The Atlantic* that asked, "Is the company destroying full-time work, entrenching us in part-time purgatory, or empowering America's most independent workers?" (Thompson 1). The conclusion was that the truth lies somewhere in the middle.

This chapter will focus on one function of technology—teaching online (including the teaching of online writing classes)—and on one group—adjunct faculty who teach far from campus. It will examine how this group has grown, how their geographic isolation has changed their interaction with the colleges and universities for which they teach, and how they are redefining the role of adjunct faculty amidst the larger landscape of a changing workforce.

For the most part, of course, the ideals expressed in the *Statement* remain the same no matter whether an instructor is teaching in a traditional or a virtual classroom. All adjunct faculty deserve to be treated as professionals, with adequate salary and benefits as well as support for professional development. Their historic and well-documented exploitation must not be tolerated. Set against the backdrop of changing times, however, in which there is less and less job "permanence," the widespread acceptance and continuing growth of distance education has created a group of instructors who do not necessarily want full-time employment and who are satisfied to be able to teach at multiple far-flung campuses in exchange for the freedom to live wherever they like and work whatever hours best suit their lifestyles.

Accordingly, is it possible that the hiring of adjunct faculty can be viewed positively in some situations? Is it still right to state that there are only "two legitimate reasons for hiring part-time faculty: (1) to teach specialized courses for which no regular faculty are available and which require special practical knowledge (e.g., hiring a distinguished reporter to teach one class in journalism); and (2) to meet unexpected increases in enrollment" (332–33)? Might it be time to consider that a cadre of online adjunct instructors—if such an arrangement meets the needs of both college and faculty—has merit for the profession of teaching post-secondary writing?

In this chapter, I argue that the *Statement* needs to include an additional legitimate reason for hiring part-time faculty: contracting with online faculty seeking only part-time employment. Circumstances have created a growing group of adjunct instructors who—by choice—teach online courses at a distance. Despite the challenges and potential for mistreatment, this situation has benefits not only for the institutions that hire them but also for the adjuncts themselves. In making my claim, I offer recommendations for minimum standards to prevent exploitation of this growing cadre of postsecondary writing teachers.

A New Class of "Professional" Adjuncts

Though growth is slowing some in the current economic climate, distance education continues to far outpace the growth of higher education enrollment overall. A 2011 report from the Babson Survey Research Group cites a 10% gain in online enrollments and growth in the number of students taking at least one online course in Fall 2010 to more than 6.1 million, a gain of 560,000 from Fall 2009 (Allen and Seaman). In contrast, the general student population grew by less than 1% (Allen and Seaman). Simply stated, more and more colleges and universities believe that online education is an important part of their institutional futures.

With the continuing decline of full-time tenure-track faculty (Larcara; Ruth et al.; Sammons and Ruth) comes an increased demand for adjunct faculty, especially in high-demand courses such as first-year writing. According to the 2008 report *Education in the Balance: A Report on the Academic Workforce in English* issued by the Modern Language Association and the Association of Departments of English (ADE), adjuncts (not including non-tenure-track full-time faculty) teaching English number 40% at four-year institutions and 68% at two-year institutions (2007 ADE).

In most subject areas, including English, the type of course making most use of adjuncts is in the area where enrollment growth is strongest: online. In "The Professional Adjunct: An Emerging Trend in Online Instruction," Laurie A. Bedford writes, "While the use of adjuncts is often seen as less desirable for both the organization and the learners, universities continue to draw upon them—particularly in their online programs—at unprecedented rates." In fact, Robert Tipple, in "Effective Leadership of Online Adjunct Faculty," cites 2008 National Center for Education Statistics data that adjuncts now make up 48% of all American college faculty, and that "the growth in online education is becoming an increasingly key factor."

What is most interesting about the growth in online teaching and learning for the purposes of this chapter are the opportunities it has created for adjuncts. One sign of the growth of academic telework is the appearance of how-to articles with titles like "A Multiple Gigs Online Teaching Guide for Adjuncts," which offer advice on how not to get overwhelmed by multiple classes at multiple colleges (Sull). Some academics have even sought new language to delineate this new role; the University of Illinois-Chicago/Great Cities Institute suggests the term "e-adjuncts," notes Susan C. Biro in "Adjunct Faculty Perceptions about Their Preparation, Support, and Value as Online Instructors."

In short, we are bearing witness to the emergence of a class of "professional adjuncts": instructors who teach online from their home offices for colleges and universities throughout the country and who, for a variety of reasons, may even prefer this arrangement to a full-time tenure-track position. While exploitation remains a serious concern, the phenomenon of those who freelance by choice has the potential to alter in profound ways the discussion about the "plight" of adjuncts. The *Statement* refers to such faculty as an "academic underclass" (330) who "work without job security, often without benefits, and for wages far below what their full-time colleagues are paid per course" (330). Though one can argue that this is an accurate depiction of many part-time appointments, the depiction of their "itinerant existence, racing from class to car to drive to another institution to teach" (330) does not apply when the adjunct is teaching online. While the distinction may seem incidental, it is in fact significant. When faculty members are able to exert some control over their work environment, they are taking a step toward independence. And if demand for their services grows, improvements may also occur in the areas of wages and benefits.

Bedford makes a solid case for a reconsideration of how adjuncts are viewed:

> The duality that informs the dialogue about the use of tenured professors versus adjunct instructors—particularly in online programs—ignores a third group of instructor. An emerging phenomenon is developing in which a new class of faculty is beginning to play a role in the nature of the organization-faculty relationship. These full-time part-timers [. . .] make up a portion of individuals who seek online, adjunct work and [. . .] are

finding that they can build a network of opportunities with an entrepreneurial spirit [. . .] They are also finding that they have negotiating power as organizations struggle to fill their teaching vacancies [. . .] Furthermore, as more online programs emerge, adjuncts are not bound by scheduling or geography to fill their employment needs [. . .] They are finding that, as they build their competencies, they are situated to capitalize on a growing market for their skills that involves multiple opportunities for part-time positions with diverse organizations [. . .] The full-time, professional adjunct needs to be explored as a career choice with the potential for diverse work, flexible scheduling, fair compensation, and professional growth for the individual. Furthermore, this trend also needs to be investigated as a possibly legitimate approach for organizations to meet their online instructional needs.

In my role as dean, I have witnessed the impact of these trends. We have hired out-of-state faculty to teach some of our online courses, and we have negotiated with adjuncts over salary and travel stipends when we have trouble filling some positions. Our part-time faculty do sometimes have negotiating power when it comes to location, scheduling, and compensation, a sign that as demand for similar services grows around the globe, professional online adjuncts should be in a better position to make demands of their own.

This new breed of adjuncts is composed of entrepreneurs making their way individually, seeking and evaluating opportunities in the same way that those in many professions do, especially at a time where job security is nearly a relic of the past. Like independent writers or contractors, their work can be viewed as freelance or project-oriented, a semester "gig" not that different from a book or building project. While an adjunct often continues to teach for an institution semester after semester, so do successful writers continue to receive assignments from editors with whom they've developed professional relationships. Bedford describes this new breed of adjuncts as taking charge of their destiny in a way that the adjunct experience is rarely described:

> Rather than find fault about their situation, these [faculty] realized the opportunity to redefine adjunct teaching and to promote the evolution of the status of [adjuncts] in the spirit of entrepreneurship. They also felt that, as entrepreneurs, they held

the responsibility for seeking alternative associations when treated unfairly.

Knowing that there are often other opportunities available gives adjuncts the freedom to walk away from unacceptable situations, a common practice for most professionals outside of academe engaged in contract work.

It's no secret that some institutions treat their adjuncts better than other institutions. Pay varies greatly from place to place, as do other important aspects of labor practices and working conditions, including continuity of employment, opportunities for promotion, funds for professional development, class size, training opportunities, and technical support. Therefore, I fully support the *Statement*'s call for part-time faculty to receive "a salary that accurately reflects their teaching duties and any duties outside the classroom they are asked to assume," as well as "the same fringe benefits and [. . .] the same cost-of-living, seniority, and merit salary increases available to full-time faculty" and "access to research support and travel funds to attend professional conferences" (334). Some institutions give these considerations to their adjuncts, but most do not, and these considerations are important for faculty who teach online as well as on-site.

The entrepreneurial adjunct, especially in a seller's market, can seek more lucrative positions when a position is viewed as inferior. Much more than in the past, part-time faculty can take matters into their own hands rather than wringing their hands as they wait for conditions to improve. This has been my experience. I have completed terms at less desirable institutions and then removed myself from their rosters of adjuncts. These were institutions where the pay was appallingly low ($900 to $1,600 per class), as well as where the class sizes were too large, the demands for adjunct time were unrealistic (regular synchronous meetings online or via phone and very frequent required training and multiple reporting requirements), the technological support was nonexistent, and/or program administrators were cold and inaccessible.

Bedford quotes a participant in her study who reports:

> As organizations grow more dependent upon our services, I see the day when we will be seen as professionals and be in a better position to negotiate for ourselves. However, this will require purposeful effort on our part. We will need to find ways to purposefully capitalize on the situation. I think that one of these ways might be to demarcate our role as unique.

I suggest that capitalizing on the demand for online adjuncts means moving beyond the perception of an "academic underclass" and the sense, as put forth in the *Statement*, that the working conditions of part-time faculty "constitute a crisis in higher education, one which dramatically affects the public interest" (330). If adjuncts can pick and choose and can fashion a satisfactory workload, then they can shed the image of being forlorn or taken advantage of and begin to demand the respect they deserve.

President Pamela Pease of Jones International University is administrator who relies on adjuncts, faculty members who outnumber her full-timers 125 to 6. Admittedly, her interests are economic, yet she recognizes that the adjuncts she hires are more entrepreneurial when she comments, "It's a new breed of faculty members who teach at multiple institutions. [. . .] They're trying to put together their own work environment. Most of them are pretty independent" (qtd. in Carnevale A31). Perhaps for online adjuncts, they are less of an academic underclass and much more professional in their approach to employment than commonly perceived.

The Benefits of Academic Telework

For institutions, the greatest incentive to hire adjuncts is obviously financial. One estimate puts the price tag for using part-timers to educate students at 36 percent lower than using full-time faculty (Holub). A reliance on adjuncts also allows for additional flexibility—albeit to the detriment of those employees—since staffing can rise or fall according to enrollment and personnel needs. The use of online adjuncts brings additional benefits to employers, most notably the ability to hire beyond the local area. Other factors worth noting are reduced needs for parking and office space.

Less recognized are the benefits of this position for the online adjuncts themselves. Foremost is freedom and flexibility, the same factors that drive student enrollment in online classes. Teaching online allows for a flexible work schedule that can accommodate all kinds of personal and family needs. Someone with commitments to care for young children or aging parents can fit work in around these demands. Someone who has had to relocate for a partner's job can keep working. Someone who travels often can continue to work as well. There are also those with health problems that make driving to a campus difficult but who are able to teach via their computer. In her dissertation, *The Emerging Academician: The Rise of the Online Adjunct Faculty*, Carolyn J. Shiffman offers the following real-life examples of online adjuncts who greatly value a flexible work schedule: a single mom caring for her children, a mother helping her pregnant daughter fight cancer, and a woman caring for her husband with ALS (67). Another faculty member interviewed by Shiffman chose online teaching as a result of a "lifestyle adjustment due to automobile accident" (63). Other online adjuncts are retired or preparing for retirement from full-time positions, as I am.

A study by Diane Chapman, "Contingent and Tenured/Tenure-Track Faculty: Motivations and Incentives to Teach Distance Education Courses," which appeared in the *Online Journal of Distance Learning Administration*, examined the motivations for teaching online. It found that a flexible schedule was the top motivator not only for online adjuncts but also for those full-time faculty teaching online. Contingent faculty in that study also noted the desire "to better balance work and family" as a motivation for teaching online. Similarly, in her dissertation, *Forecasting Online Adjunct Needs: A Delphi Study*, Marie Larcara reports that more than 92% of the 39 online adjuncts at Walden University responding to an online survey agreed that flexibility was a major reason for teaching online (87).

Tipple cites a 2008 study in which participants felt "that teaching online provided optimal working conditions as they were able to 'teach' at any time and from any place." Shiffman tries to deconstruct the popular image of "the poor adjunct" with an image of online adjuncts who "have embraced the autonomy and flexibility that their positions provide. This new professorate has found a way to express their love of teaching while maintaining balance in their lives by working from home" (40), adding that "some research indicates adjuncts experience greater overall job satisfaction than their full-time equivalents" (41). What a contrast to the language of the *Statement*, which speaks of an "academic underclass," "the worst scandal in higher education today," "an itinerant existence," "marginalized faculty," and "uncertain futures" (330).

Yes, part-time faculty must still maneuver difficult terrain. However when this terrain is virtual, it can come with compensating freedoms, such as the option to accept the most appealing teaching assignments, as noted in an interview of an adjunct who teaches for four institutions in three states (cited in Gaillard-Kenney). There can even be economic benefits for those with multiple "gigs" and for those who live in an area with limited job opportunities but a lower cost of living. That has been the case for me. I reside in South Carolina, which has the nation's twelfth highest unemployment rate as of October 2012 according to the U.S. Bureau of Labor Statistics ("Local Area") and the twentieth lowest cost of living in the second quarter of 2012 ("Cost of Living"). Fortunately, I have been able to teach online for institutions in states such as California and Maryland, where wages are higher to compensate for the higher cost of living in those areas.

Some adjuncts have reported making as much as $100,000 per year (cited in Shiffman). That's not to say that most online adjunct writing instructors are going to have six-figure salaries. Harder-to-fill positions in the sciences and engineering, for example, are going to command higher wages. In her survey, Shiffman found that although a majority of those surveyed (54.3%) earned less than $25,000 per year through adjunct teaching, thirty-three respondents (5%) had earned over $100,000 in the previous twelve months (59). So while a good salary is not the norm, it is possible and should be more so in the future as online courses and programs continue to proliferate. Since English composition courses are required everywhere, there is much opportunity.

In my role as dean, I have witnessed a trend where department heads staff on-site courses with full-time faculty and seek part-time faculty from across the country to teach their online courses. They do so not only to minimize local politics but also to search for the best online teachers. I myself have had plenty of opportunities to work as an online adjunct English instructor, which in some cases have provided contributions to my retirement fund, support for professional development, and periodic raises and promotions, concepts that should be detailed in a revised *Statement*. Let me add that those online adjunct English instructors who do a good job will continue to find work (albeit at varying rates of pay) despite what many perceive as a glut of available candidates. Yes, there are plenty of qualified English faculty out there. Many of them, however, underestimate the workload of online teaching while others determine that they prefer the face-to-face environment. The turnover of online faculty combined with the steady increase in online offerings suggests that there will continue to be opportunities for those interested in pursuing a career as a professional online adjunct.

THE CHALLENGES OF ACADEMIC TELEWORK

Despite the increasing opportunities for entrepreneurial adjuncts in postsecondary writing and other fields, an online workforce based far from campus does present significant challenges for both institutions and adjunct faculty. For institutions, the primary challenges revolve around communication with faculty working at a distance. When asked what areas of support would help adjunct retention, communication was the area most in need of improvement in a survey completed by 124 adjunct faculty at Colorado Mountain College, where 85% of the faculty are adjuncts (Recruitment and Retention Team 19). Though data is lacking on this topic, it stands to reason that communication becomes an even greater challenge with online faculty. When administrators never encounter their faculty face-to-face and rely almost exclusively on email, it's difficult to be sure that important information is relayed and understood. The *Statement*, for instance, rightly asserts that part-time faculty "should receive adequate introduction to their teaching assignments, departments, and institutions" (334). When such an introduction takes place virtually, such an introduction appears to be often inadequate.

Consider further the *Statement*'s guideline that part-time faculty "should be given a voice in the formulation of department policy regarding courses and programs in which they teach (for example, by voting at department meetings and by serving on curriculum and hiring committees)" (334). At Rio Salado Community College, for example, online adjuncts assist faculty chairs with such tasks as content and curriculum development, textbook selection, and new faculty mentoring, and the University of Illinois-Chicago/Great Cities Institute involves e-adjuncts in curriculum development and in the marketing and evaluation of online programs (Tipple). "This integrates adjunct faculty into a supportive community and increases the level of commitment for adjuncts by removing the sense of isolation that often characterizes their positions," comments Biro (21).

Even if adjuncts work for an institution at which all faculty are included in meetings and committees, some might wonder how this type of inclusion can take place at a distance. A vote might be emailed and agendas and minutes shared, but unless remote faculty are invited to participate via an online conferencing program like Skype, WebEx, or Google Hangouts, they are unlikely to truly feel like part of their units. For faculty, then, the result is typically a sense of isolation that counterbalances their sense of autonomy. Despite the connections that exist with online students, faculty teaching at a distance can feel invisible, like institutional nonentities. If they are not included on emails sent out to all faculty, then they may not be aware of issues and goals currently driving the college. If they do not have a personal connection to whom they can turn for help, then they may flounder when problems with students or technologies arise. If they are contacted only when a student complains, for example, then their experience of this particular position might be largely negative. In situations such as this, online adjuncts are "remote" in more ways than one.

In "The Isolation of Online Adjunct Faculty and its Impact on their Performance," Véra Dolan writes of how disconnected, isolated, and unappreciated adjuncts feel when they are physically removed from campus in her study of one university's twenty-eight online adjunct instructors (66). These adjuncts don't feel a sense of belonging, which is hardly surprising, especially if they "belong" to multiple institutions. "Belonging," however, does not necessarily mean being on the tenure track, as the *Statement* suggests. It is possible to feel a deep sense of connection even when teaching for more than one school as an entrepreneurial adjunct.

The keys to effective communication are genuine interpersonal interaction and frequent, friendly contact. Dolan cites research that "social connections with co-workers are a strong predictor—some would say the strongest single predictor—of job satisfaction" (67). Creating community, then, is vital; but how that happens is not as simple as creating a discussion board or chat room for online adjuncts. As Dolan suggests, the best practices of online teaching—the ones all too familiar for entrepreneurial online adjuncts—need to be applied to creating a sense of community among them. As was noted earlier, the *Statement* recommends that adjunct faculty "should be given a voice in the formulation of department policy regarding courses and programs in which they teach" (334) and "Administrators and department chairs should recognize the professional status of part-time teachers" (333). Assisting in or at least giving voice to the communities that not only support the courses and programs in which they work but also facilitate the communication and collaboration critical to their identity as professional online faculty appears to fall under this umbrella.

From my experience, online adjuncts want to be a valued part of the faculty; remote instructors want to be included. Again, communication is key. One of the easiest ways to begin this process is to provide online adjuncts with a college email address and a lead contact for online adjunct faculty. According to Biro's study, "Many interviewees described improved communication as underlying their perception of value. Overall, the more contact adjunct faculty had with a dean, administrator, trainer, or peers, the more they expressed feeling connected to, and valued by, the institution" (69). A vibrant, working online community where they can connect with peers is of great value. Active and relevant communication, on issues from technological workarounds to campus announcements to faculty forums, should be cited in any revised *Statement* as critical to the job performance of online faculty.

The communication with and availability of technical support is also vital to any faculty member's success, particularly those teaching at a distance. A 24-hour helpline is ideal, but even more important is a name, phone number, and email for an individual who can help an online instructor with problems. Technical difficulties are sure to occur, from incompatible browsers to disappearing online gradebooks to computer viruses, and a remote instructor must have access to an expert who can help address the particular issue quickly. Such access was cited as important by the adjuncts in Biro's study of online adjunct faculty from postsecondary institutions in the greater Philadelphia metropolitan region (54). Further, faculty comfort with the technology is not just important for instructors; faculty who can assist frustrated students with minor technical problems are a factor in student retention as well (Tipple). For these reasons, recommendations for technical support should be outlined in the *Statement*.

Other Recommendations

For online adjuncting to work as a career choice for individuals as well as the institutions for which they teach, these professionals need to be treated appropriately. Here are some additional suggestions to create fair working conditions for the growing online adjunct professoriate, suggestions that should be acknowledged in a revised *Statement*, if not in the specific details, then in the ethical and professional principles upon which they are grounded.

Adjuncts must receive adequate pay. As the existing *Statement* suggests, "Compensation, per course, for part-time faculty should never be lower than the per-course compensation for full-time faculty with comparable experience, duties, and credentials" (334). While salaries vary depending on credentials as well as term length, class size, and type of institution, it's clear that salaries for teaching postsecondary writing are low. A 2010 survey of 500 part-time and adjunct faculty members by Hart Research Associates on behalf of the American Federation of Teachers found that 35% receive less than $2,500 per course (13). A 2010 report by the Keystone Research Center found that contingent faculty in Pennsylvania earned an average of $3,264 per course for the 2007–2008 school year, an amount that is 30% of what tenured and tenure-track faculty are paid (Brill and Herzenberg 17). This data is a few years old as of this writing, but it is safe to assume that this situation has not changed dramatically.

When perusing the adjunct job posts on higher education employment websites, some institutions still offer $1,800 or less per course. While each adjunct will have to set his or her own baseline, of course, perhaps by using average full-time salaries for comparison, it is clear that any revision to the *Statement* should provide a formula for paying adjunct faculty that demonstrates equity with those in full-time positions. For example, a 2012 survey of 1,251 colleges by the American Association of University Professors found that the average nine-month salary for a full-time instructor is $47,842 (Curtis and Thornton 27). Similarly, the *2012–13 Faculty in Higher Education Salary Survey for Non-Tenure-Track Teaching Faculty* at four-year institutions conducted by the College and University Professional Association for Human Resources, which includes 478 private institutions and 316 public institutions, indicates the average salary for teaching assistant professors in English at $49,939. These numbers, by comparison, are much more palatable than what is commonly advertised. Further, as a matter of transparency, the pay, or at least the pay range, should be included in each job announcement, along with smaller yet still important logistical factors such as the availability of direct deposit and distributed pay. These and other matters related to compensation should be addressed in a revised *Statement*.

Similar to their full-time counterparts, part-time faculty should also have access to a "step" or promotion system, and recommendations for types of systems should be outlined in a revised *Statement*. For example, the University of California, Los Angeles promotes adjuncts from Assistant Adjunct Professor to Associate Adjunct Professor to Adjunct Professor, based on teaching, research and creative work, professional competence and activity, and university and public service ("Adjunct"). New York-based LaGuardia Community College offers the same three promotional steps, with eligibility based on having taught at least six semesters over the previous three years (*Employee Handbook: Adjunct Instructional Staff* 13). In addition, and as the existing *Statement* suggests, merit pay opportunities should be available to all faculty, not just those working full time (334). For the benefit of online adjuncts, a revised *Statement* could outline conditions of employment aimed at improving their working conditions. As articulated in the current *Statement*, transactions related to contracts, reappointments, and terminations for online adjuncts should also be conducted in writing, with adequate notice in all cases (333–34).

In addition to the conditions of employment, online adjuncts should have access to training opportunities and professional development activities in addition to "research support and travel funds to attend professional conferences" (334). While 94% of higher education administrators report that they offer some training for online faculty, such training appears to vary widely from training courses to informal mentoring (Allen and Seaman). Tipple cites research "that online adjunct faculty perceived their primary need for ongoing training included training in course management systems, pedagogical approaches to online teaching, university/institution specific student support systems, and instructional design on how to develop an online course." Similarly, a 2010 survey of 158 online writing instructors by the Conference on College Composition and Communication Committee for Best Practice in Online Writing Instruction found a need for more training, especially in online course design, which many reported having to do without any preparation (Hewett et al. 12). Thus, orientation to the institution's preferred course management system, online course procedures, and student registration processes ought to be offered at hiring and at appropriate intervals thereafter. A revised *Statement* should spell out that such training should be optional (but encouraged) and offered in both synchronous and asynchronous formats. In addition, participation in professional development activities needs to be recognized and rewarded, such as with course preference and funds for additional professional development. For example, Harrisburg Area Community College in Pennsylvania allows adjuncts to apply for up to $500 in professional development funds every other year, and the money is awarded in advance of the proposed travel. I have been an adjunct there and have been awarded one of these travel stipends.

Conclusion

The *Statement of Principles and Standards for the Postsecondary Teaching of Writing* is still valuable today for its intent to advance the profession of teaching college writing and to protect adjunct instructors from exploitation, as such exploitation remains a very real concern. However, any revision to the *Statement* must recognize that advancements in technology have created a new kind of classroom and new opportunities for adjunct instructors who might desire lifestyle flexibility over job security. Thus, it's time to consider that, given the right kind of working conditions, adjunct positions for teaching online writing courses are not by definition exploitive. They can represent a new kind of opportunity for a new class of adjunct instructors who are redefining what it means to be independent contractors in higher education.

The *Statement* needs to stop referring to adjunct faculty in negative terms. Though it's appropriate for CCCC to campaign for higher wages and better working conditions, and the nod to adjunct faculty's "extraordinary contributions" is appreciated, the use of language such as "academic underclass" perpetuates the second-class status of adjuncts (330). To assume that "it is evident that their working conditions undermine the capacities of teachers to teach and of students to learn" (330) is a refusal to acknowledge that many institutions pay decent wages and that some adjunct faculty view themselves as entrepreneurs and have fashioned a flexible professional life worthy of respect. We live in changing times in which workplace flexibility means a lot to individuals in nearly every profession.

A revised *Statement* should acknowledge that the hiring of adjunct faculty is permissible in more than very limited circumstances. Specifically, the *Statement* should be revised to include a third reason for the legitimate hiring of adjunct faculty: *when it meets the needs of both the institution and the adjunct faculty member, and the wages and working conditions are deemed fair by the instructor.* The dependence on adjunct faculty is certainly the reality, and isn't it better to campaign for improved working conditions than to fret endlessly about the proliferation of part-time positions? Wouldn't such a refocusing contribute to greater respect for these professionals and help pave the way for improvements? Isn't it time to do so in today's "Uber economy"? Administrators have heard for so long the arguments decrying the lowly status of part-time faculty that these complaints no longer register. A new approach, one that finds a way for these faculty to use the current realities to their advantage, just might find a receptive audience.

Works Cited

2007 Association of Departments of English (ADE) Ad Hoc Committee on Staffing. *Education in the Balance: A Report on the Academic Workforce in English*. Modern Language Association and Association of Departments of English, 2008, www.mla.org/Resources/Research/Surveys-Reports-and-Other-Documents/Staffing-Salaries-and-Other-Professional-Issues/Education-in-the-Balance-A-Report-on-the-Academic-Workforce-in-English.

2012–13 Faculty in Higher Education Salary Survey for Non-Tenure-Track Teaching Faculty and Researchers. College and University Professional Association for Human Resources, 2013, www.higheredjobs.com/salary/salaryDisplay.cfm?SurveyID=25.

"Adjunct Professor Series." UCLA Academic Personnel Office, 21 December 2015, www.apo.ucla.edu/policies-forms/the-call/professorial-series/adjunct-professor-series.

Allen, I. Elaine, and Jeff Seaman. *Going the Distance: Online Education in the United States, 2011*. Babson Survey Research Group, November 2011, www.onlinelearningsurvey.com/reports/goingthedistance.pdf.

Bedford, Laurie A. "The Professional Adjunct: An Emerging Trend in Online Instruction." *Online Journal of Distance Learning Administration*, vol. 12, no. 3, 2009, www.westga.edu/~distance/ojdla/fall123/bedford123.html.

Biro, Susan C. "Adjunct Faculty Perceptions about Their Preparation, Support, and Value as Online Instructors." Dissertation, Widener U, 2005.

Brill, Deirdre, and Stephen Herzenberg. *Reversing Course in Pennsylvania Higher Education: The Two Tiers in Faculty Pay and Benefits and a Way Forward*. Keystone Research Center, 2010, keystoneresearch.org/sites/keystoneresearch.org/files/1-19-11%20Reversing%20Course%20in%20PA%20Higher%20Ed..pdf.

Carnevale, Dan. "For Online Adjuncts, a Seller's Market." *The Chronicle of Higher Education*, April 2004, pp. A31–A32.

CCCC Executive Committee. *Statement of Principles and Standards for the Postsecondary Teaching of Writing*. College Composition and Communication, vol. 40, no. 3, 1989, pp. 329–36.

Chapman, Diane. "Contingent and Tenured/Tenure-Track Faculty: Motivations and Incentives to Teach Distance Education Courses." *Online Journal of Distance Learning Administration*, vol. 14, no. 3, Fall 2011, www.westga.edu/~distance/ojdla/fall143/chapman143.html.

"Cost of Living Data Series: 2nd Quarter 2012." Missouri Economic Research and Information Center, 23 November 2012, www.missourieconomy.org/indicators/cost_of_living/index.stm.

Curtis, John and Saranna Thornton. "Losing Focus: The Annual Report on the Economic Status of the Profession, 2013-14." *Academe*, March-April 2014, pp. 4-38.

Dolan, Véra. "The Isolation of Online Adjunct Faculty and its Impact on their Performance." *The International Review of Research in Open and Distance Learning*, vol. 12, no. 2, February 2011, pp. 62–77.

Employee Handbook: Adjunct Instructional Staff. Department of Human Resources, LaGuardia Community College, City University of New York, April 2015, www.laguardia.edu/uploadedFiles/Main_Site/Content/Departments/HumanResources/PDF/Adjunct%20Instructional%20Staff%20Handbook.pdf.

Gaillard-Kenney, Sandrine. "Adjunct Faculty in Distance Education: What Program Managers Should Know." *Distance Learning*, vol. 3, no. 1, 2006, pp. 9–16.

Hart Research Associates. *A National Survey of Part-Time/Adjunct Faculty. Academic American*, vol. 2, March 2010, www.aft.org/sites/default/files/aa_partimefaculty0310.pdf.

Hewett, Beth L., et al. *Initial Report of the CCCC Committee for Best Practice in Online Writing Instruction (OWI): The State-of-the-Art of OWI.* National Council of Teachers of English, 12 April 2011, www.ncte.org/library/NCTEFiles/Groups/CCCC/Committees/OWI_State-of-Art_Report_April_2011.pdf.

Holub, Tamara. "Contract Faculty in Higher Education." *ERIC Digest*, 2003, http://files.eric.ed.gov/fulltext/ED482556.pdf.

Larcara, Marie. "Forecasting Online Adjunct Needs: A Delphi Study." Dissertation, Walden U, 2010.

"Local Area Unemployment Statistics." Bureau of Labor Statistics, 23 November 2012, www.bls.gov/lau/.

Recruitment and Retention Team. "Adjunct Faculty Retention." Colorado Mountain College, Fall 2008, coloradomtn.edu/wp-content/uploads/filebase/Adjunct_Faculty_Retention.pdf.

Ruth, Stephen R., et al. "E-Learning at a Crossroads—What Price Quality?" *Educause Quarterly*, vol. 30, no. 2, 2007, pp. 32–39.

Sammons, Martha C., and Stephen Ruth. "The Invisible Professor and the Future of Virtual Faculty." *International Journal of Instructional Technology and Distance Learning*, vol. 4, no. 1, January 2007, itdl.org/journal/jan_07/article01.htm.

Shiffman, Carolyn J. "The Emerging Academician: The Rise of the Online Adjunct Faculty." Dissertation, Capella U, 2009.

Sull, Errol Craig. "A Multiple Gigs Online Teaching Guide for Adjuncts." *Distance Learning*, vol. 8, no. 2, 2011, pp. 59–63.

Thompson, Derek. "The Uber Economy." *The Atlantic*, 23 January 2015, www.theatlantic.com/business/archive/2015/01/is-uber-a-middle-class-job-creator-or-not/384763/.

Tipple, Robert. "Effective Leadership of Online Adjunct Faculty." *Online Journal of Distance Learning Administration*, vol. 14, no. 3, Fall 2011, www.westga.edu/~distance/ojdla/spring131/tipple131.html.

Vollmer, Chuck. "2016 State of the U.S. Labor Force." *Jobeconomics*, 11 January 2016, jobenomicsblog.com/2016-state-of-the-u-s-labor-force/.

11 Recognizing Realities

Barry Maid and Barbara D'Angelo

PRELUDE

When we first saw this call, we were taken by both the timeliness and the potential futility in looking at working conditions for teachers of postsecondary writing. One of us has directed writing programs at multiple institutions and written about moving part-time faculty to full-time status. The other has developed, supervised, and led the assessment of curriculum of a technical writing program staffed primarily by part-time faculty. We completely understand that the quality of writing instruction in postsecondary education is directly related to the working conditions of faculty. That is not to say that good writing instruction will always take place with good working conditions or that only bad instruction will take place with bad working conditions. However, we strongly believe that the chances of delivering quality writing instruction to students greatly increases under the right working conditions.

We also understand the need for empirical data. Yet, we feel the need to ask the question, "What kind of empirical data?" If we are discussing values, and "quality of instruction" and "good working conditions" are values, then empirical data is simply numbers used to make subjective judgments look objective. We can define "good working conditions" as the set of having X, Y, and Z. We can then look at one-hundred different college writing programs and determine which meet the criteria of having X, Y, and Z. We can then say that, hypothetically, 22 or 22% of college writing programs have "good working conditions." However, that data is based on the subjective values that X, Y, and Z represent. That's not to say that certain kinds of empirical studies might not help to understand, elucidate, and potentially ameliorate the plight of postsecondary writing instructors. However, that's not what we propose to do here.

What we propose is a statement of values or assumptions complemented by methods that institutions should employ in order to ensure productive working conditions. In doing so, we return to the *Wyoming Resolution*—especially its too often ignored third plank—where the document articulates the need for compliance and consequences (Robertson et al.; Trimbur and Cambridge). Recalling the conversation about accreditation for writing programs taking place in the late 1980s and the discussion within what was then the National Writing Centers Association to look at accreditation in the early 1990s, we contend that accreditation would have been the instrument to help professional organizations ensure compliance with "good working conditions." Of course, nothing ever happened. Still, we feel the notion of compliance as articulated in the third plank of the original resolution is crucial.

As you continue to read, you should note that much of our vision for the future of the *Statement* is incredibly close to the 1989 version—with one significant concession: We have given up the idea that the tenure line is the ideal. We also separate ourselves from the American Assocation of University Professors notion that non-tenure-line faculty are "temporary." The reality is that permanent non-tenure-line faculty have always been present in the academy. We simply embrace it. Finally, we think you will see that in the end we concur with the *Wyoming Resolution* in calling for some kind of compliance. Just as we call for faculty and curriculum to be assessed, institutions must also be held accountable.

So We Begin . . .

At the 1986 Wyoming Conference on Freshman and Sophomore Composition, a group of faculty drafted a resolution to protest the low professional status and the generally exploitive economic conditions faced by teachers of college of writing. Of course, beneath the surface of what has become known as the *Wyoming Resolution* was the assumption that the norm for working conditions for all college faculty is a full-time tenured or tenure-track position, which carries benefits and a salary based on real market value. Interestingly, that assumed norm is believed to be the case not only by academics, who clearly have a self-interest in perpetuating that assumption, but by the general public. Of course, the assumption was not the reality for most college writing instructors in 1986. In college writing programs at that time, more teaching was done by teaching assistants (TAs), part-time faculty, and full-time non-tenure-track faculty than by tenured or tenure-track faculty.

In many ways, the *Wyoming Resolution* was simply about admitting there were problems with the existing reality. If being on the tenure track is viewed as being "normal," then working conditions for faculty on the tenure track matter more than working conditions for faculty not on the tenure track. The *Wyoming Resolution* acknowledged that most faculty who teach college writing courses were not tenure-track. So, though most writing instructors were not hired to be "normal faculty," the *Wyoming Resolution* proclaimed that all faculty should have appropriate working conditions. This was seen as not only the fair and right thing to do but also the best way to ensure the delivery of quality instruction to students.

Now, thirty years after the *Wyoming Resolution* and more than twenty-five years since the resulting *Statement of Principles and Standards for the Postsecondary Teaching of Writing* (published by the National Council of Teachers of English in 1989 and referred to hereafter as the *Statement*), achieving its basic assumptions seem even more of a fantasy than they did in 1986. It's also interesting to note the current iteration of the *Statement* (updated in November 2013) only slightly continues to adequately address working conditions, opting instead to emphasize pedagogy. Higher education in the United States is undergoing a sea change. The current reality of higher education is that tenure lines may be becoming a thing of the past. It is not unlikely that there will be two distinct faculties in the future: research faculty and teaching faculty. The harsh reality is the only faculty who will be expected or allowed to do research are those who are likely to bring money to the institution as a result of their research.[1] The current climate in higher education reflects the climate in our society: All that really matters are revenue streams. Teaching faculty are cost centers who need to be cut and contained in order to increase the revenue stream. As a result, the spirit of the *Wyoming Resolution* becomes even more important, yet even more distant.

We recognize that given the current socioeconomic climate, almost anything we propose might be viewed as a fantasy scenario. Too often

---

1. Our statement is based on the assumption that all research faculty have an option to bring in external research funds. Clearly, this is not the case. Faculty in the humanities, the arts, and many applied disciplines have few external funding opportunities. Whether research will be required of faculty who do not have external funding options is a situation that remains to be played out.

people make claims and assertions that are based on hidden assumptions. Therefore, we'd like to begin by laying out our assumptions as clearly as possible. We understand that many may disagree with us.

Assumptions: Institutional and Programmatic

1. An organization has to have a mission of delivering some kind of goods or services, though recent economic history seems to have muddied this. Making money has become more important for organizations than what it is they were founded to do. Now, there's nothing wrong with an enterprise making money. Indeed, all organizations need to make money in order to survive. However, it is different to make money because you produce automobiles or provide financial services than to manufacture automobiles or provide financial services to make money. If you do the former, the goods you produce or the services you provide is primary. If you do the latter, your goods or services are always secondary to making money. Ultimately, the latter model self-destructs. As an example of how an organization that is dedicated first and foremost to its mission might also succeed financially is Apple. Apple wants to provide its customers with the best possible user experience for the consumer electronic devices they produce.

2. The primary mission of any institution of higher education must be to provide a quality education to its students. There are multiple ways to achieve this mission. Since many institutions serve a variety of student populations, the ways of providing that quality education must be tailored to local conditions. One size clearly does not fit all. However, no matter what the local conditions may be, every institution and every program within that institution must have adopted and be using an appropriate means of assessing how they are succeeding in their mission.

3. Institutions of higher education are complex entities. They teach a variety of things. An appropriate assessment for one area of learning may not be appropriate for others.

4. All academic programs must be created based on the best and most current disciplinary knowledge and be delivered using the best pedagogical practices.

5. All academic programs must maintain internal integrity. That means that, at the very least, all sections of the same course must have the same outcomes.

6. Finally, in keeping with the spirit of the *Wyoming Resolution*, all institutions must be externally accountable to ensure that they are complying with assumptions 2–5.

Assumptions: Faculty

1. All faculty must be hired because they have expertise in the content of the courses they will be teaching. This expertise may be defined in a variety of ways based on disciplinary practices and programmatic needs. Some faculty will demonstrate expertise with traditional academic credentials such as degrees. Other faculty may have a combination of academic credentials and workplace experience. All faculty, no matter their status, must be expected to remain current in the field. Therefore, all faculty must be afforded appropriate professional development opportunities. Since professional development is a condition of employment, it must be supported by the institution.

2. Teaching is not an innate ability. All faculty must receive some training in best pedagogical practices for their area of expertise. Training in best pedagogical practices should be an ongoing activity and, therefore, receive institutional support.

3. All faculty have the right to a reasonable salary that is partly determined by local markets. Understanding market realities means that both full-time and part-time faculty in engineering will make more than their counterparts in history. It also means that faculty in San Francisco will make more money than their colleagues in Omaha.

4. Since the reality of life in America at the time of this writing is that benefits (primarily health care and retirement) seem to be just as important as employment, all faculty, both full-time and part-time, must be benefits-eligible. Clearly, the implementation of the Affordable Care Act (ACA) has changed how institutions define part-time faculty in terms of benefits eligibility. If all fac-

ulty are benefits-eligible, then institutions won't have to worry about the workloads of part-time faculty and whether too many hours would force them to be benefits-eligible.

5. All faculty, both full-time and part-time, must be given the tools and spaces to do their jobs. If the faculty teach face-to-face classes, then they must be given office space in proximity to where they teach. They must be provided computers, software, and communication technologies appropriate to teaching in the digital age. We also suggest that faculty who teach online classes be provided with broadband internet services.

6. All faculty must expect to be evaluated regularly. The evaluations must be consistent and the criteria must be agreed upon. If student evaluations are used as part of the evaluation, then they must be administered in the same fashion for every faculty member and are not to be administered by the faculty member being evaluated. Consistent positive evaluations must be a condition of continued employment regardless of faculty status.

7. While it is understandable to have a large number of part-time faculty, from a programmatic view, full-time faculty have a deeper commitment to the program and the institution. It is their job, their livelihood. The program becomes their primary professional focus and, as a result, they contribute to programmatic and university missions at a higher level than part-time faculty. Part-time faculty, on the other hand, can add value to academic programs, but, ultimately in most instances, their primary commitments lay elsewhere—and should.

Our Vision: Institutions

Now some of you may think we have already started sharing our vision in our assumptions. We think not. We prefer to see our assumptions in much the same way as the "unalienable rights" section of the Declaration of Independence. They are simply the way that institutions must run if they are going to be successful. At this point, we should note that we're talking exclusively about four-year institutions. We are well aware that the number of college writing classes taught at two-year institutions exceeds the number of classes at four-year institutions, and we wish to point readers to the chapter by Holly Hassel and Joanne Baird Giordano in this collection that offers the two-year college perspective.

Still, we recognize that staffing credentials are different at two-year institutions. While some two-year schools prefer faculty with PhDs, most don't. At many, a PhD signals being over-qualified. Our ideal is written about four-year institutions, yet it should be easy enough to derive analogous ideal scenarios for two-year institutions. What we present is one potential version of how to accomplish such a vision for a post-secondary writing program. Based on the assumptions we have already presented, we want to focus our vision on three aspects of four-year institutions: faculty, curriculum, and working conditions.

Our Vision: Faculty

On the surface, it should be easy to determine who should be faculty in college writing programs. College faculty are supposed to have specific academic degrees that qualify them for their positions. In most instances, the "gold standard" has been the PhD in the discipline. For example, it would be highly unusual for an institution to hire a PhD in chemistry to teach economics. Unfortunately, those of us who have worked in or spent much time around college writing programs know that there is no "gold standard" for writing faculty. If writing programs were run like other academic programs, then the first credential that would be looked for would be a PhD in rhetoric, writing studies, or, perhaps depending on the program, technical or professional communication. These PhDs would be hired in tenure-track positions and expected to teach and engage in research. The reality is that very few college writing programs are populated exclusively with tenured or tenure-track PhDs in the field. Programs are full of TAs, part-timers with PhDs or master's degrees in a variety of fields, and even faculty with degrees in other fields. None of this is new. It was this very exigency that led to the initial drafting of the *Wyoming Resolution* thirty years ago and the *Statement* that followed it three years later.

In many ways, markets helped to determine this situation. For decades, English departments were over-producing English PhDs (and an English PhD meant a degree in literary studies—not writing studies). Though the number of programs offering PhDs in writing studies has grown, as has the number of graduates, there is still an incredible imbalance between number of sections of writing classes offered and the number of potential PhD instructors.

So then, what qualifies an individual to teach in our vision of a postsecondary writing program? The term we use is "expertise." It is important to note that there are multiple ways of gaining "expertise," and "expertise" is not static. It must be maintained or it will be lost.

We are perfectly comfortable with allowing appropriate academic credentials to constitute minimal expertise. Usually "appropriate academic credentials" refers to a graduate degree—at the minimum a master's degree, optimally a PhD. But what does possession of a graduate degree really mean—especially in light of expertise? The reality is that a PhD provides a student with theoretical knowledge and trains him/her to do research in a particular field. It does not necessarily prepare one to teach. A master's degree is more general, but it usually shows that the student has had the discipline to successfully complete advanced work in a designated field. In our vision, appropriate areas for faculty in a writing program would be degrees in rhetoric, writing studies, or technical or professional communication. While accrediting agencies, such as the Southern Association of Colleges and Schools (SACS), allow literature courses to count for people teaching writing, we believe that such coursework is not a substitute for coursework in writing. After all, SACS doesn't allow biology courses to count for people teaching physics. Just as one science doesn't substitute for or equate to another, literature does not substitute for or equate to writing.

While more and more faculty are getting some kind of preparation in writing studies, that group is still limited. With growing enrollments and reduced budgets, we recognize that an ideal vision will not happen immediately. However, what we present here is how we feel a program should be staffed, and then options that individual programs might be able to use based on their local realities.

Full-Time Faculty

Ideally, there needs to be enough full-time faculty with appropriate expertise to administer the program, develop and assess the curriculum, hire and evaluate the faculty, and create and administer appropriate professional development opportunities so that all the faculty can maintain their expertise and teach their classes. It's important to note that we're talking about a program—not a department. A department is likely to be comprised of multiple programs. This set of full-time faculty members must be present for each program. The number of full-time faculty would be dependent on the size of the program. Obviously, the larger the program, the more full-time faculty are needed to perform the basic administrative functions listed above. Any program that offers more than a mere handful of sections a term cannot effectively operate with fewer than two full-time faculty members.

We understand that there are movements to have an administrator run multiple programs and to have nothing but part-time faculty teach "canned classes." We recognize the reality that large numbers of part-time faculty with differing levels of expertise are not likely to go away. As a result, some degree of standardization in courses across sections is not necessarily a bad thing. However, the courses need to be developed and consistently revised by someone with real expertise. If the program administrator has no expertise in the field and no faculty with expertise have curricular control, then the simple fact is that there is no way the program can be delivering a quality educational experience to its students.

What kind of expertise should we expect of full-time faculty? We've already stated that a graduate degree (preferably a PhD) in writing studies is a good start, but what if there are no candidates available with that credential? We suggest then looking for candidates with the equivalent level of advanced degree and with some kind of documentable experience that proves the person knows the field of writing studies, either through some kind of relevant academic study (though not a degree) or by practitioner experience. In addition, we expect candidates for full-time positions to have some previous teaching experience. That experience might have occurred in graduate school or some other environment, but a full-time faculty member should not be a teaching neophyte given the level of responsibility she/he will take on for curriculum development and assessment.

Part-Time Faculty

Traditionally, the bar has been lower for hiring part-time faculty. In many ways, this expectation is not fair to our students. Why should some students take classes from inferior instructors? Don't we have an obligation that all our instructors meet minimal standards of expertise? Since the reality is that the minimal standard for hiring full-time instructors in this scenario is fairly minimal to begin with, we don't see how we can lower the bar for part-time instructors. Indeed, making such a statement does something interesting: It means that both full-time and part-time instructors have similar disciplinary expertise.

The difference between the two is simply that one is employed full-time and may have other programmatic responsibilities beyond teaching and one is employed part-time and teaches a limited number of classes and has no further programmatic responsibilities. As a result, faculty are not differentiated by level of disciplinary expertise; rather, they are differentiated by programmatic functions. In best-case scenarios, only part-time faculty who have a full-time job doing something other than teaching, or who do not depend on teaching for their main source of income, would be hired. (See Evelyn Beck's chapter in this collection for more discussion on the future of part-time writing faculty.) Such individuals want to teach for a variety of positive reasons and can clearly bring added value to the classroom.

Part-time faculty who piece part-time work together at multiple institutions, however, are being set up to fail. No matter how good they may be as instructors, they are working in an environment that ultimately is bad for their students. We fully acknowledge the reason many writing programs use so many part-time faculty: Part-time faculty are cheap. Institutions, in most cases, are simply more concerned with meeting their bottom line than fulfilling their primary mission. What we hope to do, then, is to present best-case possibilities of what we acknowledge to be acceptable working conditions. We also feel strongly that the only way changes in the approach to hiring and using part-time faculty will occur is when regular review, external to the institution, carries with it real consequences for the institution.

Teaching Responsibilities

It may seem strange to need to address teaching responsibilities in a visionary scenario. However, for the visionary program to work, all faculty must have specific responsibilities. They must be held accountable to meet those responsibilities. It may seem overly obvious to say that first and foremost all faculty must teach their classes. Yet, teaching their classes does not just mean meeting at the designated class times or posting assignments and material in a timely fashion in an online class. It also means teaching the courses they are assigned according to the designated curriculum, making sure their students are aware of course outcomes, and that their students work to attain those outcomes. It doesn't mean that faculty are forced into teaching a "canned curriculum," but it does mean that all assignments must be keyed to designated course outcomes. These are core responsibilities and can be achieved no matter how difficult the local situation might be.

In addition, all faculty must engage in a continuous cycle of professional development. We operate on the assumption that expertise must be dynamic and only exists when faculty are continually engaged in the conversations of the field. We acknowledge that there are multiple ways of attaining such engagement. While individual programs might designate that some kinds of professional engagement are preferred, we simply argue that all faculty must be professionally engaged. We suggest that the nature of that engagement may change from year to year and is most appropriately handled at the time of annual evaluation. Again, we feel that some kind of professional development is always possible. Even with busy part-timers who might not be able to attend daytime sessions, using online asynchronous formats should allow professional development for all faculty.

Individuals enrolled in PhD programs are rarely trained to teach. While some may have teaching responsibilities as part of an assistantship and/or take courses in pedagogy, PhD programs are designed first and foremost to engage individuals in the theory and research methods of a discipline. As a result, professional development opportunities should go beyond continual professional engagement; they must also involve development opportunities for best practices in pedagogy.

Faculty Evaluation

All faculty, both full-time and part-time, must undergo regular review. Unlike some institutions where everyone does as he/she pleases, in our vision, everyone is accountable. What's important about how we see accountability is that it is transparent. Faculty expectations should be clearly spelled out in writing at time of hire. The method of review should also be delineated. For example, if faculty members' primary responsibilities are teaching and professional development, those faculty need to know before the term begins how their teaching will be evaluated. They also need to know what kinds of professional development activities will be expected. Designating specific activities ahead of time is even better. Additionally, of course, this expectation holds for both full-time and part-time faculty. Once again, faculty evaluation is something that can occur no matter the local conditions. Indeed, when local conditions create otherwise troublesome working conditions, evaluation becomes even more important.

Our Vision: Curriculum

Each program must have one definable and assessable curriculum. We feel it makes the most sense for that curriculum to be defined by particular program outcomes. Each course in the program then must map its outcomes to meet the program outcomes. Likewise, each assignment in each class must map to the course outcomes. It is necessary that a student will meet all program outcomes by taking the required courses. Some outcomes may overlap courses, while other outcomes may be unique to a particular course.

Standardized Syllabus/Curriculum

The heart of any curriculum should be program outcomes. We have elaborated elsewhere on the use of the Writing Program Administrators' *WPA Outcomes Statement for First-Year Composition* for curriculum development and assessment (Maid and D'Angelo, "Assessing," "Rhetorical," "WPA"). In our visionary program, we believe that it is the responsibility of full-time faculty to ensure programmatic integrity through the development of a curriculum that is mapped to program outcomes, comprised of courses that meet the specific outcomes designated for them, and then continually evaluated and revised through a rigorous and recursive assessment process.

Multiple sections of the same course should use a standardized syllabus to ensure consistency of teaching and learning. In addition to standardized course policies, the syllabus should list course outcomes and grading criteria. By standardizing policies, outcomes, and evaluation across sections, we ensure that we clearly articulate to students what they will learn in the course and how they will be evaluated. In addition, since course outcomes are mapped from program outcomes, we articulate clearly how the course, as part of a degree program, fits into the broader curriculum. For those courses that serve other disciplines, outcomes articulate how the course links to writing within that discipline. Finally, depending on local circumstances and the purpose of the course, standardized assignments may be used.

As we have discussed, faculty are accountable to the program and to the mission of providing students with the best education possible. Part of this accountability is to ensure that courses are developed and designed in a way that allows for consistent delivery so that what students learn in section A is equivalent to what students learn in section B. In addition, by using this model, faculty are more clearly aligned with job functions than they are under more traditional models. Full-time faculty take on more administrative and coordination functions to develop and design courses. As the faculty who are responsible for these functions, they have the broader programmatic picture to not only ensure integrity across sections of a course but also across courses within the full curriculum. For those courses that serve other disciplines, full-time faculty are the members of the program with the time and commitment to work collaboratively across the university. Part-time faculty are then free to concentrate on what they have been hired to do: teach courses. Free of the responsibilities of course design, they are able to spend more time as facilitators and coaches so that the focus becomes enabling student learning. This model, however, does not preclude part-time faculty participation in course design (a point also taken up in this collection in the chapter by Holly Hassel and Joanne Baird Giordano).

As part of the coordination and development of courses, full-time faculty would naturally encourage a feedback loop with instructors of the course to ensure that revisions are made based on a rigorous evidence-based process with data gathered from multiple sources (e.g., feedback from teaching faculty, course evaluations, and student assessment). Any number of technologies or social networking tools could be used to ensure rigorous participation by teaching faculty while at the same time maintaining coordination of courses as the responsibility of full-time faculty. A course-specific social network could be developed, for example, to enable posting of course documents and other related information relevant to the teaching of the course. Such a site could include discussion boards or other tools to allow instructors to communicate with each other and to provide feedback to program leaders. An assignment bank within the site would allow for contribution of potential assignment ideas to be developed and coordinated by course leadership. In addition, potentially, a secured area of the network could be used for the purposes of enacting distributed grading across sections of the course and for course assessment. For courses that are taught to meet writing requirements for other disciplines, faculty from those disciplines could be invited to participate to enable cross-disciplinary collaboration and sharing of information.

Working Conditions

Course Load

Course load should be a straightforward issue and should be portable across institutions. However, the reality has always been, and remains, that course load is a highly localized affair. For years, our professional organizations have published "appropriate course load guidelines" for instructors in writing programs; and for years, institutions have blatantly ignored these guidelines. Institutions have done so because the institutions have never been held accountable. The *Wyoming Resolution* recognized the need for institutional accountability.

In our visionary program, however, we make the following suggestions regarding course load. First of all, an institution needs to create a "base number of sections" a full-time faculty member is expected to teach. We argue that this number should be based on a twelve-month calendar—not an academic year—because in our visionary scenario, all faculty are given and paid for twelve-month contracts. (We know this is never likely to happen. However, acknowledging the sense to this should help as individual programs cope with their own institutional reality.) The reality is most institutions have an active summer program. Many students, especially when given the opportunity to take online courses, enroll in summer sessions.

So then, if we start off with a hypothetical number of ten sections per calendar year, that can be broken up into 4 (fall)-4 (spring)-2 (summer), 5-5-0, 4-3-3, or other distributions. In these instances, it should be noted that this model would be for a teaching-only appointment so that the faculty member's yearly distribution for teaching equals 100% of effort. Everything else equals 0%. Having such a baseline number and tying it to distribution of effort opens up many possibilities. In institutions where there are still tenure-track research faculty, the number of yearly sections would be reduced based on different categories in the distribution of effort. For example, a full-time faculty member whose distribution of effort is 40% teaching, 40% leading program assessment, and 20% professional development would be expected to teach four sections per calendar year. Likewise, faculty charged with developing curricula, leading program professional development programs, or handling other administrative assignments would have that indicated in their distribution of effort and have their course load reduced appropriately.

This approach also helps us determine what is a full-time faculty member and what is a part-time faculty member. Historically, the real need for differentiation between full-time and part-time comes with determining benefits eligibility. The distinction for such, in most instances, was whether a faculty member's appointment was 50% or greater. Most institutions don't have a designated baseline for number of sections taught per year, and institutions used to regularly get around this by only offering part-time faculty semester by semester contracts. By doing so, if pressed, the institutions can argue that they assume the number of sections taught in any term will be the only teaching that part-time faculty member will do for the year, even when the part-timer has been teaching for a decade or more—never missing a term. However, ACA has changed the rules that institutions have played by for years. Part of ACA requires the monitoring of the number of hours of week a part-time employee works. Since institutions don't want to pay benefits to part-time faculty, they are cutting back the number of sections a part-timer can teach in a term in order to make sure they are in compliance with ACA. Institutional Human Resource offices are now dictating the number of sections that can be offered to a part-time faculty member. In our vision, however, all of this is unneeded cost and effort because all employees should be benefits-eligible.

Salary

When most people talk about salary, they tend to focus on specific dollar amounts. We think this is wrong and keeps programs from paying faculty fair and appropriate salaries. Fair salaries need to be determined based on a number of factors. As we've mentioned previously, the reality is that local conditions, such as cost of living, are real factors and must be considered. Where there needs to be more flexibility is how programs treat the salaries of full-time and part-time faculty.

The reason we began with course load rather than salaries is because we feel that course load is the key to determining salaries. When full-time faculty are hired, they should be paid based on credentials and experience. Traditionally, for tenure-track faculty, rank addresses this issue. However, when tenure-track hires may be seen as the exception rather than the rule, we feel there needs to be some reasonable guidelines. If not, institutions trying to increase profit will drive down salaries. Therefore, we propose that all full-time faculty be paid according to their course load. Since all full-time faculty should have the same course load, being differentiated only by distribution of effort, salaries for full-time faculty with the same credentials and experience should start out the same.

Let's look at what this really means. In programs where there are both tenure-track faculty (who are usually expected to do research) and non-tenure-track faculty (whose primary function is teaching), most often the tenure-track faculty are paid significantly more than the non-tenure-track faculty—even when both classes of faculty have the same credentials and experience. In order to understand how this might work and why it might work, we present this example that we expect is quite familiar. A program is advertising for two positions. The first position is for an Assistant Professor and is tenure-track. The second is for what the institution calls a Lecturer and is non-tenure-track. Both positions ask for a PhD in the field. The assumption has always been that it's to be expected to pay the tenure-track position significantly more when the only real difference between the job functions of the two positions is their distribution of effort. The tenure-track faculty member is expected to have a greater percentage of professional development (specifically research or publications) in his/her distribution of effort. The non-tenure-track faculty member will have a greater percentage of teaching in his/her distribution.

As academics, we all understand the value of research. However, we also understand that much of the current crisis in confidence in higher education is because our external constituencies don't trust us—and we suggest, perhaps, for good reasons. Hiring one faculty member at a significantly higher salary because that person will do less teaching than another faculty member hired with the same credentials sends the message that teaching is not the prime mission of the institution. All we're saying is that institutions need to "put their money where their mouth is." If teaching is primary, they need to pay for teaching.

We understand that some may argue that since research brings in dollars to the institution, such effort should be seen as primary and compensated accordingly. However, the reality is that not all research is funded, nor as we have mentioned earlier, is it likely to be. While it is possible for researchers in writing studies to bring in external funds, it is more likely that most writing studies research is either unfunded or funded through internal sources, making it a cost center instead of a revenue stream.[2] Teaching, however, which brings in tuition dollars, is always a revenue stream, and, lately, a growing revenue stream.

So far, all of this discussion has focused on full-time faculty. The reality is that part-time faculty have been a large part of who teaches in writing programs and, we expect despite our vision, will play an even larger part in the future. Historically, part-time faculty are paid by the course and work on a term by term basis. They are paid a fraction of what even non-tenure-track faculty are paid. Part-time faculty are seen as contingent even though they may have taught every term for years. The reality is that many writing programs could not survive without them.

What we propose in terms of calculating salaries for part-time faculty is to use the course load criterion once again. If the yearly course load for a faculty member is ten sections and the entry level salary for a PhD is, hypothetically, $75,000 (remember, this is a twelve-month not a nine-month salary), then faculty are paid $7,500 per section. That should then be the per section salary for a part-time faculty member with the same credentials. Pegging part-time salaries to full-time salaries does several things, all of which we feel are beneficial to the parties involved. Primarily, it means that institutions will use part-time faculty when doing so adds value to the institution—not when the institution is trying to deliver services on the cheap. The argument that part-time faculty are not required to do research, service, or whatever else doesn't carry weight when those research, service, or whatever else are accounted in the distribution of effort.[3]

---

2. It appears as though research faculty are expected to bring in external funding. While it's unlikely that writing studies faculty will consistently bring in external dollars, a reasonable way to handle research grant and contract producing faculty is to treat them like development officers and pay them a percentage of the external funds they secure.

3. In retrospect, perhaps we should have added one more assumption earlier: "You get what you pay for." We acknowledge that many, perhaps most, part-time faculty in writing programs work hard and do the best they can for their students. However, we also strongly believe that when you underpay any employee, you are asking that employee to underperform. Ultimately, except for that small group of people who view college teaching as "volunteer work," underpaid employees will either leave because they can or stay and get by. Neither situation is good for the health of an academic program. The real bottom line is that students are likely being cheated.

Office Space and Equipment

Faculty need spaces in which to work and to meet with students. All faculty, full-time and part-time, need appropriate space to meet privately with students. In some ways, the traditional model where full-time faculty have offices and part-time faculty share offices is not bad. However, offices take up lots of space and are expensive. Still, asking faculty to work in cubicles is not an option—even for part-time faculty. If for no other reason, federal laws protecting students' rights to privacy should mitigate against such a suggestion.

Equipment is another story. The digital revolution of the last several decades has created the need for every faculty member to have a networked computer and appropriate software. This need becomes even greater when faculty teach online. It is common for institutions to provide full-time faculty with networked computers and appropriate software. It is less common for institutions to provide part-time faculty with the same technologies. Often part-time faculty are asked to share computers and often they don't have access to the same software—even when some of that software might help them teach their classes. We recognize the limitations of giving every faculty member, even those who may live at a distance from campus and never come to campus, a fully-loaded computer. However, we do think it's reasonable for institutions to provide faculty with appropriate software for their home machines—regardless of whether they are full-time or part-time. Another issue is access: It is more than reasonable to expect that all faculty who teach online classes have broadband access. Given this expectation, it is also reasonable to expect the institution to provide broadband access for online faculty.

The other equipment concern is telephones. Telephones are necessary for keeping in touch with students—especially in online classes. We also know that telephones have been traditional bargaining chips when budgets get cut. Unit heads pull individual telephone lines, students complain, lines are restored. Ultimately, those kinds of battles are petty, counterproductive, and costly. Pulling and replacing phones always costs more than leaving them in place. Currently, traditional landline phones are pretty irrelevant. Providing each faculty member, full-time and part-time, with a mobile phone with unlimited texting capability, however, does make sense in terms of keeping in touch with students. For faculty, especially faculty who teach online, it allows the instructor to give students a work phone number as well as the ability to text (or

Skype or "hangout" in Google) with students, something traditional office phones do not.

Evaluation and Continuation of Employment

Every faculty member needs to be evaluated regularly. This idea should be obvious. Often though, tenured faculty are only evaluated infrequently, and part-time faculty technically don't get evaluated beyond word-of-mouth feedback and erratically-administered student evaluations. All full-time faculty need to be evaluated at least once a year by a system that has been documented in writing. The particulars of the evaluation need to be measured and considered in light of the individual faculty member's distribution of effort. Work done in each category should be mutually agreed upon as being appropriate before being undertaken. That means that each faculty member must be in regular contact with the program head to make sure he/she is spending time appropriately. Part-time faculty need to be evaluated based on predetermined and set criteria that the faculty are apprised of at time of hire. If student evaluations are to be used, then they must be administered consistently and not administered by the faculty member being evaluated.

All faculty should have an expectation of continuation of employment unless their regular evaluations determine they are failing to perform their jobs adequately. The concept of term contracts really makes no sense. If faculty are doing a good job, then it makes no sense to terminate them and hire replacements. For non-tenure-track faculty, the idea of multi-year rolling contracts makes the most sense.

Conclusion

Ultimately, we have come to realize that the *Wyoming Resolution* and the *Statement* have helped to frame our worldview on what it means to work in a college writing program. In looking back at these historical documents, we have come to believe that the faculty who framed them articulated a vision of what working conditions should be based on the primary mission of delivering a quality education to students. We understand that on the surface there may be a disconnect in recognizing current and changing realities, making assumptions, and presenting the components of an ideal scenario for a postsecondary writing program. We likewise understand that while there are some situations that can be generalized, all institutional situations are local. As a result, some things that are possible at Institution A are impossible at Institution B and are negotiable at Institution C. Only local faculty can make those determinations. Therefore, even though we understand that it is highly unlikely our ideal scenario will be adopted in full, we do think the individual pieces are good starting points within each institutional reality. We hope that we will force faculty to finally recognize which reality they, and their institution, wish to face.

Finally, we again turn to the final plank of the *Wyoming Resolution*. Without any kind of external accountability, all of this remains a fantasy. We do understand that this may be the wrong historical time for accreditation of writing programs, and perhaps the notion of programmatic accreditation is a twentieth century idea. Without accountability, though, most institutions will likely allow working conditions for writing faculty to deteriorate. Perhaps, just as curriculum in the past twenty years has become outcome-based and assessable, faculty working conditions need to become outcome-based so they, too, can be assessed. We hope that our vision, then, becomes the start for a discussion on working condition *outcomes* for postsecondary writing faculty.

Works Cited

CCCC Executive Committee. *Statement of Principles and Standards for the Postsecondary Teaching of Writing. College Composition and Communication*, vol. 40, no. 3, 1989, pp. 329–36.

Maid, Barry M., and Barbara J. D'Angelo. "Assessing Outcomes in a Technical Communication Capstone." *Handbook of Research on Assessment Technologies, Methods, and Applications in Higher Education*, edited by Christopher Schreiner, IGI Global, 2009, pp. 152–66.

—. "The WPA Outcomes, Information Literacy, and the Challenges of Outcomes-Based Curricular Design." *Writing Assessment in the 21st Century: Essays in Honor of Edward M. White*, edited by Norbert Elliott and Les Perlman, Hampton Press, 2012, pp. 101–14.

—. "Is Rhetorical Knowledge the Über Outcome?" *WPA Outcomes Statement—A Decade Later*, edited by Nicholas N. Behm et al., Parlor Press, 2013, pp. 257–70.

Robertson, Linda R., et al. "Opinion: The Wyoming Conference Resolution Opposing Unfair Salaries and Working Conditions for Post-Secondary Teachers of Writing." *College English*, vol. 49, no. 3, 1987, pp. 274–80.

Trimbur, John, and Barbara Cambridge. "The Wyoming Conference Resolution: A Beginning." *WPA: Writing Program Administration*, vol. 12, no.1–2, 1988, pp. 13–18.

12 A Focus on Reading as an Essential Component of the Next *Statement*

Alice S. Horning

Introduction

A careful reading of the *Statement of Principles and Standards for the Postsecondary Teaching of Writing* (hereafter the *Statement*), provoked by this book project, reveals an interesting point. Although the *Statement* mentions reading in its very first line and a few times thereafter, it lacks a substantial focus on reading as an essential component of excellent writing instruction. Yet there is ample evidence for an urgent need to develop students' reading abilities more directly and thoroughly. Critical reading is not only a necessary element for students learning to write but also it more generally helps them succeed in college, in their personal and professional lives, and as citizens in a democratic society.

In this chapter, I argue that all faculty, particularly teachers of postsecondary writing, should understand students' reading problems; and, they should be aware of the key elements of reading that benefit students, along with an array of useful teaching strategies to develop students' effective and efficient reading. I show how the the *Statement* can help support the achievement of these goals by integrating reading into many of its sections. Moreover, by specifically adding a focus on reading to its professional development section, the *Statement* can encourage teachers to integrate it more fully in writing courses. Ultimately, I demonstrate that the document's revised title should be *Statement of Principles and Standards for the Postsecondary Teaching of Writing and Reading*.

Focus on Reading with Writing

A rationale for expanding attention to reading comes most readily from the *Framework for Success in Postsecondary Writing*. The *Framework*, published in early 2011, is the official statement about the teaching and learning of writing from the Council of Writing Program Administrators (CWPA), the National Council of Teachers of English (NCTE), and the National Writing Project, and it should certainly inform revisions to the *Statement*. The *Framework*, in its section on "Developing Critical Thinking Through Writing, Reading and Research," encourages teachers to provide students with reading experiences relevant to their writing, including the following:

- read texts from multiple points of view (e.g., sympathetic to a writer's position and critical of it) and in ways that are appropriate to the academic discipline or other contexts where the texts are being used;
- write about texts for multiple purposes including (but not limited to) interpretation, synthesis, response, summary, critique, and analysis;
- evaluate sources for credibility, bias, quality of evidence, and quality of reasoning;
- conduct primary and secondary research using a variety of print and nonprint sources. (7)

These points all require, support, and encourage students to read. Getting students to do the reading that will make these opportunities useful is a bigger challenge. Moreover, evidence suggests that many students come to postsecondary education lacking the essential skills in reading to do such work successfully, if at all. It is for this reason that reading needs to be thoroughly integrated with writing in all composition courses. It will be difficult if not impossible to improve students' writing without also improving their reading, and for many, their reading ability needs serious work. Not only do students need help with reading, but postsecondary instructors need help to provide it for them.

The *Statement* currently does not focus on reading at all, despite its brief mention in the opening sections. While the absence of reading seems easy to see, a more objective view of how much reading is mentioned comes from the exercise of creating a word cloud for the whole document. The resulting cloud appears in the appendix, based on feeding the entire text to http://www.tagxedo.com/. The cloud reflects word frequencies within the document. Reading occurs so infrequently that it does not even appear in this cloud.

Data on Student Reading Problems

A second reason to revise the *Statement* to include reading arises from the clear and growing body of evidence concerning students' reading troubles. It comes from a variety of studies, using different approaches and methodologies, but revealing essentially the same findings. The American College Testing (ACT) organization, for example, released a report in 2010 applying ACT test scores to the Common Core State Standards for K–12 education (CCSS) (Council of Chief State School Officers and the National Governors Assocation [CCSSO/NGA]; *First*). It analyzes more than 256,000 eleventh grade students' performance on the ACT to see how many students achieved ACT's "benchmark" scores that indicate likely success in college. Only 38% of students achieved a benchmark score of 21 on the Reading section of the ACT (*First* 4).

The ACT organization itself is careful to note that the CCSS are still new, and these standards have not yet had a long-standing and widespread impact on teaching and learning in K–12 schools. Therefore, the impact of the new CCSS on ACT results should not be judged prematurely. Moreover, timed tests of students reading short passages and answering multiple-choice questions should be viewed with skepticism by themselves. However, taken together, these studies suggest that students have significant problems with reading that will limit their ability to achieve the goals listed in the *Framework* document. For all these reasons, the *Statement* should expand its focus on reading and should support the need for teachers to pursue additional professional development so that they can work with students on improving reading.

These ACT findings are consistent with those of earlier studies by ACT and other groups. For example, in 2006, ACT released a detailed study of 563,000 students who took the ACT and were subsequently followed for three years in their college experience (*Reading*). About half of the students scored below the benchmark score of 21 on the Reading portion of the test and were not successful in college. ACT defined success as a 2.0 GPA and returning for a second year of study. If the definition of "success" is raised at all, a much larger number of students have problems with reading. A similar finding is reported when students are challenged to find, read, evaluate, integrate, and document sources found online, even in untimed conditions, as is the case in the *Standardized Assessment of Information Literacy Skills* test developed by librarians and faculty at Kent State University in Ohio (Project SAILS).

This Project SAILS test warrants a bit of further explanation because it provides a different but equally important indicator of students' reading problems (Project SAILS). Those who think that students who may not have the relevant skills when working with traditional printed texts surely do better when working online are often dismayed to find that students perform equally poorly online. The SAILS instrument was developed by professional librarians, faculty, and test development experts at Kent State. It was tested carefully at eighty schools and colleges around the US and Canada and has been in use since 2006. It consists of 168 items in multiple-choice format and tied to the Association of College and Research Librarians' *Information Literacy Standards for Higher Education*. Reports on the Project SAILS website show that only about half the postsecondary students who have taken the test are able to pass it as they lack the ability to find, analyze, evaluate, use, and cite sources appropriately online. Therefore, this research suggests that students' poor reading is a problem for them whether they are reading printed or electronic sources.

It is essential to keep in mind that the ACT is only one source of data, and it is based, after all, on a timed, multiple-choice test of reading abilities; the Project SAILS results are untimed, but still result from an objective test. However, other studies provide similar evidence based on different kinds of data. For example, the American Institutes for Research (AIR) administered a direct test to students nearing graduation from a sample of colleges and universities across the country. The test used in the *National Survey of America's College Students* was the same one used in a national literacy survey commissioned by Congress and conducted by the U.S. Department of Education in 2006. It is an untimed, direct test of the ability to read, understand, and apply information. The results, based on scores of about 1,800 students, show that only a third to a half score at the proficient level in prose and document literacy. The instrument in the AIR study, which was funded by Pew Charitable Trusts, is an untimed test using set prose passages that are quite short, so it provides a limited indication of the ability to analyze, synthesize, evaluate, and apply information from texts, no indication of the ability to work with online texts, and no information on how readers deal with longer or more complex texts.

Another indicator of reading ability is reported by David J. Jolliffe and Allison Harl in *College English*, a flagship journal of NCTE, in 2008. Jolliffe and Harl paid a small group of twenty-one students at the University of Arkansas, a Carnegie Very High Research University public school of about 14,000 students in Fayetteville, to complete a background questionnaire, keep a reading journal logging their reading activities for two weeks, and write a detailed exploration of one item they read each day, responding to a prescribed series of questions (602–03). The students also participated in an interview and think-aloud protocol on textbook material used in some course they were taking during the study. This qualitative study reports much the same results, leading Jolliffe and Harl to conclude that students' reading ability is poor. Not one of these instruments is perfect; however, the array of different types of studies yielding essentially the same results provides clear evidence for the general claim that students have problems with reading that must be addressed.

Additional studies, using still more varied techniques, lead to the same essential conclusion, supporting the need for a broader integration of reading in the teaching of writing. One such study comes from the widely-publicized book that relies on the *Collegiate Learning Assessment* (*CLA*), Richard Arum and Josipa Roksa's *Academically Adrift: Limited Learning on College Campuses*. While this report has some weaknesses in methodology and relies exclusively on a single instrument, it shows students' weak development in critical thinking and writing in college.

The lack of improvement in students' scores on the reading and writing tasks of the *CLA* is closely related to faculty expectations and requirements. Arum and Roksa find that the "combination of reading and writing in coursework was necessary to improve students' performance on tasks requiring critical thinking, complex reasoning, and writing skills in their first two years of college" (94). According to the authors, the reading requirement must be more than forty pages per week and the writing requirement must be more than twenty pages over the course of a term to make a difference in students' abilities as measured by the

CLA. Even those who disagree with the approach and findings of this study need to be able to address its claim that students are not becoming better readers, writers, or thinkers in college. Doing so requires that faculty have a deeper understanding of reading and a willingness to assign more work and insure that students actually do it, issues taken up below.

A similar response is evoked by the findings presented in William G. Bowen, Matthew M. Chingos, and Michael S. McPherson's *Crossing the Finish Line: Completing College at America's Public Universities*. This book reports a study of college attainment (i.e., graduation), at sixty-eight public universities across the country. One of the many findings is that admission test scores like those from SAT and ACT do not predict college completion rates as well as high school grades (113), so it may be better not to rely much on the ACT results or perhaps even on the *CLA* results reported by Arum and Roksa. However, college attainment is "low and stagnant" (223) and needs to be improved, write Bowen and his colleagues. Reading and writing are key skills needed by students to achieve this outcome, so direct instruction in reading with writing, and professional development to help faculty understand and improve students' reading appear essential. These findings are further supported by a study of the literacy work and requirements at seven community colleges in various states around the country, reported by the National Center on Education and the Economy (*What*). The panel focused on beginning English classes and introductory courses in an array of subject areas. They analyzed the texts used in these courses, the reading tasks given to students, and the graded written work students produced. The findings show that the texts students are given are mostly at a high school level, but despite this fact, students have difficulty with them because their skills are weak and because they are not asked to access and retrieve, integrate and interpret, or reflect on and evaluate the material they read (*What* 16). Overall, poor reading preparation in high school is replicated by low expectations in the community colleges.

In writing about these large-scale studies, especially *Academically Adrift* (Arum and Roksa), columnist Thomas H. Benton from *The Chronicle of Higher Education* notes that there are ongoing changes in the forms of literacy that contribute to lower expectations, and then to lower achievement and lesser attainment. He writes:

> A generational shift is taking place in which longer forms of writing are being replaced with shorter ones, and sustained thought with shallower forms of multitasking. Those skills have

> value, but a growing percentage of students are arriving at college without having written a research paper, read a novel, or taken an essay examination. [. . .] Without a carefully structured curriculum with required courses and regulation of standards across comparable courses, it's possible to graduate without acquiring foundational skills. (A45)

On a related point, I have argued elsewhere that plagiarism is fundamentally a reading problem resulting from a lack of foundational skills ("Potential").

In short, there is ample evidence of the reading problem and its relationship to writing, college performance, and degree completion. The evidence comes from a variety of studies with different approaches or methodologies, all producing essentially the same results. Whether the findings are based on direct timed or untimed tests, surveys or qualitative data, or other kinds of information like graduation rates, all the findings point to poor reading skills for at least half or more of college students, making clear the need for faculty to understand the reading process and to teach reading in their courses. By changing the *Statement*, faculty and writing program administrators as well as other administrators can address this fundamental problem more directly.

For example, the first two sentences of the *Statement* read as follows: "A democracy demands citizens who can read critically and write clearly and cogently. Developing students' powers as critical readers and writers demands in turn the highest quality of instruction." If the following were added, the *Statement* would integrate reading more thoroughly:

> This instruction should focus on developing students' abilities to understand and analyze what they read; evaluate materials for accuracy, authority, currency, relevancy, appropriateness, and bias; and synthesize differing perspectives on an issue or topic in their own writing. Explicit instruction in critical reading must be integrated with the teaching of writing in every course.

These two sentences require direct attention to reading as part of writing instruction and would make clear from the outset the relevance of reading to the teaching of writing.

Further Studies of Reading Problems: The Transition to Online Reading

Because so much reading and writing occurs online now, it is easy to think that students' reading problems appear only when they read traditional printed texts. However, several studies suggest otherwise. A careful examination of what happens when students work with online texts indicates that they have just as much or more difficulty reading on the screen as they do on paper.

One such study was conducted by the Henry J. Kaiser Family Foundation in 2010 (Rideout et al.). This study is the third in a series of studies (prior ones in 1999 and 2004) surveying more than two thousand young people, ages eight to eighteen, across the United States. The results are based on the survey, administered in classrooms to a stratified random sample of students in public, private, and parochial schools. About seven hundred students completed a seven-day media diary in addition to the survey instrument (Rideout et al. 6). Though media use in this group has increased significantly, time spent reading books also increased, slightly, by about five minutes. However, students' grades have dropped as their use of an assortment of media (computers, cell phones, MP3 players, and others) has increased (Rideout et al. 4).

The Kaiser study relies on self-reported data, but work by web usability expert Jakob Nielsen examines teen success in finding, reading, and using information online with similarly poor results. Nielsen tested a group of eighty-four students ages thirteen to seventeen in the US and Australia, asking them to visit sites, perform specific tasks, and speak aloud about what they were doing as they did it. Nielsen reports a success rate of only 55% in completing the tasks, and he attributes the poor performance to "insufficient reading skills, less sophisticated research strategies, and a dramatically lower patience level" (48). These students are entering our college writing classrooms. Like the results of the Kaiser study, this work demonstrates that students need help with reading and the *Statement* can support teachers' readiness to work with students on their reading.

An explanation for the Kaiser and Nielsen results is offered by Mark Bauerlein, Professor of English at Emory University and author of *The Dumbest Generation: How the Digital Age Stupefies Young Americans and Jeopardizes Our Future*. Bauerlein draws on the results of the two ACT studies to suggest that students need more experience with what he calls "slow reading" in order to develop the reading skills they need to deal with complex texts ("Too Dumb"). His article, which also appears as a chapter in his book, explores the differences between the short, interactive, superficial kinds of reading and writing fostered by the Internet and the longer, more isolated, intensive, and patient reading and thinking required by complex, extended, nonfiction prose texts of the kind students are expected to read in college. Readers must be willing to take the time to "pause and probe," to work for extended periods of time without interruption, and to "take in the whole piece and grasp the implications of its contentions" ("Too Dumb"). His recommendation is that we should

> preserve a crucial place for unwired, unplugged, and unconnected learning. One hour a day of slow reading with print matter, an occasional research assignment completed without Google—any such practices that slow down and intensify the reading of complex texts will help. ("Too Dumb")

Bauerlein does not condemn continued use of electronic media, but he does suggest the need to provide students with experiences that offer extended careful reading, especially of nonfiction prose.

A deeper explanation of the results of these various studies and a stronger case for the need for more and more careful reading along with better teaching of reading comes from Nicholas Carr's *The Shallows: What the Internet Is Doing to Our Brains*, which relies on brain research for claims about the impact of new technologies on reading and learning. Carr reports on recent brain research showing the plasticity of the brain, that is, its ability to adapt and change in response to stimuli, trauma, and other influences. Plasticity in the brains of adults can be a good thing, as Carr points out in reviewing the original research on brain reorganization following trauma (27). However, there is also the possibility of a negative outcome of plasticity, which is that "just as the brain can build new or stronger circuits through physical or mental practice, those circuits can weaken or dissolve with neglect" (35). Carr claims that the more multitasking and superficial reading we do, the more our brains learn to do that and, by doing so, lose the ability to analyze, synthesize, evaluate, and apply in work with extended arguments. If Carr is right, and if these are the skills we want students to have and the skills we expect teachers to teach in college, the *Statement* should say so explicitly and support the provision of professional development focusing on what is happening with reading and how to deal with it.

Reviews of the work of Bauerlein and Carr point to some flaws in their thinking; however, critiques offered by Christine Wenderoth, the Director of the McCormick Theological Library in Chicago, and Anne Ruggles Gere, former NCTE president and University of Michigan English and Education scholar, point to several key issues that support the need for the *Statement* to integrate reading instruction with writing instruction and provide teacher training on reading. These critics point out that to help students use technology more effectively, instructors must be thoroughly tech savvy. With proper professional development, they will be in a position to help students learn to use technology in support of their reading and writing. Teacher training, then, is crucial to help students make more effective and efficient use of online texts and resources. The critics also point out that Bauerlein and Carr (though Carr to a lesser degree) do not focus on the need for more critical thinking and ways to capitalize on what the digital realm has to offer. Insofar as teaching reading and writing entails critical thinking, good teaching that develops critical thinking skills for students is crucial. Bauerlein and Carr raise provocative points about technology's impact on the teaching and learning of reading and writing, and their concerns point to the need for changes in the *Statement* to advocate the integration reading with writing in our teaching.

All of these findings serve to confirm what classroom teachers already know from their daily experience with respect to students and reading. That daily experience consists of what I refer to as the "don't, won't, can't" problem: Students don't do the reading we assign for them, and they won't unless teachers force them to do it with incentives, penalties, or other forms of coercion. More importantly, and perhaps a more useful explanation for why students don't and won't is that they really *can't* read, at least not in the ways faculty want and expect. Whether we rely on large-scale objective testing like that offered by ACT, qualitative studies like the careful, intensive journal/survey work done by Jolliffe and Harl, or technology-based studies like that done by Kaiser and Nielsen, the message is clear: Many students simply don't read as well as they could and should to be successful in college. To address this problem, the *Statement* must incorporate a deliberate focus on reading as the partner to writing; students cannot improve the one without the other. Moreover, faculty development becomes essential to insure that teachers have the knowledge and strategies to improve student reading. Writing teachers are the natural leaders for this effort, but as I have argued elsewhere, work on reading should also be going on in every discipline ("Reading").

In the *Statement*'s section that addresses teaching conditions, the following should be added:

> Teachers should have access to materials on student reading problems and strategies for addressing those problems. They should also be provided with ongoing professional development on reading and should be expected to focus their attention on reading in assignments, in online work, and in their classroom approaches.

Including a statement of this kind would encourage the thorough integration of reading with writing in college classrooms. It could also open the door to expanding the focus on reading across the curriculum.

The Benefits of Reading for the Teaching and Learning of Writing: Voice, Culture, WAC

Improving reading offers essential benefits to students in terms of their ability to complete coursework in every discipline, but it is especially pertinent to their development as writers, based on research in implicit learning and academic voice, on research across cultures, and on research on writing across the curriculum (WAC). Reading is good for students; no reader of this chapter is going to argue that point. Faculty members want students to read to understand concepts, to learn about research pertinent to course topics, to see original documents relevant to history and theory, and for a wide range of other reasons. Beyond these obvious rationales, though, reading has two specific positive effects on students' writing.

First, reading offers the opportunity for implicit learning, best defined as follows:

> The term "implicit learning" is typically used to characterize those situations where a person learns about the structure of a fairly complex stimulus environment, without necessarily intending to do so, and in such a way that the resulting knowledge is difficult to express. (Berry 1)

Reading provides precisely this situation: Students learn about academic writing, formal writing, proper voice, and so on without specific attention to these features and without being able to describe what they have learned. The "stuff" of what is learned in this way through reading comprises a second key benefit of reading: Through implicit learning, students can develop an appropriate sense of formal written language and academic voice. This sense opens the door to effective writing in college courses and beyond them in the professional world of work after graduation.

Implicit learning is hard enough to define, and whole books, like Dianne C. Berry's *How Implicit is Implicit Learning?* are devoted to ways to understand how this process works as well as capture it in specific, measurable ways. It is even more difficult to define and explain "academic voice." Here again, a number of books have been written and a number of attempts at formal definition have been made. One of the most respected definitions has come from the work of Peter Elbow, editor of a *Landmark* volume on voice. Elbow identifies five meanings of voice in writing, the most pertinent of which is what he calls voice with authority—"having a voice" (xxxii). In this meaning, voice is about "having the authority to speak or wield influence or to vote in a group" (xxxii). An example is transforming a dissertation into an article—getting the more authoritative voice of a scholar rather than the deferential voice of a student. The voice with authority comes closest to academic voice of the kind teachers want students to understand and use in their papers, and it can be learned through the processes of implicit learning, but only if there is extended, careful, analytical reading of nonfiction prose that contains such a voice.

While the *Statement* addresses specifically the work of college writing teachers, it is important that these teachers share their knowledge of reading across cultural, linguistic, and disciplinary lines. Doing so provides a second benefit of adding reading to the *Statement*. Most students learning to write in college will need their skills not only for successful completion of writing requirements but also for coursework in a variety of other disciplines across the curriculum. In this connection, the work of researchers like Ken Hyland on English for academic purposes or English for specific purposes is particularly useful. Hyland, a widely-published scholar in this field and Department Chair at the University of Hong Kong, has written about the need to see writing in a variety of disciplinary contexts (146–47). He points out that while the literacy skills students need in college and beyond might be obvious to faculty, they are not obvious to students, and especially not to second language speakers who must show their abilities "by the display of competence in a specialist written register" (146–47); moreover, they are seldom explained in any overt way:

> While it may seem self-evident to faculty what writing at the university entails, this is rarely explicitly conveyed to students. Even where they are presented with writing guidelines these rarely seek to provide them with a means of conceptualizing the epistemological frameworks within which they have to study, nor do they offer ways of recognizing that there are also different practices within the academy itself.
>
> The fact of multiple literacies within the academy is a further burden to students, particularly if they lack the vocabulary and analytical skills to distinguish the heterogeneity of the discourses and practices typical of the different disciplinary cultures they encounter. (147)

It should be clear that students can only develop the necessary skills in vocabulary, analysis, and understanding "epistemological frameworks" through reading. I have argued elsewhere that, for many students, learning to write academic prose is like learning another language (*Teaching*); they must read to get the sound of the language in their minds. Because this reading can and should go on in writing courses as well as in courses in the disciplines, teachers of writing along with those in the disciplines must include reading instruction in their work. Writing teachers need the background to provide this kind of instruction and should share their knowledge with colleagues in every field.

Support for this goal is a third benefit of adding reading to the *Statement*. This support comes in a very focused way from NCTE. In its March 2011 "Reading and Writing across the Curriculum: A Policy Research Brief," NCTE advocates for reading *and* writing in every discipline. NCTE's call arises from the CCSS, which ultimately has an impact on postsecondary education. What is most important for this discussion is that the NCTE brief specifically advocates professional development for teachers on reading and offers guidelines for such programs. Professional development should, NCTE contends,

> [e]xtend across 50 hours; connect to a school initiative; foster collaboration among teachers; and focus on teaching and learning of specific academic content. Few teachers in subjects outside ELA [English Language Arts] have been trained to provide

> effective instruction in reading and writing across the curriculum, so any serious effort to establish this kind of teaching will require significant investment in the professional development of teachers. (17)

The brief goes on to support several of the strategies discussed below, including learning communities for teacher collaboration, especially across disciplines, and opportunities for teacher inquiry and research (17).

The section on professional standards in the *Statement* is divided into sections according to expectations for various categories of full-time and part-time faculty. A revision to this section should open with a paragraph that includes reading standards all teachers should be expected to meet, such as:

> All faculty who teach writing should have or develop appropriate background in the teaching and learning of reading and should be expected to use this background to inform their classroom work. Insofar as research shows that all students need to be more efficient and effective readers, writing teachers should provide instruction to achieve this goal and should share their instructional strategies with colleagues across the disciplines.

WHAT TO DO ON MONDAY: APPROACHES TO PROFESSIONAL DEVELOPMENT

It's clear from all this discussion that the *Statement* needs to focus clearly on professional development for teachers of writing and that a good part of that professional development should be about developing postsecondary writing teachers who are confident and skilled in teaching reading. This need is growing ever more acute as the professoriate becomes increasingly part-time and untenured, as the *Statement* acknowledges. That development continues apace according to a report by Samantha Stainburn in the *New York Times* about the "vanishing full-time professor." I don't mean to suggest that non-tenured colleagues are less qualified or capable, but instead, that graduate students, part-timers, and untenured faculty who teach writing need professional development equivalent to that provided for full-time faculty, and the *Statement* should clearly address this need, specifically with regard to reading. The key question then becomes just how to provide appropriate professional development, within boundaries of time, cost, and effectiveness.

Professional development on reading should have two key goals. The first of these is to give teachers background and understanding about the nature of the reading process, including reading development and reading problems, such as dyslexia. The second goal should be to give teachers classroom strategies they can use with students to improve reading speed and efficiency so that students read well enough to get everything they need from a text in one pass. Good readers do not normally need to read a text more than once, and most students will be more successful if they fall into this category.

There are a variety of approaches that might work; the *Statement* does not have to specify these, but a brief list of suggestions seems in order. Some colleges and universities are offering faculty learning communities, for example, and my consulting meetings with a few have made clear how useful they can be, offering readings and ongoing professional development. Individual readings and discussions at staff meetings, like a common book program for faculty, is an alternative option. Materials such as *Reading in the Brain: The Science and Evolution of a Human Invention* by French cognitive scientist Stanislas Dehaene or articles such as Norwegian sociologist and media scholar Terje Hillesund's "Digital Reading Spaces: How Expert Readers Handle Books, the Web and Electronic Paper" can provide substantial information to develop teachers' understanding of the reading process. Regular staff meetings, single occasion faculty seminars, or perhaps through webinars or podcasts are other ways to encourage professional development. Common book programs for students open an opportunity for teachers to deploy what they learn about reading in work with students. I discuss these approaches and others in *Reading, Writing, and Digitizing: Understanding Literacy in the Electronic Age*.

Students cannot and will not ever be better writers unless they do a lot more reading and read better when they do. The *Statement* must recognize the need for reading *and* writing instruction and the need to provide teachers with much stronger professional development in reading so that they can work with students to improve their reading and then their writing. Professional development must help teachers understand the nature of the reading process as well as the changes happening to reading among students and in the population at large as a by-product of our interaction with technology. Students' difficulties with reading are clearly indicated by a variety of evidence and by our everyday classroom experience. There are clear benefits for writing when students read, as it is the experience of reading that sets the stage for the implicit learning of academic writing to occur. The *Statement* should and must integrate reading with writing, and must also include provisions to empower teachers with the knowledge and skills to teach reading in all classes and share their knowledge across all discipline.

Works Cited

Arum, Richard, and Josipa Roksa. *Academically Adrift: Limited Learning on College Campuses*. U of Chicago P, 2011.

Bauerlein, Mark. *The Dumbest Generation: How the Digital Age Stupefies Young Americans and Jeopardizes Our Future*. Tarcher/Penguin, 2008.

—. "Too Dumb for Complex Texts?" *Educational Leadership*, vol. 86, no. 5, 2011, www.ascd.org/publications/educational-leadership/feb11/vol68/num05/Too-Dumb-for-Complex-Texts%C2%A2.aspx.

Benton, Thomas H. "A Perfect Storm in Undergraduate Education, Part 2." *The Chronicle of Higher Education*, 8 April 2011, pp. A45–A46.

Berry, Dianne C. "Introduction." *How Implicit is Implicit Learning?* Edited by Dianne C. Berry, Oxford UP, 1997. pp. 1–12.

Bowen, William G., et al. *Crossing the Finish Line: Completing College at America's Public Universities*. Princeton UP, 2009.

Carr, Nicholas. *The Shallows: What the Internet is Doing to Our Brains*. W.W. Norton, 2010.

CCCC Executive Committee. *Statement of Principles and Standards for the Postsecondary Teaching of Writing*. College Composition and Communication, vol. 40, no. 3, 1989, pp. 329–36.

Council of Chief State School Officials and the National Governors Association (CCSSO/NGA). *Common Core State Standards Initiative*. Common Core State Standards Initiative, 2010, www.corestandards.org/.

Dehaene, Stanislas. *Reading in the Brain: The Science and Evolution of a Human Invention*. Viking Penguin, 2009.

Elbow, Peter. "Introduction." *Landmark Essays on Voice and Writing*. Ed. Peter Elbow, Hermagoras P, 1994, pp. xi–xlvii.

A First Look at the Common Core and College and Career Readiness. ACT, Inc., 2010, files.eric.ed.gov/fulltext/ED513813.pdf.

Framework for Success in Postsecondary Writing. Council of Writing Program Administrators, National Council of Teachers of English, National Writing Project, 2011, wpacouncil.org/files/framework-for-success-postsecondary-writing.pdf.

Gere, Anne Ruggles. "Review Essay: Making Our Brains." *WPA: Writing Program Administration*, vol. 36, no. 1, 2012, pp. 214–19.

Hillesund, Terje. "Digital Reading Spaces: How Expert Readers Handle Books, the Web and Electronic Paper." *First Monday*, vol. 15, no. 4, 2010, firstmonday.org/article/view/2762/2504.

Horning, Alice S. "A Potential [Solution] to the Plagiarism Problem: Improving Reading." *Journal of Teaching Writing*. 25.2 (2010): pp. 143–75.

—. "Reading Across the Curriculum as the Key to Student Success." *Across the Disciplines*, vol. 4, 2007, wac.colostate.edu/atd/articles/horning2007.cfm.

—. *Reading, Writing, and Digitizing: Understanding Literacy in the Digital Age*. Cambridge Scholars Publishing, 2012.

—. *Teaching Writing as a Second Language*. Southern Illinois UP, 1987.

Hyland, Ken. *Disciplinary Discourses: Social Interactions in Academic Writing*. Pearson Education Limited, 2000.

Information Literacy Competency Standards for Higher Education. Association of College and Research Libraries, 2000, www.ala.org/acrl/sites/ala.org.acrl/files/content/standards/standards.pdf.

Jolliffe, David J., and Allison Harl. "Texts of Our Institutional Lives: Studying the Reading Transition: from High School to College: What Are Our Students Reading and Why?" *College English*, vol. 70, no. 6, 2008, pp. 599–617.

National Council of Teachers of English (NCTE). "Reading and Writing Across the Curriculum: A Policy Research Brief." *Council Chronicle*, vol. 20, no. 3, 2011, pp. 15–18.

The National Survey of America's College Students. American Institutes of Research (AIR), 2006, www.air.org/sites/default/files/downloads/report/The-20Literacy20of20Americas20College20Students_final20report_0.pdf.

Nielsen, Jakob. "Usability of Websites for Teenagers." *The Digital Divide: Arguments for and Against Facebook, Google, Texting, and the Age of Social Networking*, edited by Mark Bauerlein, Penguin/Tarcher, 2011, pp. 44–51.

Project SAILS (Standardized Assessment of Information Literacy Skills). Kent State University, 2000–2016, www.projectsails.org.

Reading Between the Lines: What the ACT Reading Test Reveals About College Readiness. ACT, Inc., 1 March 2006, http://forms.act.org/research/policymakers/pdf/reading_summary.pdf.

Rideout, Victoria J., et al. *Generation M²: Media in the Lives of 8- to 18-Year Olds*. Henry J. Kaiser Family Foundation, 2010, kff.org/other/event/generation-m2-media-in-the-lives-of/.

Stainburn, Samantha. "The Case of the Vanishing Full-Time Professor." *The New York Times*, 3 January 2010, www.nytimes.com/2010/01/03/education/edlife/03strategy-t.html?_r=0.

Wenderoth, Christine. Review of *Now You See It: How the Brain Science of Attention Will Transform the Way We Live, Work, and Learn* by Cathy N. Davidson. *Theological Librarianship*, vol. 5, no. 2, 2012, pp. 99–100.

What Does It Really Mean to Be College and Work Ready? National Center on Education and the Economy, 2013, www.ncee.org/college-and-work-ready/.

APPENDIX: WORD FREQUENCIES WITHIN THE STATEMENT

13 Going Digital: Ideas for Updating CCCC's *Statement* for a Digital World

James P. Purdy

Introduction

As other chapters in this collection have eloquently argued, the Conference on College Composition and Communication's (CCCC) *Statement of Principles and Standards for the Postsecondary Teaching of Writing* (hereafter the *Statement*) has been a landmark document in defining and shaping institutional practice for composition instruction for more than two decades. Given revolutionary changes in writing technologies, practices, and instruction since the *Statement*'s adoption in 1989, however, the *Statement* must be revised to ensure continued relevance and influence. This chapter proposes three primary ways the *Statement* should be updated to account for these changes and to prepare for the future these changes might bring. Drawing on published studies and policy documents in rhetoric and composition[1] and considering new writing technologies, practices, and pedagogies, I contend that the *Statement* needs to account and argue for the value of digital scholarship, digitally-delivered writing instruction, and the infrastructure necessary for producing and teaching digital writing.

Digital Scholarship

Section I of the *Statement*, "Professional Standards that Promote Quality Education," lists activities of rhetoric and composition professionals that

---

1. I use the term *rhetoric and composition* to designate the academic discipline also known as *composition studies* and *writing studies* because that is the term the *Statement* uses.

should be counted "seriously" in "salary, tenure, and promotion considerations" (331). Gesturing to the 1988 "Report of the Modern Language Association's Commission on Writing and Literature," point 3 in the "Tenure-Line Faculty" section asserts that research in rhetoric and composition should be seen as legitimate as research in other areas of English studies (331). Given the focus of rhetoric and composition scholarship, opportunities, and venues for digital publication, and larger discussions about policies and requirements for tenure and promotion since then, the *Statement* should add a claim regarding research form as well. We need, in other words, to add to the *Statement*'s existing list of activities to be counted "seriously" the production of digital scholarship, both research that analyzes digital writing and research produced and disseminated in digital form.

Since publication of the *Statement* in 1989, the subfield of computers and composition has become a significant component of rhetoric and composition, and the *Statement* should reflect this area of scholarly inquiry. *Computers and Composition*, a popular journal devoted to influences of computer technologies on writing pedagogy and research, began as a newsletter in 1983 and became a journal in 1985, a few years before the *Statement*'s publication ("Brief"). Since that time, the journal and its circulation have grown, resulting in increasing influence both within and outside rhetoric and composition. This fact is already familiar to most within rhetoric and composition. That the *Statement*'s audience extends to all English studies professionals, however, necessitates explicit attention to this development,[2] particularly to substantiate a scholarly basis for digital research and writing and to frame digital technologies as more than just neutral instructional tools.

Even members of rhetoric and composition outside the subfield of computers and composition need a reminder. Despite *Computers and Composition* achieving journal status in 1985, Maureen Daly Goggin in *Authoring a Discipline: Scholarly Journals and the Post-World War II Emergence of Rhetoric and Composition* only briefly mentions computers and composition as an area of focus in rhetoric and composition as part of her history of journal development and publication in the field through 1990 (168). Moreover, she neither includes *Computers and Com-*

---

2. The field of literary studies has had an arguably parallel growth in focus on digital technologies with its subfield of digital humanities. Noting this parallel in the *Statement* might reinforce the value of explicitly drawing attention to the legitimacy of digital scholarship.

position in her list of "Journals founded in rhetoric and composition, 1950–1990" (36) nor mentions it elsewhere in her book. That work in computers and composition took several years to reach the forefront of the discipline may explain its lack of mention in Goggin's study and the *Statement* (especially as the *Statement* was published in 1989, at the end of the time period covered in Goggin's study). However, such work has become more prominent—with some scholars now calling for it to be the main focus of the discipline (McClure, *Why*; Writing in Digital Environments Research Collective [WIDE])—further substantiating the need for the *Statement* to address explicitly the role of digital scholarship in writing instruction.

Discussion of digital technologies and their pedagogical and scholarly influences have not been limited to specialized journals like *Computers and Composition*. Scholars working in computers and composition have brought a focus on digital research and writing to rhetoric and composition's leading mainstream journals, illustrated by the frequency with which their articles include language reflective of the digital turn. Table 1 and Table 2 provide data from *College Composition and Communication* (*CCC*) and *College English* (*CE*), the National Council of Teachers of English's (NCTE) two leading journals for postsecondary educators in English studies.[3]

---

3. Because the term usage statistics from 1998–2007 and 2008–July 2011 come from different sources, I separate them into Table 1 and Table 2, respectively. I gathered data on word usage for Table 1 from JSTOR, whose "moving wall" ends at 2007 as of the time of this writing. As a result, publications after 2007 are not included. To fill this gap, I gathered data on word usage from 2008–2011 from the NCTE journal database, which allows for full text searching of more recent publications. Results from both tables include only article publications; reviews, opinion essays, letters from the editor, and other journal elements are not included. The website CompPile also allows bibliographic searches for more recent publications, but has an incomplete database and does not provide full text searching, so it does not offer comparable results. The closest option is an "any field" search, which searches author, title, and keyword. An "any field" search for *digital* in *CCC* and *CE*, for example, yields five articles and one article, respectively, which, though not as accurate a gauge as the JSTOR or NCTE full text searches, still reveals sustained focus on digital technologies in these publications.

Table 1. Number of articles from 1989–2007 in which the terms *computer*, *digital*, *new media*, and *online* appear in full text

Journal	Computer	Digital	New Media	Online
CCC	143	34	16	79
CE	110	34	10	57

Table 2. Number of articles from 2008–July 2011 in which the terms *computer*, *digital*, *new media*, and *online* appear in full text

Journal	Computer	Digital	New Media	Online
CCC	25	29	18	31
CE	14	12	5	15

These statistics reveal a sustained and increasing focus on digital technologies in the field's leading journal publications. In just three and a half years from 2008–July 2011, for instance, the term *digital* appears nearly as often and the term *new media* appears more in *CCC* than in the eighteen-year period from 1989–2007. While terms like *composition*, *rhetoric*, *literacy*, and *gender* are more common, terms reflective of other influential subspecialties of rhetoric and composition (e.g., *archive*, *ESL*, *queer*) appear in approximately as many or fewer articles in *CCC* and *CE* from 1989–2007, reinforcing digital technology's shaping role in the discipline.

Term use, of course, is only one (imperfect) indication of the field's consideration of digital technologies and practices. Along with increasing attention to the digital in print publications, new digital peer-reviewed journals have arisen, including *Computers and Composition Online* (started in 1996); *Enculturation: A Journal for Rhetoric, Writing, and Culture* (started in 1997); *First Monday* (started in 1996); *Journal of Undergraduate Multimedia Projects (JUMP)* (started in 2009); *Kairos: A Journal of Rhetoric, Technology, and Pedagogy* (started in 1996); *Vectors: Journal of Culture and Technology in a Dynamic Vernacular* (started in 2005); and *The Writing Instructor* (started online in 2001), among others.

Accompanying these new digital academic journals, entirely new digital writing and publication venues have appeared, including the blogosphere (a term coined in 1999 to reflect the blogging phenomenon begun in 1997) ("Blogosphere"; Levinson 11); Facebook (started in 2004) (Levinson 120); Twitter (started in 2006) (Levinson 133); and Wikipedia (started in 2001) (Levinson 85). Especially notable is that the flagship journal of CCCC, *CCC*, now also has an online companion journal, *CCC Online* (its first issue was published in January 2012), and in May 2011, the Modern Language Association (MLA) released its "new database of scholarly web sites" ("New"), indicating recognition of the Web's significant and growing role in scholarship. Taken together, these sites and venues have changed what writing means and does, what it looks like, and who it reaches. An updated *Statement* must recognize these new opportunities and venues and argue for their relevance and legitimacy for faculty seeking tenure and promotion and for all writing faculty seeking to prepare students as writers in a world where the majority of writing (in developed nations) occurs digitally.

Discussions of digital work in tenure and promotion have also evolved since publication of the *Statement*. Other policy documents and reports of CCCC and MLA since 1989 have addressed the role of digital scholarship and publication in tenure and promotion. In particular, MLA's 2007 *Report of the MLA Task Force on Evaluating Scholarship for Tenure and Promotion* explicitly addresses the need, in light of realities regarding print monograph publication possibilities and new opportunities for peer-reviewed publication in multiple forums and formats, to recognize and value a more "capacious" definition of scholarship, one that includes digitally-produced and published work (11).[4]

While the *Statement* in itself is not a document focused primarily on tenure and promotion standards, and therefore is not expected to do the work of these other documents, it argues that research in rhetoric and composition is "fundamentally necessary to the quality of education at all levels" (332) and affirms the need for writing faculty to be tenure-line and (ultimately) tenured. Thus, an updated *Statement* must tap into the ongoing conversation about tenure and promotion and firmly assert that one of the "Professional Standards that Promote[s] Quality Education" is disciplinary and institutional valuation of scholarship produced in many forms, including the digital.

Digitally-Delivered Writing Instruction

Given the proliferation of online writing courses, including completely online degree programs, the *Statement* also needs to account for digitally-delivered writing instruction. Pushes from the public sector to increase online course offerings, such as former Governor Tim Pawlenty's

---

4. See also *CCCC Promotion and Tenure Guidelines for Work with Technology* and *Guidelines for Evaluating Work in Digital Humanities and Digital Media* (MLA).

call to have Minnesota State Colleges and Universities provide 25% of their credits via online course delivery by 2015 (Kolowich, "Political"); University of California Commission on the Future co-chair Christopher Edley Jr.'s plan to offer fully online bachelor's degrees despite massive budget cuts in the UC system (Kolowich, "California"); and Texas Governor Rick Perry's proposal to "leverage Web-based instruction" to offer a bachelor's degree that costs no more than $10,000 over four years (Kolowich, "$10,000"), will likely continue the growth of online writing instruction. Thus, we must proactively affirm the "Principles and Standards" associated with digitally-delivered writing instruction in sections I and II of the *Statement*.

The *Statement* would be more relevant and effective were it to acknowledge the growth of online instruction. In their 2010 study of 2,583 colleges and universities, I. Elaine Allen and Jeff Seaman[5] share that over 63% of chief academic officers they surveyed indicated online education is "a critical part of their institution's long term strategy" (2, 22, see also 6); that just under 75% of institutions indicated the economic recession increased demand for online course offerings (14); and that growth in online course enrollment exceeded growth in overall higher education enrollment by nearly 20% (8). They, along with Clayton M. Christensen and colleagues[6] in their 2011 study, report that nearly 30% of students now take at least one class online (8, 3, respectively). In the fall of 2009, this statistic translated to approximately 5.6 million students being enrolled in at least one online course (Allen and Seaman 8).

While neither report discusses composition courses specifically, we can safely assume that a significant proportion of these courses are writ-

---

5. One of the study sponsors, the Sloan Consortium, is explicitly "*dedicated to integrating online education into the mainstream of higher education*," though Allen and Seaman indicate that "[t]o ensure objectivity, partner organizations do not have editorial control" over the study or its data (22–23). The results of the study must be considered with the Sloan Consortium's objective in mind, though other studies (e.g., Green) also substantiate the growth of online education detailed in the Allen and Seaman report.

6. As with Allen and Seaman's report, Christensen and colleagues' report is shaped by a clear objective, which, in Christensen and colleagues' case, is using "online learning in a new business model focused exclusively on teaching and learning, not research—and focused on highly structured programs targeted at preparation for careers," that is, for-profit universities (2, 9). Its results must be considered in this context, though, again, the growth of online education it discusses is substantiated across other reports (e.g., Allen and Seaman; Green).

ing-focused, particularly given the attention online writing instruction has received in rhetoric and composition scholarship in the last two decades. Scholars have suggested pedagogical strategies and techniques for online writing instructors (Blythe; Hewett and Ehmann; Hicks; Miller-Cochran and Rodrigo; Warnock); explained challenges online writing instructors face (Anson; Blair and Monske; Hailey, Jr. et al.; Lenard; Peterson; Reinheimer); studied the efficacy of different kinds of online writing instruction with different student populations (Guardado and Shi; Hewett; Hirvela; Sapp and Simon); and explored the use of new digital technologies for such instruction (Lundin; National Writing Project [NWP] et al.; Purdy "Changing"). *Computers and Composition* even devoted a special issue to the topic in 2001 (Peterson and Savinye), and at the 2010 CCCC, the Executive Committee moved "[t]o reconstitute the Committee on Best Practices for Online Writing Instruction" ("CCCC Secretary's" 749). Referencing the Executive Committee's findings[7] in the *Statement* would help both to update the *Statement* and to present a consistent vision of best practices among NCTE documents.

Given the prevalence of online writing instruction, section I of the *Statement* must legitimate digitally-delivered instruction and explicitly address its implementation. To do so, the list of "sometimes undervalued" activities that should be "count[ed] seriously" in tenure and promotion decisions (331) must include the teaching of online course sections and the design and implementation of digital teaching spaces, including online writing labs and distance education platforms. Tenure-line faculty will be more motivated to seriously and thoughtfully engage in online education in its multiple forms if they know that these activities stand to be valued equally with face-to-face instruction for tenure and promotion. Having a policy document like the *Statement* explicitly make that case would be one important step toward establishing online writing instruction's value.

Simply including these online initiatives in a list of valued activities, however, is not enough. The *Statement* should connect such pedagogical initiatives to the increasingly globalized nature of higher education and institutional missions that reach out to student populations across the globe, often in Africa and Asia. Digitally-delivered writing instruction does not simply have value because some faculty do it; it (potentially) has

---

7. The committee released its 116-page initial report, *The State-of-the-Art of OWI*, in April 2011 (Hewett et al.).

value when it allows postsecondary institutions to achieve their educational missions. The *Statement* is an appropriate place to make this case.

The *Statement*, however, needs to do more than establish the value of digitally-delivered writing instruction. It should connect to discussions surrounding who primarily teaches such courses. One way to do so is to frankly acknowledge that part-time and temporary faculty as well as graduate students are frequently responsible for such instruction, which contributes to its (and their) marginalization. Robert Samuels eloquently discusses this problem, framing it as a "future threat to computers and composition," largely because of the poor working conditions for and exploitation of non-tenure-track instructors of (online) writing courses (63–64). Of particular concern to Samuels is how such instructors often lack ownership of their own course materials, which he contends are their intellectual property (67). Following Samuels, I argue that the *Statement* should make clear that all instructors, including part-time faculty and teachers of online classes, "own" and have control over (as much as any text is owned and controlled) the materials they create, even (and especially) those distributed online.

The marginalization of online writing instruction and online writing instructors is also frequently programmatic. By virtue of often being associated primarily (and in some programs exclusively) with contingent labor, digitally-delivered writing instruction becomes peripheral to the field—in much the same way that composition instruction itself, largely because it was mostly the responsibility of contingent non-tenure-track labor, became peripheral to many English departments, a condition that has taken decades to change (and still has not changed in too many departments). "*Recommendations for part-time faculty*" *(*333) should thereby note explicitly that composition programs should not make teaching online courses mandatory for part-time faculty or graduate students (i.e., they should be voluntary for all instructors) and should not assign part-time faculty or graduate students online writing courses without adequate training, guidance, and supervision. To be clear, my recommendation here is not that all (or even more) composition classes be offered online; it is that when such instruction is implemented, it should not be approached as appropriate only for instructors off the tenure track and further, that those who teach such classes should be afforded the employment stability, benefits, and support of full-time faculty.[8]

The *Statement* must also balance an affirmation of digitally-delivered writing instruction and a discussion of its staffing with an assertion of the conditions necessary for its success. In its 2013 report, which was adopted into an official policy statement from CCCC, the CCCC Committee on Best Practices for Online Writing Instruction acknowledges this concern: "Instructors are dissatisfied with the levels of support they receive regarding technology, course caps, training, pay, and professional development/interactions relative to OWI [online writing instruction] in both the fully online and hybrid settings" (Hewett et al. 7). Section II of the *Statement*, which lists the "Teaching Conditions Necessary for Quality Education" (335–36) should, therefore, explicitly address the needs of instructors teaching writing online. For instance, the *Statement* would do well to explicitly indicate that online course enrollments should ideally be capped at fifteen students as more instruction is provided through writing rather than lecturing or discussion—instructors Beth L. Hewett and her colleagues interviewed expressed preference for no more than twenty students (7–8)—especially as the possibility for reaching larger numbers of students (i.e., having larger class sizes) is sometimes touted as an advantage of digitally-delivered writing instruction. Indeed, the popularity of MOOCs (massive open online courses) arises at least partly from their ability to reach many students at once. Samuels provides an example of a writing instructor contract that stipulates class size cannot exceed thirty-five students (70; see also 65–67). Christensen and colleagues, moreover, offer "online learning" as the cornerstone of their higher education overhaul because it allows for "serving people who were not able to be served or were not desirable to serve" previously, resulting in reaching "many more students" (2, 6), and Perry proclaims that "Web-based instruction" is key to making higher education less expensive (Kolowich, "$10,000"). While reaching underserved populations and making postsecondary education more affordable are indeed admirable pursuits and should certainly be goals of higher education (and CCCC), the assumptions that delivering such instruction online necessarily allows for teaching more students and for teaching those students more cheaply must be tempered in the *Statement*. Based

---

8. Institutions, of course, sometimes conduct searches for instructors to teach exclusively in online settings, and instructors accept these positions knowing up front that their teaching responsibilities will be in online classes.

on a study of online education, Di Xu and Shanna Smith Jaggars provide evidence for reconsidering such claims. In their research tracking community and technical college students in Washington from 2004–2009, Xu and Jaggars found that students completing online courses (rather than face-to-face or hybrid courses) had "lower success rates on a variety of outcomes," including completion rates (19–20).

Similarly, the *Statement* should make clear that other conditions in its list also apply, with adaptations, to digitally-delivered writing instruction. For instance, online instructors, like traditional classroom instructors, require "reasonably private office space for regular conferences" (336), but they should also be provided telephones with long distance service and/or virtual conferencing software (e.g., Skype, Adobe Connect) if the online instruction requires telephone or virtual conferences. Additionally, the assertion that "The institution should provide all necessary support services for the teaching of writing, including supplies, duplication services, and secretarial assistance" (336) should be expanded to identify the particular needs of online writing instructors. Certainly all writing teachers require this equipment, but it is even more essential for online writing instructors.

Finally, to support the assertion that the "development and support" of writing centers should be an "important departmental and institutional priority" (336), work for online components of writing centers—including online tutoring and development of instructional materials for online writing labs—should also be valued and recognized for tenure and promotion and supported as a teaching activity. Doing so means listing online (and face-to-face) writing center work as labor to be counted for tenure and promotion and specifying the necessary support for this work (see Balester's chapter in this volume for more on the *Statement*'s treatment of writing center work).

Debate over the effectiveness of online education will certainly continue; however, the ever increasing role of digitally-delivered writing instruction is undeniable and requires that the *Statement* acknowledge its influence and stipulate the conditions necessary for its success. Referencing such instruction in the *Statement* may seem implicitly to support its development, and while the *Statement*'s goal is not to argue for or against such instruction, excluding it ignores the reality of writing instruction today. As Hewett and her colleagues put it in their report, "The Committee takes no position on the oft-asked question of whether OWI [online writing instruction] *should be* used and practiced in postsecondary settings because it accepts the reality that currently OWI *is* used and practiced in such settings" (2).

Digital Writing Infrastructure

The influence of digital technologies on writing instruction has extended beyond digitally-delivered courses. As Jeremiah Dyehouse, Michael Pennell, and Linda K. Shamoon assert, "Reflecting the digital turn in composition studies, multimedia writing courses have become commonplace in many writing programs" (W330). WIDE takes this assertion a step further, arguing, "It is no longer possible to teach writing responsibly or effectively in traditional classrooms. Writing instruction MUST be computer based, in some sense, to meet the needs of student writers." Thus, in addition to acknowledging the reality of digitally-delivered writing instruction, part of making the *Statement* relevant is making it applicable to digital writing instruction in all contexts—or, perhaps better said, of having it establish all writing instruction as, in some sense, digital writing instruction. The writing that students are—and will be—expected to do necessitates a robust digital writing infrastructures.

Section II of the *Statement*, which stipulates the "Teaching Conditions Necessary for Quality Education" (335–36) therefore needs to identify and argue for the material and non-material infrastructure needed for producing and teaching digital writing. Given how frequently students compose and research with digital technologies and for digital spaces (Anderson and Rainie; Lenhart et al.; McClure, "Min(d)ing"; Nicholas et al.; Purdy, "Scholarliness") and given that professional documents assert that students need to gain proficiency in digital composing for educational and professional success (Council of Writing Program Administrators [CWPA]; CWPA, NCTE, and NWP; NCTE), such infrastructure is not a luxury but a necessary element of composition instruction.

Articulating the materials necessary for students to achieve postsecondary writing success and to become literate citizens in the twenty-first century would allow the *Statement* to be consistent with NCTE's other policy documents. For example, *The NCTE Definition of 21st Century Literacies* asserts:

> Because technology has increased the intensity and complexity of literate environments, the 21st century demands that a literate person possess a wide range of abilities and competencies,

> many literacies. [. . .] Active, successful participants in this 21st century global society must be able to [. . .] [d]evelop proficiency and fluency with the tools of technology [. . . and] [c]reate, critique, analyze, and evaluate multimedia texts.

The *Statement* should reflect these 21st century "demands" and use of "tools of technology."

Similarly, in 2011, CWPA, NCTE, and NWP issued a joint statement on the *Framework for Success in Postsecondary Writing*. The *Framework*, which "describes the rhetorical and twenty-first-century skills as well as habits of mind and experiences that are critical for college success," emphasizes that one of the ways teachers can (and should) help students succeed as writers is to provide students with opportunities to compose in multiple environments, including digital spaces.

To reinforce the importance of this goal for first-year composition students and beyond, CWPA, in the second instantiation of its own *WPA Outcomes Statement for First-Year Composition* in 2008, added a fifth set of outcomes for "Composing in Electronic Environments." The third instantiation, adopted in July 2014, eliminates this separate section and more fully integrates attention to digital composing. The second paragraph of the Introduction reads:

> In this *Statement* "composing" refers broadly to complex writing processes that are increasingly reliant on the use of digital technologies. Writers also attend to elements of design, incorporating images and graphical elements into texts intended for screens as well as printed pages. Writers' composing activities have always been shaped by the technologies available to them, and digital technologies are changing writers' relationships to their texts and audiences in evolving ways.

This opening assertion that digital technologies shape all aspects of composing reinforces that writing with digital technologies should not only be a foundational component of first-year writing courses but should also permeate students' entire postsecondary educational experience rather than be limited to one class or unit.

The *Statement* should stipulate that to meet this goal, teachers need equipment, including, but not limited to, computer hardware and software that allow for composing in and for digital spaces, network access that affords accessing and publishing to the Internet, and projection peripherals that facilitate the simultaneous viewing and sharing of digital texts by teachers and students. Richard J. Selfe provides an example of these infrastructural expenditures for one "computer-rich" teaching environment:

1. servers
2. computer workstations and monitors
3. network connectivity (Internet service provider charges, telephone charges)
4. printers
5. toner cartridges
6. backup mechanisms (e.g., tape system)
7. scanners
8. cables
9. surge protectors
10. mice and keyboards
11. security and anti-virus software
12. multimedia authoring software
13. video editing software
14. word processing software
15. optical character recognition software
16. ergonomic chairs
17. round tables
18. storage cabinet
19. conference tables (166–69)

Such a list can seem daunting, but these items are as integral to composing processes as the lead pencil once was. The reality, of course, is that such physical infrastructure can be expensive. Yet the reality also is that such equipment defines the writing environment we and our students inhabit.

This necessary infrastructure extends beyond the material. As Dànielle Nicole DeVoss, Ellen Cushman, and Jeffery Grabill; Dyehouse and colleagues; and James P. Purdy and DeVoss argue, infrastructure extends beyond "what" to include "when," "where," and "who." The *Statement*'s discussion of infrastructure, then, must also affirm the need for nonphysical infrastructure to ensure quality writing instruction in a digital age. Namely, the *Statement* should affirm that the demands of doing digital scholarship, working with digital technology, and teaching digital writing (online and off) are best met by full-time tenure-line faculty or faculty with equivalent status and benefits who have the time and resources necessary to learn to use, teach with, and produce texts with digital technologies.

Teachers need support—in the form of training and human support staff. Yet this component of infrastructure is often missing. In his 2010 study of 183 colleges and universities, Kenneth C. Green reports that 61% of institutions cite lack of training and support services as a major impediment to expansion of online instruction. The CCCC Committee on Best Practices for Online Writing Instruction reports similar results:

> Training is needed in pedagogy-specific theory and practice in both fully online and hybrid settings, but particularly in fully online settings because of its unique complete mediation by computers. In most cases, it appears that 'writing' and how to achieve strong writing and identifiable student results are left out of online writing instructional training. (Hewett et al. 7)

In other words, updated computer technology, software, and Internet access in office and classroom spaces are necessary but not sufficient. Instructors asked to teach digital writing (online and face-to-face) must receive training and be given opportunities to test out and play with the digital technologies they will be expected to use (e.g., Blackboard, Moodle, Sakai, Skype, MediaWiki). They also should be trained in using these technologies in pedagogically effective ways and have access to pedagogical models addressed in published scholarship and used by other instructors at the same or comparable institutions. While this argument regarding the need for training is certainly not new (e.g., see Savenye at al.; Selfe; among many others), it must again be made within the context of the *Statement* to reinforce that such infrastructure is essential to quality writing instruction in the digital age.

In an era marked by budget cuts and constraints, an explication of the infrastructures necessary for digital writing instruction may seem futile. However, such a public statement during this time of drastically-reduced budgets is even more necessary to reaffirm what should not—indeed, cannot—be eliminated for writing instructors to effectively prepare students to succeed as writers in the digital age. A revised *Statement* need not provide the level of detail offered above, but it should affirm the multiple facets of infrastructure (e.g., human, technological, material, and financial) involved in digital writing instruction.

Conclusion

Making these changes asks for expanding the current premise of the *Statement*: proficient writing abilities are essential for the effective functioning of a democracy (329). This rationale is certainly still true, but the networked, digital world we now live in calls for a revised *Statement* that addresses how digital technologies have changed and enhanced opportunities for widespread, instantaneous, and global written communication. In other words, a revised *Statement* is necessary not only for a functioning democracy but also for a "flat,"[9] globalized world. Through their writing, our students can quickly reach a large and diverse audience across the globe, and it is incumbent upon us to provide the conditions necessary for them to learn to do so effectively. The *Statement* offers an important opportunity for us to stipulate publicly what those conditions are. While in some sense the *Statement* represents an ideal, it is an ideal that must reflect the conditions that characterize our current technological world and educational climate.

Works Cited

Allen, I. Elaine, and Jeff Seaman. *Class Differences: Online Education in the United States, 2010.* Babson Survey Research Group/The SLOAN Consortium, 2010, files.eric.ed.gov/fulltext/ED529952.pdf.

Anderson, Janna Quitney, and Lee Rainie. "The Future of the Internet IV." *Pew Research Center's Internet and American Life Project*, 19 February 2010, www.pewinternet.org/2010/02/19/future-of-the-internet-iv/.

Anson, Chris M. "Distant Voices: Teaching and Writing in a Culture of Technology." *College English*, vol. 61, no. 3, 1999, pp. 261–80.

Blair, Kristine L., and Elizabeth A. Monske. "Cui Bono?: Revisiting the Promises and Perils of Online Learning." *Computers and Composition*, vol. 20, no. 4, 1993, pp. 441–53.

"Blogosphere." *Wikipedia*. Wikimedia Foundation, 10:35, 10 June 2011, en.wikipedia.org/wiki/Blogosphere.

Blythe, Stuart. "Designing Online Courses: User-Centered Practices." *Computers and Composition*, vol. 18, no. 4, 2001, pp. 329–46.

"A Brief History of *Computers and Composition*." *Computers and Composition: An International Journal*, 2008, computersandcomposition.candcblog.org/html/history.htm.

---

9. Thomas L. Friedman popularized use of the word "flat" to describe an increasingly globalized world in his popular history *The World Is Flat*.

CCCC Executive Committee. *Statement of Principles and Standards for the Postsecondary Teaching of Writing.* College Composition and Communication, vol. 40, no. 3, 1989, pp. 329–36.
"CCCC Secretary's Report, 2009–2010." *College Composition and Communication*, vol. 62, no. 4, 2011, 746–52.
Christensen, Clayton M., et al. *Disrupting College: How Disruptive Innovation Can Deliver Quality and Affordability to Postsecondary Education.* Center for American Progress/Innovate Institute, 2011, cdn.americanprogress.org/wp-content/uploads/issues/2011/02/pdf/disrupting_college.pdf.
Conference on College Composition and Communication Committee on Computers and Composition. *CCCC Promotion and Tenure Guidelines for Work with Technology.* Conference on College Composition and Communication, National Council of Teachers of English, November 1998, www.ncte.org/cccc/resources/positions/promotionandtenure.
DeVoss, Dànielle Nicole, et al. "Infrastructure and Composing: The When of New-Media Writing." *College Composition and Communication*, vol. 57, no. 1, 2005, pp. 14–44.
Dyehouse, Jeremiah, et al. "'Writing in Electronic Environments': A Concept and a Course for the Writing and Rhetoric Major." *College Composition and Communication*, vol. 61, no. 2, 2009, pp. W330–W350.
Framework for Success in Postsecondary Writing. Council of Writing Program Administrators, National Council of Teachers of English, and National Writing Project, 2011, wpacouncil.org/files/framework-for-success-postsecondary-writing.pdf.
Freidman, Thomas L. *The World Is Flat: A Brief History of The Twenty-First Century.* Farrar, Strauss, and Giroux, 2005.
Goggin, Maureen Daly. *Authoring a Discipline: Scholarly Journals and the Post–World War II Emergence of Rhetoric and Composition.* Erlbaum, 2000.
Green, Kenneth C. *Managing Online Education.* Western Cooperative for Educational Telecommunications—Campus Computing Project, 2010, wcet.wiche.edu/sites/default/files/ExecSummary-ManagingOnlineEd-2010.pdf.
Guardado, Martin, and Ling Shi. "ESL Students' Experiences of Online Peer Feedback." *Computers and Composition*, vol. 24, no. 4, 2007, pp. 443–61.
Guidelines for Evaluating Work in Digital Humanities and Digital Media. Modern Language Association (MLA), January 2012, www.mla.org/About-Us/Governance/Committees/Committee-Listings/Professional-Issues/Committee-on-Information-Technology/Guidelines-for-Evaluating-Work-in-Digital-Humanities-and-Digital-Media.
Hailey, Jr., David E., et al. "Online Education Horror Stories Worthy of HALLOWEEN: A Short List of Problems and Solutions in Online Instruction ." *Computers and Composition*, vol. 18, no. 4, 2001, pp. 387–97.

Hewett, Beth L. "Synchronous Online Conference-based Instruction: A Study of Whiteboard Interactions and Student Writing." *Computers and Composition*, vol. 23, no. 1, 2006, pp. 4–31.

Hewett, Beth, and Christa Ehmann. *Preparing Educators for Online Writing Instruction: Principles and Processes*. National Council of Teachers of English, 2004.

Hewett, Beth L., et al. *Initial Report of the CCCC Committee for Best Practice in Online Writing Instruction (OWI): The State-of-the-Art of OWI*. National Council of Teachers of English, 12 April 2011, www.ncte.org/library/NCTEFiles/Groups/CCCC/Committees/OWI_State-of-Art_Report_April_2011.pdf.

Hicks, Troy. *The Digital Writing Workshop*. Heinemann, 2009.

Hirvela, Alan. "Computer-based Reading and Writing across the Curriculum: Two Case Studies of L2 Writers." *Computers and Composition*, vol. 22, no. 3, 2005, pp. 337–56.

Kolowich, Steve. "The $10,000 Question." *Inside Higher Ed*, 14 February 2011, www.timeshighereducation.com/news/inside-higher-ed-the-10000-question/415192.article.

—. "California Dreamer." *Inside Higher Ed*, 3 August 2010, www.insidehighered.com/news/2010/08/03/california.

—. "A Political Online Push." *Inside Higher Ed*, 17 June 2010, www.insidehighered.com/news/2010/06/17/pawlenty.

Lenard, Mary. "Dealing with Online Selves: Ethos Issues in Computer-Assisted Teaching and Learning." *Pedagogy*, vol. 5, no. 1, 2005, pp. 77–95.

Lenhart, Amanda, et al. "Writing, Technology, and Teens." *Pew Research Center's Internet and American Life Project*, 24 April 2008, www.pewinternet.org/2008/04/24/writing-technology-and-teens/.

Levinson, Paul. *New New Media*. Pearson, 2009.

Lundin, Rebecca Wilson. "Teaching with Wikis: Toward a Networked Pedagogy." *Computers and Composition*, vol. 25, no. 4, 2008, pp. 432–48.

McClure, Randall. "Min(d)ing the Changes: Research on Secondary and Postsecondary Students in the Digital Information Age." *The New Digital Scholar: Exploring and Enriching the Research and Writing Practices of Next-Gen Students*, edited by Randall McClure and James P. Purdy. Information Today, Inc., 2013, pp. 51–72.

—. "Why Rhetoric and Composition Must Become Computers and Writing: A (Re)Visionary Statement." Annual Meeting of the Great Plains Alliance for Computers and Writing, April 2005, Minnesota State University, Mankato.

Miller-Cochran, Susan K., and Rochelle L. Rodrigo. "Determining Effective Distance Learning Designs through Usability Testing." *Computers and Composition*, vol. 23, no. 1, 2006, pp. 91–107.

National Writing Project, et al. *Because Digital Writing Matters: Improving Student Writing in Online and Multimedia Environments*. Jossey-Bass, 2010.

NCTE Definition of 21*st* Century Literacies. National Council of Teachers of English (NCTE), February 2013, www.ncte.org/positions/statements/21stcentdefinition.

"New Database of Scholarly Web Sites." Modern Language Association, 12 May 2011, https://www.mla.org/news_from_mla/news_summary.

Nicholas, David, et al. "The Google Generation: The Information Behaviour of the Researcher of the Future." *Aslib Proceedings*, vol. 6, no. 4, 2008, pp. 290–310.

Peterson, Patricia Webb. "The Debate about Online Learning: Key Issues for Writing Teachers." *Computers and Composition*, vol. 18, no. 4, 2001, pp. 359–70.

Peterson, Patricia Webb, and Wilhelmina C. Savenye, editors. *Distance Education: Promises and Perils of Teaching Writing Online*. Special issue of *Computers and Composition*, vol. 18, no. 4, 2001, pp. 319–430.

Purdy, James P. "The Changing Space of Research: Web 2.0 and the Integration of Research and Writing Environments." *Composition 2.0*. Special issue of *Computers and Composition*, vol. 27, no. 1, 2010, pp. 48–58.

—. "Scholarliness as Other: How Students Explain Their Research-Writing Behaviors." *The New Digital Scholar: Exploring and Enriching the Research and Writing Practices of NextGen Students*, edited by Randall McClure and James P. Purdy, Information Today, Inc., 2013, pp. 133–59.

Purdy, James P., and Dànielle Nicole DeVoss, editors. *Making Space: Writing Instruction, Infrastructure, and Multiliteracies*. Sweetland Digital Rhetoric Collaborative and University of Michigan Press, 2016, www.digitalrhetoric-collaborative.org/makingspace.

Reinheimer, David A. "Teaching Composition Online: Whose Side Is Time On?" *Computers and Composition*, vol. 22, no. 4, 2005, pp. 459–70.

Report of the MLA Task Force on Evaluating Scholarship for Tenure and Promotion. *Profession*, 2007, pp. 9–71.

Samuels, Robert. "The Future Threat to Computers and Composition: Non-tenured Instructors, Intellectual Property, and Distance Education." *Computers and Composition*, vol. 21, no. 1, 2004, pp. 63–71.

Sapp, David Alan, and James Simon. "Comparing Grades in Online and Face-to-Face Writing Courses: Interpersonal Accountability and Institutional Commitment." *Computers and Composition*, vol. 22, no. 4, 2005, pp. 471–89.

Savenye, Wilhelmina C., et al. "So You Are Going to Be an Online Writing Instructor: Issues in Designing, Developing, and Delivering an Online Course." *Computers and Composition*, vol. 18, no. 4, 2001, pp. 371–85.

Selfe, Richard J. *Sustainable Computer Environments: Cultures of Support in English Studies and Language Arts*. Hampton Press, 2004.

Warnock, Scott. *Teaching Writing Online: How and Why*. National Council of Teachers of English, 2009.

WPA Outcomes Statement for First-Year Composition. Version 3.0. Council of Writing Program Administrators, July 2014, wpacouncil.org/positions/outcomes.html.

—.. Version 2.0. Council of Writing Program Administrators, 2008, wpacouncil.org/positions/outcomes.html.

Writing in Digital Environments Research Center Collective (WIDE). "Why Teach Digital Writing?" *Kairos: A Journal of Rhetoric, Technology, and Pedagogy*, vol. 10, no. 1, 2005, english.ttu.edu/kairos/10.1/binder2.html?coverweb/wide/index.html.

Xu, Di, and Shanna Smith Jaggars. "Online and Hybrid Course Enrollment and Performance in Washington State Community and Technical Colleges." *CCRC Working Paper No. 31*. Community College Research Center, Teachers College, Columbia University, 2011, ccrc.tc.columbia.edu/media/k2/attachments/online-hybrid-performance-washington.pdf.

14 Out of Print: Revising the *Statement* for More Inclusive Storytelling

Joseph Janangelo

> 1. Recension: *A critical revision of a text incorporating the most plausible elements found in varying sources.*
> 2. *A text so revised.*
>
> —The Free Dictionary.com

INTRODUCTION

This chapter suggests ways that the *Statement of Principles and Standards for the Postsecondary Teaching of Writing* (hereafter the *Statement*) can be rhetorically reimagined for effective online delivery and circulation. I suggest crafting a revision that is less polished and declarative than the current *Statement*, and composing one that reveals the text's key streams of input and evolving composition history. Such a revision would involve rhetorical reconceptualization. It would include detailed storytelling about how the *Statement* was recrafted and how ideas concerning content were debated, accepted, revised, or discarded. These revelations would, in turn, make the text more transparent to readers and more responsive to their situated institutional contexts, intellectual queries, and evolving professional needs. Such a revision would also move the text from one that is best suited to hard-copy presentation to one that performs optimally and dialogically in digital and online forums. To argue for redesigning the *Statement* in ways that would make it revelatory of its own production history, I draw on ideas from textual criticism, particularly concepts of clear and inclusive text practices. I then suggest how these concepts might help the *Statement* receive and sustain a more inclusive, if vulnerable, rhetorical redesign.

To sketch the contours of this project, I offer an argument composed as a triptych. One "panel" discusses clear text practices as an assumed best practice. Another panel reviews inclusive text practices as a critique of that assumption. The central panel, then, does not seek to champion or castigate either strategy. Rather, it keeps both arguments in play while outlining the necessarily limited value of each approach. In describing the vulnerabilities and strengths of both positions, I try to explain what is lost—and envision what might be gained—as we endeavor to imagine and achieve a reborn digital *Statement* that would serve more, if not all, of us well.

The Sway of Clear Text

Textual critics have historically concerned themselves with issues of recension and redaction. Some of their work involves restoring texts' lost passages; comparing extant versions to discern their contributions to meaning; dating and distinguishing sources for accuracy; locating streams of manuscript input; reconciling inconsistencies among drafts and manuscripts; examining textual creation, distribution, revision, and circulation; and revising and editing manuscripts in order to present correct and definitive editions of the material. Simply put, these scholars sought (and sometimes still seek) to publish texts in accurate and definitive ways. Textual critics call these publications "clear text" editions. As defined by David Greetham in *The Pleasures of Contamination: Evidence, Text, and Voice in Textual Studies*, "a *clear text* is one in which all signs of editorial intervention have been removed, and the apparatus of variants and editorial emendations is available only in a separate tabulation" (247).

Not surprisingly, these methods have often been applied to important literary texts and other long-term texts of distinction, such as religious scripture. Simply put, textual critics tend to work with and on texts that count for a great deal in their given communities. It thus makes sense that a central goal of textual studies has been to establish the clearest and most stable version of the text possible, thus "securing" (Eggert) its future and legacy by ensuring that it is presented and circulated free of inconsistencies, errors, and digressive commentary. For many textual critics, clear text practices became a strategy of choice. That strategy, in turn, became standard practice and eventually a tacit "gold standard" among many influential editors and redactors.

Recently, that popular and vaunted practice has received articulate critique and attack. Greetham characterizes clear text practice in terms of nostalgia. He remembers, not particularly fondly, that "[d]uring the great period of positivist, definitive editing [. . .] editors could take a proprietary responsibility for and delight in the 'clear text,' unsullied, newly pristine text pages of multivolume editions of the great canonical authors, while burying any possible evidence for unweaving discreetly and discretely in the back of the book" (*Pleasures* 247). That once popular strategy of discretion, which presented immaculate and inviolate texts, reflected discernible ambitions, intentions, and power moves as editors controlled how much and which version of the work readers could see.

Mindful of this concern, I see a certain rhetorical fit between clear text practice and works of public discourse such the *Statement*. Let's reflect back on Greetham's critique. He criticizes "clear-text idealism," arguing that it "may be seen as a manifestation of the 'well-wrought urn' of the culturally isolated and artistically self-referential modes of Russian Formalism and Anglo-American New Criticism" (*Pleasures* 255). This association may sound damning, but in crafting public discourse—where clear, prescriptive discourse and memorable sound bites hold sway—I detect a value that may be *of* value.

I see clear text as clean text; I also see it as easy-to-read text. These features can offer considerable utility to those who compose public discourse. For example, following clear text practices can help create a unified, standardized, and stable text. That strategy can add strength when the text covers issues in which readers are heavily invested. It may also undergird the rhetorical force of prescriptive texts. Let's consider policy statements like the *National HIV/AIDS Strategy*[1] as a model for texts that merit clear text treatment. I argue for a parallel—that in some ways public texts like the *Statement* are of comparable cultural consequence

---

1. Policy statements like the *National HIV/AIDS Strategy* tend to be directive. Consider the language of the following "Action Steps": Increasing Access to Care and Improving Health Outcomes for People Living with HIV

- Establish a seamless system to immediately link people to continuous and coordinated quality care when they learn they are infected with HIV.
- Take deliberate steps to increase the number and diversity of available providers of clinical care and related services for people living with HIV.
- Support people living with HIV with co-occurring health conditions and those who have challenges meeting their basic needs, such as housing.

and import. They have similar work to do in that they point to meritorious examples that could and should guide responsible behavior.

In Composition Studies, our best practice and policy statements are inherently advisory and prescriptive. Consider the *Statement*'s comment about graduate student labor:

> Graduate students' teaching experience should be understood as an essential part of their training for future professional responsibilities. They are primarily students and should never, for mere economic expediency, be used to replace tenure-line faculty in the staffing of composition programs. Graduate students' teaching loads should not interfere with their progress toward their degrees: an average of one course per term is ideal; more than two courses per term is unreasonable. (332)

Serving as the defining word ascribed to a committee of fair-minded experts, these capacious miniatures trumpet intellectual guidelines and professional practice in relatively clean and clear terms. Clear text presentation suits prescriptive rhetorical projects. Such projects may become more forceful and effective as representatives of professional organizations (e.g., the Conference on College Composition and Communication [CCCC] and the Council of Writing Program Administrators [CWPA] speak in a collective voice to craft professional statements that present ideas in a united front. Furthermore, ideas that are presented in smooth and polished prose often appear to reflect careful and considered thinking. The seamless look of clear texts sustains an ambience of agreement, without distracting backstory or discordant backchannel ideas and conversations. Such presentation moves things strictly forward by displaying tempered best thinking largely uninflected by compelling data or input that might undermine the text's central concept, purpose, or argument.

While there is certainly something restrictive about clear text practices, there is also something protective as well. By protective, I mean that clear texts offer guarded disclosure; they are generally "on point" and minimally framed. Most policy documents, best practices, and outcomes statements, for example, tend to offer a brief word from their creators and sponsors. Then the text is generally published without too many debatable or distracting sidebars or embellishments, and any embellishments that do appear are deployed with restraint. That streamlined presentation suggests "that an edition is the more decorous if its scholarly pudenda have been kept out of sight" (Greetham, *Pleasures* 34). Where there is streamlined presentation and textual clarity, there is at least the appearance of intellectual and ethical certainty, and intellectual accord.[2] Yet this familiar practice, despite its long history and for all its adherents, has recently received extended scrutiny and critique, something I discuss in the next section.

The Way of Inclusive Text

The practice of creating clear text editions has fallen under articulate critique. While some textual scholars admire the streamlined effects of clear text presentation, others argue that it is predicated on pretense and prevarication. For example, in *From Gutenberg to Google: Electronic Representations of Literary Texts*, Peter L. Shillingsburg critiques one of the alleged benefits of clear text—that it offers us a streamlined reading experience. Of this, Shillingsburg writes,

> A scholarly edition that puts all its editorial and historical apparatus at the back, keyed to page and line number in the text is said to be a 'clear text' edition because it does not interrupt the reader with note numbers or intrude with footnotes on the text page. This clarity of presentation suggests by its form—its body language—that the text has been 'established' and the reader need not access the record of alternative forms except perhaps as a curiosity or to verify the editor's work. Editions with at least some apparatus on the text page seem to declare by their form that they are editions of the work, rather than the work itself. (18)

Yet what if some readers feel a need to access that information? Clear text leaves them little choice; the best they can do is follow some links that may or may not be there or may fail to lead them someplace useful (Pemberton). So while clear text practices have (largely had) their admirers, their practitioners now garner cutting criticism. For example, Greetham

---

[2]. In addition to undermining consensus, offering readers a substantial amount of material poses further challenges: "We can see this if we reflect on two dangers, recognized very early, that threaten digital textspace: the interface may become a confusion of options for the user; and the user may get lost in navigating the looped and linked network of materials" (McGann 279).

suggests that the act of presenting clear text can be understood as a strategy predicated on deception and containment. He notes that the

> pristine transparency of those clear-text editions—in which the text itself asserts its logistic and phenomenological superiority over the record of variance embedded in the deliberately invisible, or occluded, apparatus—sought to render culturally impotent the margins of discourse, whether bibliographic or political, and to separate the Platonized *textus* of the 'text that never was' from the accreted social detritus that too often accompanied the text proper in this fallen world. (*Pleasures* 277)

Greetham evinces little nostalgia for the custodial practices of editors and other redactors who polished texts by ridding them of their embedded variance and withholding vital, potentially incendiary information and material from readers. Instead, he proffers practices that ask editors to be less controlling, less intent on crafting immaculate master texts that offer obscured (e.g., end notes) traces of textual input and revision. The world Greetham describes posits editors who admit, without feeling pressured to do so, "that texts are variable and can always also be otherwise" (Gabler 95). It also posits readers who are curious about texts' histories, variants, and versions and who don't sustain the belief that published policy statements are without contested input or excised data. Such readers (e.g., CCCC members and other individuals who access policy statements online) may be wary of the genre's traditional focal elements and moves. They may welcome inclusive text practices that invite them to see and study previously unavailable document histories, drafts, and versions that may answer their questions and fuel new ones.

The idea of increasing readers' access to draft material helps Greetham explain the value of inclusive text, a discourse that is "contaminated" because it flaunts the text's apparatus by making it easily accessible and productively intrusive. He praises invaded, embellished, and "'mixed' discourse" (*Pleasures* 2) because it lets the seams of the argument show. Readers see final decisions (e.g., the "finished copy") as well as points of selection, disagreement, and perhaps lingering dissonance. We might recognize this inclusive text approach from DVD culture where directors and other contributors include telling bonus features such as alternate takes and extended scenes, outtakes, auditions, and voice-over commentary that explains mutated or rejected draft material or other creative concepts.

Inclusive text provides readers with detailed information about textual history and revision, thus offering more detailed storytelling than clear text. The inclusive text approach fuels viewers' thirst for information (Lanham); it also undermines the text's authority by making it more "unfinished" (Lunenfeld). Shillingsburg explains how inclusive text promotes candor and visibility: "It would present each [text] in multiple facsimiles of manuscript and printed historical forms and provide as supporting materials a range of the 'things that went without saying' for most contemporary readers but which no longer go without saying with most students." He adds that "the idea would be that students could use such information to help them to imagine the empowering meaning-generating 'not-saids'" (7). More than that, inclusive text lets readers see what was once written and then criticized or excised from a work or document. Inclusive text presentation allows these words and ideas to remain legible and in place and play. An inclusive text approach thus offers increased transparency that yields storied windows into processes of creation and revision that are often hidden from readers of professional best practice and policy statements.

Digital Design and Inclusive Storytelling

Deciding to tell and share more of the story is in league with practices of online textual design and delivery. Some might view this move as the work of "reshaping historic texts for a new market" (Greetham, *Pleasures* 71). I regard it as a both a marketing and rhetorical tool, one that helps us deliver messages effectively in online forums. As I see it, the *Statement* is very much an artifact of print-based design that is best suited to hard-copy presentation and dissemination. I am suggesting, therefore, ways that contemporary authors might make deep use of the rhetorical affordances and design aesthetics (Gibson) of online discourse so that the *Statement* (if they wish to preserve that term) can be rhetorically reimagined and revitalized for optimal online delivery and circulation.

Moving purposefully from print to digital practice could involve deliberately designing the *Statement* for its Web appearance. This would mean using design elements that give insight into the text's backstory and reveal streams of interests and input. Salient design elements might include a frequently asked questions page, and links to drafts, data, and definitions along with comments and revisions from task force members. The *Statement* might also offer drop-down menus that would offer testimony, strategies, and advice, perhaps in video form and designed for online audiences (McClure and Goldstein), for making the findings and advice more responsive to various institutional contexts. The drop-down menus would help the text's descriptions and advice become more inclusive and situated, if less centered.

By moving from "*paginal* space" (Kaufmann 41) to screen space, the new *Statement* could first become the newest and then the newer iteration as its designers seek and incorporate input from various situated users. The text could potentially in turn become more responsive to (among others) two-year college faculty, graduate students doing WPA work, and writing center directors who could bring their situated experiences, advice, and needs into conversation with what is now a rather prescriptive statement that inveighs a "one size fits all" approach to an understandably (remember the *Statement* was published in 1989) proliferating range of programmatic and institutional practices.

Designing the statement for online presentation could result in expanded presentational options that provocatively discomfit and transcend the affordances of streamlined print appearance. I describe the complications of such moves later in this essay, but now I discuss the positive changes such moves might bring. Unfettered by "closed surfaces" (Gibson 135) and working within the four corners of the printed page, authors could push the *Statement* beyond its current clear text capacities. For example, authors and compositors might also offer other windows into the recension process including drafts with extant track changes and paratextual (Genette) evidence of intellectual input, collaboration, and due diligence such as a copy of the committee charge as well as email and committee listserv exchanges that may show points of consensus, investment, and disagreement. Designed for multimodal presentation and viral circulation, the *Statement* might also offer annotations and a running commentary of its production notes and history. Such a text might well include images and sounds, excerpts from committee meetings, focus groups, and conference presentations that fueled the formal composition.

Several textual critics have noticed the growing interest in texts' backstories and compositional histories.[3] Neil Fraistat and Julia Flanders recognize "broader effects in the growing interest in collaborative editing environments." They note that "[a]nother newly emerging paradigm in the era of electronic editing is the practice of treating editorial debate (whether with oneself or with other editors) as something that can itself be formalized and incorporated into the edition's data." Fraistat and Flanders explain that "the use of text markup (for instance, the TEI Guidelines) to create electronic editions makes it possible to represent the editorial work itself—decisions, uncertainties, forms of evidence, alternative possibilities and viewpoints—in a comprehensive way as part of the formal data of the edition." They add that "[a]s a result, [the data] can be incorporated into the edition's interface and made visible to the reader: for instance, revealing passages about which there is significant debate, or decisions for which the evidence is contested." That "increased transparency" (13) offers readers a more inclusive picture of the text's and authors' journey by including scenes of "inscription, graphic representation, transmission, error/variant, authenticity, [and] reception" at least by committee members, focus groups, and sponsoring institutions such as CCCC (Greetham, "History" 17). That detailed rendering suggests that "a far denser web of history [than initially suspected or apparent on the clear text page] informs every action and every artifact" (Sutherland 45).

What I am suggesting is more invasive than the minimal framing (e.g., front matter and end matter) that professional statements usually offer and receive. This approach would make the *Statement* less polished and more porous. The *Statement* would become less clean and more candid and revelatory of debate, trial, use, reception, input, contributions, and critique. The text would likely become more communicative because we would see more of the insights, discussions, and decision-making that informed and that did not make it into the definitive revision. These changes are potentially viral because they would course and teem in and throughout the text. They are also viral in that they may serve to

---

3. In "A History of Textual Scholarship," Greetham suggests that disclosing moments of inscription and revision creates as sense of "text as history" (17) of recension rather than timeless artifact. Matthew G. Kirschenbaum and Doug Reside describe a market for such information and ask, "What scholar of American letters would not want to read Walt Whitman's MySpace page, if such a thing existed?" (260) Discussing the archival material of *RENT*, they also suggest that "a bit of trivia" (267) can portend "the future of cultural heritage" (262).

contaminate the *Statement*'s inviolate appearance and authority. I realize this approach may well put public texts, especially position statements, at important and lingering risks. I discuss these risks in the next section.

Salient Risks of Abandoning Clear Text Practices

Inclusive text has its merits, and the idea of creating more porous and revelatory texts sounds both desirable and contemporary. Furthermore, presenting a record of textual input and modifications and letting readers see what went into as well as what did not make it into the text's final cut sounds democratic, and such a method of composing comports with the transparency afforded by online communication. Design overhaul introduces new variables and complications, though. Participating in inclusive text practices would move us from discretion to disclosure. Readers could see who did, said, or changed what and why.[4] They could trace and question a text's gestations and incubations. Putting texts at risk to reveal untold moments of input also sounds like inclusion. It reflects the glamorous aspects of the contamination metaphor. Who wants pristine and declamatory text when inclusive text is far more transparent and candid?

---

4. Such efforts are already in play when composing and revising digital texts. Consider Wikipedia's explanation of its page history function:

> A page history shows the order in which changes were made to any editable Wikipedia page, the difference between any two versions, and a menu of special external tools. A page history is sometimes called revision history or edit history. It is accessed by clicking the "View history" tab at the top of the page.
>
> The page history contains a list of the page's previous revisions, including the date and time (in UTC) of each edit, the username or IP address of the user who made it, and their edit summary. For example, the page history for this help page shows that it was first created on September 20, 2004, and that it had been changed more than 500 times during the last ten years. ("Help:Page history")

While I am not envisioning the *Statement*'s iterations occurring as often as Wikipedia page revisions sometimes do, Wikipedia models public text's ongoing inscription. Furthermore, readers can see older versions and mine them for their specific purposes. That, in turn, supports the idea that "The ways in which form can attest to politics suggests that 'old' and 'inadequate' editions may have important stories to tell as witnesses to histories of power relations" (Warren 125–26).

Here I see a conundrum: If inclusive text is candid text, then it is also vulnerable text. As a genre, best practice and policy statements have important rhetorical work to do. They trumpet the way things should be in clear ways. Dissonance and disagreement are largely muted and relegated to the use of quick qualifiers such as "sometimes" and "exceptions." Consider these examples from the *Statement*:

- "Whenever possible, faculty professionally committed to rhetoric and composition should coordinate and supervise composition programs" (331).
- "The commitment to quality education requires that the number of part-time writing teachers in the second category be kept to a minimum. We recognize, however, that at the present time many administrators and department chairs have become dependent on part-time faculty lines" (331).
- "Whenever possible, part-time instructors should be hired as much in advance of their teaching assignments as possible" (333–34).

One might argue that these streamlined texts work because they to speak simply and strategically.[5] These qualities reflect the aforementioned utility of using collective voice and projecting accord. These carefully crafted texts are often tasked with reflecting unity and providing direction. Their contributors are asked to take a team approach; they must produce encapsulated, concentrated, focused texts that can stand up for colleagues in need of guidance and/or help.

Since best practice and policy statements are tacitly required to stand for a discipline and speak for a profession in united and predicative ways, a clear text approach may serve a mandate and need. Furthermore, people who judge colleagues or whose work is valued according to terms described in these statements (e.g., the CWPA statement on *Evaluat-*

---

5. See "On Strategizing" (129–32) in Charlton and colleagues' *GenAdmin: Theorizing WPA Identities in the Twenty-First Century* for a nuanced discussion of the philosophical complications of speaking strategically to advance one's program and administrative credibility. The authors describe a WPA who "finds success by tapping into her skills as a rhetorician," and write that "By being strategic, by carefully considering her audience and framing her argument to reach that audience, the strategic WPA is one who plans, manages, and controls her discourse with colleagues in a measured, intentional way" (129). The authors deftly question the value of that once prized scenario where the WPA is the clearest, most persuasive expert in the room. They critique that approach to conversation by asking "But what if 'winning' isn't the goal?" (131).

ing the Intellectual Work of Writing Administration) may well need these texts to be direct and prescriptive. Using a bit of declaration and consensus—creating texts that team with solidarity instead of teeming with dissonance—may serve the project of outlining possibilities, drawing lines (e.g., about exploitive labor practices, as Randall McClure and colleagues do in this volume) and suggesting viable ideas and paths that can and should be followed by intellects of informed professional practice and generous collegiality.

Important design renovations, especially conceptual ones, may introduce new variables and ongoing complications. For one thing, some readers may see inclusive text, with its emphasis on substantial disclosure, as obtrusive and overwrought. The perception of too much embellishment (even in terms of links) can clutter texts, especially ones that have historically profited from being sleek and lean. Indulging in textual abundance might actually vitiate the *Statement*'s rhetorical power. While some readers may call clear text policy statements too grand and directive, others may deem inclusive iterations too granular and distracting to do the leadership work of describing and defending specific action plans.[6] Greetham speaks to the perception of overkill: "By contaminating my text with the exorbitance of the annotation, I have both subjugated it and yet allowed it to participate—as provocateur, as conspirator, as addressee—with a circle of rhetoric that, while it may never hope to be pre-hermeneutic or foundational, may form a sort of ground for more

---

6. This moment of potential and indecision leads some textual scholars to evince suspicion about what works best. Kathryn Sutherland argues that "we put faith in what has been called screen essentialism—an uncritical endorsement of the computer's power to reproduce the real, uncompromised and undistorted by its own materiality" (55). Yet Sutherland does not pine for clear text practices. Instead, she suggests that "Both ways of thinking need to be recognized for their timeliness rather than their essential truth; both are responses to the burden of media consciousness, informed by new technologies, by which the materiality of our traditional literary culture (the functions of type, paper, format, book structures etc.) comes into sharper focus" (55–56). Other critics express nuanced celebration. For example, Kirschenbaum and Reside find the relative incipience of digital textuality appealing, noting "We look forward to textual scholarship's embrace of this moment when the material foundations of the field are so completely in flux, even as practitioners equip themselves with the knowledge and training necessary to carry their discipline forward into the new century" (273). Hans Walter Gabler also perceives "a fresh conceptual departure" where "[. . .] gains are most likely to be secured through intense debate between orthodox attitudes and new beginnings" (95).

exorbitance" (*Pleasures* 55). In terms of the *Statement*, a plethora of annotation could potentially redirect readers' attention from the document's once central point (its message about principles and standards) to the story of how the committee conducted its work.

The point about exorbitance is well-taken. It makes me wonder if texts can become too telling and revelatory. For example, spotlighting internal processes and debates may undermine a text's coherence (e.g., by presenting many possibilities and differences of opinion) and may diminish the *Statement*'s reputation as being a definitive or even authoritative "go to" document that reflects the sought-after professional best thinking. Worse than indecorous, revealing extensive backstory and conversation can resemble indecision and indiscretion (Lamos).[7] That, in turn, can undermine professional statements' authority and utility when they are seen as eliding their mandate of providing clear directions and specific action plans.

I also wonder about how much candor and transparency is productive. My thought is that extensive revelation of what was/not discussed, who abstained, and any pronounced disagreements or stalemates might catalyze some readers, leading them to focus on *who* said, supported, or criticized what rather than on the ideas themselves. Ethically, this raises problems if such exchanges were conducted with the expectation of privacy or confidentiality. Some participants may not want all of their discussion points made public. That leads to further complications. Once readers can source ideas and input, might they tend to prioritize or devalue it according to their perceptions and judgments of the speaker? Would the focus on identity work to further undermine inclusion and diversity?

Moreover, I suspect that transparency can become a powerful breeding ground for textual dissonance. Remember the assertion Mary Douglas repeats in *Purity and Danger: An Analysis of the Concepts of Pollution and Taboo* that "dirt is matter out of place" (35). The problem here is that inclusive text could put "the dirt" of who said or voted for what on prominent display. Matter out of place would soon become matter very prominently placed. There would be little relegated to behind-the-scenes

---

7. For John D. Niles, discretion is a key concern. Writing about oral textual scholarship, he raises questions about quality and privacy. Niles contends that "the technical quality of some archival recordings is so wretched as to render them almost unusable." He adds, "Moreover, some audio recordings contain sensitive personal materials that, from an ethical perspective, ought not to be made available indiscriminately" (221–22).

status. Such public sharing and spillage, with its emphasis on protracted backstory, might disrupt the genre's clean, action-oriented purpose and distract and potentially detract from the once central point, which is now made peripheral, or at least relational, to other textual material.

Finally, would the plot of the recension subsume interest in the *Statement* itself and undermine its intended impact? Sharing details of inscription and mutation may yield a less guarded text that fuels readers' thirst for information. It may make the text more vulnerable as readers engage in auguries, wondering aloud (e.g., on listservs and professional Facebook groups) about the value of or bias toward what was inserted, dislodged, amended, or appended. That information would likely inspire more conversation and debate; it could also expose controversial editing decisions that reflect the composers' use of due process or lack thereof. Could candor then comprise the working process? By that I mean would all contributors speak freely and creatively if they knew that their input would be memorialized and circulated? Or would they work even more assiduously and responsibly?

If the inclusive text approach advocated here represents an example of democracy in action, that ambitious project is not without its complications and compelling counterarguments. Such arguments cause me to wonder how and when inclusive text strategies are optimal and for whom. In the lives of public documents, what was once "done" persuasively and perhaps definitively may be dramatically undone and rendered nugatory by the public revelation of drafts, draft information, "sidebar" and truncated discussions, and dissonant or devalued data. My point is that whatever is visible and accessible is also available for scrutiny and criticism.

Discerning Return on Investment

Having outlined some complications of undermining clear text's dominion over best practice and policy statements, I wish to counter my own arguments. What might our professional organizations gain by making integral use of online rhetorical affordances and risking the potential candor and vulnerability that digital textuality offers? How might we, as a community of colleagues, envision integral online design as offering valuable return on investment? I can think of two ways.

1. Redesigning the Statement *for online presentation would help professional organizations increase credibility and community with readers by evincing transparency and collegiality.*

Clear text practices allegedly add value by promoting a smooth and uncluttered reading experience. In terms of literary works, they represent the authoritative version of the text. In the case of policy statements, they serve readers' professional needs by offering the best thinking on the topic in streamlined presentation. Discussing the goal and strategy of keeping things simple and clear, Greetham writes that "one might object that this is no more or less than textual critics have been claiming for a century and more: that their labors were to allow the text 'to speak for itself'" (*Pleasures* 35).

I contend that this method works because we have been conditioned to read these professional statements as finished and authoritative documents, ones that brook little criticism due to their designers' expertise, extensive vetting by executive committees, and the official imprimatur of our professional organizations. We expect this genre to be clear and authoritative. Its declarative nature serves as a marker of quality and unity of thought. Yet, some textual scholars challenge their predecessor's clear text practices, deriding them as controlling and attributing that strategy to "a pernicious desire to do good" (Willis 3). Discerning a power play where readers are only allowed to see the final text but not its versions or drafts, they help us to understand that clear text's strength of method is predicated on overplayed acts of discretion and effacement. That method can, in turn, sustain at least two important deceptions.

The first deception is that the published version of a text represents complete unity on the part of its authors and sponsoring organizations. Textual scholars often focus on drafts and versions; they have serious interest in material (e.g., words, passages, ideas) that was once in the text, but is no longer visible or present. When Williams William Proctor and Craig S. Abbott ask "[w]hat does the book contain?" (39), they refer to extant and excised source material as well as histories and circumstances of textual inscription, transmission, redaction, and dissemination. Analyzing textual fragments and comparing drafts leads them to ask "[w]hat is known, from bibliographical analysis and other sources, about the printing and publishing of the book, its variant states, and the irregularities of particular copies?" (39)

This inquiry into access to drafts and other excised or revised material pertains to position statements because clear text strategies place readers on a need-to-know basis in terms of information about textual history, a document's source material, its streams of input, and the decision-making that yielded the final version. Simply put, authors, editors, and redactors often deny readers access to text that didn't make it into the final cut. If we believe that our colleagues (the professionals who will use these documents to improve their own and others' pedagogical practices and working lives) deserve to see that material, we might be glad that the rhetorical affordances of digital discourse can make that happen. Along with the finished *Statement*, our organizations could make available evidence of committees and editors at work. That could include email exchanges, minutes from meetings, videotaped committee conversations, narratives of composition, records of abandoned ideas and approaches, as well as other edits and excisions.

Using online affordances to release and circulate this material would undermine the suppressive aspects of clear text in the service of extending collegiality to readers. Sharing textual versions and variant texts would constitute an act of trust that builds community and credibility. Inviting readers to review the *Statement*'s input streams would send a message that sponsoring organizations see readers as colleagues who both need and deserve to know how these texts were conceptualized, drafted, debated, and revised. Think of the goodwill and ethos-building that act could encourage among readers who are National Council of Teachers of English members. Such sharing could well engender questions and conversation as well as intense and ongoing scrutiny and critique, as readers may focus on who said what and what went on behind the once closed doors of committee meetings and conversations. At the very least, such revelations would signify a deliberate and risky departure from business as usual. Whatever the risks (e.g., fomenting partisanship and driving attention to backstory and histories of textual composition rather than the unified on-point messaging this genre has hitherto sustained), such openness could potentially help our professional organizations accrue increased integrity. If readers could see how committees came to frame arguments, debate insights, and make decisions, might we not have even more trust in them, their due diligence, and responsible service to our profession?

The second deception is that policy statements reflect unilateral consensus on the part of their authors. On that note, detractors of clear text may reasonably argue that it portrays excessive agreement among community members. Skeptics may ask the following questions: Was there no or so little counterevidence or disagreement in the committee's deliberations and findings? What considerations and concessions occurred between the original committee charge and the vetted public version? How did the committee devise and negotiate its conceptual approach? Were there any catalytic moments of input, critique, or revision? Was there any data that did not comport with the committee's ultimate assertions? What happened to that data and [when] will it be available for public scrutiny?

By making a commitment to disclosure and visibility and evincing a willingness to put detailed information and even committee "dirt" on public display, our professional organizations could use online design to revise and release position statements candidly and with transparency. Whereas clear text practices assert a unilateral and perhaps dubious accord, inclusive text practices could serve as markers of due diligence and nuanced thinking. Refusing to suppress troubling data or arguments could potentially enhance these texts' credibility with persuaded readers and detractors. It could show that our committees and organizations work without ruse and deception. It could also show that we share our source material and disagreements in the project of working thoughtfully, ethically, publicly and responsibly.

2. Just as transparency would support collegiality and credibility by positioning readers as stakeholders in an openly collaborative process, sharing the Statement's draft material and textual versions would be a constructive act that fuels readers' future projects and work.

The CCCC homepage helps us "Find a Position Statement." The wording is apt. Given its static PDF presentation, the most one can do is locate and read these texts as they are. Thinking about the *Statement* and discussing it must occur off-site. Revising the *Statement* for online presentation could constructively render the text less immaculate and inviolate. By giving readers access to extant, excised material, perhaps through links or menus, the revised *Statement* could represent both the public text and its archive.

Not surprisingly, some scholars find such repositories to be of tremendous value, arguing that "narratives of textual history, variation, adaptation and appropriation would provide other kinds of guidance to the interpretive richness of the archive" (Shillingsburg 78–79). In researching print-based texts, readers who seek more information can always try consulting an archive. Yet access is often granted under specific conditions and rules. Even digital archives may appear on password-protected sites. Online design could constructively change that. By displaying both the text and its archive, perhaps with portals where committee members articulate and explain their choices, the revised *Statement* could circulate material that readers could use to address their curiosity and fuel their own projects. By relinquishing static online presentation and restricted access, the revised *Statement* (and writ larger, its genre) might portend a more porous design scape, one that has much to tell and little to hide. Both textual passages and individual words could appear *sous rature*, "under erasure," yet still present and legible. Increasing legibility and offering access to once restricted material would constitute generous, collegial, and perhaps inspirational acts of risk and trust on the part of our professional organizations.

Offering access to previously unavailable material would configure readers as welcome stakeholders in an invitational and participatory project of reading position statements, appreciating and critiquing their insights, and moving their ideas forward in diverse and unpredictable ways. By serving readers' hunger for information, authors would render visible their source material and rhetorical decisions so that readers could ask questions, contest and contribute perspectives, and engage, re-mine, and redeploy that data in future projects. By evincing an openness that beckons and supports scrutiny, use, and revision, the revised *Statement* would become both reflective and anticipatory. It would represent a forward-looking archive that would show what happened in committee in order to fuel ongoing iterations and work.[8] Readers would no longer just "Find a Position Statement" and surmise the thought that went into

---

8. Some critics characterize textual plenitude as inherently democratic. Michael G. Sargent writes that "[l]ike a manuscript, an electronic edition can present a heteroglossic text: but where the textual polyglossia of manuscripts lies in the fact that each speaks the text with a different voice, an electronic edition can present all of these voices simultaneously" (234). Yet the presence of archival material does not guarantee change. As Roger Chartier and Peter Stallybrass conclude, "The question that remains is whether the proliferating materials that are now brought together and made available through electronic archives will be used to recreate the platonic ideal of the authorial book or to explore the multiple human agencies and material forms that have shaped the literary text and will continue to reshape it in new and unforeseeable ways" (202). For provocative discussions of the stakes and responsibilities of stewarding and curating digital archives, see Kirschenbaum's "Electronic Literature as Cultural Heritage (Confessions of an Incunk)" and Reside's "What is a Digital Curator?"

it. These online texts would offer increased return on investment by acknowledging the investments of their committee members and sponsoring organizations (perhaps by including drafts of the authors' official charge) and inspiring readers to go forward with that material in their own invested (e.g., laudatory, critical, and imaginative) ways. Made more credible and accessible by the rhetorical affordances of online design, the revised *Statement* would likely become less authoritative because what was "done" in committee could be undone by the revelation of drafts, and redone by readers/writers who may use the finished text and its public archive as draft material for ongoing projects of assessment, replication, and contestation. I find that idea both risky and valuable, something I discuss in the conclusion.

Conclusion: Discerning Integrity

Fraistat and Flanders describe integrity eloquently, contending that "What is at stake here is an increased transparency and an interest in what we might almost term 'negative capability': a desire to treat the edition not as a final resolved statement but as a field of intelligently structured possibility, whether the edition is produced in print or electronically" (13). Regarding the *Statement*'s potential digital redesign, I still see value in nurturing inclusive storytelling and believe that the project of pursuing transparency is worth the potential dissonance and complexity we may experience. There is no doubt that creating inclusive text can be invasive and risky, but it can also be incendiary and fueling.[9] A starting point for envisioning and preparing the *Statement* for online circulation might be to examine the web presence of the *Common Core State Standards Initiative* (Council of Chief State School Officers and the

---

9. Michael A. Pemberton offers a nuanced account of the ethical and professional complications of defining and securing textual integrity once a work has been published. He persuasively charts the dilemma's contours:

> An important ethical question for journal editors, then, is whether their desire to help researchers locate scholarly references as quickly and efficiently as possible outweighs their desire to protect and maintain the integrity of original source documents. In other words, do they see reference lists as *tools* whose value depends on accuracy and currency, or do they regard them as *historical artifacts* whose value depends on stability and integrity? The same question might be legitimately applied, as I suggested earlier, to the full corpus of any scholarly article: Does it achieve the greatest value through ongoing modification or perpetual stasis?

National Governors Assocation). Despite the claims of some of the *Initiative*'s opponents to the contrary, the document uses an inclusive text approach (though in a minor key) to reveal a project's multiple streams of input. We see some authors' contributions and some readers' reactions as well as evolving drafts. This "extratextual" material productively undermines "the firm structuralist bipolarity between the text itself and its margins" (Greetham, *Pleasures* 277). Some textual critics endorse this idea wholeheartedly. Greetham frames the imperative, saying that "A choice must be made from culturally plausible responses to the contaminated text, and the criticism must take account of both the new integrity of the contamination and the elements from which it could be made" (314). He also expresses things with more nuance, suggesting "it may be that 'contamination' will provide us with at least the possibility of choice, and thus of criticism" (314).

A choice could be made, but that choice would not be uncomplicated. The revisions I suggest would ruin the texts' seamless construction and stimulate a more dissonant reading experience. What I call collegiality in action may be perceived as "a text so revised" ("recension") that it is unrecognizable and ineffective. Discerning integrity and utility in light of digital design engenders important questions:

- Would presentational capacity influence rhetorical disposition on the part of the *Statement*'s authors and sponsoring organization(s)?
- Why might authors welcome public scrutiny and criticism of their ideas, drafts, and responses to other committee members? How can we create a professional culture that sustains and supports such transparent practices? How can we build that sensibility into graduate preparation and professional development for seasoned faculty?
- Regarding return on investment, what is the presage for disseminating data, backstory, and versions for all to see and use? Some critics already offer committees faint praise and generous criticism for the work they do.[10] So, why might authors want future critics seeing their drafts?
- As we cull rhetorical strategies to support digital authors, might we cultivate reading strategies that understand and welcome that

---

10. Consider Micheal Callaway's observation that "the 2008 revision of the [*WPA Outcomes Statement for Firist-Year Composition* . . .] does not move much beyond the 1999 version in terms of its focus on technology as a tool" (275).

work? Traditionally, we might ask: How can we help readers cope with the plenitude of information that could be made available? Less traditionally, we might see millennial readers as capable of engaging texts that are more contrapuntal than melodic. By simultaneously directing, throwing, and splitting attention, the revised *Statement* would challenge and enhance readers' ability to toggle effectively (Davidson) among its various texts, paratexts, and threads. Wary of policy statements offering mostly distillations and directives, these readers would not just gloss the *Statement* for action items. Instead, they would want to learn and discuss how the document was conceptualized, debated, drafted, received, and rebuilt.

- If we deride strict clear text practices, are there tipping points to help us understand how much contamination is welcome (and by whom) and when texts are deceptively distilled or gratuitously bloated? Would focus groups help us access that information? Yet what if those presumed fault lines are fictional? What if the very concept of tipping points is a default scare tactic used to shutter democratic digital design and foment clear text privilege?

For some and for now, it remains expedient and familiar to "Find a Position Statement" and quote from it. That comports with our print-based reading traditions and habits. Practitioners of clear text policy statements will likely keep many of their adherents due to the seamless construction and intellectual/emotional solace their work provides. Alternatively, implementing integral digital redesign into the *Statement*, which I can see being called "radical" in many senses of the word, would likely involve the risky work of promoting transparency while yielding more dissonant and complicated storytelling. Those activities would involve a new way of doing business and of getting "it" done again and anew. They would move the *Statement* from a fixed and finished text to an open and vulnerable one that is more revelatory of its inscriptions and more participatory in terms of the work we (writers and readers who become writers) might do separately and together. Such projects can be risky because they may destabilize a genre of expressly-purposed, very purposeful texts. For some, they may also proffer at bit too much choice and criticism. Even Greetham, who champions contamination and the interplay of choice and criticism, suggests that "there will, one hopes, be limits on both of these activities" (*Pleasures* 314).

It is this critical note—the nexus of rhetorical possibilities and ethical dilemmas—that makes the endeavor intriguing and worthwhile. Shillingsburg argues for "a general methodology of relational complexities." He says "*that* can be the aesthetics of scholarly editing in the twenty-first century if we understand that the emerging oneness does not consist of simplification or elimination of the complexity but instead that it arises from our recognition of the textual condition understood whole" (23–24). Understood whole and wholly understood may be parallel things, both of which can influence and impinge upon the potential practice of revising the *Statement* in ways that are hospitable to inclusive storytelling, contributory to community building, and relevant to online circulation. Having wondered how much dissonance the genre of best practice and position statements can contain, we might ask how much can it sustain. What might the newest take on the "new integrity" become as these texts are imagined, made, and remade? We have some sense of what the *Statement* meant in its initial time of composition and reception. We might wonder what the revised text will come to mean in our time and in the future iterations we envision, design, contest, and steward.[11]

Works Cited

Callaway, Micheal. "The WPA Learning Outcomes: What Role Should Technology Play?" *The WPA Outcomes Statement—A Decade Later*, edited by Nicholas M. Behm et al. Parlor Press, 2013, pp. 271 84.

CCCC Executive Committee. *Statement of Principles and Standards for the Postsecondary Teaching of Writing. College Composition and Communication*, vol. 40, no. 3, 1989, pp. 329–36.

"CCCC Position Statements." *Conference on College Composition and Communication*. National Council of Teachers of English, www.ncte.org/cccc/resources/positions.

Charlton, Colin, et al. *GenAdmin: Theorizing WPA Identities in the Twenty-First Century*. Parlor Press, 2011.

Chartier, Roger, and Peter Stallybrass. "What is A Book?" *The Cambridge Companion To Textual Scholarship*, edited by Neil Fraistat and Julia Flanders, Cambridge UP, 2013, pp. 188–204.

---

11. I am grateful to Dayna V. Goldstein, Randall McClure, and Michael A. Pemberton for their careful reading and fine advice. I thank Yola C. Janangelo, Farrell J. Webb, and Joyce Wexler for generously sharing their insights and perspectives.

Council of Chief State School Officials and the National Governors Association. *Common Core State Standards Initiative*. Common Core State Standards Initiative, 2010, www.corestandards.org/.

Davidson, Cathy N. *Now You See It: How the Brain Science of Attention Will Transform the Way We Live, Work, and Learn*. Viking: 2011.

Douglas, Mary. *Purity and Danger: An Analysis of the Concepts of Pollution and Taboo*. Routledge & Kegan Paul, 1966.

Eggert, Paul. *Securing the Past: Conservation in Art, Architecture and Literature*. Cambridge UP, 2009.

Evaluating the Intellectual Work of Writing Administration. Council of Writing Program Administrators, 1998, wpacouncil.org/positions/intellectualwork.html.

Fraistat, Neil, and Julia Flanders. "Introduction: Textual Scholarship in The Age of Media Consciousness." *The Cambridge Companion To Textual Scholarship*, edited by Neil Fraistat and Julia Flanders, Cambridge UP, 2013, pp. 1–15.

Gabler, Hans Walter. "Late Twentieth-Century Shakespeares." *The Cambridge Companion To Textual Scholarship*, edited by Neil Fraistat and Julia Flanders, Cambridge UP, 2013, pp. 79–96.

Genette, Gérard. *Paratexts: Thresholds of Interpretation*. Translated by Jane E. Lewin, foreword by Richard Macksey, Cambridge UP, 1997.

Gibson, James J. *The Ecological Approach to Visual Perception*. Lawrence Erlbaum Associates, 1986.

Greetham, David. "A History of Textual Scholarship." *The Cambridge Companion To Textual Scholarship*, edited by Neil Fraistat and Julia Flanders, Cambridge UP, 2013, pp. 16–41.

—. *The Pleasures of Contamination: Evidence, Text, and Voice in Textual Studies*. Indiana UP, 2010.

"Help:Page history." *Wikipedia*. Wikimedia Foundation, 4 April 2016, en.wikipedia.org/wiki/Help:Page_history.

Kaufmann, Michael. *Textual Bodies: Modernism, Postmodernism, and Print*. Bucknell UP, 1994.

Kirschenbaum, Matthew G. "Electronic Literature as Cultural Heritage (Confessions of an Incunk)." 6 April 2013, mkirschenbaum.wordpress.com/2013/04/06/electronic-literature-as-cultural-heritage-confessions-of-incunk/.

Kirschenbaum, Matthew G., and Doug Reside. "Tracking The Changes: Textual Scholarship and the Challenge of Born Digital." *The Cambridge Companion To Textual Scholarship*, edited by Neil Fraistat and Julia Flanders, Cambridge UP, 2013, pp. 257–73.

Lamos, Steve. "'What's in a Name?': Institutional Critique, Writing Program Archives, and the Problem of Administrator Identity." *College English*, vol. 71, no. 4, 2009, pp. 389–414.

Lanham, Richard A. *The Economics of Attention: Style and Substance in the Age of Information*. U of Chicago P, 2006.
Lunenfeld, Peter, editor. *The Digital Dialectic: New Essays on New Media*. MIT P, 2000.
McClure, Randall, and Dayna V. Goldstein. "Different Paths to the Same Goal: A Response to Barbara Cambridge." *WPA: Writing Program Administration*, vol. 35, no. 2, 2012, pp. 190–95.
McClure, Randall, et al. "Strengthening the *Statement*: Data on Working Conditions in College Composition." *Labored: The State(ment) and Future of Work in Composition*, Parlor Press, 2017, pp. 268-284.
McGann, Jerome. "Coda: Why Digital Scholarship Matters; or, Philosophy in a New Key." *The Cambridge Companion To Textual Scholarship*, edited by Neil Fraistat and Julia Flanders, Cambridge UP, 2013, pp. 274–88.
National HIV/AIDS Strategy. The White House, July 2010, www.whitehouse.gov/sites/default/files/uploads/NHAS.pdf.
Niles, John D. "Orality." *The Cambridge Companion To Textual Scholarship*, edited by Neil Fraistat and Julia Flanders, Cambridge UP, 2013, pp. 205–23.
Pemberton, Michael A. "The Ethics of Digital Publishing: Do Online Texts Threaten History?"*Ethics in a Digital Age: Ethics and Digital Media in the Writing Classroom*. Special issue of *Computers and Composition Online*, edited by Toby Coley, vol. Fall 2011, www2.bgsu.edu/departments/english/cconline/ethics_special_issue/pemberton/.
"Recension." *The Free Dictionary.com*, www.thefreedictionary.com/recension.
Reside, Doug. "What is a Digital Curator?" New York Public Library, 4 April 2011, www.nypl.org/blog/2011/04/04/what-digital-curator
Sargent, Michael G. "Manuscript Textuality." *The Cambridge Companion To Textual Scholarship*, edited by Neil Fraistat and Julia Flanders, Cambridge UP, 2013, pp. 224–35.
Shillingsburg, Peter L. *From Gutenberg to Google: Electronic Representations of Literary Texts*. Cambridge UP, 2006.
Sutherland, Kathryn. "Anglo-American Editorial Theory." *The Cambridge Companion To Textual Scholarship*, edited by Neil Fraistat and Julia Flanders, Cambridge UP, 2013, pp. 42–60.
Warren, Michelle R. "The Politics of Textual Scholarship." *The Cambridge Companion To Textual Scholarship*, edited by Neil Fraistat and Julia Flanders, Cambridge UP, 2013, pp. 119–33.
Williams, William Proctor, and Craig S. Abbott. *An Introduction to Bibliographical and Textual Studies*. Modern Language Assocation, 2009.
Willis, James. *Latin Textual Criticism*. U of Illinois P, 1972.
WPA Outcomes Statement for First-Year Composition. Council of Writing Program Administrators, July 2014, wpacouncil.org/positions/outcomes.html.

15 Strengthening the *Statement*: Data on Working Conditions in College Composition

Randall McClure, Dayna V. Goldstein, and Michael A. Pemberton

Introduction

The Wyoming Conference and the *Resolution* it produced marked "the formation of a political will among writing teachers—a collective decision that we do not have to accept second class status because we are interested in the study and teaching of writing and that together we can determine our own fate as a profession and pursue our hopes as writing teachers, scholars, and program administrators" (Trimbur and Cambridge 13). Conceived formally as the *Statement of Principles and Standards for the Postsecondary Teaching of Writing* (hereafter the *Statement*), the *Wyoming Resolution* advocates for equitable labor practices for all writing teachers at all levels—including tenure-track faculty, graduate students, and part-time instructors—and details working conditions that facilitate successful teaching of writing. Despite the best efforts of concerned scholars and practitioners to craft both a powerful call to action and a useful strategic tool for writing professionals, however, the problematic labor practices addressed by the *Statement* remain unresolved issues for composition nearly thirty years later. The question we have to ask ourselves is "Why?"

The *Statement* has been a go-to document for the field since its creation, and National Council of Teachers of English (NCTE) and Conference on College Composition and Communication (CCCC) members have been vocal and vociferous for years about the deplorable conditions many full-time, part-time, and adjunct instructors labor under. Despite some small victories here and there, however, the general status of composition teachers nationwide has not changed and, in many cases, has only gotten worse. Thus the question still remains: "Why?" As a partial answer to that question, we argue that the discipline's ongoing preference for qualitative site- and context-dependent research (as opposed to quantitative site- and context-independent research) has contributed, perhaps inadvertently, to the *Statement*'s lack of effectiveness in ameliorating many of these conditions. Put more bluntly, the discipline has been historically disinclined to view quantitative, data-driven studies into topics such as staffing conditions as a part of its core research mission or preferred epistemology.

The problems associated with working conditions for composition teachers (e.g., low pay, large class sizes, lack of job security, and adjunct status) are not new. They seeded the creation of the *Statement* in the late 1980s, they reappeared with some tenacity in the late 1990s, and they came on full force a decade later. The problems and their histories have been discussed at length, but their solutions remain distant and, in the minds of many, may be unachievable. In 1997, Joseph Harris, citing Lester Faigley's "Chair's Letter to CCCC Members," labeled the subject of working conditions "the most pressing question of location in our field today" (332). Harris went on to note that, as editor of *College Composition and Communication* (*CCC*), he tried to publish a special issue on transforming the working conditions in composition, but the response to his call for papers was "surprisingly small," and the proposals that were submitted were "better at offering narratives defining the problems associated with unfair working conditions than in proposing new ways to respond to them" (332).

Harris concluded that responding to concerns over staffing and work conditions "as they impact on our more traditional concerns with teaching and the curriculum is still something that, as a field, we need to learn how to do" (332–33). We concur, and we believe the "traditional concerns" Harris refers to still comprise the predominant set of research interests in the discipline; developing a comprehensive research agenda that works to address staffing and work conditions is something that our field has yet to embrace.[1] Admittedly, the kind of data-oriented research we call for in this chapter—research that is likely to be the most persuasive to stakeholders outside the discipline—is not the kind of research many rhetoric and composition professionals have been trained to pursue. However, we believe, as does Harris, that "unless we teach ourselves how, we will continue to labor under constraints others have set for us" (333).

In the thirty years since the Wyoming Conference, rhetoric and composition as a field has been extraordinarily successful in achieving one of its major goals: the accoutrements of disciplinarity. It has constructed curricula at multiple levels and built thriving PhD programs at major institutions (Downs and Wardle 31). Its members conduct theoretical and pedagogical research, publish that research in an expanding number of international journals, and present their work at regional, national, and international conferences annually. Nevertheless, rhetoric and composition has been far less successful in fulfilling the other major goal that emerged from Wyoming: guaranteeing that institutions of higher learning nationwide hire well-trained professionals to teach writing courses and provide them with appropriate, equitable working conditions. A major economic recession, declining state appropriations for higher education in the last decade, and the impact of the Affordable Care Act have only worsened composition's labor crisis and made the issues of staffing and workplace equity more pressing than ever before. In the face of this exigency, then, it is imperative that we work from positions of strength, making the strongest arguments we can that are supported by reliable,

---

1. A 2013 special joint issue of the *ADE Bulletin* and the *ADFL Bulletin* (Editorial Subcommittee) a 2011 issue of *College English* (Palmquist and Doe) are dedicated to the status of contingent faculty. These publications are certainly an indicator of continuing interest in research on working conditions, though much of what is presented in both issues is based on qualitative loci. Still, it is worth noting that one article in the *ADE & ADFL Bulletin*, "A Profile of the Non-Tenure-Track Academic Workforce," offers an analysis of data on contingent faculty. Another essay in the bulletin, "An Evolving Discourse: The Shifting Uses of Position Statements on the Contingent Faculty," and one from the *College English* issue, "The Spirit and Influence of the Wyoming Resolution: Looking Back to Look Forward," consider the history and value of professional statements on labor, including but not limited to the *Statement*. Another *College English* article, "The Current Status of Contingent Faculty in Technical and Professional Communication," offers survey data in one sub-specialty that should be of interest to composition researchers.

convincing data. We believe, therefore, that the best and most effective strategy for improving the collective working conditions of composition professionals in the current political and economic climate is to rely more strongly on quantitative research and the data it provides than on qualitative research which, though a mainstay of composition work, can be—and has often been—dismissed for its lack of generalizable results.

We want to be clear that it is by no means our intent to devalue the importance of qualitative research and discrete, context-specific studies in rhetoric and composition. We recognize that every composition program is unique, much like every writing student, and that qualitative research informs our theory and praxis in meaningful ways. However, we believe that the ongoing and pervasive preference for qualitative research loci in rhetoric and composition has left the discipline vulnerable to legislative and administrative decisions that tend to be based largely on quantitative data. It seems incumbent upon us as trained rhetoricians, then, to adapt to the needs and expectations of our audiences and to provide the kinds of data-driven arguments that will be most persuasive to those who make decisions that directly impact the working conditions of writing instructors.

The Qualitative Agenda around Labor Issues in Composition

One way to understand the distinction between quantitative and qualitative research agendas is through what Chaïm Perelman and Lucie Olbrechts-Tytecha call "loci of the preferable." These loci are "premises of a general nature that can serve as the basis for values and hierarchies" (84), and two of the six loci they discuss are "quantity" and "quality." The "locus of quantity" asserts that something that is good for (or applicable to) a greater number is better than a similar good that affects or applies to a smaller number. The "locus of quality," by contrast, contends that the unique and exceptional is of greater value than that which is common. When applied to working conditions, then, quantitative loci encourage us to examine common features across varied contexts and make the best decisions for the most people on the basis of those shared features (e.g., pay, hours, courses, and number of positions at multiple institutions). Qualitative loci, by contrast, push us to examine each person in an unstable employment condition as an isolated, yet context-dependent, case and determine what is best for that person in his or her particular circumstances.

The tension between these loci, then, is due to fundamental philosophical differences about which is more important: "the needs of the many or the needs of the few (or the one)," to appropriate a pop culture cliché. In terms of working conditions in composition, these two loci push against each other when, on the one hand, we argue for national standards that might be applied to writing instructors across institutions (the quantitative locus) or for the working conditions of individual writing professionals in particular institutions (the qualitative locus). The *Statement* was heavily premised on the side of quantitative loci, advocating positions that applied to all composition teachers collectively (e.g., that composition professionals should gradually move into tenured and more economically stable positions); but implementation and enforcement was left to each institution and department, thereby embracing a qualitative, context-sensitive approach. Though this was certainly a pragmatic path to follow at the time, in keeping with political and institutional realities, the lack of ongoing quantitative research to support the claims and assertions about working conditions detailed in the *Statement* has, over time, lessened its value as a tool to effect real change.

Quantitative Loci and Research into the Teaching Conditions of Postsecondary Writing Teachers

The *Statement* has certainly aided many rhetoric and composition professionals in addressing the mistreatment of writing teachers, which at the time was identified as "the worst scandal in higher education" (330). In providing principles for the staffing of composition programs and standards for the working conditions of teachers in them, the *Statement* professionalized the field of rhetoric and composition and elevated the professional status of composition teachers. In a quantitative though incomplete move, the *Statement* also prepared composition for research into teaching conditions that would be replicable, aggregable, and data-supported (Haswell 201). These principles stood to be examined, quantified, and returned to over time.

Yet despite the fact that the *Statement* has been subject since its publication to an increasing need for data substantiation in order to maintain its visibility and increase its credibility in local, state, and national discussions, this imperative has not been taken up as a serious area of study.

Data has been slow to accrue, leaving those who champion composition teachers vulnerable to competing arguments about working conditions. In fact, most of the data about working conditions has come from sources outside of the discipline, such as the College and University Professional Association for Human Resources (CUPA-HR), the American Association of University Professors (AAUP), and the National Center for Education Statistics (NCES). Though this data can certainly be adapted to our own circumstances and needs, we strongly encourage rhetoric and composition professionals to pursue research agendas that are grounded in and informed by our own disciplinary perspectives and theories.

To illustrate the need for such quantitative research into employment conditions, we turn to a *CCC* article from 1998, "After Wyoming: Labor Practices in Two University Writing Programs," by Jennifer Seidel Trainor and Amanda Godley, which discusses the ways in which administrators on the campus of "Oakdale University" used the "very discourse [of rhetoric and composition]—of the teacher as specialist—to justify their policy decisions" (153), which included outsourcing basic writing to a nearby community college and firing their own full-time faculty in the program. Both of these decisions were made in response to a system mandate to remove remedial courses from university campuses (167), but the authors make clear that the unfortunate outcome was also due, in part, to the stakeholders' inability or unwillingness to make a strong case for retaining permanent faculty using quantitative data and relying perhaps a bit too heavily on the trope of individual teacher heroics that has historically pervaded Composition Studies.

In the case of Oakdale, efforts in rhetoric and composition to improve the working conditions of part-time faculty—of labeling them "teacher-heroes" not only out of respect for them but also in an attempt to improve their working conditions—backfired, allowing decision makers to use the discipline's own arguments to justify the claim that part-time faculty, particularly community college teachers, were just as, if not more, qualified and "more specialized than enfranchised [full-time] faculty" (167). Because the full-time lecturers in writing believed they did not have the interest and support of the tenure-line faculty on campus and, more importantly from our perspective, because they were unable themselves to construct a convincing argument that basic writing students benefit more from working with full-time faculty, the Oakdale administration turned a labor discussion into an issue of student need, citing that students benefit more from the invested, part-time teaching corps at the community college who willingly teach such students and are, therefore, specialists in working with them (162–63).

The mistreatment of faculty at Oakdale University related by Trainor and Godley is a story familiar to many readers. Tales like this one appear on discussion lists,[2] programs for national conferences like CCCC and WPA, and on occasion in the professional literature. Along these lines, Trainor and Godley note the purpose of their essay is to "intervene productively in the growing debates over the erosion of faculty working conditions in higher education by examining how, at *local* levels, such erosion takes place" (154; emphasis added). Trainor and Godley contrast the ugly outcome at Oakdale with the somewhat more palatable outcome at "Bridgewater," in which basic writing was saved from outsourcing, though the staffing model for basic writing and the working conditions for teachers in the composition program did not improve in the ways the faculty expected. A win for the curriculum and students, but not so much for the faculty involved and their working conditions.

We believe that these unfortunate outcomes might have been averted had the faculty had knowledge of, commitment to the integrity of, and access to discipline-specific quantitative research data on the teaching of composition. Several kairotic moments existed that, with a little gamesmanship, could have altered the outcome for the better. To respond, for example, to the romanticized notion of the part-time teacher as heroic figure, the full-time faculty could have shown, supported by quantitative evidence, that instructors in part-time positions are less effective teachers across a variety of metrics than their full-time counterparts—not because they lack ability or expertise, but because their working conditions substantially mitigate the impact they can have on students and student learning.

Data from several studies support this position. Ronald Ehrenberg and Liang Zhang in "Do Tenured and Tenure-Track Faculty Matter?" find that six-year graduation rates diminish proportionally to the percentage of non-tenureable faculty, and several studies (Benjamin; Jaegar and Egan; Umbach) indicate that increasing percentages of non-tenure-

---

2. An August 2011 discussion on the WPA-L Listserv highlights the enduring popularity of qualitative loci in discussions on working conditions in composition. Over a three-day period, at least fourteen direct or related responses discussing *local* conditions were posted to a query on the subject of *national* data on employment conditions for full-time non-tenure-track faculty. Few responses worked in any way along quantitative loci.

track faculty diminish the time tenured or tenureable faculty spend on course preparation and work with students outside of scheduled class meetings. Overall, assumptions about the advantages of part-time faculty were in this case *factually incorrect*. They are not typically experts in the sense of expertise deriving from advanced education. Data from the Integrated Postsecondary Education Data System (IPEDS) indicate that the vast majority of those teaching with only a master's degree in part-time positions are educated widely within the humanities, including but limited to degrees in literature, creative writing, journalism, law, mass communication, and theater. Unfortunately, IPEDS and other such data resources, as mentioned earlier, remain buried in the literature of higher education administration, generally unknown and/or inaccessible to the composition professionals who need them most when wrestling with long-term labor practices.

Addressing the Conditions through Research

Methods beyond position statements and local narratives must be used to respond persuasively to prevailing teaching conditions. Aggregated research from inside and outside the discipline is currently available and can easily be brought to bear on working conditions for composition professionals. At the end of this book, in an annotated appendix, we offer an enhanced version of the *Statement*, supported where possible by data offered in more than a dozen reports and national studies conducted over the past decade.

These reports, ranging from the National Survey of Student Engagement (NSSE) to the *Initial Report on Survey of CCCC Members*, provide positive support for improving the working conditions of composition faculty. Of course, more research on staffing models and labor practices along several lines of inquiry is needed, and we have identified several lacunae in a number of conditions articulated in the *Statement*. For example, the following sentences of the *Statement* cannot be supported by national quantitative research at the present time:

> Part-timers should be eligible for the same fringe benefits and for the same cost-of-living, seniority, and merit salary increases available to full-time faculty. Part-time faculty should be given mailboxes, office space, telephones, and clerical support. They should be given a voice in the formulation of department policy regarding courses and programs in which they teach (for

> example, by voting at department meetings and by serving on curriculum and hiring committees). They should have the same right as full-time faculty to participate in the design of evaluation procedures. They should have access to research support and travel funds to attend professional conferences. (334)

Affordances for part-time faculty, along the lines of those listed above, may be among the most crucial labor concerns encountered by the discipline currently, but they remain largely unresearched on a national level.

In fact, the only report that mentions institutional or departmental research support for part-time faculty that we have been able to identify is the *2012–13 Survey of Humanities Departments at Four-Year Institutions*, and the data offered is not favorable to part-time faculty. Whereas 93% of full-time tenured or tenure-track faculty and 70% of full-time non-tenured or non-tenure-track faculty are reported to have access to research support, only 27% of part-time faculty do (White et al., 66). As this example illustrates, the conditions of part-time (and other) faculty are measurable. Fringe benefits, seniority, merit salary, and research and travel support are all quantifiable and can be reported in simple numerical terms. Other affordances, from mailboxes and office space to voting rights and input on evaluation processes, can be accounted for with surveys and corresponding percentages that report the results. The needed research is achievable, which makes its absence all the more conspicuous.

Despite several such gaps in the research on working conditions, rhetoric and composition professionals *do* have a tremendous amount of data available that can help make strong cases for improvement. Though we do not have the space in this chapter to provide a detailed discussion of every area in our data-enhanced *Statement*, we can offer several examples of how we have augmented the *Statement* with national data. For example, the *Statement* contains principles and standards for staffing and teaching composition, with the majority of the document committed to staffing, particularly a call for the hiring of tenure-track composition faculty and respect for their work as both teachers and researchers in the maturing field of rhetoric and composition. Other sections are dedicated to the conditions of employment for graduate students and the occasional necessity of hiring part-time faculty. The latter portion of the *Statement* is dedicated to working conditions. Albeit much shorter and less descriptive, this part of the *Statement* articulates standards for such things as class size, secretarial support, and writing centers.

The opening sentence in the "Professional Standards" section of the *Statement*, which begins with tenure-line faculty, says: "To provide the highest quality of instruction, departments offering composition and writing courses should rely on full-time tenured or tenure-track faculty members who are both prepared for and committed to the teaching of writing" (331). Mining reports such as *The CCCC Strategic Research Survey*, the Faculty Survey of Student Engagement (FSSE), the *2014 –15 Faculty in Higher Education Salary Survey for Four-Year Colleges and Universities* (CUPA-HR), and the *2004 National Study of Postsecondary Faculty* (*NSOPF:04*; Cataldi et al.), we can provide the following data relevant to this position:

1. The *NSOPF:04* suggests 44% of faculty teaching sections of first-year composition are employed full time, with 37% of those tenured or tenure-track (Cataldi et al.).

2. *The 2012–13 Survey of Humanities Departments at Four-Year Institutions* suggests that 69% of English faculty are full-time, a figure that has remained stable for since 2008. Additionally, this survey reports that 52% of English faculty are tenured or tenure-track, representing a 4% increase since 2008 (White et al. 6).

3. While salaries for English tenured and tenure-track faculty continue to lag behind those in related disciplines, salary increases for tenured and tenure-track faculty are keeping pace with the annual Consumer Price Index (CPI-U). According to *2014 –15 Faculty in Higher Education Salary Survey for Four-Year Colleges and Universities*, the average increase for tenured and tenure-track faculty was 2.0% for the 2014–2015 academic year, and this number compares favorably with a CPI-U of 1.6% in 2014 (CUPA-HR 8). Another document, one relying on data from both the AAUP *Faculty Compensation Survey* and the NCES's IPEDS Data Center, reports the increases for all faculty and continuing faculty for 2014–2015 at 2.2% and 3.7%, respectively (Barnshaw and Dunietz 6).

4. More than 90% of those who administer first-year composition programs are employed full time, with 73% of all WPAs tenured or tenure-track, according to the *Initial Report on Survey of CCCC Members* (Q17).

5. More than 90% of WPAs also hold terminal degrees (PhD, DA, EdD, MFA), with 83% of WPAs holding PhDs, according to the *Initial Report on Survey of CCCC Members* (Q15).

6. In a study conducted by Jonikka Charlton and Shirley K Rose, 53% of WPAs indicate "Rhetoric and /or Composition" as the field or focus of the coursework for their most advanced degree; up from 15% in 1986 (122–23).

7. Three-fourths (75%) of first-year composition faculty hold advanced degrees, with half (49%) holding a terminal degree and more than a third (36%) holding a PhD, according to the *Initial Report on Survey of CCCC Members* (Q16).

8. Charlton and Rose report in their 2007 survey of WPAs that more than 91% of those administering writing programs hold terminal degrees (122).

These data suggest that an increasing, parallel emphasis on disciplinarity and full-time employment status characterizes the field. If a university today wants to be competitive with its rhetoric and composition hires, then the trend is toward increasing commitment to the preparation and maintenance of dedicated full-time specialists in rhetoric and composition. Further, despite the economic challenges faced by higher education since the *Statement* was written, the data suggest that institutions have remained committed, slowly and consistently, to staffing their composition programs with well-prepared, full-time faculty. As advanced degree holders continue to professionalize the teaching of first-year composition and the administration of writing programs, the overall trend is an increase in specialization, expert leadership, and compensatory advantage.

The instructional demands placed on composition teachers has a long, rich history in higher education, and the authors of the *Statement* acknowledge these demands. For example, the authors note that "writing instruction requires so much individual attention to student writing" (336). To illustrate how rhetoric and composition professionals can use quantitative research to support improved working conditions, we offer the following examples. Data provided in response to the twenty-seven supplemental questions developed by the Consortium for the Study of Writing in College (CSWC)[3] for the NSSE reveals that in

---

3. CSWC is a partnership between CWPA and NSSE. More information on CSWC is available at http://comppile.org/wpa+nsse/.

2009 more than ten thousand students, or 67.9% of respondents, indicate they work with their writing instructor to develop ideas on some, most, or all of their major course assignments. This finding is supported by NSSE annual results from 2009, which indicate 73% of students respond positively to their relationships with faculty members, identifying them as available and helpful, along with findings in the *Your First College Year Survey 2012* from the Higher Education Research Institute (HERI), which indicate very positive experiences for first-year students. "The majority," conclude the HERI researchers, "81%, were 'satisfied' or 'very satisfied' with their academic experience [. . . including] their general education and core curriculum courses (76%), the overall quality of instruction (76%), and the amount of contact with faculty (69%)" (Hurtado et al. 1). Students report they want feedback on their writing, and composition teachers are not only doing so helpfully but also making themselves available to do so, even despite other demands placed on their time.

The high demand for teacher feedback on writing can be documented through both faculty and student reporting on workload. According to the 2009 FSSE, 62% of faculty spend at least five hours per week grading papers, with one in four (29%) spending at least nine hours a week. This time does not include hours spent each week providing written and oral feedback to students, of which 44% of faculty spend at least five hours each week. The significant amount of time on task reported by faculty is confirmed by the 2009 NSSE, which indicates that nearly a third (31%) of college students compose at least eleven papers of fewer than five pages; 34% compose at least five papers between five and nineteen pages in length; and 20% compose a paper of twenty pages or more *during their first year of college*. On these projects, 93% of first-year students report on the 2009 NSSE that they receive prompt written or oral feedback from their teachers, feedback that 89% of faculty report that they provide "often" or "very often." In addition, half of all faculty responding to the 2009 FSSE (50%) believe it important or very important that students prepare two or more drafts. Of course, the annual NSSE and FSSE do not ask students specifically about their experiences in first-year composition (certainly one inspiration for the creation of the CSWC), but they do focus one set of questions on the first-year experience.

High demands on faculty, including composition specialists, extend far beyond creating traditional writing assignments for students and providing individualized feedback. First-year students report, for instance, learning many other fundamental principles of effective writing including: writing in the disciplines (81%); visual rhetoric (74%); and writing with multi-media (77%) (Paine et al. 2). Moreover, students report on the 2009 NSSE that their teachers spend a great deal of time with them beyond their scheduled class time: 93% take time to discuss grades or assignments; 60% discuss readings with students outside of class; 77% talk to them about career plans; 43% work with students on learning activities other than coursework; and 62% work with students on research projects outside of course or program requirements. Faculty members report a high level of engagement as well. For example, 79% of faculty report on the 2009 FSSE that they spend time outside of class with at least one out of every four students.

As a final example, consider the data that support the work of writing program administrators. Another professional standard offered in the *Statement* concerns the administration of composition programs:

> Whenever possible, faculty professionally committed to rhetoric and composition should coordinate and supervise composition programs. Evidence of this commitment can be found in research and publication, participation in professional conferences, and active involvement in curriculum development and design. Those who supervise writing programs should also be involved in determining policy and budget for their programs. (331)

As mentioned above, what we have been able to determine so far is that rhetoric and composition professionals frequently serve as administrators of composition programs. Data clearly illustrate that training in and commitment to the discipline of rhetoric and composition are indeed the professional standard for writing program administrators at this time. In 1987, only 15% of those involved in writing program administration pursued advanced degrees in rhetoric and composition. Twenty years later (2007), more than half (53%) held terminal degrees in rhetoric and composition. These professionals provide leadership, sometimes simultaneously, for a variety of composition programs including first-year composition (41%); writing across the curriculum (31%); basic writing (23%); and writing centers (22%) (Charlton and Rose 121–22). Higher education institutions also recognize the professional standing of writing program administrators, as annual salaries of more than $86,000 have been reported on national surveys, along with a mean annual salary for writing program administrators at $63,616 (*Initial Report*).

The data offered above is just some of what is available to the composition community. More importantly, we join with other contributors to this book in emphasizing that conducting research on working conditions for its own sake misses the point. Instead, we must be "Going Public" with it, as Peter Mortensen implored in his 1998 *CCC* article.[4] Mortensen argues that the discipline suffers for only speaking internally and makes clear his hope that we don't "consign ourselves to mere spectatorship in national, regional—and, most importantly, local—struggles over what counts as literacy and who should have opportunities to attain it" (183). His point applies equally well, possibly even more cogently, to what counts as satisfactory working conditions for postsecondary teachers of writing.

Conclusion

In order to maintain visibility and increase credibility in local, state, and national discussions around the labor practices addressed in the *Statement*, rhetoric and composition professionals must come to a quantitative consensus about the extant working conditions of postsecondary writing teachers. The highly conservative, data-driven, financially-strained environment in which many staffing decisions in higher education are made creates an increasing need for data substantiation in support of the *Statement*. Accumulated, rigorous scholarship on the valuation of quality teaching and its relationship to student learning could provide much of the support needed on labor conditions in composition that decision makers will find compelling.

That being said, the *Statement* as it sits cannot be the end point for research into working conditions for composition; instead, we believe it should become the beginning of a new quantitative agenda. Simply put, strong data is advantageous. It strengthens the discipline as a whole and improves its ability to support the kinds of phenomenal teaching that lead to real literacy learning. We began this project with the belief—one that remains common in the field today—there was little research on the labor conditions of writing teachers that could be persuasively used to

---

4. McClure and Goldstein discuss the idea of "YouTube Writing Research" as one form of "going public" in their article "Different Paths to the Same Goal: A Response to Barbara Cambridge."

make arguments that support their work. We sought to understand why, despite the evident need underscored by the *Statement*, this research was not being accrued by the discipline. What we discovered was that much of the research we wanted to see already existed, but rhetoric and composition, as a field with a strong preference for qualitative rather than quantitative loci, is not generally aware of this research and as a consequence does not often access it, employ it, or incorporate its methodologies to generate new knowledge.

The lack of a concrete research agenda into the teaching conditions of composition constrains our ability to improve them. Using quantitative loci requires not only a research question but also awareness of the relevant dimensions that could lead to potential answers. As yet, composition has made little headway in this regard. The infrastructure and support mechanisms that allow for data collection, aggregation, analysis, and synthesis are occasionally called for but largely absent in composition; hence, what is there comes from outside of the field. It is time for a change—a new "resolution," as it were, to recognize the value of quantitative research in rhetoric and composition and to conduct it in the service of equitable working conditions for our colleagues and ourselves. By doing so, we will be best positioned to make good on the promises from nearly thirty years ago at the conference in Laramie.

WORKS CITED

Barnshaw, John, and Samuel Dunietz. "Busting the Myths: The Annual Report on the Economic Status of the Profession, 2014–15." *Academe*, March–April 2015, pp. 4–19.

Benjamin, Ernst. "How Over-Reliance upon Contingent Appointments Diminishes Faculty Involvement in Student Learning." *Peer Review*, vol. 5, no. 1, 2002, pp. 4–10.

Cataldi, Emily Forrest, et al. *2004 National Study of Postsecondary Faculty (NSOPF:04) Report on Faculty and Instructional Staff in Fall 2003* (NCES 2005 –172). National Center for Education Statistics, U.S. Department of Education, 2005, nces.ed.gov/pubs2005/2005172.pdf.

CCCC Executive Committee. *Statement of Principles and Standards for the Postsecondary Teaching of Writing. College Composition and Communication*, vol. 40, no. 3, 1989, pp. 329–36.

Charlton, Jonikka, and Shirley K. Rose. "Twenty More Years in the WPA's Progress." *WPA:Writing Program Administration*, vol. 33, no. 1–2, 2009, pp. 114–45.

Conference on College Composition and Communication. *The Strategic Research Survey*. 2008, https://s.zoomerang.com/sr.aspx?sm=UnpQG0Bgoxm AEerZv8H%2fDvg72ZhKeQnC8DKhZXzT65k%3d.

Downs, Doug, and Elizabeth Wardle. "Teaching about Writing, Righting Misconceptions: (Re)Envisioning 'First-Year Composition' as 'Introduction to Writing Studies.'" *College Composition and Communication*, vol. 58, no. 4, 2007, pp. 552–84.

Editoral Subcomittee of the Committee on Contingent Labor in the Profession. *Non-Tenure-Track Faculty Members in English and the Other Modern Languages: Issues and Directions. ADE & ADFL Bulletin. ADE* vol. 153, 2013; *ADFL* vol. 42, no. 3, 2013.

Ehrenberg, Ronald, and Liang Zhang. "Do Tenured and Tenure-Track Faculty Matter?" *Cornell Higher Education Research Institute Working Paper #53*, 2004, digitalcommons.ilr.cornell.edu/cgi/viewcontent.cgi?article=1051&context=workingpapers.

Faculty in Higher Education Salary Survey Executive Summary for the 2014–15 Academic Year. College and University Professional Association for Human Resources (CUPA-HR), 2015, www.cupahr.org/surveys/files/salary2015/FHE4-2015-Executive-Summary.pdf.

Faculty Survey of Student Engagement (FSSE). *Grand Total Frequencies: Frequency Distributions August 2009*. Indiana University Center for Postsecondary Research, 2009, fsse.indiana.edu/pdf/FSSE_IR_2009/FSSE09%20Reports%20%28Total-TS%29.pdf.

Harris, Joseph. "Location." *College Composition and Communication*, vol. 48, no. 3, October 1997, pp. 331–33.

Haswell, Richard. "NCTE/CCCC's Recent War on Scholarship." *Written Communication*, vol. 22, no. 2, 2005, pp. 198–223.

Hurtado, Sylvia, et al. *HERI Research Brief: Your First Year College Survey 2012*. Higher Education Research Institute, UCLA, January 2013, ww.heri.ucla.edu/briefs/YFCY2012-Brief.pdf.

Initial Report on Survey of CCCC Members. James R. Squire Office of Policy Research in the English Language Arts, 2009, www.ncte.org/library/NCTEFiles/Groups/CCCC/InitialReportSurveyCCCCMembers.pdf.

Jaeger, Audrey J., and Kevin M. Eagan. "Effects of Exposure to Part-time Faculty on Associate's Degree Completion." *Community College Review*, vol. 36, no. 3, 2009, pp. 167–94.

McClure, Randall, and Dayna V. Goldstein. "Different Paths to the Same Goal: A Response to Barbara Cambridge." *WPA:Writing Program Administration*, vol. 35, no. 2, 2012, pp. 190–95.

Mortensen, Peter. "Going Public." *College Composition and Communication*, vol. 50, no. 2, 1998, pp. 182–205.

Murphy, Michael. "New Faculty for a New University: Toward a Full-Time Teaching-Intensive Faculty Track in Composition." *College Composition and Communication*, vol. 5, no. 1, 2000, pp. 14–42.

National Survey of Student Engagement (NSSE). *Assessment for Improvement: Tracking Student Engagement Over Time—Annual Results 2009*. Indiana University Center for Postsecondary Research, 2009, nsse.indiana.edu/NSSE_2009_Results/pdf/NSSE_AR_2009.pdf.

Paine, Charles, et al. *Writing Item Aggregated Results, 2009*. Consortium for the Study of Writing in College, 2009.

Palmquist, Michael, and Sue Doe, editors. *Contingent Faculty*. Special issue of *College English*, vol. 73, no .4, 2011, pp. 353–454.

Perelman, Chaïm, and Lucie Olbrechts-Tyteca. *The New Rhetoric: A Treatise on Argumentation*. Translated by John Wilkinson and Purcell Weaver, U of Notre Dame P, 1969.

Seibel Trainor, Jennifer, and Amanda Godley. "After Wyoming: Labor Practices in Two University Writing Programs." *College Composition and Communication*, vol. 50, no. 2, December 1998, pp. 153–81.

Snyder, Thomas D., and Sally A. Dillow. *Digest of Education Statistics 2010*. National Center for Education Statistics, April 2011, nces.ed.gov/pubs2011/2011015.pdf.

Trimbur, John, and Barbara Cambridge. "The Wyoming Conference Resolution: A Beginning." *WPA: Writing Program Administration*, vol. 12, no. 1–2, 1988, pp. 13–18.

Umbach, Paul D. "The Effects of Part-Time Faculty Appointments on Instructional Techniques and Commitment to Teaching." 33rd Annual Conference of the Association for the Study of Higher Education, Jacksonville, FL, 2008.

White, Susan, et al. *The 2012–13 Survey of Humanities Departments at Four-Year Institutions*. Statistical Research Center, American Institute of Physics, 2014, www.humanitiesindicators.org/binaries/pdf/HDS2_final.pdf.

16 Afterword

Joseph Harris

I've long felt that there have been two heroic moments in the history of the Conference on College Composition and Communication (CCCC)—the first in 1974 when we adopted the *Students' Right to Their Own Language* and the second in 1987 when we adopted the *Wyoming Resolution*. The essays in this book begin with that second moment, when our field rose up in anger at the mistreatment of so many teachers, and then go on to try to explain why the clarity and conviction of 1987 has led to so little real change.

There is no single, agreed-upon narrative that accounts for what went wrong. As a group, though, the essays in this book illustrate a tension upon which our attempts to act in the spirit of Wyoming have consistently foundered—and that is the question of whether the key problem we face has to do with working conditions or with the quality of teaching. Let me quickly note the obvious—that these two problems are closely intertwined. Indeed, following the lead of Holly Hassel and Joanne Baird Giordano in this book, I'd argue that we can't address one issue without taking on the other. But I think it may be useful to first note how they differ.

We can get at their differences through looking at the opening words of the 1987 *Wyoming Resolution* and the 1989 CCCC *Statement of Principles for the Postsecondary Teaching of Writing*—the document meant to operationalize the *Wyoming Resolution* and the focus of this book. The first words of the *Wyoming Resolution* are, "Whereas, the salaries and working conditions [. . .]" (Robertson et al. 278). This is a document that presents itself as a labor grievance. It assumes that most writing teachers are doing good work for which they are not being paid fairly. In contrast, the first sentence of the *Statement* is: "A democracy demands citizens who can read critically and write clearly and cogently" (329). This is a document about providing a quality education for students. There is no necessary contradiction between these two texts. We need to pay and support teachers fairly if they are to help students succeed. There is, however, a difference in emphasis, and I suspect this difference has been crucial and divisive.

I must resort a bit to conjecture to explain why. My sense is that the staunchest advocates of the *Wyoming Resolution* tend to feel that teaching writing is hard but not especially complex intellectual work—the kind of thing that a reasonably intelligent person with a master's degree can do pretty much as well as anybody else. As James Sledd put it, memorably, "[T]he best evidence of commitment to the teaching of writing is just its devoted teaching" (278). Practice makes perfect, evidently, even when that practice is not informed by reading in the field. Seen as a labor issue, then, the basic question is ethical: Are these workers being paid and treated fairly?

In contrast, I suspect that a driving force behind the drafting of the *Statement* was a sense that teaching writing is a true profession, one that requires training, mentorship, and disciplined effort to enter. I am puzzled by the ambivalence of many on the academic left on this point—since, in arguing on behalf of the right of instructors with little training in the field to teach composition, they seem to downplay the right of working-class students to be offered a rigorous and informed introduction to academic writing. It strikes me as one thing to argue for the rights of workers in an industrial context, but quite another to advocate for the rights of minimally-trained teachers to help students at a critical juncture in their education. The moments in my career I most regret have come when, as a writing program director, I've had to assign courses to people whom I've known were not much good at or even interested in the teaching writing simply because there was no one else to turn to. The *Wyoming Resolution* makes no distinction between teachers who are professionally trained in composition and those who are not. This indifference shortchanges students who find themselves in courses with unqualified teachers. Viewed as a professional issue, then, the question is: Are these people well prepared to teach writing?

The solution that the *Statement* offered to this problem was tenure. We should evaluate writing teachers the same way we assess Chaucerians and Miltonists. The strength of this proposal was that it called upon a mechanism for ensuring quality teaching that academics already knew and valued. Yet the *Statement*'s endorsement of tenure has also been criticized as an attempt to exalt the few at the expense of the many, to establish the authority of a small group of "boss compositionists" in the managed university. I think such criticisms are wrongheaded, that there is little reason to doubt the intentions of scholars eager to draw on an emerging body of research to try to improve the quality of teaching in their writing programs. Nevertheless, I also agree with those, like Jeanne Gunner in this book, who argue that such sweeping calls for tenure are less realistic than nostalgic, that they respond to current problems with appeals to past practices.

We need to confront the fact that most writing programs depend on the good work of teachers who will never be considered for tenure. We need to pay those teachers fairly and to offer them the best working conditions we can. We need to pay attention to and respect the intellectual work they do with students in classrooms and writing centers and online. And we also need to find ways to help them continue to develop as teachers over the course of their careers. We need to support; we need to professionalize.

My view is that the *Statement* mistook a means for an end. Tenure can be an effective way to support the work of teachers, and thus the intellectual growth of students. But it cannot be the only way, or we are in deep trouble. We have to develop a diverse repertoire of strategies of support and professionalization. When we can move writing teachers to the tenure track, we should leap at the chance to do so. At the same time, though, we need to work at creating good teaching jobs off the tenure track. This will involve pressing for better working conditions, full-time positions, longer contracts, regular and transparent systems of review, support for research and travel, and the like. Even so, there's more to good jobs than such economic concerns. People want to feel part of an intellectual community. We need to learn how to recognize and value the contributions made to our programs by writing teachers at all ranks—and to have high, rather than contingent, expectations for their work. Doing so will require a profound shift in the culture of the academy.

The debilitating irony of the *Statement* was that in positing tenure as a kind of absolute good, it ended up marginalizing many of the people it had hoped to argue for: adjuncts, part-timers, grad students, and tutors. I was moved in reading this book by how so many of the authors in it seem to write out of a continuing sense of pain and exclusion. For them, the *Statement* represents a failed chance for change. Yet many other authors in this book seem far more cheerfully ready to tinker with and amend the *Statement*—to revise its phrasings, to cite data to support its claims, to make connections to other statements on working conditions, to add to its list of stakeholders, and to suggest new ways of circulating it online. And most of these suggestions make very good sense indeed.

If I can, I'd like to agree with both groups. I see no point in rejecting the *Statement*, but neither do I think we can simply tweak its phrasings to support writing teachers both on and off the tenure track. The document, as written, is simply too invested in a defense of tenure. Rather, I think we should say that the 1989 *Statement* is a document of its time, honor what it attempted, and then call for a new statement—one that outlines the kinds of support, both material and intellectual, that all writing teachers need to do their jobs happily and well. (Why do I feel, as I write these words, that I am volunteering for a committee?) The good news is that the essays in this book suggest that we now have a more detailed and nuanced sense of what those forms of support need to be than we did in 1989. We no longer need to be tied to dreams of writing programs where everyone is on the tenure track. But we can be hardheaded about the things writing programs ought to do to improve the conditions of work for all their teachers.

Works Cited

CCCC Executive Committee. *Statement of Principles and Standards for the Postsecondary Teaching of Writing. College Composition and Communication*, vol. 40, no. 3, 1989, pp. 329–36.

Robertson, Linda R., et al. "The Wyoming Conference Resolution Opposing Unfair Salaries and Working Conditions for Post-Secondary Teachers of Writing." *College English*, vol. 49, no. 3, March 1987, pp. 274–80.

Sledd, James. "Why the Wyoming Resolution Had to Be Emasculated: A History and a Quixotism." *Journal of Advanced Composition*, vol. 11, 1991, pp. 269–81.

Appendix: Data Enhanced Version of the Statement of Principles and Standards for the Postsecondary Teaching of Writing (1989)

The editors are proud to offer you this data-enhanced version of the 1989 *Statement of Principles and Standards for the Postsecondary Teaching of Writing* (hereafter the *Statement*).[1] We envision it as one of many possible ways to make the *Statement* more relevant to today's labor discourse and the arguments that must be made to improve the working life of postsecondary writing teachers. It is our hope that this version of the *Statement*, unlike the revision approved in 2013, facilitates the making of those arguments in an empirical, administratively-constructive way. To this end, we make more than fifty data enhancements to the 1989 *Statement*.

Several conditions were decided upon when we considered what data to add. First, we imagined how this document may be used as a tool in the fight for equitable labor conditions for teachers of writing across the country. Given this exigency, the data selected to support this statement are both national and relevant to English departments and more narrowly-defined institutional niches where teachers of writing are employed. Second, local findings were excluded from supporting this version of the *Statement*, but the authors heartily encourage their inclusion for any arguments made in order to improve working conditions for teachers of writing at a specific institution. Third, although the impact of history is difficult to overstate, we have only included data from the twenty-first century.

Several reports were consulted in order to develop the framework for a data-backed *Statement*, including the following:

- The College and University Professional Association for Human Resources (CUPA-HR) *2014–15 Faculty in Higher Education Salary Survey for Four-Year Colleges and Universities*

---

1. This work was sponsored by a 2009 CCCC Research Incentive award for the project, "*The Principles and Standards for the Postsecondary Teaching of Writing*: Providing a Data-Based Framework for the 21st Century," by Randall McClure and Danya Goldstein.

- *Annual Report on the Economic Status of the Profession, 2014–15* (Barnshaw and Dunietz)
- *Digest of Education Statistics 2014* (Snyder et al.)
- *The 2012–13 Survey of Humanities Departments at Four-Year Institutions* (White, Chu, and Czujko)
- *A Portrait of Part-Time Faculty Members* (2012)
- *2011–2012 Faculty Salary Survey by Discipline*
- *Undergraduate Teaching Faculty: The 2010–2011 HERI Faculty Survey* (Hurtado, Egan et al.)
- *Your First Year College Survey 2011* (Hurtado, Pryor, DeAngelo, and Blake)
- *Your First Year College Survey 2012* (Hurtado, Pryor, Blake et al.)
- *Initial Report on Survey of CCCC Members* (2009)
- The CCCC *Strategic Research Survey* (2008)
- National Survey of Student Engagement (NSSE), 2009
- Report from the Consortium for the Study of Writing in College (2009)
- Faculty Survey of Student Engagement (FSSE), 2009
- "Twenty More Years in the WPA's Progress" (Charlton and Rose, 2009)
- *AAUP Contingent Faculty Index 2006*
- *Release Time for Writing Program Administrators: A Survey* (Bowden, 2005)
- *TYCA Two-Year College Facts and Data Report 2005* (Millward and TYCA Research Committee)
- *2004 National Study of Postsecondary Faculty* (*NSOPF:04*; Cataldi et al.)

In compiling and applying the data used to support the *Statement*, three issues became apparent. First, there are limited national data on the status of contingent laborers. Second, the data that is available details current labor problems in more general terms, as seen by the preponderance of support for the early section of the *Statement*. Long past the identification of problems in labor practices and working conditions and now long past time to generate data-defensible solutions that will support the recommendations in this or any similar statement, the available data points to the need for empirical exemplars of equitable, successful labor conditions. Third, the warrants that connect long-term employment and improved learning require significant disciplinary substantiation.

To facilitate our and future work with the *Statement*, each line of the document has been numbered. In one instance, line 107, the sentence was further divided given not just its length but also its reference to several issues related to working conditions. All other aspects of the 1989 document, including headings and paragraph breaks, have been maintained.

Introduction: Writing Instruction in American Colleges—The Commitment to Educational Quality

1. A democracy demands citizens who can read critically and write clearly and cogently.
2. Developing students' powers as critical readers and writers demands in turn the highest quality of instruction.[2][3]
3. This quality is the goal to which the Conference on College Composition and Communication (CCCC), the learned society founded in 1949 to serve as the professional association for college teachers of writing, is committed.
4. And yet the achievement of this goal is at risk, for the quality of writing instruction is today seriously compromised.[4][5][6]
5. The purpose of this document is to examine the conditions which undermine the quality of postsecondary writing instruction and to recommend alternatives to those conditions.
6. Quality in education is intimately linked to the quality of teachers.

---

2. According to the *NSOPF:04*, 33% of English faculty have a PhD in field, 49% have an MA, 9% have an MFA, and 7% have a bachelor's degree or less. The other percentage is some type of professional degree.

3. According to the *NSOPF:04*, 58% of English faculty members spend 80% or more of their time on undergraduate instruction, with only 3.5% of English and literature instructors spending less than 20% of their time on undergraduate instruction. In contrast, 84.4% of English faculty members spend less than 40% of their time instructing graduate students.

4. According to the *NSOPF:04*, 84.4% of English faculty members require multiple drafts of student writing in some of their classes, and 64.8% require multiple drafts in all of their classes.

5. According to the *NSOPF:04*, a high percentage of English faculty spend between one and five hours per week "individually" instructing undergraduates (82.7%) and graduate students (91.5%).

6. Despite claims of interdisciplinary activity, 98.8% of English faculty do research exclusively in field, according to the *NSOPF:04*.

7. Higher education traditionally assures this quality[7] by providing reasonable teaching loads,[8] research support,[9] and eventual tenure[10] for those who meet rigorous professional standards.
8. Such standards are applied and such support extended to virtually all faculties in higher education—but rarely to those who teach writing.
9. At all levels of the academic hierarchy, current institutional practices endanger the quality of education that writing teachers can offer their students.[11] [12] [13]

---

7. According to the *NSOPF:04*, only 2.5% of English faculty of all employment conditions were very dissatisfied with their job, and 89.1% were somewhat (44.3%) or very satisfied (44.8%) with their job.

8. Nearly all English faculty surveyed in the *NSOPF:04* (99.1%) teach fewer than twenty credit hours a semester and 69% teach fewer than ten credit hours per semester; 95.7% taught five classes or fewer per semester.

9. Satisfaction with support for teaching improvement is high for English faculty, with 29.1% very satisfied and 41% somewhat satisfied, according to the *NSOPF:04*.

10. Jonikka Charlton and Shirley K. Rose's "Twenty More Years in the WPA's Progress" indicates that 94% of those WPAs on the tenure track replied that they were either more or most likely to receive tenure. This is reported as a 14% increase since 1987.

11. English faculty members are noticeably active in the fight for more humane labor practices. For example, part-time faculty in English constitute 16% of the respondents in the *A Portrait of Part-Time Faculty Members* from the Coalition on the Academic Workforce.

12. According to *The 2007–08 Survey of Humanities Departments*, "[P]rograms that award degrees in English employ about 20,390 faculty members in full-time positions and 10,290 faculty members in part-time positions. There are approximately 11,700 tenured faculty members and 3,910 tenure-track faculty members [. . .] English departments and programs recruited about 900 tenure-track, or permanent faculty members for 2008–09 and had hired about 920 for 2007–08. This represents about 4% of the full-time faculty workforce. The 530 faculty members who were granted tenure comprise about one-seventh of the tenure-track faculty corps. An additional 5% of those in tenure-track positions were either denied tenure or left before the tenure decision was made" (White, Ivie, and Czujko 33).

13. According to the AAUP's *Annual Report on the Economic Status of the Profession 2012–13* authored by John W. Curtis and Saranna Thornton, English faculty earn on average between $39,503 and $45,708 per year.

10. The teaching, research, and service contributions of tenure-line composition faculty are often misunderstood or undervalued.
11. At some postsecondary institutions, such faculty members are given administrative duties without the authority needed to discharge them;[14] at others, they are asked to meet publication standards without support for the kind of research that their discipline requires.[15]
12. The English graduate students who staff many writing programs are regularly assigned teaching duties[16] [17] that they cannot responsibly discharge without neglecting their own course work.
13. More disturbing still is the situation of those college teachers of writing who now constitute an enormous academic underclass.
14. More than half the English faculty in two-year colleges, and nearly one-third of the English faculty at four-year colleges and universities, work on part-time and/or temporary appointments. [18] [19]

---

14. Charlton and Rose found that 82% of the sample answered "Yes" to their status as a current WPA, 4% responded that they were doing WPA work without a formal position, and slightly less than 10% of respondents have never held a WPA position, though they still identified with the work of WPAs. Something in the work of composition appears to breed administrative tendencies.

15. The *NSOPF:04* provides a rich picture of the scholarship in English. In a given year, 75% of English faculty complete between one and three book reviews, chapters, or creative works, and 19% produce between four and six of these types of scholarship. One to three books, monographs, and reports are published per year by 87% of English faculty. Incredibly, 95% make at least one conference presentation per year. English faculty are clearly active scholars.

16. While assisting a professor in teaching at least one credit bearing undergraduate class is reported by only 6% of graduate students in the *NSOPF:04*, more than 42% of graduate students have been the teacher of record for at least two undergraduate classes per year.

17. The *Initial Report on Survey of CCCC Members* found that 25% of the 44,173 sections of college writing were taught by graduate students.

18. The CCCC *Strategic Research Survey* indicates that 23% of respondents are on contingent, temporary, and part-time appointments.

19. In his analysis of the 2011 *Employees by Assigned Position* report from the U.S. Department of Education, a survey of more than 1.5 million faculty, David Laurence finds that 43% of faculty at four-year institutions and 69% of those at two-year institutions work part-time, a double-digit increase for both categories since what was reported in the 1989 *Statement*.

15. Almost universally, they are teachers of writing, a fact which many consider the worst scandal in higher education today.[20] [21] [22]
16. These teachers work without job security, often without benefits,[23] and for wages far below what their full-time colleagues are paid[24] per course.
17. Increasingly, many are forced to accept an itinerant existence, racing from class to car to drive to another institution to teach.[25] [26]

---

20. According to the CUPA-HR *2014–15 Faculty in Higher Education Salary Survey for Four-Year Colleges and Universities*, English is the fifth lowest paid discipline across all ranks, and the second lowest paid at the non-tenure-track instructor level. Tenured or tenure-track faculty in English are the third lowest paid of all the disciplines for new assistant professors.

21. The CUPA-HR *2014–15 Faculty in Higher Education Salary Survey* reports the average salary for tenured and tenure-track English faculty at $69,221, or roughly 12% less than the average for similar faculty across all disciplines when compared with the average salary of $78,625 for all "full-time instructional faculty" in 2014–2015 as reported by the National Center for Education Statistics (Synder et al.).

22. Half of all English faculty (51%) do not start their first postsecondary teaching position with tenure or on the tenure track, according to the *NSOPF:04*.

23. According to *The 2010–2011 HERI Faculty Survey* (Hurtado, Egan et al.), only 15% of voluntary part-time faculty and 25% of involuntary part-time faculty responded that they are in positions that provide the benefits (e.g., health insurance and retirement) they need.

24. The *2011–2012 Faculty Salary Survey by Discipline* indicates that the average Professor of Law earns 60% more than the average Professor of English. On average, full professors in English earn 13% less than all other full professors, and 17% less than those in the social sciences. The only comparable field within 5% of English is labeled in the study as "Fine Arts."

25. According to the *NSOPF:04*, only 18% of English faculty have another full-time job.

26. *The 2010–2011 HERI Faculty Survey* (Hurtado, Egan et al.) reports that "more than a quarter of voluntary part-time faculty (29%) report holding part-time teaching appointments at multiple institutions, whereas just under half (46%) of involuntary part-time faculty have strung together multiple part-time teaching appointments."

18. The CCCC recognizes, with respect and gratitude, the extraordinary contributions that so many of these teachers have made to their students and schools.[27][28][29]
19. But it is evident that their working conditions[30][31] undermine the capacities of teachers to teach and of students to learn.
20. These conditions constitute a crisis in higher education, one which dramatically affects the public interest.
21. "The responsibility for the academy's most serious mission . . . should be vested in tenure-line faculty."
22. This crisis must concern all faculty and administrators at postsecondary institutions.
23. As the American Association of University Professors has affirmed, when institutions depend increasingly on faculty whose positions are tenuous and whose rights and privileges are unclear or nonexistent,[32] those freedoms established as the right of full-time tenurable and tenured faculty are endangered.

---

27. According to the *NSOPF:04*, 13% of surveyed faculty would not choose an academic career again. This is the highest number in the humanities by more than one-third.

28. When queried on the *NSOPF:04* whether part-time faculty were treated fairly by their institution, 42% of those in English indicated disagreement.

29. According to the *NSOPF:04*, 44% of the English faculty planned to retire after age 66.

30. According to the *NSOPF:04*, 20% of English faculty were dissatisfied with their institution's equipment and facilities.

31. Less than 75% of English faculty across all ranks are satisfied with the support for teaching improvement, according to the *NSOPF:04*.

32. When queried on the *NSOPF:04* whether part-time faculty were treated fairly by their institution, merely 22% of those in English indicated strong agreement.

24. Moreover, the excessive reliance on marginalized faculty[33] damages the quality of education.[34]
25. Even when, as is often the case, these faculty bring to their academic appointments the appropriate credentials and commitments to good teaching, their low salaries, poor working conditions, and uncertain futures mar their effectiveness and reduce the possibilities for loyalty to the institution's educational goals.
26. All lose: teachers, students, schools, and ultimately a democratic society that cannot be without citizens whose education empowers them to read and write with critical sophistication.
27. With these considerations in mind, and in response to the many educators who have requested our help in developing standards for effective writing programs,[35] we provide the following guidelines.
28. These guidelines are based on the assumption that the responsibility for the academy's most serious mission, helping students to develop their critical powers as readers and writers, should be vested in tenure-line faculty.
29. That is the standard to which every institution should aspire.
30. Because assumptions to the contrary have become well entrenched in institutions of higher learning during the past fifteen years, however, we offer guidelines as well for the professional recognition and treatment of part-time and temporary full-time faculty during the period when these positions are being transformed to the tenure track.
31. It is our hope and expectation that this period of transition will be brief. Ultimately, every institution should extend to teachers

---

33. The *Initial Report on Survey of CCCC Members* indicates that 39.44% of the classes taught across the respondents are taught by part-time faculty.

34. In "Do College Instructors Matter? The Effects of Adjuncts and Graduate Students on Students' Interest and Success," Eric Bettinger and Bridget Terry Long found that first exposure to adjunct and graduate students as instructors in English decreased students' likelihood of choosing English as a major by approximately 15%. It was also found that first-year exposure to adjunct and graduate student faculty resulted in the students taking fewer courses in English.

35. More than half (53%) of those who responded to the CCCC *Strategic Research Survey* had time assigned to administrative or other "managerial" responsibilities. That quantity of writing professionals doing managerial work necessitates informed practices.

of writing the same opportunities for professional advancement (e.g., tenure and promotion) and the same encouragement of intellectual achievement (e.g., support for research and reasonable teaching responsibilities) that they extend to all other faculty.
32. As colleges have the right to expect of writing specialists the highest level of performance, so they have the obligation to extend the greatest possible support.
33. To do less is to compromise writing instruction for future generations of American students.

34. I: Professional Standards That Promote Quality Education

35. Tenure-Line Faculty

36. To provide the highest quality of instruction, departments offering composition[36] and writing courses should rely on full-time tenured or tenure-track faculty members[37] who are both prepared for and committed to the teaching of writing.
37. The teaching of writing courses need not be limited, however, to those faculty members whose primary area of scholarship is rhetoric and composition.
38. Because of the significant intellectual and practical connections between writing and reading, composition and literature, it is desirable that faculty from both areas of specialization teach in the composition program.

---

36. Several types of departments house composition. As reported in the *Initial Report on Survey of CCCC Members*, 68% of writing programs are housed in English departments, 4.6% in humanities programs, approximately 2% each in rhetoric departments, writing centers, or composition departments, and nearly 20% in the provost's office or support services.

37. While the *2012–13 Survey of Humanities Departments at Four-Year Institutions* suggests that 52% of faculty in English are full-time tenured or tenure-track (White, Chu, and Czujko 6), tenured or tenure-track faculty only accounted for 16% of those teaching college writing classes according to those answering the *Initial Report on Survey of CCCC Members*.

39. Ideally, faculty from each area should have the training and experience necessary to teach in both the literature and composition programs.[38]
40. Whenever possible, faculty professionally committed to rhetoric and composition should coordinate and supervise composition programs.[39] [40]
41. Evidence of this commitment can be found in research and publication, participation in professional conferences, and active involvement in curriculum development and design.[41]
42. Those who supervise writing programs should also be involved in determining policy and budget for their programs.
43. Research in rhetoric and composition is a legitimate field of scholarship with standards comparable to other academic fields.[42]
44. In salary, tenure, and promotion considerations, research and publication in rhetoric and composition should be treated on a par with all other areas of research in English departments.
45. As recommended in the "Report of the Modern Language Association's Commission on Writing and Literature" (MLA/Profession 88, 1988: 70–76), postsecondary institutions should count seriously certain kinds of professional activity, sometimes undervalued within current measures of scholarly achievement, that are particularly important to this field.

---

38. Of Charlton and Rose's 188 survey participants not enrolled in graduate school at the time of the survey, 53% reported rhetoric and /or composition; 27% literature; 6% English education; 5% speech/communications; 1% linguistics; 2% creative writing; and 11% "other" as their main coursework area.

39. Charlton and Rose found those who are WPAs are three times more likely to have chosen rhetoric and composition over literature as the focus for their coursework.

40. The WPA's highest academic degree is a PhD for 83% of those surveyed in the *Initial Report on Survey of CCCC Members*.

41. The *Strategic Research Survey* reveals that the average CCCC member joins after three years and doesn't leave the organization until they've been in the profession for more than twenty-five years. There is always room for professional development in the discipline.

42. More than a quarter (27%) of those who answered the *Strategic Research Survey* have been in rhetoric and composition for more than twenty-five years. Another quarter (25%) have been in the profession from 16–25 years. This is a profession one can make an academic career.

46. These activities include: (1) the publication of composition textbooks as a primary form of original research; (2) collaborative research on articles and books that draw on diverse scholarly backgrounds and research orientations; (3) professional activities such as workshops and seminars for faculty at all levels; and (4) the particularly demanding administrative service that is often a regular part of a composition specialist's responsibilities.
47. These are "measures of evaluation and standards of practice that do justice to the professional achievements of teachers of rhetoric and composition" (MLA/Profession 88, 73).
48. Because it is fundamentally necessary to the quality of education at all levels, research in rhetoric and composition should be supported not only at research institutions but also at those institutions primarily dedicated to teaching.[43]
49. While insisting on the importance of research in rhetoric and composition, we join with those professional associations and learned societies who have affirmed that postsecondary institutions should develop flexible standards governing tenure, standards that accurately reflect the mission of the institution.
50. At the vast majority of colleges and universities, and even at research institutions, distinguished teaching and service should warrant serious consideration for tenure and promotion.

51. Graduate Students

52. Graduate students' teaching experience should be understood as an essential part of their training for future professional responsibilities.
53. They are primarily students and should never, for mere economic expediency, be used to replace tenure-line faculty in the staffing of composition programs.
54. Graduate students' teaching loads should not interfere with their progress toward their degrees: an average of one course per term is ideal; more than two courses per term is unreasonable.
55. "Teaching loads should not interfere with progress toward degrees."

---

43. *The 2012–13 Survey of Humanities Departments at Four-Year Institutions* reports that 93% of full-time tenured or tenure-track faculty in English have access to either institutional or departmental research support (White, Chu, and Czujko 66).

56. Graduate teaching assistantships for writing courses should be awarded only to students (1) who demonstrate superior writing ability and (2) who present evidence of successful experience in the teaching of composition or who have had training in the teaching of composition.
57. The standards for admitting graduate students and for awarding teaching assistantships should not be compromised by the need to staff the composition program.
58. Each institution should provide adequate training and supervision of graduate writing instructors, and this training should be conducted by someone with appropriate preparation or experience in rhetoric and composition.
59. Nearly all graduate students teaching writing in English departments are fully in charge of their classes.
60. Because the university entrusts to them such serious responsibility, their special status among graduate students should be recognized and their compensation, benefits, class size, and course load should be adjusted accordingly.
61. In this adjustment, attention should be given to hours spent inside[44] and outside of class[45] and to the increased responsibility for grading, classroom management, and preparation.[46]

62. Part-Time Faculty

63. CCCC and other professional associations generally recognize two legitimate reasons for hiring part-time faculty: (1) to teach specialized courses for which no regular faculty are available and

---

44. More than 20% of English faculty surveyed in the *NSOPF:04* teach four or more classes a semester. A full 50% of those surveyed teach at least one class with fifty students or more in it.

45. This next statistic drawn from the *NSOPF:04* is a bit complicated, but if one spends three hours a week with twenty-five students, then one has seventy-five student contact hours per week. Among English teachers, 34% have between 100–200 total student contact hours per week, and 23% have between 200–300 contact hours.

46. According to the NSSE results from 2009, 20% of first-year students wrote papers of twenty pages or more. In that same report, 34% of first-year students responded that they write at least five papers of five pages in length or more during their first year, and 31% write at least eleven papers of fewer than five pages. Teachers provided "prompt" written and oral feedback to 93% of first-year students, according to the survey.

which require special practical knowledge (e.g., hiring a distinguished reporter to teach one class in journalism); and (2) to meet unexpected increases in enrollment.
64. Abuses in this second category are cause for the most serious concern. Assuring and sustaining quality in education is incompatible with relying, purely for fiscal expediency, on part-time faculty appointments in rhetoric and composition.
65. The commitment to quality education requires that the number of part-time writing teachers in the second category be kept to a minimum.[47]
66. We recognize, however, that at the present time many administrators and department chairs have become dependent on part-time faculty lines.
67. In the process of transforming these lines to the tenure track, administrators should impose severe limits on the ratio of part-time to full-time faculty.
68. The percentage of part-time instructors in writing programs should not exceed what is necessary to meet unexpected increases in enrollment.
69. When more than 10 percent of a department's course sections are taught by part-time faculty, the department should reconsider its hiring practices.
70. "Assuring and sustaining quality in education is incompatible with relying, purely for fiscal expediency, on part-time faculty appointments."
71. To assure that students receive the instructional excellence to which they have the right, the educational qualifications and experience of all part-time faculty should meet the highest professional standards.
72. Part-time teachers of writing should (1) demonstrate superior writing ability, (2) demonstrate professional involvement with composition theory and pedagogy, and (3) present evidence of successful experience in the teaching of composition.

---

47. According to the *TYCA Two-Year College Facts and Data Report: 2005* (Millward and TYCA Research Committee), two-year colleges enrolled 96,785 international students. This number accounts for just under a 60% increase since 1994. Given this growth and the increased effort necessary to read and comment on the papers of international students, the *Statement* should provide support for the need to pay attention to class size, teaching load, and other conditions necessary for effective teaching.

73. Recommendations for part-time faculty.
74. Administrators and department chairs should recognize the professional status of part-time teachers.
75. Recommendations 1–5 (see below) apply to all part-time faculty, even those hired only occasionally to meet truly unexpected increases in enrollment.
76. Recommendations 6–10 apply especially to part-time faculty who are regularly employed, even when departments abide by the 10 percent guideline recommended above.
77. These faculty members, described by AAUP guidelines as those "whose contribution to the academic program of the institution and to its academic life is equal to that of a full-timer except for the proportion of time given to the position," deserve special consideration in matters of governance, job security,[48] and incentives for professional development.
78. That we recommend the following guidelines for the just treatment of part-time faculty should in no way be construed as condoning the practice of relying on part-time positions instead of full-time, tenure-track positions.
79. Expectations for part-time instructors' teaching, service, and research should be made clear, in writing, at the time of hiring, and these instructors should be evaluated according to those written expectations.
80. Whenever possible, part-time instructors should be hired as much in advance of their teaching assignments as possible.
81. We recommend the preceding term.
82. They should receive adequate introduction to their teaching assignments, departments, and institutions.
83. They should receive a salary that accurately reflects their teaching duties and any duties outside the classroom they are asked to assume.
84. Compensation, per course, for part-time faculty should never be lower than the per-course compensation for full-time faculty with comparable experience, duties, and credentials.

---

48. According to *The 2010–2011 HERI Faculty Survey* (Hurtado, Egan et al.), more than eight of ten (81%) voluntary part-time faculty and close to nine of ten (89%) involuntary part-time faculty responded that they have "no guarantee of job security."

85. Part-timers should be eligible for the same fringe benefits and for the same cost-of-living, seniority, and merit salary increases available to full-time faculty.
86. Part-time faculty should be given mailboxes, office space, telephones, and clerical support.[49]
87. They should be given a voice in the formulation of department policy regarding courses and programs in which they teach (for example, by voting at department meetings and by serving on curriculum and hiring committees).
88. They should have the same right as full-time faculty to participate in the design of evaluation procedures.
89. They should have access to research support and travel funds to attend professional conferences.[50]
90. During the period when departments are converting part-time positions to full-time tenured lines, departments should offer long-term contracts to part-time faculty who have demonstrated excellence in teaching.
91. Part-time faculty who have been employed for six or more terms or consecutively for three or more terms should not be terminated without a full term's notice.
92. Taking into account recommendations made by the AAUP ("The Status of Part-Time Faculty," 1980), we recognize that some institutions have responded innovatively to requests for tenure-line part-time positions.
93. Where such positions are entirely the equal of full-time positions in terms of eligibility for tenure, prorated salary, fringe benefits, merit raises, support for research, participation in governance, and so on, we find this practice acceptable.
94. But such positions are and should be exceptions. The quality, integrity, and continuity of instruction and the principle of academic freedom are best ensured by a full-time tenured or tenure-track faculty.

---

49. *The 2010–2011 HERI Faculty Survey* (Hurtado, Egan et al.) reports that part-time faculty's access to institutional resources is highest for access to institutional email (90%), and roughly half (48%) of part-time faculty have access to a phone with voicemail and a personal computer.

50. The *2012–13 Survey of Humanities Departments at Four-Year Institutions* reports that only 27% of part-time faculty in English receive support for research (White, Chu, and Czujko 66).

95. Full-Time Temporary Faculty

96. The permanent use of temporary faculty is a contradiction in terms and should be avoided.
97. As the AAUP repeatedly insists, the regular employment of full-time temporary faculty is "unjust and inequitable" and represents "a threat to academic freedom" ("On Full-Time, Non-Tenure-Track Appointments," 1978).
98. Two guidelines should be followed.
99. Full-time temporary appointments should be used only to fill non-recurring instructional needs (e.g., short-term visiting professorships or replacements for tenure-line faculty on leave).
100. The use of these positions to provide instruction that is a regular part of the institution's curriculum is exploitative.
101. The rights and privileges afforded to individuals with full-time temporary appointments ought to be congruent with the policies of the AAUP, and their working conditions and salaries ought to be in compliance with those outlined in this document for teachers of writing.
102. "The permanent use of temporary faculty is a contradiction in terms."
103. We recognize that where an institution has relied heavily on part-time positions, their transformation to full-time tenure-track lines may have to proceed in stages.
104. Except in the cases noted above (visiting professorships and leave replacements), full-time temporary positions are tolerable only as a stage in converting part-time to full-time tenure-track positions.

105. II: Teaching Conditions Necessary for Quality Education

106. The improvement of an individual student's writing requires persistent and frequent contact between teacher and student both inside and outside the classroom.
107A. It requires assigning far more papers than are usually assigned in other college classrooms; it requires reading them and commenting on them not simply to justify a grade, but to offer guidance and suggestions for improvement;

107B and it requires spending a great deal of time with individual students,[51]

107C. helping them not just to improve particular papers but to understand fundamental principles of effective writing that will

107D. enable them to continue learning throughout their lives.

108. The teaching of writing, perhaps more than any other discipline, therefore requires special attention to class size,[52] teaching loads, the availability of teaching materials, and the development of additional resources that enhance classroom instruction.

109. For these reasons, we offer the following guidelines, widely supported by professional associations in English.

110. "The teaching of writing . . . requires special attention to class size, teaching loads, the availability of teaching materials, and the development of additional resources that enhance classroom instruction."

111. No more than 20 students should be permitted in any writing class.

112. Ideally, classes should be limited to 15.

113. Remedial or developmental sections should be limited to a maximum of 15 students.

114. No English faculty members should teach more than 60 writing students a term.

115. In developmental writing classes, the maximum should be 45.

116. The effectiveness of classroom writing instruction is significantly improved by the assistance students receive in writing centers.[53]

---

51. *The 2010–2011 HERI Faculty Survey* (Hurtado, Egan et al.), a study of close to 24,000 full-time faculty teaching undergraduate courses at more than 400 four-year colleges and universities across the US, reports that 44% of faculty spend nine hours or more teaching and 59% of faculty spend more than nine hours preparing to teach each week. These figures are for preparation and class time only and do not include time responding to or grading student writing.

52. The single most common class size cap for a writing course is twenty-five students, although 20% of institutions responding to the CCCC *Strategic Research Survey* reported a cap of 18 or lower and 47% have a cap between 19–24 students.

53. In the *Your First Year College Survey 2012* (Hurtado, Pryor, Blake et. al) of more than 14,000 first-year students from more than sixty colleges and universities, 51% of first generation and 45% of non-first generation students visit the writing center "occasionally" or "frequently," up from 44% and 39% respectively just a year earlier.

117. Centers provide students with individual attention to their writing and often provide faculty and graduate students with opportunities to learn more about effective writing instruction.
118. Because these centers enhance the conditions of teaching and learning, their development and support should be an important departmental and institutional priority.
119. Because rhetoric and composition is a rapidly developing field, all writing instructors should have access to scholarly literature and be given opportunities for continuing professional development.
120. Because writing instruction requires so much individual attention to student writing,[54] it is important that all instructors have adequate and reasonably private office space[55] for regular conferences.
121. The institution should provide all necessary support services for the teaching of writing, including supplies, duplication services, and secretarial assistance.

Works Cited

2011–2012 Faculty Salary Survey by Discipline. Office of Institutional Research and Information Management, Oklahoma State University, 2012, http://www.montana.edu/opa/restricted/OSUSalaries12F.pdf.

AAUP Contingent Faculty Index 2006. American Association of University Professors (AAUP), 2006, www.aaup.org/aaup-contingent-faculty-index-2006.

Barnshaw, John, and Samuel Dunietz. "Busting the Myths: The Annual Report on the Economic Status of the Profession, 2014–15." *Academe*, March–April 2015, pp. 4–19, www.aaup.org/sites/default/files/files/2015salarysurvey/zreport.pdf.

---

54. According to a report from the Consortium for the Study of Writing in College, 78% of the 12,026 first-year student respondents indicated that they received feedback from their writing instructor on a draft for at least some of their assignments. The same report notes that 16% of those 12,026 students received feedback on *all* of their drafts before submitting them. This data supports the conclusion that writing teachers, by and large, are offering ample guidance for the improvement of student writing.

55. *The 2010–2011 HERI Faculty Survey* (Hurtado, Egan et al.), reporting the results from analyses of more than 3,500 part-time faculty members working at more than 250 four-year colleges and universities, finds that two-thirds (66%) of part-time faculty have access to office space, with close to one in five a private office.

Bettinger, Eric, and Bridget Terry Long. "Do College Instructors Matter? The Effects of Adjuncts and Graduate Students on Students' Interest and Success." *NBER Working Paper No. 10370*. National Bureau of Economic Research, March 2004, www.nber.org/papers/w10370.

Bowden, Darsie. *Release Time for Writing Program Administrators: A Survey*. July 2005, comppile.org/profresources/releasetime.htm.

Cataldi, Emily Forrest, et al. *2004 National Study of Postsecondary Faculty (NSOPF:04) Report on Faculty and Instructional Staff in Fall 2003* (NCES 2005 –172). National Center for Education Statistics, U.S. Department of Education, 2005, nces.ed.gov/pubs2005/2005172.pdf.

CCCC Executive Committee. *Statement of Principles and Standards for the Postsecondary Teaching of Writing. College Composition and Communication*, vol. 40, no. 3, 1989, pp. 329–36.

Charlton, Jonikka, and Shirley K. Rose. "Twenty More Years in the WPA's Progress." *WPA: Writing Program Administration*, vol. 33, no. 1–2, Fall/Winter 2009, pp. 114–45.

Conference on College Composition and Communication. *The Strategic Research Survey*. 2008, https://s.zoomerang.com/sr.aspx?sm=UnpQG0Bgoxm AEerZv8H%2fDvg72ZhKeQnC8DKhZXzT65k%3d.

Curtis, John W., and Saranna Thornton. "Here's the News: The Annual Report on the Economic Status of the Profession 2012–2013." *Academe*, March—April 2013, pp. 4–19.

Faculty in Higher Education Salary Survey Executive Summary for the 2014–15 Academic Year. College and University Professional Association for Human Resources (CUPA-HR), 2015, www.cupahr.org/surveys/files/salary2015/FHE4-2015-Executive-Summary.pdf.

Faculty Survey of Student Engagement (FSSE). *Grand Total Frequencies: Frequency Distributions August 2009*. Indiana University Center for Postsecondary Research, 2009, fsse.indiana.edu/pdf/FSSE_IR_2009/FSSE09%20 Reports%20%28Total-TS%29.pdf.

Hurtado, Slyvia, Kevin Eagan, et al. *Undergraduate Teaching Faculty: The 2010–2011 HERI Faculty Survey*. Higher Education Research Institute, UCLA, 2012, heri.ucla.edu/monographs/HERI-FAC2011-Monograph.pdf.

Hurtado, Sylvia, John H. Pryor, Laura Palucki Blake, et al. *HERI Research Brief: Your First College Year Survey 2012*. Higher Education Research Institute, UCLA, January 2013, www.heri.ucla.edu/briefs/YFCY2012-Brief.pdf.

Hurtado, Sylvia, John H. Pryor, Linda DeAngelo, and Laura Palucki Blake. *HERI Research Brief: Your First College Year Survey 2011*. Higher Education Research Institute, UCLA, January 2012, www.heri.ucla.edu/PDFs/pubs/briefs/YFCYBrief2011.pdf.

Initial Report on Survey of CCCC Members. James R. Squire Office of Policy Research in the English Language Arts, 2009, www.ncte.org/library/NCTEFiles/Groups/CCCC/InitialReportSurveyCCCCMembers.pdf

Laurence, David. "A Profile of the Non-Tenure-Track Academic Workforce." *ADE Bulletin*, vol. 153, 2013, pp. 6–22.

Millward, Jody, and TYCA Research Committee. *TYCA Two-Year College Facts and Data Report: 2005*. TYCA, September 2005, www.ncte.org/library/NCTEFiles/Groups/TYCA/TYCA_DataReport.pdf.

National Survey of Student Engagement (NSSE). *Assessment for Improvement: Tracking Student Engagement Over Time—Annual Results 2009*. Indiana University Center for Postsecondary Research, 2009, nsse.indiana.edu/NSSE_2009_Results/pdf/NSSE_AR_2009.pdf.

Paine, Charles, et al. Writing Item Aggregated Results, 2009. Consortium for the Study of Writing in College, 2009.

A Portrait of Part-Time Faculty Members. Coalition on the Academic Workforce, June 2012, www.academicworkforce.org/CAW_portrait_2012.pdf.

Snyder, T.D., et al. *Digest of Education Statistics 2014* (NCES 2016–006). National Center for Education Statistics, Institute of Education Sciences, U.S. Department of Education, 2016, nces.ed.gov/pubs2016/2016006.pdf.

White, Susan, Raymond Chu, and Roman Czujko. *The 2012–13 Survey of Humanities Departments at Four-Year Institutions*. Statistical Research Center, American Institute of Physics, 2014, www.humanitiesindicators.org/binaries/pdf/HDS2_final.pdf.

White, Susan, Rachel Ivie, and Roman Czujko. *The 2007–08 Survey of Humanities Departments*. Statistical Research Center, American Institute of Physics, 2008, archive201406.humanitiesindicators.org/binaries/humanitiesDepartmentalSurvey.pdf.

Contributors

Chris Anson (www.ansonica.net) is Distinguished University Professor and Director of the Campus Writing and Speaking Program at North Carolina State University, where he teaches graduate and undergraduate courses in language, composition, and literacy and works with faculty across the disciplines to reform undergraduate education in the areas of writing and speaking. He has published fifteen books and more than one hundred and twenty articles and book chapters relating to writing and has spoken widely across the US and in close to thirty other countries. He is a Past Chair of the Conference on College Composition and Communication, and past President of the Council of Writing Program Administrators.

Valerie M. Balester, Professor of English at Texas A&M University and Assistant Provost for Undergraduate Studies, serves as the Executive Director of the University Writing Center, which houses the writing-and-speaking-in-the disciplines program, and as Executive Director of the Academic Success Center. Her 1993 *Cultural Divide: Case Studies of African American College-Level Writers* (Boynton/Cook-Heinemann) earned an Honorable Mention for the W. Ross Winterowd Award for best book on composition theory. More recently, she co-edited, with Michelle Hall Kells and Victor Villanueva, *Latino/a Discourses: On Language, Identity and Literacy Education* (Boynton/Cook, 2004) and contributed "How Writing Rubrics Fail: Toward a Multicultural Model" to *Race and Writing Assessment* (edited by Asao B. Inoue and Mya Poe, Peter Lang, 2012), which received the 2014 CCCC Outstanding Book Award in the Edited Collection category.

Evelyn Beck has a BA and an MA from Florida State University. She has taught college English for many years in both adjunct and full-time positions and is retired from Piedmont Technical College in Greenwood, South Carolina.

Barbara J. D'Angelo is Assistant Clinical Professor of Technical Communication at Arizona State University. She has served as Director of Assessment and Curriculum for the undergraduate technical communication degree program. She has presented on topics related to information literacy, technical communication, writing assessment, and curriculum development at the Conference on College Composition and Communication, the Association for Business Communication annual convention, and the International Writing Across the Disciplines conference among others. Her publications include several book chapters and articles on the use of outcomes for curriculum development and assessment and on information literacy. She is the recipient of the 2011 Francis W. Weeks Award of Merit from the Association for Business Communication.

Timothy R. Dougherty is Assistant Professor of English and Direcor of the First-Year Writing Program at West Chester University of Pennsylvania, where he teaches general education classes in writing and upper-division classes in rhetorical theory, cultural rhetorics, and writing studies. His work on the labor politics of writing instruction has also appeared in *College Composition and Communication*. He has also published work on transnational constitutive rhetoric in *Rhetoric Society Quarterly* and decolonial rhetorical history in *Enculturation*.

Casie J. Fedukovich is Assistant Professor of English and Associate Director of the First-Year Writing Program at North Carolina State University. She mentors teaching assistants and teaches graduate seminars in composition research, theory, and pedagogy. Her research explores labor practices, teacher training, writing program administration, and activism in composition. She has published in *WPA: Writing Program Administration*, *Workplace: A Journal for Academic Labor*, *Composition Studies*, and *Composition Forum*.

Joanne Baird Giordano is the Developmental Reading and Writing Coordinator for the University of Wisconsin Colleges (a statewide, two-year institution) and a senior lecturer at the University of Wisconsin Marathon County. She has graduate degrees in English and TESOL from Brigham Young University. Her research interests focus on the experience of students at open-access institutions, especially multilingual writers and significantly underprepared students.

Risa P. Gorelick's background as a compositionist can be characterized as a combination of collaborative-based and community-based work; her research has always impacted her teaching and service. She has published fifteen articles/chapters in scholarly blind-reviewed journals and given more than sixty presentations at professional conferences. Gorelick has taught composition courses at several institutions and served as a writing program administrator. Her research focuses on service-learning, the rhetoric of food writing, and the importance of mentoring in composition. Since 1995, Gorelick has served as the Chair/Co-Chair of the Research Network Forum at the Conference of College Composition and Communication. Currently, she is on the alt-ac track working as a Dissertation/Writing Coach for Defend & Publish, LLC where she assists writers at all stages of their dissertations, scholarly works, and other writing projects.

Jeanne Gunner is retired from Chapman University in Orange, California. She served as writing program administrator at UCLA and Santa Clara University; was a member of the Council of Writing Program Administrators executive and editorial boards; was co-facilitator of the WPA Summer Workshop; and a past editor of *College English*. Her recent publications include *The Writing Program Interrupted*, co-edited with Donna Strickland, and an article in the *Journal of Advanced Composition* on the branding of writing programs and the loss of disciplinarity.

Joseph Harris (josephharris.me) is Professor of English at the University of Delaware, where he teaches academic writing, critical reading, and creative nonfiction. He was previously the founding director of the Thompson Writing Program at Duke University—an independent, multidisciplinary program noted for its approach to teaching writing as a form of intellectual inquiry. His books include *A Teaching Subject: Composition Since 1966* (updated 2012), *Teaching With Student Texts* (2010), *Rewriting: How to Do Things With Texts* (2006), and *Media Journal* (1998). He served as editor of *College Composition and Communication* from 1994–1999 and of the Studies in Writing and Rhetoric book series from 2007–2012. He is currently at work on *Dead Poets and Wonder Boys*, a book on how the teaching of writing has been depicted in film and fiction.

Holly Hassel is Professor of English at the University of Wisconsin-Marathon County. She earned a PhD in English from the University of Nebraska-Lincoln and her scholarship has appeared in *College English*, *Pedagogy*, *The International Journal for the Scholarship of Teaching and Learning*, *Feminist Teacher*, *College Composition and Communication*, and *Teaching English in the Two-Year College*. Her research interests focus on the transition of students from high school to college, particularly in their development as first-year college writers, and in teaching and learning in introduction to women's and gender studies courses.

Alice S. Horning is Professor of Writing and Rhetoric at Oakland University, where she holds a joint appointment in Linguistics. Her research over her entire career has focused on the intersection of reading and writing, focusing lately on the increasing evidence of students' reading difficulties and how to address them in writing courses and across the disciplines. Her work has appeared in the major professional journals and in books published by Parlor Press and Hampton Press. Her most recent book is *Reading, Writing, and Digitizing: Understanding Literacy in the Electronic Age* published in 2012 by Cambridge Scholars Publishing.

Joseph Janangelo is a Past President of the Council of Writing Program Administrators, an Associate Professor of English at Loyola University Chicago, and co-founder of The CWPA Mentoring Project. His books include *A Critical Look at Institutional Mission: A Guide for Writing Program Administrators* (Parlor Press 2016), *Resituating Writing: Constructing and Administering Writing Programs* (with Kristine Hansen) and *Theoretical and Critical Perspectives on Teacher Change*. His work has appeared in *College Composition and Communication*, *College English*, *Computers and Composition*, *Journal of Teaching Writing*, *Kairos: A Journal of Rhetoric, Technology, and Pedagogy*, *Teaching English in the Two-Year College*, *The Writing Center Journal*, and *WPA: Writing Program Administration*.

James C. McDonald is Professor of English at the University of Louisiana at Lafayette and one-time Co-Chair of the CCCC Committee on Contingent, Adjunct, and Part-Time Faculty. His research covers the history of rhetoric and literacy, composition faculty labor issues, writing centers, and composition theory and pedagogy. He is the author of the textbook *The Reader* (Longman, 2009), the editor of *The Allyn & Bacon Sourcebook for College Writing Teachers* (2nd ed., 2000), and co-editor of *Mardi Gras, Gumbo, and Zydeco: Readings in Louisiana Culture*. His articles and reviews have appeared in such journals as *The Writing Center Journal, The Writing Lab Newsletter, English Journal, Kairos, Forum*, and *The Journal for College Writing*. He and co-author Valerie Balester received the International Writing Centers Association Outstanding Scholarship Award for Best Article in 2001 for "A View of Status and Working Conditions: Relations Between Writing Program and Writing Center Directors."

Barry Maid is Professor of Technical Communication at Arizona State University, where he served as Program Head for ten years. Previously, he taught at the University of Arkansas at Little Rock where, among other things, he helped in the creation of the Department of Rhetoric and Writing. For more than twenty years, he has been actively participating in online communities and using them as teaching/learning spaces. Along with numerous articles and chapters focusing on technology, outcomes assessment, information literacy, independent writing programs, and program administration, he is a co-author, with Duane Roen and Greg Glau, of *The McGraw-Hill Guide: Writing for College, Writing for Life*.

Susan Miller-Cochran is Professor of English and Director of the Writing Program at University of Arizona, where her research focuses on the intersections of technology, multilingual writing, and writing program administration. She is currently President of the Council of Writing Program Administrators, and her publications include *Rhetorically Rethinking Usability* (2009), *The Wadsworth Guide to Research* (2014), and *Keys for Writers* (2014).

James P. Purdy is Associate Professor of English and Director of the University Writing Center at Duquesne University, where he won the Presidential Award for Excellence in Teaching in 2016. He has edited four collections with Randall McClure, *The New Digital Scholar* (2013), *The Next Digital Scholar* (2014), and *The Future Scholar* (2016), and one with Danielle DeVoss, *Making Space* (2016). His research has appeared in *College Composition and Communication, Computers and Composition, Kairos, Pedagogy*, and *Profession*, as well as several others. With co-author Joyce R. Walker, he won the 2011 Ellen Nold Award for the Best Article in Computers and Composition Studies and the 2008 Kairos Best Webtext Award.

Brent Simoneaux holds a PhD in Communication, Rhetoric, and Digital Media from North Carolina State University. At the time of writing, he was a graduate student who regularly taught courses in first-year composition, rhetorical theory and history, and digital media. He now works in the tech industry as a writer, editor, and content strategist.

Robin Snead holds a PhD in Communication, Rhetoric, and Digital Media from North Carolina State University. She is currently a Lecturer in the English, Theatre, and Foreign Languages Department at UNC-Pembroke, where she teaches composition courses and advises in a program for at-risk students. She regularly presents her research in multimodal communication and composition pedagogy at conferences such as CCCC, and has published in *Computers and Composition* and *Across the Disciplines*.

Susan Wyche serves as the founder and Director of the Office of Grant Development at University of Hawaii Maui College. After graduating from University of Washington in the 1980s with a PhD in Rhetoric and Composition, she taught at several West coast universities, directed the Writing Program at Washington State University, and founded the University Writing Program at California State University, Monterey Bay. In 2001, she left academe and returned to school at University of California Berkeley to study sustainable landscape design, a program she dropped out of to build a successful design business, which she eventually expanded to Maui. She returned reluctantly to academe during the Great Recession, accepting a job as a developer of externally-funded projects for the Chancellor's Office. She marvels that she is now officially paid to bring innovative disruptions to campus instead of doing it for free.

About the Editors

Randall McClure has taught writing at several universities, including Miami University, Georgia Southern University, Cleveland State University, and Minnesota State University, Mankato. He researches in the areas of information behavior and academic writing, teaching and learning online, and academic policy. He has published articles in *The Writing Instructor, Inside Higher Ed, portal: Libraries and the Academy, Computers and Composition Online, Academic Exchange Quarterly, Computers and Composition, Writing Spaces, WPA: Writing Program Administration, Writing & Pedagogy*, and the *Journal of Literacy and Technology*. He is co-editor with James P. Purdy of *The New Digital Scholar, The Next Digital Scholar,* and *The Future Scholar*. He recently edited *Rewired*, a collection of essays on library-writing partnerships for the Association of College & Research Libraries.

Dayna V. Goldstein is an Assistant Professor of English at Texas A&M University Texarkana. Her interests include writing assessment, labor, qualitative research, and network theories of composing. Her scholarship includes publication in *College Composition and Communication, Writing Spaces, WPA: Writing Program Administration*, and presentations of quantitative data at national and international writing conferences including CCCC, WPA, and Writing Research Across Borders. She serves on the CCCC Committee on Part-time, Adjunct or Contingent Labor.

Michael A. Pemberton is Professor of Writing and Linguistics at Georgia Southern University and director of the University Writing Center. He has published five books, including *The Ethics of Writing Instruction: Issues in Theory and Practice, The Center Will Hold: Critical Reflections on Writing Center Scholarship*, and *Bookmarks: A Guide to Research and Writing*, as well as more than fifty articles on writing center theory, tutoring ethics, and writing technologies in journals such as *College Composition and Communication*, the *Writing Center Journal*, and numerous book chapters. He serves on the editorial and governing boards of the WAC Clearinghouse, *Computers and Composition, Praxis, Prompt*, and the *Journal of Writing and Pedagogy*, and is current editor of the journal *Across the Disciplines* and the series *Across the Disciplines Books*.

Index

academic labor, xv, 71, 127, 128, 130, 148
ADE Guidelines for Class Size and Workload for College and University Teachers of English: A Statement of Policy, 74, 90
Adjunct Project, The 139–140, 142
adjuncts, x, xvi, 14–15, 25–27, 34, 53, 55, 81, 83, 90–91, 108, 118, 120, 125, 139–140, 153, 169, 170–174, 176–186, 269, 296
administrators, ix–11, 24, 31, 35, 71–73, 75, 86, 88–89, 95, 111, 116, 131, 135, 141–142, 152, 161–162, 174, 178, 182, 213, 254, 268, 280, 295, 301
Affordable Care Act, 153, 191, 270
American Association of University Professors (AAUP), 25, 27, 58, 59, 65, 69, 70–73, 75, 84, 108, 130, 181, 273, 277, 290, 292, 295, 302–304, 306
American College Testing (ACT) organization, 209–210, 212, 214, 216, 222–223
American Institutes for Research (AIR), 210, 223
Anson, Chris, xiii, xvi, 14, 122, 128, 130, 133, 144, 231, 239
assessment, 4, 23, 30, 32, 37, 45–46, 63, 77–80, 95, 100, 102, 120, 122, 137–138, 156, 161, 164, 187, 190, 195, 198–200, 262
Association of Departments of English (ADE), 70, 72, 74–81, 90, 92, 133, 144, 150, 152, 162, 165, 171, 184, 270, 283, 308
AWP Guidelines for Creative Writing Programs & Teachers of Creative Writing, 75, 86, 90

Balester, Valerie, xiii–xiv, 29–30, 36, 41, 47, 234
basic writing, 88, 159, 273–274, 280
Beck, Evelyn, xvi, 83, 91, 169, 196
benefits, x, xvii, 15, 23–24, 69–70, 74, 81, 84, 86–87, 102–103, 106–109, 120, 128, 134, 141, 147, 153, 170–172, 174–176, 188, 191, 201, 217, 222, 233, 238, 248, 275–276, 294, 300, 303
Boquet, Elizabeth, 42, 44–45, 47
boss compositionists, 7, 21, 57, 121, 287

CCCC Promotion and Tenure Guidelines for Work with Technology, 76, 78, 80, 91, 229, 240
CCCC Writing Program Certificate of Excellence, xv, 127, 137, 139, 144–146
censure, 120, 122, 128–130, 133, 137

class size, xviii, 70, 75–76, 86, 103, 128, 137, 159–161, 174, 180, 233, 269, 276, 300–301, 305
clear text, 245–251, 252, 254–255, 257–260, 264
Coalition on the Academic Workforce (CAW), 71–73, 81, 92, 140, 146, 166, 308
College English (journal), xii, xix, 6, 9, 47, 50, 66, 91, 92, 113, 125, 140, 144–146, 153, 165–166, 206, 211, 223, 227, 239, 267, 270, 284, 288
Collegiate Learning Assessment (CLA), 211–212
Committee on Professional Standards, 10, 19, 47, 70, 91, 124, 129, 131, 144–145
Common Core State Standards for K-12 education (CCSS), 209, 219
compensation, xvii, 4, 17, 21, 37, 53–54, 60, 61, 69–71, 73–75, 78, 81–83, 86–87, 97, 99, 106–107, 120, 128–129, 132, 139–140, 153, 170, 173–174, 177, 180–181, 184, 188, 191, 201–203, 226, 275–278, 280, 285, 294, 296, 298, 300, 302–304
compliance, 20, 120, 130, 133, 188, 201, 304
composition instruction, 23, 225, 232, 235
composition studies, 4, 19, 20–24, 44, 65, 69, 77, 81, 87, 225, 235
Computers and Composition (journal), 91, 226–228, 231, 239–242, 267
Conference on College Composition and Communication (CCCC), ix, xi, xiii–xv, xix, 4, 9–11, 19–20, 27, 36, 39, 47, 52, 54, 56, 58–59, 63–65, 69–72, 75–78, 80–81, 88–89, 91, 93, 112, 115–116, 118–119, 122–125, 127–131, 137, 138–146, 153–154, 156, 162, 165, 182–185, 206, 222, 225, 228–229, 231, 233, 238, 240–241, 247, 249, 252, 260, 265, 268–269, 274–275, 277–278, 282–283, 285, 288–291, 293, 295–298, 300, 305, 307–308
Connors, Robert J., 20, 27
conservatism, 56–57
contingent labor, x, xvi, 139, 148, 151–152, 155, 232, 290
contract faculty, x, xv–xvi, 20, 23, 55, 58–60, 62–64, 69–71, 73–74, 81–86, 89, 92, 120–121, 123–124, 126–129, 133–141, 146, 148–157, 161–162, 166,169, 181, 203, 232, 270, 287, 290, 293
conventional institutional model, 63–64
Council of Writing Program Administrators (CWPA), xix, 4, 23, 28, 33, 35, 73, 86, 88, 93, 96, 99–100, 106, 110–112, 114, 157, 161, 165, 166, 208, 222, 235, 236, 240, 243, 247, 254, 266–267, 278
course load, 4, 6, 75–76, 83, 86, 110, 134, 157, 200–201, 203, 300–301
creative writing, 72, 75, 87, 275, 298
Crowley, Sharon, 6, 9, 10, 19–20, 27, 126, 130–131, 145
curriculum development, 4, 41, 77, 84, 178, 195, 198, 280, 298

data substantiation, 272, 281

democracy, 56–57, 121, 207, 213, 239, 253, 257, 261, 264, 285, 291, 296
Demography of the Faculty: A Statistical Portrait of English and Foreign Language (MLA/ADE), 150, 165
department chairs, ix, x, 24, 33, 73, 77, 79, 162, 179, 254, 301–302
digital redesign, 255, 262, 264
digital technologies, xvii, 52, 58, 77, 80, 117, 136, 192, 204, 216, 225–229, 231, 235, 236–239, 244–245, 248, 250, 253, 255, 257, 259, 261–264
digital writing, xvii, 225–228, 235, 238
disenfranchisement, 4, 61
Dougherty, Timothy R., xiv, 93

economic model, xvii, 11, 12, 24–25, 52, 55, 57, 59, 60–62, 86, 107, 136, 142, 151–152, 159, 171, 175–176, 188, 190, 230, 247, 270, 278, 287, 299
Elbow, Peter, 12, 218, 222
empirical research, 31, 45, 77, 161, 187, 289–290
English as a Second Language (ESL), 37, 58, 72, 74, 87, 88, 117, 139, 218, 223, 228, 240
English departments, 11, 20, 29–31, 34, 36, 39–40, 69, 72–73, 78–79, 81, 84, 87, 89, 121, 134, 143, 155, 164, 193, 232, 289, 292, 297, 298, 300

Ensuring the Quality of Undergraduate Programs in English and Foreign Languages: MLA Recommendations on Staffing, 85, 91

ethics, 62, 95, 97, 110, 126–128, 136, 138, 141–142, 180, 248, 256, 262, 265, 286
evidenced-based practice for writing centers, x, 42, 45–46, 161, 199
exclusion, 25, 35, 154
expertise, 16, 99, 135, 154–155, 163–164, 191, 194–197, 258, 274–275

faculty development, 25, 64, 82, 86, 216
faculty evaluation, 77, 79
Fedukovich, Casie J., xiii, xv–xvi, 81, 126
first-year composition, xi, 33, 130, 236, 277–280
first-year writing, xi, 20–21, 26, 34, 57, 98, 126, 129, 133–135, 138, 148–151, 154–155, 158, 162–164, 171, 236, 277–280, 296, 300, 305–306
folklore research, 72, 77–78
formal writing, 78, 217–218, 251–252, 293
four-year colleges, ix, 3, 30, 127, 152, 158, 162, 171, 181, 192–193, 293, 305–306
freeway flying, 18, 26
funding, 12, 31, 44–45, 110–111, 133–134, 142, 151, 156, 189, 203

Giordano, Joanne Baird, xvi, 147, 151, 165, 193, 199, 285
globalization, 57, 60, 109, 231, 236, 239
Goldstein, Dayna V., ix, xviii, 44, 111, 251, 265, 267–268, 283, 289
Google Hangouts, 178, 205, 215, 223, 242, 248, 267

Gorelick, Risa P., xv, 81, 115
graduate students, 5–7, 10–11, 29, 34, 43, 46, 55, 62, 73, 76, 86–87, 96, 115–116, 119, 121, 123–124, 163–164, 220, 232, 251, 268, 276, 291, 293, 296, 300, 306
Great Recession of 2008, 134
Gunner, Jeanne, xiv, 19, 23, 27, 52–53, 65, 66, 287

Hairston, Maxine, 19, 64, 66
Hale, Connie, 5, 13
Harris, Joseph, x, xviii, 23, 26, 27, 34–35, 39, 41, 48–49, 134, 145, 269, 283, 285
Hassell, Holly, xvi
Henry J. Kaiser Family Foundation, 214, 216, 223
Hesse, Doug, 34–35
hierarchical system, 20, 22, 55, 65, 73, 292
higher education, ix–x, xvi, 9, 12, 21, 24–26, 40, 52–53, 59–62, 65, 70, 74, 79–81, 86, 90, 119, 121, 123, 126, 138, 140, 148, 152, 163, 171, 175, 176, 181–183, 189–190, 202, 230–231, 233, 270, 272, 274–275, 278, 281, 292, 294–295
Horning, Alice S., xvii, 94, 96–98, 111–113, 207, 223

identity, 5, 9, 19, 27, 44, 46, 52–53, 63, 99, 179, 256
implicit learning, 217–218, 222
inclusive text, 244–245, 249–250, 253–257, 260, 262
individualized instruction, 25, 33, 46, 280
inequities, x, xii, 4, 7, 97, 129
inkshedding, 8, 12

institutional infrastructure, xvii, 155, 225, 235, 237–238, 282
International Writing Centers Association (IWCA), 34, 35, 42, 73, 86, 87, 88, 89
Irmscher, William, 10

Janangelo, Joseph, xvii, xviii, 49, 51, 112, 161, 244, 265
job security, x, xvii, 30, 69, 73, 83–86, 90, 93–94, 98, 101, 103, 108–109, 114, 127, 134, 172–173, 183, 269, 294, 302

Kezar approach, 62–63, 66
KnowledgeWorks, 26–27

labor issues, xii–xv, xviii, 20, 71, 86, 89, 105, 116–124, 136, 174, 255, 268, 271, 275, 281, 290, 292
labor pool, ix–x, 12
labor practices, xii–xv, 86, 105, 116–124, 136, 174, 255, 268, 275, 281, 290, 292
laboratory approach, 33–34
Ladder of Abstraction (S.I. Hayakawa), 138
lecturers, xi, 4, 7, 11, 12, 273
Lerner, Neal, 32–34, 44–45, 47, 49
liberal arts, 12, 30
listserv, xi, 48, 98, 251
literacy, 31, 34, 39–40, 46, 52, 57, 88, 121, 158, 160, 210, 212, 218, 228, 281
literature, 5, 21, 24, 31, 34, 39, 41–42, 44, 55–56, 63–64, 72, 76, 87, 89, 99, 121, 136–137, 140, 163, 194, 274–275, 291, 297–298, 306
locus of quality, 270–271, 274

locus of quantity, 271–272, 274, 282
Lunsford, Andrea, 6, 10, 32, 49

Maid, Barry, xvi, 40, 49, 161, 187, 198, 206
marginalization, 287; of faculty, 14, 38, 54–57, 60, 132, 153, 176, 296
Marxist rhetoric, 7, 19
Massive Open Online Courses (MOOCs), 60, 117, 233
material conditions, xiii, 18, 107, 134–136, 148–149, 157, 161
McClelland, Ben W., ix–x, xix, 93–94, 112, 129
McClure, Randall, ix, xviii, 44–45, 49, 53, 91, 99, 111, 113, 146, 161, 227, 235, 241–242, 251, 255, 265, 267–268, 283, 289
McDonald, James C., xiv, 18, 31, 35, 41, 47, 54, 66, 69–70, 85, 91, 94, 96, 104, 109, 113, 120–121, 125, 128, 130–131, 145
Miller-Cochran, Susan, xv, 126, 146, 231, 241
MLA Recommendation on a Minimum Wage for Full-Time Entry-Level Faculty, 74, 83, 91
MLA Recommendation on Minimum Per-Course Compensation for Part-Time Faculty Members, 82, 91
MLA Statement on the Use of Part-Time and Full-Time Adjunct Faculty, 81, 92
Modern Language Association (MLA), xii, xix, 4, 9, 59, 66, 70–72, 74–75, 77, 79–83, 85–86, 88, 91–92, 119–121, 125, 133, 144–145, 150, 152, 165, 171, 184, 226, 229, 240, 242, 298–299
Mullin, Joan, 37–39, 49
Murray, Donald, 22

National Conference on Peer Tutoring in Writing, 42
National HIV/AIDS Strategy, 246, 267
National Study of Postsecondary Faculty, 150, 277, 282, 290, 307
National Writing Centers Association, 34, 69, 188
NCTE (National Council of Teachers of English), 13, 72, 75, 80, 81, 82, 88, 119, 132, 136, 208, 211, 216, 219, 223, 227, 231, 235–236, 242, 268, 283
New Faculty Majority, 135–136, 140, 146
Nielsen, Jakob, 214, 216, 223
noncompliance, 20, 54, 122, 129, 133
non-tenure-track faculty (NTTs), ix–x, xviii, 14–26, 34, 41, 52, 57, 59, 60, 62, 75, 81, 83–84, 102, 107–109, 119, 127, 133–136, 138–139, 141, 152, 154–155, 188–189, 202–203, 205, 232, 274, 276, 293, 296, 304; *see also* part-time faculty
nontraditional students, 159
North, Stephen, 34, 37, 39, 46, 50, 143

Olsen, Tillie, 14
online writing centers, xvi, 30, 33, 37, 39, 170, 182–183, 229, 231–234, 238
online writing instruction, xvi, 3, 30, 37, 39, 47, 59–61, 78, 80, 83, 170–183, 192, 196–197, 200, 204, 210–211, 214, 216–

322 *Index*

217, 228–234, 238, 244, 249, 250–251, 253, 257–262, 265, 287–288
outsourcing, 60, 273–274

part-time faculty, ix–xi, xvi, xix, 7, 12, 15, 18–20, 22, 25–26, 34, 41, 55, 74, 80, 82–84, 92, 103, 108, 115, 121, 127, 130–133, 140, 141, 146, 149–150, 152–154, 156, 166, 169–181, 183, 187, 189, 191–197, 199, 201, 203–205, 220, 232, 254, 268–269, 273–276, 284, 287, 290, 292–296, 300–304, 306, 308
pedagogy, xii, xix, 12, 22, 25, 46, 56, 58, 63–64, 77, 80, 132, 136, 148–150, 156–157, 162–164, 182, 189–191, 197, 226–227, 231, 238, 259, 270, 301
Pell Grant, 160
Pemberton, Michael A., ix, xviii, 34–35, 42–44, 48–50, 111, 248, 262, 265, 267–268
Porter, James, xi, xii, xix
Portland Resolution (CWPA), xiv, 73, 86–89, 91, 93–97, 100–101, 102, 104–105, 107–111, 113–114
Position Statement on Professional Equity for the Field of Teaching English to Speakers of Other Languages (TESOL), 86, 92
Position Statement on the Status and Working Conditions of Contingent Faculty (NCTE), 80, 82, 92, 132, 136, 146, 153, 166
power, xiv, 7, 11, 21, 23, 31–32, 40, 45, 57, 65, 73, 104, 120–124, 131, 137, 143, 149, 173, 246, 253, 255, 258

Principles for the Postsecondary Teaching of Writing, xii, xix, 285
private universities, xv
professional development, xvi–xvii, 46, 84, 95, 110, 120, 126, 129, 149, 155–156, 163, 170, 174, 177, 182, 191, 194, 197, 200, 202, 207, 209, 212, 215–217, 219–221, 233, 263, 298, 302, 306
program review, 4
Project SAILS (Kent State University), 210, 223
public universities, xv, 26, 151, 212
Purdy, James P., xvii, 52, 80, 225, 231, 235, 237, 241–242

qualitative research, xi, 271
quantitative research, xi, 79, 110, 123, 143, 269, 271–275, 278, 281–282

Raymond, James, 6, 9, 129, 308
reading, xvii, 22, 52, 55–56, 64, 72, 84, 98, 156, 159, 163, 207–221, 223, 248, 258, 261, 263–265, 286, 287, 297, 304
recension, xix, 53–54, 245, 251–252, 257, 263, 267
recession, x, 4, 12, 230, 270
reform, 21, 70–71, 95, 107, 111, 133, 136
Reither, Jim, 7–8
Research Network Forum (RNF), xv, 115–119, 122–125
retention, xi, 12, 39, 46, 97, 159–160, 178, 180
retirees, 15–16, 25, 60, 74, 82, 84, 176–177, 191, 294
Rhetoric and Composition (field), ix, 132, 137, 226, 240–241

Robertson, Linda, 9, 10, 128, 146, 188, 206, 285, 288
Rose, Shirley K, 11, 48, 122, 142, 146, 278, 280, 282, 290, 292–293, 298, 307

salary, xvii, 4, 17, 21, 54, 61, 74–75, 78, 82–83, 97, 129, 139, 170, 173–174, 177, 181, 184, 188, 191, 201–203, 226, 275–277, 281, 294, 298, 302–303
Schell, Eileen, 13, 54, 66, 70, 85, 91, 109, 112–113, 120, 121, 125–126, 128, 130–131, 145–146, 152, 166
scholarship, xvi–xvii, 21–23, 25, 33–34, 40–44, 55, 64, 69, 71–73, 77–81, 86–87, 90, 93, 120, 127, 142–143, 151, 155, 225–227, 229, 231, 237–238, 255–256, 281, 293, 297–298
Simoneaux, Brent, xv, 126
Simpson, Jeanne H., 34, 36–37, 50, 70, 73, 86, 88, 92
Skype, 178, 205, 234, 238
Sledd, James, 7, 11, 20, 28, 57, 64, 66, 121, 125, 128, 130, 134, 136, 146, 286, 288
Slevin, Jim, 9–11, 19, 70, 92, 120, 122, 129
Snead, Robin, xv, 126, 144
social media, 8, 117, 119–120, 199
specialization, 5, 55, 72, 278, 297
staffing, ix, x, 34, 71, 87, 108, 114, 133–134, 152, 175, 193, 233, 247, 269–270, 272, 274–276, 278, 281, 299
Statement, The and *Scholarship in Composition*, 78
Statement, The in *College Composition and Communication* (*CCC*), xiii, 70
Statement of Mutual Expectations (SME), 143

status quo, xiv, 57–58, 61, 131
Stay, Byron, 36–37, 46–51
StraighterLine (website), 61, 64
Survey of Earned Doctorates, 5

Task Force to Revise the CCCC Principles and Standards for the Teaching of Writing, xii, xix
technologies, 33, 37, 77–78, 80, 192, 204, 234, 236–238
tenure, xi, xiv, 4–5, 7, 10, 14, 16, –18, 21, 23–24, 26, 29, 31, 33, 35–36, 39–43, 45, 53, 55, 57–60, 62–64, 70, 73, 76–79, 85–86, 90, 94–100, 103, 105, 107–110, 120–121, 126, 130–134, 136–137, 143, 147–150, 152–156, 162–163, 172, 179, 181, 188–189, 193, 205, 226, 229, 231–232, 234, 238, 247, 272–273, 275, 276–277, 286–288, 292–299, 301, 303–304
tenure-track positions, x–xi, xiv, xviii, 5, 18–22, 24–26, 33, 36, 41, 53, 56–57, 61, 63, 70, 73–75, 81–86, 88–90, 94–97, 99, 102–103, 105, 106, 108–110, 120, 127, 130, 132–133, 141–143, 147, 150, 152–153, 155–156, 171–172, 181, 188–189, 193, 200–202, 238, 247, 268, 273, 276–277, 292, 294–297, 299, 302–304
testing, xvii, 88, 216
Texas A&M University, 37, 43
Two-Year College English Association, 155, 165
two-year colleges, ix, 30, 37, 127, 148, 149, 150–152, 155, 158–163, 171, 192–193, 251, 293, 301

U.S. Bureau of Labor Statistics, 169, 177

Uber, 169, 183, 186
undergraduates, 76, 160, 291
untenured writing program administrators, xiv, 94–98, 100, 101, 103–111, 114
utility, xvii, 106, 246, 254, 256, 263

voting privileges, 135, 142

Warnock, Tilly, 9, 231, 242
What Lies Ahead for Writing Centers: Position Statement on Professional Concerns (IWCA), 50, 86, 88–89, 92
workforce, ix, 71, 135, 169, 170, 178, 292
working conditions, ix–x, xiii, xv–xix, 4–5, 7–11, 14–15, 18, 20–21, 23–24, 26, 30–32, 46, 52, 54, 56–57, 60–63, 69, 70–73, 76, 78, 81, 83, 86–87, 89, 93–95, 102, 106–107, 108, 111, 116–120, 122–124, 127–129, 131–132, 135, 140–142, 148–149, 152–153, 156–158, 164, 174–176, 180, 182–183, 187–189, 193, 196, 198, 205–206, 232, 268–276, 278, 281–282, 285, 287–291, 295, 296, 304
work-in-progress, xv, 116–119, 122–124
WPA: Writing Program Administration (journal), ix, xix, 47, 51, 66, 91, 112–113, 125, 146, 206, 223, 267, 284, 307
WPA Summer Conference, 110
writing center, xiii, 29–32, 34–36, 37–46, 73, 88, 106, 116, 163, 202, 234, 305
writing center directors, 31–35, 37, 40–41, 43, 46, 70, 86–89, 99, 105, 251

Writing Center Journal, 38, 42, 45, 47–50
writing centers, xiii, 29–51, 73, 86, 92, 160, 189, 234, 276, 280, 287, 297, 305–306
writing instruction, x–xiii, xvii, 29, 31, 33, 36, 56, 88, 131, 149, 155, 187, 207, 213, 216, 221, 225, 227, 229, 231, 232–235, 237–238, 278, 291, 297, 305–306
Writing Lab Newsletter, 36, 42, 49–50
Writing Program Administrator's Resource, 35, 48, 124
writing program administrators (WPAs), ix–x, xvii, 26, 34–35, 40, 48–49, 57, 66, 73, 78, 81, 86–89, 93–94, 96–99, 101, 104–105, 107, 110, 112–113, 120, 122, 129, 138, 161, 198, 213, 277–278, 280, 290, 292–293, 298, 307
Writing Program Certificate of Excellence, xv, 128, 137–142, 144
Wyche, Susan, xiii, 3, 128, 146
Wyoming Conference, ix, xiii, 3–4, 6, 9, 56, 64, 66, 70, 91, 96, 115, 120, 123, 125, 129, 140, 144–146, 188, 206, 268, 270, 284, 288
Wyoming Conference on English, 6, 56, 115
Wyoming Conference Resolution, xiii–xiv, 3–4, 8–9, 11, 13, 19–20, 27–28, 52–57, 64, 66, 69–70, 91–92, 96, 113–114, 121–123, 125, 127–131, 133, 136–138, 140, 144–146, 188–189, 191, 193, 200, 205–206, 268, 270, 284–285, 286, 288

Yancey, Kathleen Blake, 34–35, 137, 146

www.ingramcontent.com/pod-product-compliance
Lightning Source LLC
Chambersburg PA
CBHW031434230426
43668CB00007B/529